Russian War
Films

Russian War Films

On the Cinema Front, 1914–2005

Denise J. Youngblood

University Press
of Kansas

Published by the University

Press of Kansas (Lawrence,

Kansas 66045), which was

organized by the Kansas

Board of Regents and is

operated and funded by

Emporia State University,

Fort Hays State University,

Kansas State University,

Pittsburg State University,

the University of Kansas, and

Wichita State University

Library of Congress Cataloging-in-Publication Data

Youngblood, Denise J. (Denise Jeanne), 1952–
    Russian war films : on the cinema front, 1914–2005 /
Denise J. Youngblood.
    p.   cm.
    Includes bibliographical references, filmography and
index.
    ISBN 0-7006-1489-3 (cloth : alk. paper)
    1. War films—Soviet Union—History and criticism.
2. War films—Russia (Federation)—History and criticism.
3. World War, 1939–1945—Soviet Union—Motion pictures
and the war.   4. Motion pictures—Soviet Union.
5. Motion pictures—Russia (Federation)   I. Title.
    PN1995.9.W3Y68   2006
    791.43′658—dc22

                                              2006023563

British Library Cataloguing-in-Publication Data is available.

Printed in the United States of America

10 9 8 7 6 5 4 3 2 1

CONTENTS

LIST OF ILLUSTRATIONS

PREFACE AND ACKNOWLEDGMENTS

Cinema is for us the most important of all arts.
Attributed to V. I. Lenin and emblazoned on every movie theater in the USSR

This book examines nearly a century of Russian fiction films about wars and wartime, focusing on Russia's twentieth-century wars: the two world wars, the Russian Civil War, and the conflicts in Afghanistan and Chechnya.[1] Pride of place naturally falls to the Great Patriotic War, as World War II was known in the Soviet Union. This work emerges from two abiding passions.

The first is my deep affection for Russian cinema. From art to entertainment to kitsch, Russian cinema is, for me, "the most important of the arts." Apart from a few scattered periods (the 1920s, the Thaw, glasnost), Russian/Soviet cinema might not have existed as far as standard film histories and cultural histories are concerned. (The rest was allegedly "propaganda," after all.) Entrenched stereotypes notwithstanding, this is a rich trove of work that deserves more comprehensive study by historians, as well as by film scholars.

The second is my fascination as a historian and teacher with war and wartime. This obsession is not pathological, as director Aleksei Gherman, whose films will figure prominently in later chapters, explained in a 1979 essay. War interests him as a filmmaker, he wrote, because of its "extreme situations" and "profound drama."[2] "War is a distillation [*sgustok*] of life," he continued. "You learn who is who."[3] Because war (and the preparations for it) became a way of life in the USSR, war was arguably more important as an organizing principle for state authority than it was anywhere else in Europe. Because the Soviet film industry was nationalized, a war film could never be "only" a movie.

Intellectual Contexts

This work emerges from, and is intended to contribute to, multiple scholarly contexts and dialogues. Cinema study is hotly contested territory. Over the past two decades there has been considerable debate among historians engaged in the scholarly study of the cinema about how best to use movies as historical sources. The film and history movement was pioneered by two French historians, Pierre Sorlin and Marc Ferro.[4] In the United States, two basic schools of thought have emerged. The "Toplin school" (my term), represented by the work of Robert Brent Toplin, John J. O'Connor, Peter Rollins, and others, argues for the importance of Hollywood and popular film, in the historical enterprise.[5] The "Rosenstone school" (also my term), represented by the work of Robert Rosenstone, Leger Grindon, Marcia Landy et al., draws from critical studies theory and tends to focus on the art film.[6]

Although I have contributed to "Rosenstonian" texts,[7] in this book I attempt to steer a middle ground. I intend *Russian War Films* to be an illustration of what Hayden White has dubbed *historiophoty*[8]—a "historiography" based on an analysis of filmic rather than written texts, but one that draws primarily on the Soviet equivalent of Hollywood films, that is, mainstream films for a mainstream audience.

Film scholars may not recognize the ways I have adapted the language of film analysis to the language of history, but their influences on my thinking are significant nonetheless. Frank Manchel's magisterial *Film Study* is the essential starting point for anyone studying the history of film scholarship.[9] There are many important genre studies about American war films. The one that has contributed the most to the shape of this book is Jeanine Basinger's *The World War II Combat Film*, although I do not limit my discussion to combat films and use the term *genre* very loosely.[10] For purposes of narrative analysis, I have adapted David Bordwell's typology of Hollywood classical film narration from his seminal work *Narration in the Fiction Film*.[11] Not surprisingly to readers familiar with the tenets of socialist realism, most of the movies to be discussed follow the framework of the classical Hollywood narrative (linear and character- and goal-centered), with the striking exception that few Soviet war films have a "happy ending."

Moving from theoretical and methodological to historical influences, this work draws on a number of different themes that have been important in the historiography of the USSR, particularly its cultural and social aspects. Katerina Clark's pathbreaking work on socialist realism is essential for anyone studying the culture of the Stalin period.[12] Roger Pethybridge's analysis of the impact of the Civil War on the militarization of Soviet society has influenced a generation of social historians.[13] Military historians, especially Roger Reese and David R. Stone, have also situated their analyses of the Soviet military squarely in the sociopolitical context.[14] Three Soviet film scholars—Yury Khaniutin, Vatslav Smal, and Aleksandr Kamshalov—lay the groundwork for this book by arguing that war movies played an important role in inculcating patriotism in the late Soviet period.[15]

Many gaps in our understanding of culture and society in the Stalin era have been filled in over the past twenty years. Much interesting work has emerged since the end of the USSR, due in part to greater access to previously closed archives. Exceptionally important for this work, especially in the later chapters, is Nina Tumarkin's remarkable book on the cult of World War II.[16] Sheila Fitzpatrick's scholarship on the social history of the 1930s has charted new territories, as has the growing body of scholarship on Stalinist public culture, for example, Jeffrey Brooks's work on newspapers and public rhetoric, David Hoffmann's on Stalinist values, and Karen Petrone's on Stalinist celebrations.[17] Richard Stites's studies of Soviet popular culture have also broken considerable new ground for research.[18] As a result, it is now clear that Stalinist society and culture, even in its darkest hours during the Great Terror, was considerably more dynamic than was previously assumed.

Over the past two decades, American and British scholars have rewritten most of the history of Soviet cinema as it had been known in English, with the Brezhnev era as the only one still awaiting its scribe.[19] My own primary research in the history of the Soviet film industry stops at 1935.[20] For background on more recent periods, I have relied heavily on the work of Peter Kenez for the 1930s to the death of Stalin, Josephine Woll for the Thaw, and Anna Lawton for the glasnost era and post-Soviet period.[21] Richard Taylor's extensive scholarly publications on various aspects of cinema in the Stalin era have also been essential sources of background information.[22]

Additional insight is provided from "within." Since the end of the Soviet Union, Russian film scholars have been freed from their political restraints. The past decade has seen a flowering of Russian scholarship on Russian cinema, especially the cinema of the Stalin era. For example, one of the new film journals, *Notes on Cinema Studies* (Kinovedcheskie zapiski), provides the kind of forum for intellectual debate about cinema that has not been seen since the 1920s. Among significant recent scholarly books that are germane to this study are three sponsored by the Scientific Research Institute on Cinema Art (Nauchno-issledovatel'skii Institut Kinoiskusstva): *Russian Illusion* (Rossiiskii illiuzion), which revises the canon of Soviet cinema by including many previously marginalized or banned films; *Cinema: Politics and People in the 1930s* (Kino: Politika i liudi, 30-e gody), which utilizes long-unavailable archival material to reevaluate a particularly difficult period in the history of Soviet cinema; and *Cinema in the War: Documents and Evidence* (Kino na voine: Dokumenty i svidetel'stva).[23] Sergei Zemlianukhin and Miroslava Segida's *Domestic Cinémathèque: National Cinema, 1918–1996* (Domashniaia sinemateka: Otechestvennoe kino, 1918–1996) is an invaluable source of box office information.[24]

I am pleased to acknowledge the individuals and institutions that have helped me bring this project to fruition. For their inspiration, I thank Michael Paris, who invited me to write about Russian war films for his anthology *The First World War and Popular Cinema*, and Jeffrey Wasserstrom, who asked me to contribute an article on Soviet World War II films for a forum in the *American Historical Review*. Michael Briggs encouraged me to expand this work into a book and has waited patiently as the project developed more slowly than either of us would have liked.

During the six years that I conducted the research for this book, I worked in two administrative assignments at my home institution, the University of Vermont. Academic administration often makes maintaining an active research agenda difficult, but I was fortunate in serving with two scholar-administrators who encouraged me to persevere. The late Dean of the College of Arts and Sciences, Joan M. Smith, and the university's Provost, A. John Bramley, provided research dollars and release time, as well as moral support. I am particularly grateful to the Provost's Office for the administrative leave that allowed me to complete the writing. I also thank the University Scholars Program of the UVM Graduate College for its financial assistance and recognition of my research and the College of Arts and Sciences Dean's Discretionary Fund for defraying some of the costs of obtaining the stills.

Librarians and archivists have of course been essential to the completion of this project. The Summer Research Laboratory at the University of Illinois, Urbana-Champaign is overseen by the university's Russian, East European, and Eurasian Center and is partly funded by a Title VIII grant from the U.S. Department of State. It offers access to one of the United States' leading Russian-language collections. This program and the UIUC Slavic Reference Service (which provided answers to some of my last-minute questions) are essential for Slavists who teach at universities that lack specialized research collections. Likewise, the staff of the European Reading Room at the Library of Congress provided exemplary assistance that enabled me to accomplish a great deal during relatively short research trips. I was fortunate to screen some of the rarest titles discussed herein at the Hungarian National Film Archive in Budapest, which houses a significant collection of Soviet films and offers good access to foreign scholars; Blanka Szilágyi, who staffs the Archive's international desk, was most helpful. In Budapest I also benefited from the resources of the Open Society Archives at Central European University; Oksana Sarkisova, who oversees OSA's film section, went far beyond the call of duty. Nina Harding of the Stills Department at the British Film Institute facilitated my review and selection of the stills included in this book.

I am deeply indebted to the intellectual generosity of my colleagues— Peter Kenez, Anna Lawton, Frank Manchel, Richard Taylor, and especially Josephine Woll—who gave detailed, sharp (and sometimes irritating) critiques of the manuscript in its thorny early stages and continued to answer my questions and offer wise counsel right up to the end. Kevork Spartalian, who has been hearing the "pop, pop, pop" of Soviet war films for more years than he cares to remember, served as a devoted and sharp-eyed lay reader and critic. As the project neared completion, it benefited from a thorough and thoughtful reading from Vida T. Johnson and Susan Ecklund's skillful copyediting. Two former graduate students, Eric A. Hutchinson and Clayton J. Trutor, provided research assistance at various points. My UVM colleagues Sean Field, Jonathan Huener, Wolfgang Mieder, and Kenneth Nalibow helped with various translation and transliteration questions.

This book is dedicated to Josephine Woll, whose strength of spirit in the face of adversity is truly inspiring.

MECHANICS

All translations from the Russian are my own unless otherwise indicated. In the text, English titles for films, books, and journals are employed throughout; the transliterated Russian title is given in the first reference. I have sometimes retranslated a title in order to give the non-Russian-speaking reader a better sense of the literal meaning of a title. In such cases, I have included the alternate English versions of the title. Source notes and bibliography entries in Russian have not been translated due to space considerations and the assumption that they will be useful only to those who read Russian. The filmography is organized by English translation, with details in Russian for specialist reference.

Transliteration from the Cyrillic alphabet to the Latin poses difficulties that cannot be easily or consistently resolved. For personal names and proper nouns in the text, I have adopted a simplified (but not entirely consistent) system intended to give readers who do not know Russian a better idea of how to pronounce the word: for example, "Semyon," not "Semën" or "Yalta" rather than "Ialta." Three generations of the "German" family (Yury, Aleksei, and Aleksei Alekseevich) appear as "Gherman" in order to avoid unending confusion as to whether we are speaking of the artists or the enemy. The names of famous personages are spelled according to common usage: for example, "Peter Tchaikovsky," rather than "Pyotr Chaikovsky" or "Pëtr Chaikovskii." In the notes, filmography, and bibliography, however, the Library of Congress system has been strictly applied, to facilitate spelling back into Russian for the specialist.

All film details are from my personal screening notes, unless otherwise indicated. Especially for older films, it is often not possible to establish a definitive version, a problem that is not unique to Russian cinema.

I have tried to avoid Russian coinages and Soviet acronyms insofar as possible. Russian is, however, a marvelously economical and flexible language. It seems so much more sensible to employ *frontovik* rather than "front-line soldier" or *komsomolets* instead of "member of the Communist youth league" when the context is clear. The following terms appear in the text:

agitki	agit-films (Civil War)
Cheka, NKVD	Soviet secret police; precursors of the KGB

frontovik/frontoviki	Frontline soldier/soldiers
Goskino, Sovkino, Soiuzkino	Various names for the state film trust
kino-sbornik/kino-sborniki	Cinema anthology/anthologies (WWII)
kombat	Battalion commander
kombrig	Brigade commander (Civil War)
Komsomol	Young Communist League
komsomolets/komsolmoltsy	YCL member/members
Narkompros	Commissariat of Enlightenment
NEP	New Economic Policy period (1921–1928)
the Party	Communist Party of the Soviet Union
politruk	Political instructor
TsOKS	Central Union of Cinema Studios (WWII)
VGIK	All-Union State Institute of Cinematography
VNIIK	All-Union Scientific Research Institute of Film Art

The following abbreviations appear in the source notes and bibliography:

DS	*Domashniaia sinemateka* (Domestic Cinémathèque, book)
IK	*Iskusstvo kino* (Art of the Cinema, journal)
KZ	*Kinovedcheskie zapiski* (Notes on Cinema Studies, journal)
RI	*Rossiiskii illiuzion* (Russian Illusion, book)
SE	*Sovetskii ekran* (Soviet Screen, journal)

Introduction:
"Waiting for the Barbarians"

What are we waiting for, assembled in the forum?
The barbarians are due here today.
C. P. Cavafy, *"Waiting for the Barbarians"*[1]

To a remarkable degree, Russia's twentieth-century history can be interpreted in terms of the state's relationship to the "barbarians": preparing for them, waiting for them, engaging with them. The barbarians were a constantly shifting target; sometimes the enemies were real, sometimes imagined or concocted.[2] For the czarist government, the barbarians could be variously defined as the Japanese, the revolutionaries, the Jews, or the Germans. For the new Soviet government, the "barbarians" were capitalists, aristocrats, Romanovs, competing Socialist parties, the British, the Germans, kulaks, spies, returning prisoners of war, and so forth. There were as many kinds of wars in twentieth-century Russia as there were enemies: European wars, world wars, civil wars, revolutions, insurrections, and finally "cold war." Movies were made about all of these, and as we shall see, these films not only *reflected* their times but also *shaped* their times.

Parameters

Russian War Films is a study of the filmic history of Russia's most important twentieth-century "hot" wars: the Great War (1914–1918), the Civil War (1918–1921), the Great Patriotic War (1941–1945), the war in Afghanistan (1979–1989), and the Chechen wars (1994–1996, 1999–2000).[3] Its central focus is Russian *fiction* films about combat (both regular armed forces and partisans) and wartime (home front), with a few spy thrillers and films about "prewar" and "postwar" added to the mix.[4] My approach is selective rather than encyclopedic. I have chosen 160 titles for inclusion, films that met at least two of the following criteria: engagement in key issues of war and wartime (e.g., heroism, sacrifice, resistance, suffering, leadership, responsibility, collaboration); representation of key themes and trends in war films; box office success or significant promotion efforts; critical acclaim.

Although most of the period under consideration in this book is "Soviet," the focus is Russian, with limited examples from Belorussian/Belarusian, Georgian, and Ukrainian cinemas. For all the multiethnic brigades seen in Soviet war films, with concomitant depictions of multiethnic friendships among soldiers, Soviet cinema was "Great Russian" in its orientation, as directors from the ethnic minorities were all too aware. Many important directors of Russian-language films were not ethnic Russians. As much as they might have wanted to make movies in their own regional studios, they understood that such a move would have dramatically limited their exposure as artists. Exploration of the history of the resistance to this hegemonic culture is under way, especially with regard to Ukrainian cinema, where archival access has become much easier since independence.[5] "Minority" films are included only when there is evidence of wide-scale promotion and distribution, for example, Aleksandr Dovzhenko's *Shchors*, which will be discussed in chapter 3, or Rezo Chkheidze's *The Father of a Soldier*, in chapter 6.

Goals

This rich body of work invites multiple modes of interpretation. My areas of emphasis are, therefore, far from definitive. In addition to describing, analyzing, and contextualizing a significant body of films, *Russian War Films* has three central aims: (1) to chart the evolution of the Russian war film over the course of the twentieth century; (2) to apply Hayden White's neologism "historiophoty" to an analysis of the cinematic history of Russia's twentieth-century wars; and (3) to interrogate the art/entertainment paradigm in Russian cinematic history. I hope the study will stimulate further research and analysis into this and other genres.

Previous Western scholarship on Soviet cinema (including my own) has tended to focus on *periods*, *styles*, and *auteurs*. Remarkably little work has been done outside Russia on Soviet film genres apart from the extensive studies of the revolutionary films made during the storied 1920s. Genre analyses fall into two basic types—formal analysis and content analysis—that are not necessarily mutually exclusive. Film scholars privilege the former, historians the latter. Although issues of form and style certainly come into play in this book, it is primarily an analysis of the evolution of content and themes in their historical context and over the *"longue durée."*

War-themed films were exceptionally important to Soviet cinema and remain important in the post-Soviet era. They are a remarkable source for the study of Soviet society and politics. War films had the potential to reinforce or undermine the state-sanctioned stories the Party wanted citizens to hear about their past. More important, however, war films provided a highly contested space for supporting and challenging official views of Soviet history. Some were indeed useful tools of political persuasion, but many others were much more than that.

There are four major reasons for the special place the war film occupied in Soviet cinematic history. First, the USSR was born in war (World War I and the Civil War). It might also be argued that it effectively ended in war (Afghanistan). Second, wars in both their factual and mythologized incarnations served as the rationale for maintaining the hypercentralized authoritarian state: "We are surrounded by enemies who seek to destroy us." Third, the rhetoric of Soviet power was as much militaristic as socialist: society was organized in "brigades" for the purpose of carrying out "campaigns" on various "fronts." *Cinema front* (Kino-front) was not only a term used to describe the film industry; it was also the title of an important film journal in the 1920s. Finally, given the centrality of war and wartime to Soviet history, war films gave filmmakers the opportunity to subvert official history in the guise of art or entertainment, a luxury that Soviet historians did not have. It is emphatically not true, as one American film scholar has written recently, that Russian and Soviet war films "are neither historically accurate or [sic] particularly good cinema."[6] Indeed, as I have argued in previous work and as we shall see demonstrated herein, many Soviet directors took the historical enterprise and their role as quasi historians very seriously.

The second central theme is, therefore, to examine the history of Russia's twentieth-century wars as written on film, that is, its historiophoty, which White defines as "the representation of history and our thought about it in visual images and filmic discourse."[7] Cinema is not a particularly efficient vehicle for transmitting "facts," but a well-made historical film *can* evoke the flavor and feeling of an era more effectively than the written word. As White noted in his pathbreaking *American Historical Review* essay, history on film is not a supplement to written history but a distinctive form of historical discourse.[8] For this study, therefore, *authenticity* is more important than *accuracy* in assessing the historical merits of a particular film. To what extent were these films authentic evocations of Russian experiences of war and wartime? To what extent did they celebrate the militarized, patriotic society that Stalin and Brezhnev so ardently desired? To what extent did they construct a "usable past" for public consumption?

Given that the Soviet film industry was state-controlled from its nationalization in 1919 to the end of the USSR in 1991, all film production was, of course, official, that is, state-funded and at least nominally intended to support the Party's policies and programs. As film scholar Petre Petrov has written, "Cinema—taken as a whole and not in its individual texts—was the art most closely synchronized with the historical being of the Soviet state."[9] Like the other Soviet arts, cinema was subjected to review before, during, and after production. Depending on the decade and the political climate, however, this "censorship" ranged from lax to extremely stringent. As we shall see, it is a fallacy to assume that most Soviet films were no more than propaganda or that most directors were mere tools of the state's cinematic bureaucracy.

Despite cinema's nationalization, central control of the enterprise was far from easy. Films are complicated cultural products, much harder to censor than the written word. War films deviated from the Party line with surprising frequency, and although they can be construed as "political" (like all art), they were not necessarily intended to be propaganda. Even subtle digressions from the "general line" can, therefore, be quite illuminating, illustrating the complex dynamics of Soviet cultural production during the most authoritarian times. In the late Soviet period, as the system was in decline, filmmakers often strayed "off message," telling stories about the Civil War and World War II that were complex and ambiguous.

The final goal of this book is to understand how Russian war films functioned as art and entertainment. The "art or entertainment" dichotomy entered Soviet cultural discourse in the 1920s, a subject that I have addressed in earlier work.[10] The war genre provides a particularly interesting case study for interrogating this analytical paradigm because the most significant works in Soviet cinema, in terms of artistic merits, sociopolitical impact, or box office appeal, have been films about war and wartime. Some of them—Chapaev, The Cranes Are Flying, Come and See—are well known outside Russia, but most of the films discussed in this book are popular films intended to appeal to the mass audience. Few of these were exported. Yet even the least successful among them was seen (and seen again) by millions of Soviet citizens, especially true for the blockbusters.

Art films are typically privileged by scholars because they are the films that offer the most complexity for analysis—and also because they are the films we usually prefer to see. The best entertainment films, however, have more widespread *social* impact than the best art films because they appeal to millions more people. The reason for the greater popularity of entertainment films can be easily understood by comparing what David Bordwell calls the "classical narrative" of the Hollywood entertainment film to art film narrative. From the 1930s on, socialist rhetoric notwithstanding, Russian war films conform closely to Bordwell's models. This is not as paradoxical as it might seem. In structural terms, the recipe for the classical narrative that Bordwell describes is virtually the same as Katerina Clark's typology of the socialist realist narrative.[11]

The structure of the classical narrative is ideally suited to telling war stories. The story (*fabula*) is character-centered and action-oriented. The plot (*siuzhet*) consists of three parts: the status quo (peacetime) is established; it is then violated (invasion); and, finally, set right ("victory"). In the Russo-Soviet context, however, victory rarely means an American-style happy ending, but rather, a Soviet version of "happiness": achieving martyrdom through death. There are typically at least two story lines: the "mission" (the collective goal) and the "personal" (individual leaders or comrades). The story unfolds chronologically, with restrained use of flashbacks and crosscutting. The film's visual style is realistic, drawing from a limited palette of devices. The goal is an easy-to-follow story, with a clear message.

Art film narration is especially well suited to the war film when the message is intended to be antiwar.[12] The art film's main goal is to deconstruct the notion of a single reality that can be explained through a linear narrative. Art film directors leave gaps in their stories, manipulate and disrupt time, and use stylistic devices to unsettle rather than to clarify. Art films have protagonists rather than heroes, and, as Bordwell writes, their "prototypical characters . . . tend to lack clear-cut traits, motives, and goals."[13] The message is fragmented and ambiguous in order to provoke the viewer into engaging with the film's issues.

For decades, because of the isolation of the USSR, Soviet cinema was considered sui generis. The USSR was never, however, as hermetically sealed as cold war rhetoric implied. Fans of Hollywood and British war films will find the structure and themes of many Russian war films quite familiar; a comparative analysis would be an interesting subject for a different book.

My intention here, however, is not to compare and contrast Russian war films with their Anglo-American counterparts but, rather, to consider the particularities of Russian war films in their sociopolitical context. By interrogating the traditional bifurcation between elite and popular moviemaking in these pages, I demonstrate that this dichotomy can be artificial when considering *themes* rather than style and structure. In thematic terms, the best-known Soviet art films about war and wartime actually have a great deal in common with their mass-market counterparts (and vice versa).

This is not surprising. Most important Soviet filmmakers studied at the same school, the All-Union State Institute for Cinematography (VGIK), under the tutelage of major directors (or cinematographers, scenarists, etc.). After graduation, they competed to be assigned to Mosfilm or Lenfilm (the largest, most prestigious studios). When their careers were established, they also taught at VGIK, repeating the cycle.

Overview

Insofar as possible, I have sought to write a "classical" narrative, straightforward and accessible, with enough description to allow readers who have not seen these films to come to their own judgments (and, perhaps, to be inspired to seek them out for viewing). I try to avoid jargon, hyperanalysis, and equivocation (the last has been banished to the notes).

The book's overall structure is chronological in order to demonstrate change (or lack thereof) over time and to analyze the extent to which political and social changes actually impacted production. As a historian, I readily confess to being a captive of what Petrov calls the "determining background of historical meteorology."[14] That said, the nature of the material guides the shape of individual chapters. Chapters are introduced with an italicized historiophoty, that is, a brief summary of how the history of the wars is interpreted for the screen—not "what happened" (which is unknowable) but the points of view presented on-screen. This is followed by a concise overview of the political and cultural context. "Art" and "entertainment" films are divided into their customary categorizations, in order to underscore their thematic similarities, as well as their stylistic differences.

Chapter 1 lays the foundation: an overview of the first thirty-six years of Russian cinema from its beginnings in 1896 to the end of the silent era around 1932. In these years, Russia lived through three wars (Russo-Japanese, World War I, Civil War) and three revolutions (1905, February 1917, October 1917), with an embryonic patriotic culture marked by the absence rather than the presence of a rich body of war films. This chapter also establishes the peripheral role of the war film in Soviet cinema's golden age from the midtwenties to the end of the Cultural Revolution of 1928–1932.

Chapter 2 examines the relationship between Stalinism, socialist realism, and filmmakers in the first steps toward the creation of a war film genre. It focuses on three classic Civil War films: *Chapaev, We Are from Kronstadt,* and *Shchors*. This era was marked by increasing militarization, a drive toward conformism, and the widespread state terror, culminating in the massive purge of the Party and the army, known as the Great Terror. Stalin's obsession with movies caused great difficulties for filmmakers, and yet they persevered in preserving a degree of artistic autonomy.

Chapter 3 looks at the war films made during the Great Patriotic War, focusing on the centrality of cinema to the wartime propaganda effort and the remarkable feminization and humanization of the genre despite the pressing political imperatives. Because the Soviet Union was fighting the enemy on its own territory for most of the war, it was essential that the entire population be mobilized for combat. Until late in the war, when the Red Army was on the offensive, most Soviet war films featured partisans and women, not soldiers. By 1944, however, women and guerrillas were being replaced as characters by uniformed officers, the higher ranking, the better.

Chapter 4 traces the Stalinist regression of the postwar years to the death of Stalin, a period marked by a "film famine," in which Soviet film production came almost to a halt for reasons both political and economic. The frigid cultural climate particularly affected the production of war films, as Stalin sought to displace commemoration of the war with increasingly overwrought celebrations of the Stalin of his dreams. By the late forties, Stalin had become the "hero" of most World War II films.

Chapter 5 examines the films of the Thaw, the period of cultural relaxation that more or less coincided with Khrushchev's rule, although it had no clear-cut end after Brezhnev took over in October 1964. Soviet cinema underwent a significant artistic renascence from the midfifties to the late sixties, and many of the most artistically important movies of the Thaw were war films that reexamined the legacy of the Great Patriotic War, a key aspect of de-Stalinization. War movies intended for the mass audience also flowered at this time. Whether art or entertainment, Thaw war films gave World War II a human face.

Chapter 6 looks at the first years of the Stagnation, as Soviet intellectuals dubbed the Brezhnev era. The late 1960s were indeed a difficult period for makers of war films, as Brezhnev sought to reinforce his authority by developing a cult surrounding the commemoration of World War II that would promote patriotism and militarism. Directors were now discouraged from making intimate war films in favor of overblown war epics, culminating in Ozerov's *Liberation*, commissioned for the twenty-fifth anniversary of Victory Day in 1970. Directors also tried their hand at making war comedies, which proved popular with a public hungering for escapist entertainment. As a result of these changes, some war film directors returned to the Civil War as a topic, with mixed results.

Chapter 7 "revisions" the cinematic landscape of the 1970s, usually regarded as a low point for quality Soviet films, regardless of genre. In some respects, Brezhnevian "philistinism" proved harder to combat than Stalinist authoritarianism. Although superficial combat epics continued to be churned out, famous Thaw directors like Grigory Chukhrai and sparkling younger talents like Aleksei Gherman and Larissa Shepitko made a number of challenging war films. In terms of the war film genre, the period 1972–1979 marked the apogee of the Soviet war film.

Chapter 8 examines the unsettled 1980s. Until Gorbachev unveiled his grand plans for restructuring Soviet society in 1986, Soviet cinema, like every other aspect of Soviet life, was in decline. The fortieth anniversary of Victory Day in 1985 produced only one important war film, Elem Klimov's *Come and See*. The reorganization of the film industry and the beginnings of glasnost seemed to sound the death knell for the war film genre. Directors turned to previously forbidden topics, and at least initially, the audience's appetite for exposés was insatiable. With the opening of the Soviet film market to exports, however, domestic production collapsed, and the Soviet film industry was moribund when the USSR came to an end on 25 December 1991.

Chapter 9 marks the beginning of new life for Russian cinema in general, but especially for the Russian war film. In the late 1990s, a new crop of directors turned to the Afghan and Chechen wars as subjects, and since 2000, films about World War II have dominated domestic production, especially films made for television. On the one hand, the Putin government hopes to revive patriotism and national pride; romanticized versions of the Great Patriotic War might help in this enterprise. On the other hand, every nostalgic or thrilling cinematic vision of the war seems to be countered by an exposé of the war's dirtiest secrets.

As these pages will demonstrate, Russian cinema is a cinema of endings and beginnings that both mirrors and influences the fate of the nation, as well as that of the state. When its death seems almost certain, it rises again like the phoenix from the ashes. The revival of interest in the World War II film in the twenty-first century promises a significant new chapter in the historiophoty of Soviet wars.

1 The Revolutionary Era, 1914–1932

By the 1920s, the historiophoty of the Great War and the Civil War that followed the revolutions presents a thoroughly Bolshevik point of view. The Great War is an imperialist war fought by the many for the benefit of the few, carried on by the treacherous Provisional Government after the autocracy is overthrown early in 1917. After the peace-loving Bolsheviks sign a separate treaty with the Germans, foreign interventionists join the counterrevolutionary Whites in a terrible Civil War that tears families and lovers apart. Because of the self-sacrifice and discipline of the Bolsheviks, both male and female, the Reds win the Civil War and thereby save the Revolution.

The groundwork for the development of the Soviet war film was laid some twenty years before the Revolution, with the birth of the Russian film industry. It is important to understand that the pioneering Soviet filmmakers did not start with a tabula rasa but in fact inherited a well-developed urban film culture. This chapter provides an overview of the early days of Russian and Soviet cinema and charts the tentative first steps toward the creation of a war film genre. Russia was in a state of constant warfare from 1914 to 1921, with revolution and civil war emerging seamlessly from world war. Directors and scenarists had plenty of material from which to draw, but as we shall see, they also faced political constraints that militated against critical interpretations of this painful period of conflict.[1]

Beginnings: 1896–1914

The movie age began in Russia on 6 May 1896, in St. Petersburg's Aquarium amusement park, with a screening arranged by Lumière. The empire's unstable political situation did not augur well for the development of a new industry, as over the next decade Russia was racked by rural famine, strikes from the rising industrial class, peasant rebellions, a catastrophic war with

Japan, and the Revolution of 1905–1907. Although American and British entrepreneurs also moved in early to "colonize" Russian cinema, the French companies Lumière, Pathé, and Gaumont persevered in the face of daunting obstacles to lay the foundations for the Russian film industry—and to dominate it.

In 1908, Aleksandr Drankov, a photojournalist and portrait photographer in St. Petersburg, opened his own studio to challenge French control. After the triumph of his first film, *Stenka Razin* (Stenka Razin, 1908), native-owned production and distribution companies proliferated. The balance of power began slowly to shift, stimulated by the rise of nationalist sentiments as the political right strengthened in response to the rise of various socialist, revolutionary parties. The number of pictures produced by Russian companies grew rapidly, from 19 in 1909 to 129 in 1913, an impressive increase considering the strong competition from well-financed foreign studios.[2] Foreign films continued to dominate Russian screens before World War I, but after 1908, the French had to compete with imports from Germany, Sweden, Denmark, and Italy, often brought in by Russian-owned distribution companies.

Films required venues for screening them—and audiences to watch them. Although temporary installations and traveling shows dominated, on the eve of war in 1913, the empire counted 1,500 movie theaters, mainly in cities.[3] Concrete sales and attendance figures for the cinema are hard to come by, but one 1914 account, looking back at the previous year, reported 108 million tickets sold and estimated that regular patrons numbered some 12 million.[4] This seems like a minuscule number for a country with 140 million people until one considers that it represents nearly *half* of Russia's urban population. Regular moviegoing continued to be a primarily urban pastime throughout the life of the USSR.

Censorship was less of a problem for studios before the Revolution than after it. Although the Russian imperial censorship was the most stringent in Europe, it was primarily political in its focus. Censors rarely concerned themselves with issues of morality, sexuality, or violence in the arts. After the Revolution of 1905, with the establishment of the constitutional monarchy, state censorship relaxed considerably and became even more narrowly political, focused on preventing the spread of socialist ideas. In the cultural community, the practice of self-censorship was long ingrained.

In any case, no Russian studio head had socialist sympathies, so it was relatively easy to avoid running afoul of censorship regulations in imperial

Russia. Practically speaking, there were two ways for a film to get into censorship trouble. The first was religious censorship, centering on screen adaptations of Leo Tolstoy's work. The second was the Romanovs' claim to a monopoly on the production and distribution of their own image and policies. This is likely the reason that there were so few war films before 1914, and none that were well known apart from Vasily Goncharov's *The Defense of Sevastopol* (Oborona Sevastopol'ia, 1912), a picture about the Crimean War produced by the Khanzhonkov Studio. The first "full-length" (i.e., 2,000-meter) film made in Russia, *The Defense of Sevastopol* not surprisingly focused on the heroism of the defenders, rather than on Russia's defeat in the war.

The Great War, 1914–1917

The Great War marked a turning point in the history of early Russian cinema.[5] Up to this time, the Russian film industry had evolved in the same way as cinema in Europe and America. Native Russian production skyrocketed after the outbreak of the war in 1914. German imports were entirely cut off, leaving Russian audiences without their favorite German film stars—and Russian producers without German film stock and equipment. Importing other foreign films became increasingly difficult as the war deepened and land routes became harder to traverse.

Nevertheless, Russian producers rose to the challenges and opportunities the war presented. Production nearly doubled from 1913 to 1914 (from 129 to 230 titles) and then doubled again, to 500 titles by 1916.[6] Given the explosion of the film industry after the outbreak of war, it is not surprising that exhibition sites increased as well. By 1916, there were about 4,000 movie theaters in Russia serving 2 million viewers daily.[7] According to one Soviet film historian, the cinema outsold the stage ten to one, a marked shift in viewer preferences.[8]

Russia's wartime movie business was an island of prosperity in the midst of a national economy in collapse. The government, frantically searching for new sources of revenue to finance the war, sought to exploit the successes of the film industry by dramatically increasing taxes, which led to the formation of a producers' association as well as a theater owners' association and the politicization of formerly apolitical businessmen.

One of the most interesting aspects of Russian cinema during the Great War is the absence of patriotic films from the repertory, particularly as the war dragged on with little success and faith in the government of Nicholas II plummeted. Initially, Russians responded with the same degree of cheerful jingoism as did the citizens of the other combatant nations. Filmmakers were pleased to have new subject matter—and new villains. For the first time, not only was it politically safe to make movies about a modern war, it was encouraged as a patriotic duty. From 1 August 1914 to the end of the year, nearly half the films made (50 of 103) concerned the war, but two years later, in 1916, the figure was only 13 titles out of 500.[9] Part of this shift can be attributed to moviegoers' understandable desire for escapist entertainment as the brutal war dragged on. However, it probably also illustrates the public's disaffection from the czarist government and its disastrous war effort—as well as the government's difficulty in organizing cinematic propaganda effectively (the impact of which the Bolsheviks surely noted).

The failure of the government's efforts at political persuasion were not, of course, limited to cinema. But the government's inability to mine cinema's propaganda potential is particularly noteworthy given the czar's well-known personal interest in film and photography. This led in 1915 to the creation of the Skobelev Committee, named in honor of a nineteenth-century Russian general, which was intended to stimulate the production of patriotic films to support the flagging war effort. Nicholas II seriously considered nationalizing all film production to create, as Viktor Listov has noted, a "moral state cinema which would be free of the pernicious influence of the Western democracies."[10] Commercial producers were not pleased to have state-financed competition from the Skobelev Committee, but it quickly became clear that they had no reason to worry. The state fared no better at filmmaking than it did at war-making.

Russian producers made films on patriotic themes when they felt so inclined, and only as long as war movies would attract paying customers to the theaters. Studio head Aleksandr Khanzhonkov, Russia's most successful producer, recounted in his memoirs that in October 1914, he "had to give in" to pressure to make a movie supppporting the war effort, despite the fact that he was "not a supporter of tendentious war films, lacking in art and unconvincing."[11] The result was The King, the Law, and Freedom (Korol', zakon i svoboda), which was based on a play by the popular writer Leonid Andreev. This movie was better received critically than the play itself, in part because Khanzhonkov staged a dramatic flooding of the fields of Belgium, which obviously could not be re-created on a stage in a traditional theater.[12]

Few of the patriotic films made during the Great War survive, but based on their titles and descriptions, we can imagine that they were, as Khanzhonkov suggested, "lacking in art and unconvincing." As Peter Kenez dryly notes, "The Germans in Russian films committed extraordinary atrocities before they had time to do so in real life."[13] The film *By Fire and Blood* (Ognëm i krov'iu, 1914), to name only one of many examples, also went by the alternate and more descriptive title *The Atrocities of the German Major Preisker* (Zverstva nemetskogo maiora Preiskera). The best of the extant specimens of wartime patriotism in cinema are the over-the-top melodrama *Glory to Us, Death to the Enemy* (Slava nam—smert' vragam, 1914) and the charming "trick" film *The Lily of Belgium* (Liliia Belgii, 1915).

Glory to Us, Death to the Enemy, directed by one of early Russian cinema's most gifted filmmakers, Yevgeny Bauer, falls below the aesthetic and dramatic standards of his finest work. It is, however, noteworthy in prefiguring the "violent woman" of the Soviet war film. The picture starred Dora Chitorina as a woman who joins the Red Cross to avenge herself upon the Germans for the death of her huband, played by the Russian screen idol Ivan Mozzhukhin (known in emigration as "Mojoukine"). The idea of a nurse as a murderous avenging angel might strike those familiar with the conventions of Western, especially American, cinema of this period as strange, but the strong, independent, even murderous heroine was a recurring motif in prerevolutionary Russian film melodramas, the genre in which Bauer excelled.

The Lily of Belgium provides a sharp contrast. This is a propaganda film that renders the "rape of Belgium" suitable for viewing by children and the tenderhearted, through the magic of Władysław Starewicz's animation of insect "puppets." In *Lily*, the rape of Belgium is portrayed through a battle between gentle winged insects and loathsome, ugly German beetles. A single battered lily escapes the treacherous onslaught of the beetles.

By 1916, however, producers no longer felt that they "had to give in" to any demands the government might make to produce patriotic films. Audiences were no longer feeling particularly patriotic, and studios returned to the production of the contemporary melodramas, historical costume dramas, and literary adapations that drew spectators to the movies in droves.

Movie producers rejoiced when the autocracy fell in February 1917.[14] The overthrow of the Romanov dynasty in February ended media censorship, which naturally pleased filmmakers. Their joy was short-lived. It soon became clear that the quasi-democratic Provisional Government, which was determined to continue the war, could not provide political, economic, or social stability to a country on the brink of total anarchy. By fall 1917, shortages of electricity left theaters dark most of the week, and after the Bolshevik takeover in October/November of that year, movies theaters were closed by order of the new government. Bolshevik proclamations made clear that the new government intended to implement a Marxist program, starting with the abolition of private property, but as long as the Bolsheviks stayed in Petrograd (St. Petersburg's wartime name), filmmakers felt protected by the distance between the capital and Moscow, then Russia's Hollywood.

When the nation's capital moved from Petrograd to Moscow in March 1918, production companies in Moscow began packing up and evacuating their studios and personnel to the Crimea, where the counterrevolutionary White forces were marshaling strength. All-out civil war followed. By late 1919, it was obvious to most filmmakers that the Reds would win the Civil War. As the fighting wound down in 1920, most of the Russian film industry's leaders were in exile, primarily in Paris, Berlin, and Prague, although a few made their way to Hollywood. Some, like Yakov Protazanov, eventually returned to Soviet Russia and reestablished their careers.

Filmmaking in Revolutionary Russia, 1918–1924

The Bolsheviks understood that force alone would not save their revolution. Their recognition of the agitational potential of the movies was prescient, particularly in a country with the lowest literacy rates in Europe. In 1918, workers' councils ("soviets") began to form revolutionary film committees in a mostly futile attempt to resume production. On 27 August 1919, in a largely symbolic gesture, the Bolshevik government nationalized the film industry, turning it over to Narkompros, the People's Commissariat for Enlightenment, the ministry of education. Commissar Anatoly Lunacharsky, a cultivated "Westernizer" (zapadnik), became cinema's great champion among the Bolshevik leadership.

The Civil War of 1918–1921 devastated European Russia.[15] Filmmaking took place under extraordinarily difficult conditions of famine, cold, and brutality. Trained cameramen and projectionists vanished, along with film stock and spare parts to fix broken-down equipment. Since by 1919 most established directors, producers, and actors had already fled central Russia for territories controlled by the White armies, young men and women with artistic talent found themselves rapidly rising to positions of prominence in the revolutionary cinema. These young people were drawn to film as the art of the future, the art of the masses, the art that for them exemplified the opportunities inherent in a socialist revolution.

Crisis sparked innovation. In addition to battle footage from the front, the Civil War repertory consisted of general newsreels and "agit-films" (*agitki*). *Agitki* were schematic one- or two-reel melodramas, with clear, simple, and direct political messages attacking the bourgeoisie and supporting the worker-peasant revolution. Colorfully decorated "agit-trains" traveled the country, carrying portable electric generators, a necessity in rural areas without electricity (i.e., most of the country). The screen for these impromptu shows was usually no more than a linen sheet. The agit-trains also carried Bolshevik propagandists to read the titles, explain the films, and monitor the political allegiances of the audiences.[16]

A semblance of order was restored to most parts of the country by 1921, although fighting and rebellion continued sporadically until 1922. Early in 1921, Lenin decided to end the draconian system of fixed prices, rationing, requisitioning, and forced labor known as War Communism in favor of a mixed economy known by its acronym, the NEP (the New Economic Policy). The NEP had the same salutary impact on the Soviet film industry that World War I had had on the prerevolutionary cinema. In 1922, the first state film trust, Goskino (State Cinema), formed under the titular control of Narkompros; it was renamed Sovkino in 1924, after the formal establishment of the Union of Soviet Socialist Republics. Movie theaters slowly reopened, and new ones were built. Eventually, the traveling exhibition circuit was reestablished, although with the aim of "enlightening" the rural masses rather than entertaining them. Initially, however, most of the movies screened were recycled hits from the old Russian film industry.

By the end of the Civil War, Soviet Russia's future filmmakers had converged on Moscow, which once again became the center of movie production; Petrograd (renamed Leningrad in 1924) became the capital of a cinema "counterculture." Because film stock was carefully rationed until the postwar economy recovered (in relative terms) in 1924–1925, young would-be directors contented themselves with theory instead of practice. They also competed with leading directors from the old regime who were reinventing themselves as Soviet filmmakers. Film censorship during the NEP was loose enough to allow all kinds of "bourgeois" artists to work, so long as they were not openly counterrevolutionary.

Little Red Devils: Dunya is interrogated by Makhno and his men. Courtesy BFI Stills.

It is not, therefore, as surprising as it might seem that the first box office success of Soviet cinema, the phenomenally popular *Little Red Devils* (Krasnye d'iavoliata, 1923), came from the experienced hands of one of these bourgeois directors, Ivan Perestiani, a fine movie actor who had worked with imperial Russia's master director Yevgeny Bauer. This first Soviet "hit" was set during the Civil War, rather than the Revolution. Perestiani's delightful film is only superficially political. This is war-as-rollicking-adventure, with a trio of lively children as the protagonists.

The story concerns an orphaned brother and sister, who join forces with the Negro boy, "Tom Jackson," to fight a gang of "Greens" associated with the evil Ukrainian anarchist leader Nestor Makhno (who sports sunglasses). *Little Red Devils* is an enjoyable pastiche of styles: comical escapades alternate with scary ones. (The young girl Dunya is actually tortured on hot coals.) The villains are deliciously villainous; the spunky children make great heroes. The story is easy to follow, quick-witted and fast-paced. The Reds triumph; their opponents die.

The contrast with the Civil War's true brutality could not have been more marked, which is, of course, entirely the point. The war's survivors needed no reminders of its horrors scarcely a year after the conflict's end. What they needed was escapist entertainment, and Perestiani cheerfully provided it. Critics enthusiastically applauded.[17] The film enjoyed a remarkably long life; one veteran of the Stalingrad campaign recalled that it was screened for the soldiers on 7 November 1942 (the twenty-fifth anniversary of the October Revolution) and many times thereafter.[18]

The Great War during the "Golden Age," 1925–1932

Despite the success of Little Red Devils, war films were only slightly less tangential to the history of early Soviet cinema than they were to imperial Russian cinema. An examination of the depiction of the Great War and the Civil War during Soviet cinema's golden age illuminates the problems directors faced. The year 1927 marked the tenth anniversary of the Russian Revolution, and a number of celebratory films were commissioned from major directors to commemorate the event. Therefore, many of the best examples of the role the Great War played in the revolutionary film come from 1927–1928.

The most famous anniversary film was Sergei Eisenstein's October (Oktiabr', 1928), in which the war is no more than a sidebar to the main action of revolution. Even though soldiers and sailors are the main characters, they are revolutionaries rather than combatants. The only exception is a very brief scene of fraternization near the beginning of the picture. Russian and German soldiers embrace, brother to brother, proletarian to proletarian, until shrapnel fire drives them back into the trenches. The Provisional Government has committed the Russian worker-soldier to fighting a losing war, for a "cause" that no one understands and that only the effete officer class still embraces for the sake of its crumbling honor.[19]

Another film commissioned to celebrate the tenth anniversary of "Great October," Vsevolod Pudovkin's masterpiece The End of St. Petersburg (Konets Sankt-Peterburga, 1927), provides a slightly more detailed view of the Great War, while remaining clearly revolutionary in its purpose. The End of St. Petersburg is set at a munitions factory and focuses on the conflicts between the plant's workers and its unprincipled manager and greedy owners in order to illustrate rising class consciousness and heightening class tensions in Russia on the eve of revolution. (An interesting secondary theme shows the close connection between this "military-industrial complex" and the czarist government.)

Depictions of the war itself occupy only about ten minutes of the film's footage, with a few standard, if well-shot, scenes of soldiers in the trenches. The pandemonium of battle is crosscut with the pandemonium of the scene on the floor of the stock exchange as the value of shares in Lebedev Munitions rises dramatically because the firm has obtained an exclusive government contract. An intertitle informs the viewer that the war is a provocation to divert attention from the growing revolutionary movement. Pudovkin demonstrates how cleverly the imperial government manipulates the masses to patriotic fervor (an irony that was overlooked by Soviet censors and critics in 1927, the year of a fabricated war scare with Britain).[20]

Another interesting though atypical example of the Great War's representation in early Soviet cinema comes from Fridrikh Ermler's *The Fragment of the Empire* (Oblomok imperii, 1929). The story of an amnesiac (the result of a war injury) who suddenly recovers his memory to discover that Russia has been replaced by the USSR, this was Ermler's most experimental film to date, skillfully employing unusual camera angles and cutting to show the man's overwhelming confusion at the disappearance of his world. The eight-minute opening sequence, set during the Civil War, offers a nightmare vision of combat's aftermath: bodies are unceremoniously dumped on stretchers, soldiers pile onto trains. The befuddled protagonist Filimonov (played by the brilliant silent film actor Fyodor Nikitin) is stealing boots from the corpses, one from a soldier who is still alive.

The film then flashes forward to 1928. Filimonov's memory is stirred by a glimpse of his wife at a train window. A packet of cigarettes, and then the sound of a bell, triggers a new rush of memories. In a ten-minute tour de force of silent film art, we see Filimonov assaulted by a kaleidoscope of images from the Great War: from his service cross, to the crosses on graves; crawling on the battlefield, with a tank coming in his direction; finding himself in no-man's-land face-to-face with a German soldier. They smoke and chat together before they are fired upon. Tellingly, Nikitin plays both parts; indeed, he plays all the soldiers in the flashbacks. This famous scene ends with his declaration of identity: "I am *unter-officer* Filimonov." Although the rest of the film concerns his efforts to find his wife and build a new life (as part of Ermler's ongoing critique of the NEP society), Filimonov continues to have occasional flashbacks to the war, of bombed-out buildings, maimed soldiers, barren fields, soldiers dying from typhus.[21]

This great film became a cause célèbre during the Cultural Revolution of 1928–1932, a period in which both avant-garde and entertainment films were attacked as unnecessary for a socialist society.[22] After initially strong reviews in the "realist" Moscow film press (closely aligned with the goals of the Cultural Revolution), *The Fragment of the Empire* was pilloried, more for its avant-garde style than its content.[23] The film regularly appeared in lists of the dreaded "formalist" films; by 1930, one of its early admirers, the well-known critic Ippolit Sokolov, had seen the political (if not moral) wisdom of revising his evaluation. Ermler's movie was now seen as emblematic of the "most basic danger in Soviet cinema."[24]

Given the increasingly regimented and intolerant cultural climate of the Cultural Revolution, exemplified by the case just presented, it is easy to understand why Soviet directors, like their counterparts in the war years, showed little interest in making films about the Great War. At a time of state-building and rapid economic transformation, no one could expect the Soviet government to encourage nostalgia for a cause so clearly linked to the interests of the old regime. Nor was the pacifist message of the typical European film about the Great War useful to the goals of a state that was rapidly militarizing to protect itself from the "capitalist encirclement." If anything, the virtual abandonment of internationalist policies in order to focus on the domestic economic front and the building of "socialism in one country" made cinematic examinations of the war less palatable than before. There was, therefore, no reason to expect that Soviet cinema would ever produce an important film about the Great War.

The Civil War as Entertainment and as Art

In sharp contrast to the Great War, the Civil War was a truly national conflict that marked Red victory rather than Russian capitulation. Soviet Russia was forged in the fires of the Civil War, a war that was both devastating and awe-inspiring. Much has been written about the cult that developed around the Civil War and its "fighting brotherhood,"[25] but little about the failure of early Soviet cinema to reinforce in any meaningful way the Bolshevik interpretation of the war. The culture of absence surrounding World War I is understandable; the culture of absence in cinema surrounding the Civil War in the 1920s requires more explanation.

As we have seen above, the first box office success of Soviet cinema, Georgian director Ivan Perestiani's phenomenally popular *Little Red Devils*, was set during the Civil War. Although no other Civil War movie matched the box office success of *Little Red Devils*, which remained a favorite through the decade, the "middling" directors of what we now call B pictures developed their own formulas for the Civil War as adventure. These generally forgettable films focused mainly on the depredations of the Cossack bands that allied with both the Reds and the Whites and also exploited the extreme violence of the war for sensational effect.

Among the better-known examples of this type of Civil War film are two from 1926: *Wind* (Veter) and *The Tripol Tragedy* (Tripol'skaia tragediia).[26] *Wind*, directed by L. Sheffer, was written by Abram Room (soon to become an important director) and Nikolai Saltykov, who also starred in the main role of Commander Guliavin. Guliavin, an officer in the Red cavalry, is seduced by an *atamanka*, the female leader of a Cossack band. The *atamanka* recalls the violent women of prerevolutionary Russian melodramas, but not their motivations. She kills because she enjoys killing—and because it arouses her. The sexual undercurrents in this film are quite strong. The more tempestuous her anger, the more Guliavin is attracted to her.

Foreshadowing the relationship between commissar and commander in *Chapaev*, to be discussed in the next chapter, a staff officer from headquarters attempts to warn the unsophisticated Guliavin of the dangers this woman presents to their cause. Aware that this officer has been attempting to influence Guliavin against her, the *atamanka* coolly murders him. Guliavin finds him lying in a pool of blood, shot in the head. Jolted to his senses, Guliavin begs forgiveness from his comrades ("I sold a brother for a woman") before she is executed, and the Reds ride off into the sunset. The combination of melodrama, sex, and violence doubtless made this film a guilty pleasure with audiences.[27]

Another film that used the Civil War as an excuse for staging strongly violent scenes was *The Tripol Tragedy*, directed by Aleksandr Anoshchenko, a Ukrainian filmmaker who had made a name for himself as a conservative critic of the avant-garde. Set in the Ukrainian village Tripol, the film presents a political message that critiques Ukrainian nationalism, but this message was completely consumed by the relentless orgy of violence that the Cossacks unleash upon the village. Essentially plotless (save for an unbelieveable romance between a sweet young girl and a bestial *ataman*), the film moves from one hanging, looting, shooting, fire, rape, and so forth, to the next. The Cossacks beat up old ladies. They bury their enemies alive and dance on their graves. *The Tripol Tragedy*'s over-the-top violence led to an extensive critical discussion in the cinema press about the negative social impact of excessive violence on screen, even if "historically accurate."[28]

The other major Civil War film category in the 1920s was the family drama. Like any civil war, the Russian Civil War divided families. This subject was not only painful, it was also dangerous in the postwar political climate. Anyone with relatives among the Whites sought to sever or hide such ties.

This fraught theme inspired no masterpieces so soon after the war's end. One of the better examples came from Abram Room, *Death Bay* (Bukhta smerti, 1926), another from Ukrainian director Georgy Stabovoi, *Two Days* (Dva dnia, 1927).[29] In both films, the political divide is generational, a tale of fathers and sons. Although neither father is actually a White, each is apolitical, which allows him to continue working for the Whites. Their sons, however, clearly support the Reds. In both cases, the fathers are eventually aroused to action against the Whites. Room's film, which is set on a battleship, is more successful as a "war film"; this father, a ship's mechanic, eventually sinks the ship. In *Two Days*, on the other hand, personal tragedy, not political conviction, motivates the father—the gentry child he has saved from the Reds betrays his own son to the Whites. The old servant torches his master's house, an action on an entirely different order of magnitude from the destruction of a battleship.

Another variation on this theme of divided loyalties can be found in Yevgeny Cherviakov's *Cities and Years* (Goroda i gody, 1930), adapted from Konstantin Fedin's novel by the same name.[30] War and revolution divide friends, rather than family members, with the "nationality question" providing an additional point of contention. A young Russian artist, who lived and worked in Germany for a number of years, returns home. Allied with the Reds, he nevertheless helps a German acquaintance who is fighting with the Whites escape capture. Another German friend, a staunch communist, discovers the artist's treachery; faced with the threat of execution, he commits suicide. Soviet critics noted that the "salon-poetic" treatment of this melodramatic tale scarcely fit the demands of the Cultural Revolution; the weak-willed protagonist was more like the "superfluous man" of a century earlier than a model hero for the new society.[31] By 1930, politically astute filmmakers understood that friendship—and even family—needed to be subjugated to the transformation of state and society.

The three best (and best-known) films of the Civil War after *Little Red Devils* all appeared in the late 1920s, at the end of the silent era. These were Yakov Protazanov's *The Forty-first* (Sorok pervyi, 1927); Vsevolod Pudovkin's *The Heir to Genghis Khan* (Potomok Chingis-khana, 1928, also known in English as *Storm over Asia*); and Aleksandr Dovzhenko's *Arsenal* (Arsenal, 1929). Each views the Civil War from a different vantage point.

The veteran Protazanov, who had been working in Russian film almost from its inception, brought his well-honed talents to this adaptation of the eponymous novella by Boris Lavrenev, a popular writer of pulp fiction.[32] Protazanov stays close to the skeletal plot that may have drawn some inspiration from George Bernard Shaw's play *The Admirable Crichton*, with the introduction of a gender reversal. Mariutka, an unschooled and coarse young woman from a working-class background, is a skilled sharpshooter, so skilled that she has claimed her fortieth victim by the time that the handsome White lieutenant Govorukhin, who is carrying a message from Admiral Kolchak to General Denikin, is captured by her unit. They are eventually stranded on an island in the Caspian Sea, where, predictably, they fall in love. But, unpredictably, at least to Western eyes, when a White ship appears on the horizon to rescue them, Mariutka unhesitatingly claims her forty-first victim, although she is overcome by grief after the deed is done.

The Forty-first is a skillfully blended mixture of two genres popular in early Soviet cinema. First and foremost, it is a melodrama: the pretty girl finds her femininity and emerges from the chrysalis of her soldier's uniform to bask in the love of a handsome young man. The lieutenant, too, is transformed. He overcomes his class prejudices to see the innate goodness in the girl, who saves his life when he is dying of fever and sacrifices her precious poems to give him cigarette paper.

The film is also an "Eastern." European Soviets (like European Russians before them) were fascinated by the "exoticism" of the vast expanses of the Asian USSR. The first half of *The Forty-first* is set in the Kara-Kum Desert. Military service there is brutal; the Red brigade has to contend not only with the Whites but also with nomads and brigands who spirit their camels away. (Some of the natives do, however, shelter the Red survivors.) Nature in the East is unfriendly to the Reds, and the desert, with its blinding light, extreme heat, and lack of water, becomes an enemy more powerful than the Whites. So, too, are the waters of the wild and stormy Caspian, which claim the lives of the men sent with Mariutka to accompany Govorukhin to headquarters.

Protazanov had previously proved capable of laying a communist patina over virtually any subject, but here the obligatory political commentary is organic to the content and therefore aesthetically more palatable. Exhortations to save the Revolution shore up the defeatists in the ragtag band. The natives who help the Whites are unscrupulous and lascivious; those who aid the Reds are open-faced and hospitable. Until he learns better, Govorukhin cares more about form (like table manners) over substance; he grimaces watching Mariutka gobbling her food.

The final scene is exceptionally well edited in a series of short takes: they see a ship; Govorukhin fires shots to attract its attention; the ship closes in; he is ecstatic when he recognizes it as a White vessel; she shoots him as he exults; she kisses his body, trying to bring him to life; the soldiers come; she sees their epaulets; her face freezes. Protazanov seems to be posing questions to the audience: Is this Mariutka's victory as a Bolshevik? Or her defeat as a woman?

The Forty-first is a classic of Soviet entertainment filmmaking in the silent era. It was advertised as a hit before it even opened, perhaps due to the advance ticket sales, perhaps due to the Mezhrabpom studio's unerring commercial instincts. The film ranked third in the top ten list of 1928 and received generally good reviews, although one of the new hard-line critics labeled it a "socially primitive" and "decadent" example of the "Western adventure" film.[33]

Pudovkin's *The Heir to Genghis Khan* presents a different kind of revolutionary subject from *The End of St. Petersburg*. Like *The Forty-first*, *The Heir to Genghis Khan* is a Civil War "Eastern," but the enemy is the British imperialist invaders rather than the counterrevolutionary Whites.[34] Bolshevik partisans, led by a miner from the Donbass, engage in guerrilla warfare with well-armed and impeccably uniformed British regulars. A "Mongol," the native Bair, is inadvertently drawn into a conflict that is not his own. Shot trying to rescue a British officer, he in turn is rescued by the partisans and embraces their cause. Bair does not understand what "revolution" means, but he realizes that the Bolsheviks, unlike the British, are "of the people."

Fighting alongside the partisans, Bair eventually is taken prisoner by the British, who are puzzled by his involvement with the Reds (an accurate reflection of the fact that the indigenous peoples of Russia's eastern regions found little stake in the Bolshevik cause). At first the British plan to execute Bair but then decide to exploit him by making him head of the puppet government they are establishing in the region. Bair does not, however, remain a puppet for long and leads his people in rebellion against the British.

In terms of narrative development, this is the least successful of Pudovkin's silent films. The plot is neither well developed nor particularly coherent. The first half of the movie is dominated by scenes intended to establish that the British are motivated by greed. They need to support their lavish lifestyle (cars, jewels, servants, women), which contrasts sharply with the straits in which the partisans struggle to survive. Visually, however, The Heir to Genghis Khan is a masterpiece. The East is a force of nature. Its physical geography presents an obvious challenge to would-be conquerors, but so do its "simple" people, as we see in the final scene.

Costumed as an oriental potentate, Bair sits on his throne, inscrutable. When one of his people is executed by British soldiers before his very eyes, Bair suddenly springs to life, denouncing them as "robbers, bandits, thieves" before escaping on horseback. The British give chase, but Bair has picked up a veritable army of natives along the way. A dust storm blinds the British. The wind bowls them over; their guns are blown away. Bair's troops are completely unaffected. They speed ahead, to the future. "Death to the dogs of imperialism!" reads the final intertitle.

Given that The Heir to Genghis Khan appeared in theaters as the attack on "formalism" in cinema was gearing up, it is curious that critics ignored its undeniable formal artistry.[35] (As noted above, Fridrikh Ermler was not so lucky with The Fragment of an Empire.) Pudovkin experimented with symbolism in this picture to a greater extent than ever before. He also utilized a stylistic device dubbed "thingism" (veshchizm), an emphasis on objects for symbolic purposes, like the loving shots of the luxurious furs being sold at the bazaar. Unlike Pudovkin's previous films, The Heir to Genghis Khan lacks obvious mass audience appeal. But the film's attack on the British, coming on the heels of the War Scare of 1927, made it politically timely, regardless of its aestheticism.

The final important film about the Civil War era made during the 1920s, Dovzhenko's Arsenal, is particularly interesting for our purposes because it moves seamlessly from the Great War to the Civil War, essentially eliding the Revolution.[36] Arsenal also marks the transition from the 1920s to the 1930s. Finally, unlike any of the other films discussed in this chapter, it is almost wholly a combat film.

The Great War serves as *Arsenal*'s prologue, fifteen minutes or about one-quarter of the film's total length. The opening, establishing low-angle shot shows tangled barbed wire—no soldiers in sight. The second shot shows a woman standing alone in a bare room. The third shot returns to the front. Then the first intertitle reads: "A mother had three sons." This is followed by four highly abstract shots of the front, then the title: "There was a war." The woman walks through a desolate village before being confronted by a soldier. Title: "The mother had no sons."

This prologue is unusual because its Great War narrative is abstract rather than personalized. Dovzhenko presents a rapid montage of images, from the impoverished village to the czar sitting at his desk writing inane entries in his diary ("Today I shot a crow. The weather is fine.") to the battlefields, where a one-armed soldier stands. The continuous crosscutting becomes increasingly rapid and hysterical. Soldiers run through the barbed wire. Smoke obscures vision and understanding. A hideously laughing soldier. Gas attack. Arm protruding from the soil. Smiling corpse. "But where is the enemy?" reads the title. Soldiers march in silhouette, faceless, anonymous, insignificant.

The Great War serves as prelude to the Civil War. Soldiers deserting the battlefield return home to find that their wives have new babies, another symbol of the war's impact on the home front. They also see that the revolution in Ukraine has been co-opted by predatory nationalists, here represented by the elderly, the church, and the Cossacks, led by Hetman Petliura. Dovzhenko now introduces the enigmatic Timosh (played by the broodingly handsome Semyon Svashenko), identified simply as a "Ukrainian worker." The action becomes intentionally difficult to follow as Dovzhenko emphasizes the rapid flux of events in Ukraine, which was the main battleground of the Civil War, and the confusion over which "ism" would better serve the desire of the Ukrainian people for freedom: nationalism or communism? It is often difficult to tell which side is which during the battle scenes—or which side the director is on, until the end. Timosh, initially uncertain about taking a stand, joins the Reds against the nationalists. In the final, very famous concluding scene, Timosh, who is manning a machine gun, runs out of bullets. The counterrevolutionaries keep firing, but they cannot kill him. Defiant, he bares his chest for the bullets. The message is too obvious to require explanation.

As in *Arsenal*'s prologue, Dovzhenko privileges the horror and pathos of war over its glory or heroism. The wounded, the "lucky" ones, crowd the

Arsenal: Timosh defiantly prepares for death. Courtesy BFI Stills.

hospital. Corpses are everywhere, sometimes buried, mostly not. Dovzhen-ko's tracking shots of corpses and riderless horses are particularly com-pelling, as are the juxtapositions of shots and titles. (The riderless horse, which augurs death in Russian folklore, becomes a poignant trope of Civil War films.) To provide one excellent example of Dovzhenko's technique, the film cuts from the battle to a woman standing by a freshly dug grave, waiting for the body. Title: "Here he is, mother! There's no time for ex-planation." As a different example, a three title card sequence—"Where is father? / And husband? / And son?"—is followed by a shot of men being executed. Dovzhenko also uses titles to emphasize, trenchantly, the degree to which war has consumed men's souls, as well as their lives: "Four years of service, four years of war, one year of civil war," and then, "Bury me at home, brothers. I haven't seen it in nine years."

This movie found its detractors. Dovzhenko's negative depiction of the Ukrainian nationalists as narrow-minded and self-serving was continually undercut by Timosh's repeated identification as a *Ukrainian* worker. But even the film's most strident critics had to admit its powerful originality. As in the case of *Fragment of the Empire*, this originality was seen as a shortcoming. According to one observer, *Arsenal* was a film neither "understood by the million, nor oriented toward the millions."[37] Could the USSR, in the throes of accelerated economic transformation, afford to finance films that required "highly qualified" viewers?

The Problem of War Films in Soviet Silent Cinema

As we can see from the movies discussed here, defining a "war film" was difficult in the 1920s. Nearly 200 silent feature films (15 percent of the decade's total) were made on revolutionary topics, a figure that excludes the propaganda shorts produced during the Civil War to mobilize the population for the Bolshevik cause.[38] Most revolutionary features included some references to, or episodes about, the Great War and/or the Civil War. It would be misleading, however, to dub them "war films" because war served as little more than the "backstory" to the main story, revolution.

Second, for political reasons, the Great War never captured—nor was allowed to capture—the Russian imagination. Despite the massive loss of Russian life on the eastern front—casualty figures may have been as high as 6 million, with deaths ranging from 1.5 to 2 million—World War I was "the war that wasn't" in terms of postwar Russian cultural production. For the Bolsheviks, it was, of course, an imperialist war that pitted members of Europe's proletariat against one another, but as noted earlier in this chapter, the resistance to mythologizing the war began during the war itself.

Third, Soviet Russians had a competing war that was politically privileged over the Great War. War did not end in Russia after the Bolshevik Revolution in October 1917, not even after the Treaty of Brest-Litovsk in 1918. The Great War and the Russian Revolution evolved into an even greater calamity, the greatest test of the social fabric that any society can face: the brutal Civil War that claimed several million combatant lives, including perhaps as many as 7 million civilians.[39] The Russian Civil War was complicated by a variety of foreign interventions, including a war with neighboring Poland, newly independent and expansionistic, that lasted to the end of 1920. The events of 1917–1920, loosely dubbed "the Revolution," supplanted the memory of the Great War and became the stuff of myth-making in art, theater, literature, and the movies. For Soviet Russians, in marked contrast to the Germans, French, or British, the Great War was no more than a prelude to the even greater cataclysm that followed.[40] In fact,

"Great" was an appellation reserved for the October Revolution, as in the oft-used "Great October" (Velikii Oktiabr').

Finally, there is typically a lag in the cultural interpretation and representation of important historical events. Even in the West, important films about the Great War did not begin to appear until the midtwenties. Given that combat did not end until 1920–1921 in Soviet Russia, it is understandable that the delay would be a bit longer, to the late twenties. And at this point, unfortunately, directors of all political and aesthetic orientations faced the hurdle of the Cultural Revolution that urged directors to be present-minded, if not future-minded.

By 1932, as the Cultural Revolution was winding down, it was unclear whether any of the themes developed in these first attempts at a Soviet war film would survive. Given Stalinism's emphasis on the public over the personal, it was highly unlikely that there would be room for more films like *The Forty-first* or *The Fragment of the Empire*. Given Stalinism's emphasis on guilt by association, it was even more unlikely that the theme of divided families would have much traction. Films saturated with violence or sexual innuendo were also unlikely to find favor in puritanical Stalinist culture. But the heroes-who-will-not die, like Timosh in *Arsenal* and Bair in *The Heir to Genghis Khan*, could serve as a paradigm for future films, if stripped of formalist trappings and placed in more realistic narrative films.

It is no accident, therefore, that the dawning of this new age in Soviet cinema was marked by its first true combat film: *Chapaev*. Not only was *Chapaev* the most popular film of the 1930s, it was also the paradigm for a "movie for the millions," a film that was entertaining and politically sound at the same time. *Chapaev* and the birth of the Soviet war film genre are the subjects of the next chapter.

2 Socialist Realism, 1933–1940

In the historiophoty of recent Russian wars, the imperialist war of 1914–1918 recedes even further into the past. By the 1930s, it is a minor event, no more than a primary school for raising the class consciousness of worker-soldiers. The Russian Civil War, on the other hand, has become a university for political education. In the 1930s, or so the Civil War films tell us, Bolshevik "consciousness" tamed the revolutionary spontaneity of the masses and channeled it into victory. The message is clear. With Party and people working together, the USSR possesses the will to win any war.

As the Cultural Revolution wound down in 1932, filmmakers understood that the era of relative creative freedom was over. The artistic innovation that flourished during the Revolution and the NEP had ended. To quote from some of Stalinism's many slogans, movies and their makers were "in the service of the state," producing art that must appeal to "the millions."

Cinema was now supposed to support the state's social, political, and economic goals in addition to entertaining and educating the moviegoing public. This was a time of industrial transformation, widespread state terror, rising nationalism, and increasing militarization. More stringent control over cinema—before, during, and after production—ensued, and as a result, by 1933 production had plummeted to a mere thirty-five films.[1] This chapter examines the changing contours of Soviet cinema, the birth of a war film "genre," and the extent to which the war films of the 1930s supported the militarization of Stalinist culture. As we shall see, despite increasing obstacles, directors were able to maintain a surprising degree of artistic autonomy.

Filmmaking in the Stalin Era

"Socialist realism" was officially proclaimed the state's aesthetic paradigm for writers in 1934. Contrary to some cold war stereotypes, socialist realism was never a rigid formula but rather a set of mutable guidelines. In general, however, socialist realist art was characterized by simplicity of form and content, easily accessible messages that conformed to the goals of Party and state, action-oriented "positive heroes," and clearly recognizable enemies. It was formally adopted by the film industry in 1935 at the All-Union Creative Conference on Cinematographic Affairs. Some politically astute directors had foreseen the inevitable and for several years had practiced "self-censorship" by making movies set in factories or on collective farms that were only slightly more sophisticated than the *agitki* of the Civil War era.[2]

Socialist realism posed significant but not insurmountable artistic challenges to filmmakers less willing to compromise, especially the leading avant-garde directors of the silent era. The advent of sound cinema also posed difficulties that severely constrained the experimental talents of these artists. Because of the limitations of early sound technology, movies became much more static, with the quick cutting of the silent era giving way to "realistic" story films.

By the mid-1930s, the USSR moved into the era of purges, denunciations, arrests, show trials, and executions known as the Great Terror. As nervous directors tried to navigate the constantly changing "Party line," film production continued to plummet, falling well short of the target announced in the annual plans. Many projects were aborted midproduction. Stalin's intense personal interest in movies and his direct involvement in moviemaking greatly exacerbated the tense atmosphere in the film industry.[3]

Some films in this period indirectly supported the Terror by depicting upright Soviet citizens vanquishing the enemy within, but even "enemy movies" did not exempt their directors from the vagaries of an arbitrary and capricious censorship.[4] It would be a serious mistake, however, to assume that movies in the 1930s consisted mainly of enemy films devoid of moral integrity, artistic merit, or entertainment value. While art may have been an afterthought to the bureaucrats, entertainment films were central to the plans of Soiuzkino (Union Cinema, as Sovkino had been renamed) to revive Soviet cinema, as articulated by its head, Boris Shumiatsky.[5] Some of the first generation of Soviet filmmakers, who had been damned for their formalism during the Cultural Revolution, eventually rebuilt their careers by making revolutionary adventure films and historical films celebrating Stalin's favorite heroes from Russia's storied past.[6] Critical for the evolution of the Soviet film industry, a new genre, the musical comedy, also became quite popular at this time.[7]

As important as were musical comedies, historical costume dramas, and enemy films to the cinematic repertory in the 1930s, the revolutionary film also saw a revival. Indeed, 20 percent of the 308 Soviet feature films produced in the period 1933–1940 revisited the origins of the USSR.[8] Most of these aimed to "revision" the history of the Revolution and Civil War in order to cement the Lenin cult and strengthen the foundations for the rapidly growing Stalin cult.[9] Even though a number of these films are set during the Civil War, their focus is narrowly political, and war is no more than a backdrop.

The complicated political climate notwithstanding, three major war films appeared from 1934 to 1939: *Chapaev* (Chapaev), *We Are from Kronstadt* (My iz Kronshtadta), and *Shchors* (Shchors). Three less famous but also noteworthy pictures serve as counterpoint: *Borderlands* (Okraina, also known in English as *Patriots* or *Outskirts*), *Girlfriends* (Podrugi), and *Riders* (Vsadniki, also known as *Guerrilla Brigade*). Each contributed in important ways to the shaping of a war film genre in Soviet cinema, even if as an example *not* to follow.

The Great War's Swan Song: *Borderlands*

In 1933, the Great War found its poet in Boris Barnet (1902–1965), a popular young director of adventure serials and comedies who seemed an unlikely candidate to make any war film, let alone a great one. *Borderlands*—the most unusual film to emerge from this fraught decade—is the only Soviet movie made before World War II to deal exclusively with World War I. Of the six films to be discussed in this chapter, *Borderlands* alone makes an uncontested claim to "art." It is, therefore, an anomaly, but an important one.

When Barnet received the assignment to adapt Konstantin Finn's eponymous novella, his career was faltering. His Western-style entertainment films were distinctly out of step with the "Bolshevik tempo" of Stalinism. *Borderlands* concerns both war (combat) and "wartime" (the home front). Set in a Russian town that the opening title informs the viewer could be "anywhere," it was filmed in Tver.[10] Constructed in three discrete parts, *Borderlands* follows the contrasting fortunes of two families, the Greshins and the Kadkins. Cobbler Greshin, a man with some bourgeois pretensions, owns his small shop and lives with his feckless young daughter, Manka, and a German tenant. On the other hand, the Kadkins, a father and two sons, are proletarians working in the town's boot factory.

The film begins on the first day of the war. Barnet skillfully introduces both families through rapid crosscutting and minimal dialogue. To the despair of Kadkin senior, his sons Kolya and Senka, swept up by the wartime rhetoric, decide to enlist. The Greshins are also immediately affected by the outbreak of war. Barnet's Greshin becomes a mindless "patriot"; consumed with anti-German fervor, he ejects his longtime German boarder and friend. (In Finn's original story, Greshin was an intelligent skeptic and a cultural Germanophile, not a knee-jerk patriot.)

The second, central part of the film cuts back and forth between the battlefront and the home front. The battlefront scenes are exceedingly well done; Barnet may have drawn from his own frontline experiences as a medic during the Civil War. The Kadkin brothers languish with their comrades in the trenches, their boredom distracted by crude horseplay and sporadic shelling. When the time comes to charge out of the trenches and fight, Senka cowers in the bunker, weeping about his toothache. An officer drags him, screaming and crying, out of the trench and throws him into no-man's-land. He is shot and killed.

Meanwhile, the town hums with prosperity. German POWs and children are pressed into the service of the bustling wartime economy. Greshin's daughter, Manka, has become attracted to one of the Germans, Müller. At first, life looks good for Müller. Unaware that his younger son is dead, Kadkin offers the young German work and a bed in his home. An embittered, crippled veteran brings a gang of "patriots" to beat Müller up, savagely kicking and punching him until he is bloody and unconscious. Manka rushes into the fray to rescue Müller, assisted by Kadkin, even though he now knows that Senka has been killed in battle by the Germans.

The action of the third and final part is set in 1917 between the February and October revolutions. Soldiers in the trenches learn that the czar has abdicated. Kolya Kadkin once again enters the picture. He has beaten the odds and survived into the war's fourth year. After a pitched battle, all is quiet on the eastern front. Russian survivors lie exhausted in their trenches, while a badly wounded German soldier crawls toward them, piteously begging for his life. The Russians understand his meaning, if not his words; like them, he does not want to fight.

Kolya impetuously climbs out of his trench waving a white handkerchief on his bayonet. Alone against the scarred landscape, he slowly walks to the German side, met by a single German soldier. Troops spill over the embankments in a spontaneous, joyous, and short-lived moment of fraternization.

Borderlands: Kolya invites the
Germans to a cease-fire. Courtesy
MOMA Stills.

Kolya is executed for his role in this encounter; "barbarians" cannot be acknowledged as human.

Ending this war will not be easy. In the town an assembly has gathered
to hear their local socialist declare himself the representative of the Provisional Government, to the loud strains of "The Marseillaise." With the boot
factory owner leering at his side, he rants against Bolshevik incitements to
desertion and fraternization. At home, everyone rebels: Manka against her
father; Kadkin against the Provisional Government; Müller against loyalty
to nationality. The film closes with a montage of the townspeople march-
ing, led by Kadkin and Manka, intercut with shots of an old soldier kneel-
ing by Kolya's body, urging him to get up. The dead man's face seems to
wear a slight smile.

The tendentiousness of *Borderlands* is more obvious than its genuine icono-
clasm. If one were to judge by the plot alone, it sounds like a fairly predictable
propaganda film. Certainly, it bears no resemblance to the war films made
during the war itself, where all enemies were German, not Russian.

Barnet understood the essential social and political messages that he
needed to convey. The heroes in *Borderlands* are workers; the villains are not
the Germans so much as the bourgeoisie (the exploitative factory owner), the
socialist intelligentsia (the ubiquitous, upwardly mobile patriotic agitator),

and the czarist officer corps (the sniveling coward who orders Kolya's death while he is lying in the dust where Kolya knocked him). The male characters are perfectly typecast, especially Nikolai Bogoliubov's tall, strong, and ruggedly handsome Kolya, who could serve as the physical model for the Soviet New Man of the 1930s.

The film's attitude toward the Provisional Government is also politically correct: betraying the will of the people, the Provisional Government committed itself to continuing the war, a meaningless conflict pitting worker against worker. The Provisional Government is presented, more or less accurately, as an implacable foe of the Bolsheviks and a friend of what we would call today the military-industrial complex.

Finally, Barnet repeatedly privileges socialist internationalism and class solidarity over nationalist patriotism, but his timing is slightly off. Given the rise to power of the Fascists and National Socialists in Europe—and their appeal to working-class Italians and Germans—Barnet's internationalist message was becoming suspect.

Borderlands received mixed reviews.[11] By 1933, the journal Cinema (Kino) held sway, a very different situation from the diversity in the film press in the 1920s. Although Cinema initially praised Borderlands for its technical achievements, a few months later the "line" had changed. The Leningrad critic and scenarist Mikhail Bleiman, for example, complained that Barnet's understanding of ideological issues was weak at best and insinuated that the worst might be too awful for words.[12] These attacks certainly discouraged any other filmmakers who might have considered the Great War a viable topic.

Bleiman's suspicions about Borderlands' political platform had a valid foundation. Barnet's tale is not as straightforward as it might seem on the surface; its complex relationship between content and form directly challenged the newly articulated socialist realist aesthetic. Although (as already noted) socialist realism was not formally adopted as the official Party policy for the arts until 1934, it was well entrenched in practice by 1930. Truly Soviet, truly socialist art needed to present "life as it should be," in a form that was intelligible to the "millions."

Kadkin and his older son, Kolya, are admirable representatives of two generations of the working class. Both manage to control their emotions to do the right thing; they have, therefore, harnessed spontaneity in the service of consciousness. Kadkin recognizes that Müller, although a German, is not emblematic of the evil that claimed Senka's life. Kolya neither shrinks from his execution nor accepts it passively, which is demonstrated when he calmly knocks the officer threatening him to the ground.

Apart from these two iconographic portraits, however, we see a complicated view of class and class behavior in *Borderlands*. Most of the "little people" in the film, especially Greshin, represent pure spontaneity as they are swept up in the jingoism of the war. They resent Manka and Kadkin for their evenhanded attitude toward the German POWs. Furthermore, the depiction of Senka's death is a perfect example of the kind of brutal realism that inspirationalist socialist realist art intentionally ignored. Senka's fear as he is dragged whimpering to his death is palpable—and difficult to watch.

The idiosyncratic depiction of women in the film also deserves mention. Manka presents a particularly thorny interpretive challenge because she does not conform to the developing model of Soviet womanhood. In Finn's original version, Manka was a thirty-six-year-old spinster who ends up marrying the German POW. Barnet's Manka, on the other hand, is depicted as a girl in her midteens, still in short skirts and braids. The talented Yelena Kuzmina was badly miscast as Manka.[13] She looks considerably more mature than her twenty-four years, nothing like a child, which makes her giddily flirtatious behavior with the dazed Müller odd and disconcerting. Furthermore, Manka's decision to join the Revolution at the end of the film has no ideological underpinnings or glimmerings of class consciousness, unless resistance to patriarchy counts. She is piqued at her domineering father.

In stylistic terms, *Borderlands* displays a high degree of individualism and originality. These qualities were not prized in Soviet official culture in the 1930s. The narrative depends on crosscutting and parallel structures that become increasingly sophisticated as the story progresses. The montage is associational as well as relational. For example, Barnet frequently comments on the war's progress by cutting to the activity on the boot factory floor—or by cutting from the speechifying warmongers back to the trenches. This technique admittedly becomes a bit treacly at the end of the film as Barnet intercuts shots of Mother Russia's peaceful landscapes with those of the kindly peasant soldier who has befriended Kolya.

In pictorial terms, Barnet's visualization of combat is quite remarkable given the technical limitations of Soviet cinema in the early sound period. Despite his undeserved reputation in the 1920s as a lightweight director of commercial entertainment, Barnet here reveals his facility with the techniques developed by his better-known contemporaries in the cinematic avant-garde. A good example is his use of the extreme close-up and fast-motion cinematography as the soldiers are photographed flying over the trenches. (The design of the battle scenes is reminiscent of those in *The End of St. Petersburg*, not surprising given that Sergei Kozlovsky served as art director for both films.)

Barnet's effective utilization of sound montage exemplifies the principles outlined in the famous treatise on sound written by Eisenstein, Pudovkin, and Grigory Aleksandrov.[14] *Borderlands'* combat scenes are filled with sounds—explosions, sirens, whistles, and so forth—that are deliberately asynchronous with the visual effects. Barnet also employs sound as transition, cutting on sound, as when Greshin's smashing of Robert Karlovich's framed photograph becomes the thunk of boots on the factory floor.

Finally, the movie's quirky humor, though characteristic of Barnet's style, is unexpected. It is most evident in Müller's scenes; in his first meeting with Manka, for example, he does not notice that because of his abrupt departure, the bench they have been sharing becomes a seesaw, and she lurches to the ground. A talking horse that comments on the foolishness of patriotism near the beginning of the film is a particularly extreme example of Barnet's offbeat humor, but there are many others.

These factors combine to make a memorable picture, one of the most interesting early sound films as well as the only important Soviet movie about the Great War.[15] As an antiwar war film, it presents a Russian variation of themes being developed by directors such as Lewis Milestone (*All Quiet on the Western Front*, 1930) and G. W. Pabst (*Westfront 1918*, 1930).[16] However, in its denunciation of patriotism and militarism, *Borderlands* was also a cinematic dead end that revealed how politically problematic any Soviet film about the Great War was likely to be. The Civil War, on the other hand, was a different matter.

The Civil War: *Chapaev, We Are from Kronstadt, Shchors*

Chapaev was the biggest box office hit of the 1930s, selling more than 50 million tickets in the five-year period from its release to the end of the decade.[17] Directed by the self-styled "Vasilev Brothers,"[18] Georgy Vasilev (1899–1946) and Sergei Vasilev (1900–1959), Chapaev opened on 7 November 1934, the seventeenth anniversary of the Bolshevik Revolution. This movie attracted

Soviet audiences in droves and was well received abroad, particularly in the United States.[19] Stalin loved the picture; recent research has indicated that he watched it at least thirty-eight times.[20]

The film is still enjoyable, largely due to the screen personality of Boris Babochkin. He effortlessly inhabited the role of Vasily Chapaev (1887–1919), the brash commander of the Red Army's Twenty-fifth Infantry Division. Chapaev was an appealing hero, an uneducated peasant soldier elevated to leadership by the Revolution and his native talent. The historical Chapaev was killed in action late in the summer of 1919 after his brigade participated in repelling Admiral Kolchak's counterrevolutionary forces. He would likely have been a sidebar to the military history of the Civil War had it not been for Dmitry Furmanov's thinly fictionalized 1923 novel based on his experiences as the Chapaev Brigade's political commissar.[21]

Chapaev the book became an immediate best seller. Considered by literary historians to be a socialist realist novel *avant la lettre*, the novel doubtless provided readers a welcome alternative to the less accessible works by more famous avant-garde writers. Furmanov's book became a phenomenon of early Soviet popular culture, spawning a veritable Chapaev industry of songs, games, jokes, and postcards. The novel was still in print a decade after its publication, but the movie's success certainly extended its shelf life and completed the canonization of the Red Army commander in the pantheon of revolutionary heroes.

Furmanov's Chapaev was an unlikely prototype for "Homo sovieticus," especially given Stalinism's emphasis on conformism and absolute obedience to authority. This Chapaev, who we can assume bore some resemblance to the man himself, was unruly, impulsive, and politically ignorant. He is a model of the "spontaneity" of the people that needed to be tamed by the "consciousness" of the Party. Given Chapaev's background and circumstances, this is likely an authentic representation. Furmanov emphasizes it in order to glorify his own role as a frontline political commissar (modestly renamed "Klychkov" in the novel). In Furmanov's view, Chapaev blossomed as a leader only under his wise tutelage. (These commissars, not surprisingly, were the bane of many a commander's existence, in World War II as well as in the Civil War.) The Vasilevs emphasized these characteristics as well, but Chapaev comes alive in the film in a way that he does not on the page: rash and even foolhardy, perhaps, but courageous and full of life, infinitely preferable to the all-knowing and patronizing commissar.

The main plot—showing how Chapaev's relationship with Commissar Furmanov evolves from one of suspicion to mutual admiration—comes straight from the book. The Vasilevs wisely added two subplots that contribute greatly to the film's heart at a time when human interest was relatively rare in Soviet films. The first concerns the burgeoning romance between Petka, Chapaev's young right-hand man, and Anka, a "girl" machine gunner in the troop; the second is the relationship between the White colonel, who leads the counterrevolutionary army attacking Chapaev's division, and his batman, the subservient Russian peasant Petrovich.

We first see the legendary Chapaev division as a disorderly, ragtag band. Commander Chapaev does not set a good example for his men—not only is he slovenly (his shirt is not tucked in) he is also prone to shouting and tantrums. He overlooks breaches in military discipline; it is implied that he has condoned looting. Despite Chapaev's undoubted success as a warrior, there have been complaints about his arbitrary actions from the "pigeons" among his men.

The Party, in the person of the smug political commissar, comes to the rescue. Given the buttoned-up traditionalism of emerging Stalinist culture, Furmanov's role is as much about correcting Chapaev's personal behavior as about monitoring his political views. Furmanov smirks condescendingly as he observes Chapaev's methods, especially when the unlettered commander moves potatoes around a table to illustrate military tactics. Furmanov encourages Chapaev to smarten up his appearance and, in general, to lead by stellar example rather than by tantrums and bombast.

The brewing conflict between the two men comes to a head when the commissar orders the arrest of one of Chapaev's men, a soldier whom the villagers have accused of stealing a pig. Chapaev angrily confronts the commissar: "Who's the head of the division? You or I?" Furmanov calmly responds: "You. And I." When the peasants thank Chapaev for putting a stop to his men's thievery, Chapaev sees the wisdom of this and accepts credit for the order that was actually his commissar's.

Of course, Furmanov must provide Chapaev with political instruction as well as advice on grooming and etiquette. At a meeting to which Chapaev calls the villagers, one peasant asks him: "Are you a Bolshevik or a Communist?" As confused as his interlocutor, the commander responds vaguely: "I am for the International," which prompts Furmanov to retort, with a sly grin, "For the Second or the Third?" Chapaev is not, however, a complete political naïf. He wants to know which International Lenin favored and thereby saves face by also selecting the Third.

Chapaev: Chapaev as frontline commander, with Petka. Courtesy BFI Stills.

On the surface, the Chapaev-Furmanov relationship conforms to the desired political stereotypes. The disciplined Furmanov saves the unruly Chapaev from himself. The political message is, however, undermined by the fact that Furmanov is not a particularly likable character in the film—certainly not when compared with Chapaev.

One suspects that youngsters watching the film in the 1930s wanted to grow up to be a Chapaev, not a Furmanov. Chapaev is willing to learn from Furmanov when the latter proves he has something to teach, but he refuses to accept without question the authority of a man lacking in military experience. When Furmanov smugly informs the bewildered Chapaev that "Aleksandr Makedonsky" (Alexander the Great of Macedonia) is not a living general but one from the ancient world, Chapaev informs him, with dignity, that he only learned to read two years earlier and is trying to "catch up" as quickly as he can. The viewer's sympathies lie entirely with Chapaev.

The Petka-Anka subplot is the first full-fledged example of a love story in the Soviet combat film.[22] Although nurses often figure as the love interest in Soviet war films (as they do elsewhere), Anka foreshadows what would become a staple of the frontline love story; she is neither a nurse nor a telegraph or radio operator, but a soldier. Anka asks Petka for a lesson in operating the Maxim machine gun. As he instructs her, he fondles her breast and tries to kiss her. Indignant, she pushes him away, protesting, "I'm not a *baba*" (a pejorative term for a peasant woman). When we next see the two of them, Anka demonstrates that she has learned to assemble the gun. Now wise to the ways of the New Woman, Petka restrains his desire to kiss her and shakes her hand instead. As he takes his leave, she watches him with a confused smile. This is true love, Soviet style.

But Anka provides much more than romantic interest. She takes a major role in the battle scenes in the final third of the film as she "mans" the Maxim alone in the midst of a melee. She also brings in the reinforcements that rescue what is left of the Chapaev division at the end, too late to save the lives of Chapaev and Petka, but in time to save the Revolution. Anka represents the future: prior to the final debacle, Chapaev urges her to live and to stay strong for the cause.

The second subplot centers on another paired relationship, that between the White colonel and his batman, Petrovich. The colonel is an interesting and even surprising character for a Soviet film of this period in that, although he is an enemy, he is not entirely unsympathetic. Unlike the other White commanders, who dismiss Chapaev as a buffoon based on his class background alone, this colonel rightly regards Chapaev as a worthy adversary. When Petrovich's brother has been sentenced to be executed as a deserter, the colonel accedes to Petrovich's humble request for a reprieve (although the substituted penalty, to run the gauntlet instead, still leads to the brother's death from the savage beating). There is also a lovely scene in which the colonel plays Beethoven's "Moonlight Sonata" on the piano while Petrovich sways to the music, polishing the floor with a foot cloth. (Lenin's love of Beethoven's music and his irritation at the emotion it caused him was well known to the Soviet public.) But after the death of his brother, Petrovich crosses over to the Red side (earlier Petka has captured and released him) to reveal the Whites' battle plan to Chapaev. And it is Petrovich who in true melodramatic fashion eventually kills the colonel in battle, but, unfortunately, not before the Whites inflict grievous damage to the Chapaev brigade.

The first two-thirds of the film focus on developing the three sets of relationships described here, but the final third consists almost entirely of combat scenes. The only immediate points of comparison to *Chapaev*'s battle scenes are those in *Borderlands,* and the contrast is obvious. Although contemporaneous, these two sound films differ sharply in terms of visual and aural style. Barnet experimented with sound in the context of silent film aesthetics. The Vasilevs, on the other hand, made a genuine "talkie," with all its advantages and limitations. Sound is naturalistic (lots of singing and gunshots) rather than experimental. Even though the Vasilevs occasionally utilized the extreme close-ups and rapid montage of classic Soviet silent style, most of *Chapaev*'s battle scenes are long shots in longer takes that impart the *action* of open battle (as opposed to static trench warfare) very effectively. Despite the problems with Soviet sound technology, the Vasilevs succeeded in creating some exciting battle sequences, especially in the film's finale. Chapaev and his surviving men are forced to scramble down a cliff and into a river. We last see Chapaev swimming strongly, his rifle held high, until he is shot.

Chapaev received widespread press coverage and critical acclaim comparable only to that of Eisenstein's *Battleship Potemkin* (Bronenosets Potëmkin) a decade earlier. The Vasilevs received "noisy applause" when they met with the press to discuss the film.[23] The Leningrad studio was hard put to keep up with the demand for copies: the film was showing in sixteen theaters in Moscow and ten in Leningrad. Within two weeks of its release, 4 million people had already seen the movie, especially noteworthy given that this audience was almost entirely urban. Although there were 28,000 silent projectors in the rural cinema network, there were only 20 sound systems in the countryside at the end of 1934.[24] Stalin's veritable obsession with the film—from 7 November to 20 December 1934, he saw it *sixteen* times—put additional pressure on the studio to keep up with the demand.[25]

What was really new about *Chapaev* was how long it remained in the spotlight. To the end of the Stalin era, it remained *the* canonical film—not only of the Civil War but as the paradigm for socialist realism. It figured prominently in the commemorative photo album of Soviet cinema published for the twentieth anniversary of the Revolution.[26] It was widely shown at the front during World War II, to the reported and remembered delight of the *frontoviki.*[27] It also became an object of "scientific" study for the first generation of Soviet film scholars, to be analyzed and reanalyzed for the next fifty years.[28] In 1977, it came in twenty-fifth in *Soviet Screen*'s readers' survey of the old movies that should be shown again.[29]

It is noteworthy, therefore, that Soviet scholars and critics "overlooked" *Chapaev*'s significant deviations from the tenets of socialist realism, which emphasized the sacrificial positive hero, the Party over the individual, and "life as it should be." Chapaev dies for the cause, to be sure, but as we have seen, he is an individualist, not a conformist. He never appears to be ideologically motivated; indeed, he is unsure whether there is a difference between Bolsheviks and "communists." Although reinforcements appear at the end, the Reds have lost this battle. And why? Because they were *sleeping!* Even the sentries are sleeping, which has been a motif throughout the film, the one change that Furmanov was not able to enforce. How good a commander can Chapaev really be?

Stalin certainly ignored the cinematic Chapaev's political shortcomings. It is plain from Shumiatsky's record of Stalin's remarks after his near-nightly screenings in the 1930s that Stalin was a genuine film buff. He derived deep pleasure from watching movies, and especially from *Chapaev.* No other film came close for him. After his twenty-seventh viewing (on 10 November 1935), he observed to his cronies that "the more one watches it, the more one likes it"; after his thirty-eighth viewing (on 9 March 1936), he remarked with satisfaction, "This is, of course, the best film."[30]

By the standards of Hollywood or Paris or Berlin in 1934, *Chapaev* is a fairly average "B" picture. But it is a rather extraordinary example of an entertainment film as a political-cultural phenomenon. The next important Civil War film, *We Are from Kronstadt* (1936), could not possibly match *Chapaev*'s popularity, but it came close, for reasons that are instructive in the development of the genre as well as the politics of the times.

Just as *Chapaev* catapulted the Vasilevs to the front ranks of Soviet film directors, so did *We Are from Kronstadt* elevate its director, Yefim Dzigan (1898–1981), to prominence. Dzigan began his directorial career with Mikhail Chiaureli, the Georgian director who became infamous for his cinematic odes to Stalin. Dzigan had not, however, garnered much notice, critical or otherwise, for the five films he made prior to *Kronstadt.*

This movie, based on a screenplay by the well-known playwright Vsevolod Vishnevsky, was publicized in *Pravda* six months in advance of its premiere, a signal that it was intended as an "event."[31] Nevertheless, Dzigan faced many difficulties getting the picture from script to screen, a subject he was not free to discuss in print for another twenty-five years.[32] *Kronstadt* presented Soviet movie audiences with a fictionalized rendition of a famous chapter in the history of the Civil War, General Yudenich's assault on Petrograd in the fall of 1919. As we learn early in the film, Lenin has ordered Peter's city, the former capital, defended "to the last drop of blood."

There are two narrative threads. The first is the story of how citizens and soldiers banded together to repel the attack and save the city. The second, which holds more political import, is a conversion narrative demonstrating how the Party, represented by Commissar Martynov, saves the soul of Artyom, a "non-Party" sailor whom the other Red soldiers and sailors have scornfully labeled too "undisciplined" to join the unit that has been quickly assembled to save the city.

As in *Chapaev*, behavior management appears to be as important as ideological indoctrination for the Bolshevik leadership. We initially see Artyom as a thug who ogles and stalks a woman and then picks a fight with a man who tries to stop him (even though this man is accompanied by his young son). Artyom boastfully promises revenge: "You wait; I'll pay you back."

Yudenich's forces rapidly approach the city, so Commissar Martynov attempts to organize a defense brigade combining soldiers, sailors, and civilian volunteers. Each man's social background is carefully examined. Artyom, to his chagrin, fails this test, but Martynov nevertheless decides to "let him [Artyom] show what he can do." Martynov, carefully identified as a "Party member since 1901," is beyond reproach (although real Old Bolsheviks learned otherwise in the Great Terror).

Martynov's hastily assembled division needs to be transformed into an effective fighting unit. There is a great deal of dissatisfaction in the ranks, particularly concerning the lack of bread (one loaf for twenty men) and the need to share it equally among themselves, not to mention the possibility of giving up their food to provide for the starving children in a nearby orphanage. Instinctive communism is not much in evidence (they definitely dislike having to share), although a Party-minded sailor chides the grumblers: "Where's your revolutionary spirit?"

In their initial contact with the Whites, Martynov's division meets success. The men march into battle confidently singing "The Internationale." But when faced with a tank assault, they scatter in disorderly retreat until Martynov shouts "Communists! Stop!" Shamed, they do stop. Although the enemy advances in waves, the Reds heed Martynov's warning, "Not one step back."

The film's turning point occurs when Martynov, Artyom, and several other Reds, including a young boy, are captured by the Whites. This is where Artyom learns the stuff of which Communists are made. When Martynov is asked by his White captors to identify himself, he replies simply: "Member of the Party." The Whites offer "non-Party men" the chance to survive,

We Are from Kronstadt: "Mademoiselle" offers the orphanage as refuge. Courtesy BFI Stills.

but the prisoners, including Artyom and the boy, stalwartly step forward as Communists (whether they are or not). Stones tied around their necks, they walk calmly to their deaths, pushed off a cliff into the sea. The Whites refuse to spare the child.

Artyom alone manages to wrest free of his bonds before drowning. He fails to save Martynov but manages to drag the commissar's body to shore. He carefully preserves Martynov's Party card, reflecting that the safeguarding of one's Party card had become paramount for Party members. (A campaign to sanctify the Party card was under way, most famously celebrated in Ivan Pyrev's movie *Party Card* [Partiinyi billet, 1936].)

At this point *Kronstadt*'s subplot is foregrounded. A children's home for war orphans has found a makeshift shelter in an abandoned mansion. The orphanage, located in the center of the battle zone, becomes a place of refuge for Artyom as well. When Artyom addresses the stern (but beautiful) headmistress as "Mademoiselle," she retorts that she is not a "mademoiselle" but, rather, a member of the Party (later she is also revealed as the wife of a Red commander). She helps Artyom escape, disguised as a peasant woman.

Now he gets a taste of his own sexism as he is eyed by other soldiers. This marks the final stage in his conversion from lumpenproletarian to the Soviet New Man.

Fully reborn, Artyom assumes Martynov's role. Inspired to leadership, he urges non-Party men to join the Communists in avenging their commissar. He helps the Reds organize their counterattack, with soldiers in the front as decoys and sailors in the rear, all former rivalries set aside in favor of their common cause. Now it is the Whites who are driven off the cliffs to their deaths. The ending is triumphant: "Who else wants to take Petrograd?!"

This fast-paced movie proved to be a crowd-pleaser.[33] Its combination of pathos, humor, and adventure attracted the attention of audiences and critics alike. Its political message, while obvious and perhaps heavy-handed, was nevertheless appealing. Unlike Chapaev, Artyom actually needed to be "saved." Comparing Kronstadt to Chapaev, Pravda immediately proclaimed the success of Dzigan's film, which played in thirteen Moscow theaters simultaneously, only slightly fewer than for Chapaev.[34] Stalin pronounced it "good and extremely interesting" and watched it at least three times.[35] The film was exported and was particularly well received in France, which the Soviet press reported with some satisfaction.[36] It won a prize at the International Film Exhibition held in Paris in 1937.

The only sour notes came from rival filmmakers, and then only privately. For example, Sergei Eisenstein had been commissioned to write a laudatory review of the film (never published) in which he dutifully compared it to his masterpiece, Battleship Potemkin. At the end of March 1936, a few weeks after the film opened, he wrote sadly in his diary: "I saw We [Are] from Kronstadt. But somebody has got to preserve cinema culture. What I saw isn't even another level. It's like heaven and earth."[37]

Eisenstein was right, of course. Kronstadt is "earth," not "heaven," but it provided honest entertainment, which was more necessary than ever in the gray 1930s. Like Chapaev, Kronstadt continued to be rereleased and praised in commemorative articles for decades after its original release.[38] Dzigan's film was shown at the Stalingrad front in 1942 and remained a hit.[39]

Both pictures demonstrated that ideological conformity and entertainment value were not necessarily mutually exclusive, but neither film offered a surefire formula for other directors to follow. Indeed, neither the Vasilevs nor Dzigan ever made another film quite the equal to these early triumphs; their difficulties may be attributed largely to the unpredictable political climate, rather than to lack of talent. By the late 1930s, the dangers of interpreting the Civil War on-screen were obvious, as the case of *Shchors* painfully illustrates. In fact, Dzigan's next attempt at a Civil War film, *The First Cavalry* (Pervaia konnaia, 1941), was banned.[40]

As a number of scholars have noted, the history of the making of *Shchors* serves as a perfect illustration of the vagaries of film production under Stalin.[41] In 1935, Stalin himself suggested to director Aleksandr Dovzhenko that he should consider making a film about the "Ukrainian Chapaev," Nikolai Shchors (1895–1919), founder of the Bogun Brigade and commander of the First Soviet Ukrainian Division.[42] Dovzhenko was an unlikely choice to make a film about a Red Army hero: for a period during the Civil War, Dovzhenko had served with the forces of the Ukrainian nationalist Petliura, archenemy of the Bolsheviks and Shchors.[43] Most likely, Dovzhenko hoped that the project would bring him some measure of protection from his past and perhaps something akin to the adulation from Party and people that *Chapaev* had brought the Vasilev Brothers. The gifted, but politically hapless, director soon learned otherwise; the filmmaking took four trying years and countless revisions before coming to the screen in 1939.

Unlike Vasily Chapaev, who had been commemorated in Furmanov's novel nearly a decade prior to the Vasilevs' film, Nikolai Shchors was unknown to most Soviet moviegoers. But as George Liber has demonstrated, as soon as Stalin's mention of Shchors became public, the Soviet propaganda machinery jumped into motion, rapidly creating a larger-than-life Shchors who bore little relation to a commander whom his superiors considered problematic at the time of his death.[44]

Dovzhenko took this commission very seriously. He assiduously studied the historical materials available about Shchors and sought to include many real-life characters in the film, including Ivan Dubovyi. Dubovyi, who had been Shchors's lieutenant and served as military consultant on the film, was arrested on suspicion of espionage and executed in 1938 as part of the purge of the Soviet military. (Dubovyi ultimately confessed under torture to the ludicrous charge of murdering Shchors.) A month after Dubovyi's execution, Dovzhenko was in a serious (and suspicious) car accident; the steering column of his car had been cut. All the while, Stalin was meeting with Dovzhenko and criticizing various aspects of the script. In the final version of the film, Dubovyi and most of the other historical characters had been excised. Shchors, now played by the third actor to be cast in the role, was allowed to live on in the picture, even though he was actually killed. Not surprisingly, Dovzhenko suffered a severe nervous collapse before the film-ing was completed.[45] Shchors was finally approved for release in March 1939: Stalin, the only viewer whose opinions mattered, was pleased.[46]

Given the tortuous history of the production, which was not public knowledge for many years, it is no surprise that Shchors cannot be counted among Dovzhenko's major films.[47] Indeed, the director's distinctive lyrical visual style recedes into the background after a promising prologue. This opening montage—bombs exploding in a field of sunflowers, riderless horses, hand-to-hand combat, villages in flames, women and children flee-ing in terror—is vintage Dovzhenko. Especially memorable is the shot of terrified horses entangled in the sheets that unsuspecting housewives have hung out to dry. The spell is broken when we see Shchors: ramrod straight, impeccably uniformed, beard neatly trimmed, he is the model commander of the Stalin era. In his recent study of the Stalinist value system, David Hoffmann writes that by the late thirties the Party had "established a strict definition of the proper values and behavior of Party members: sobriety, sexual propriety, honesty, openness and loyalty."[48] The cinematic Shchors is all these.

Compared with the bare-bones narrative structure of Shchors, the plots of Chapaev and We Are from Kronstadt seem almost sophisticated. Shchors's di-vision must expel the Germans, Poles, and their local collaborator Petliura from Ukraine. His well-disciplined, well-dressed, well-equipped soldiers should have no trouble defeating these ill-assorted enemies, but Shchors apparently needs to deliver many, many speeches and lectures before his troops can spring into action.

Dovzhenko's Shchors is Civil-War-hero-as-professor. When not inspect-ing his troops, he sits at a desk in a book-lined room. From beginning to end, he is the hectoring, buttoned-down teacher, whose gestures from the rostrum recall newsreel footage of Lenin, from whose writings Shchors co-piously quotes. Shchors even lectures the family and guests at a village wed-ding that is unaccountably taking place in the midst of a battle.

Shchors also wears an air of martyrdom. His pained expressions in the midst of the human imperfection of wartime seem Christlike; his narrow face, neat beard, and burning dark eyes resemble the iconography of Jesus in Orthodox churches. His personal sacrifices for the cause are exemplified by an unwittingly humorous scene in which he dictates a letter to his wife. Whereas Chapaev might have done this because he was illiterate, for the bookish Shchors, this symbolizes his nearly complete separation from his former private and corporeal life. Ascetic in all ways, Shchors even refuses to smoke.

Shchors does have a foil in Hetman Bozhenko, a kindly, disheveled old man who always wears a peasant's embroidered shirt, the distinctive Cossack cloak (burka), and a peaked sheepskin hat. Bozhenko brings a little warmth and humor to this chilly movie. When Bozhenko is devastated by news of his son's death in battle, Shchors attempts to comfort him, but stiffly, as if grief is alien to him.

This is a very talky war film. When Dovzhenko is able to take the action outside, to the battlefront, he demonstrates the skill for staging combat scenes that he had first shown in Arsenal a decade earlier. But he fails to build dramatic tension effectively because at this point in Soviet history, the Germans, Poles, and Petliura cannot be depicted as the powerful, menacing obstacles to Red victory that they actually were. The main obstacle that Shchors faces, therefore, is not the enemy but the panic that engulfs the town of Vinnitsa when the populace hears that Petliura's troops are converging on the city. Shchors struggles for once with a genuine crisis: how to reestablish order in the crowd. A second crisis, but one that is not developed, is Bozhenko's death in battle.

The film ends shortly after Bozhenko's stately funeral procession. In fact, Shchors was killed a few days later, but the viewer receives no hint of that fact. We last see Shchors reviewing his troops, who suddenly appear as a real modern army. Unlike the soldiers in Chapaev or We Are from Kronstadt, these neatly uniformed automata march in disciplined, orderly rows. His dark eyes burning, his face alight with ecstatic fervor, Shchors announces that "Lenin told me" of the future victory.

In January 1939, about two months before Shchors officially opened in Moscow, Pravda prepared viewers (and critics) for the film's imminent arrival by announcing the film's genesis at Comrade Stalin's suggestion.[49] Given that the idea for the movie had now been publicly identified as Stalin's, Shchors could not be other than well received regardless of any shortcomings.[50] Indeed, the progression from Chapaev to We Are from Kronstadt to Shchors provides a textbook illustration of Stalinism's drive to create a disciplined citizenry and a disciplined military from the remnants of a revolutionary society. Chapaev is controlled, but never really tamed, by his commissar; Artyom is not only saved by his commissar but truly transformed; Shchors does not need a commissar because he already embodies the Party's principles.

Shchors: Shchors sees the future victory. Courtesy BFI Stills.

Counterpoint: *Riders* and *Girlfriends*

As the history of *Shchors* illustrates, by the end of the thirties, Soviet film-makers were in an unenviable position. A subject that was safe one day, approved by one set of bureaucrats, could ruin a career (or end a life) the next. Although *Shchors* ultimately succeeded in political terms, it failed not only as art and entertainment but also as a paradigm for subsequent war films. As the example of *Riders* indicates, directors were in no hurry to emulate *Shchors.*

In 1939, the same year that *Shchors* at last appeared on Soviet screens, another Ukrainian director, Igor Savchenko (1906–1950), released an entertaining film about the Civil War in Ukraine entitled *Riders* (Vsadniki). *Riders* is the only Civil War movie I have seen that successfully reframes *Chapaev.* The film, which opens in 1918, seeks to connect the concept of Ukrainian nationalism with the Ukrainian aristocracy who are linked with, and manipulated by, German imperialists. *Riders* was withdrawn after the Molotov-Ribbentrop Pact of 1939, but for a few months it provided Soviet moviegoers with rollicking entertainment.

Savchenko pits a Donbass miner, the brave and resourceful Red partisan Chubenko, against Gurkovsky, a Russian (probably Russo-Polish) officer whom the Germans "plant" among the partisans. Gurkovsky skillfully insinuates himself among the partisans as a medic, but his perfidy is defeated not by the Party as much as by the people. In cinematic terms, Chubenko, not Shchors, is truly the "Ukrainian Chapaev." Like Chapaev, Chubenko is a man of action, not words. His partisans easily rescue a boy whom the Germans are planning to hang. Resourceful and brave, Chubenko is worth the price of 5,000 *gold* rubles that the Germans offer for him "dead or alive." Even when the Germans surround the building where the underground Central Committee meets, Chubenko manages to escape. And the scene in which he jumps off the cliff into the Black Sea, swimming until he is rescued by a fisherman, is an obvious homage to the final scene in *Chapaev*, except, of course, that Chubenko survives to fight another day.

In addition to presenting a positive hero through Chubenko, director Savchenko aims to demonize Germans, a major goal of the USSR's anti-fascist foreign policy prior to the amazing about-face in August 1939. These Germans are easily the most villainous of any Civil War film. They steal from the peasants, offering receipts rather than money for confiscated goods. They try to execute a child. They raze a village, killing every tenth inhabitant ("Tell them what the German army does to people who rebel"). They force peasant women to front for them. (Of course, the fact that such barbaric behavior was routine during the Civil War and not limited to the Germans could not be acknowledged.)

Savchenko takes care to develop the character of the native collaborator Gurkovsky. Gurkovsky easily passes as a medic among the gullible partisans. When Chubenko rejoins his partisan unit, bringing his new friends from the seaside town to reinforce their ranks, Gurkovsky attempts to warn the Germans by "accidentally" discharging his weapon. He fails. But when Chubenko succumbs to typhus, Gurkovsky has his chance. He tries to "save" Chubenko by taking him out from under the cover of the woods. His delirium notwithstanding, Chubenko manages to shoot and kill the duplicitous Gurkovsky.

Savchenko also stresses the alliance (*smychka*) between the miners and the sailors in defeating the foreign invaders. The emphasis on nationality rather than class is typical of the late thirties, indicative of rising international tensions. The film's climax inserts peasants and gender into the mix: Ukrainian peasant *women* successfully warn the partisans of danger.

At film's end, Chubenko is supremely confident of victory, although unlike Shchors he never refers to any ideological props. While the German general calls for his surrender, Chubenko sends a telegram to Lenin predicting victory. The soon-to-be-defeated Germans protest, "We came at the invitation of the Ukrainian government" (an ominous sign to real-life Ukrainians harboring nationalist sympathies), but Chubenko issues a final, defiant warning: "We will drive you off until you are exterminated."

Although *Riders* did not figure prominently in Savchenko's career, he became an important director of war films—as well as an important teacher of those who made them in the 1950s and 1960s. In an article about Savchenko's work that appeared posthumously, *Riders* was praised as a "heroic poem" about the Civil War.[51] An entertaining commercial film squarely in the *Chapaev* mode, *Riders* is important because it suggests the variety that was still possible in Soviet war films on the eve of World War II. The 1935 feature *Girlfriends* (Podrugi), directed by Leo Arnshtam (1905–1979),[52] likewise expands the parameters of the possible—and foreshadows the centrality of women in the films of the war that lay just around the corner.

Girlfriends opens in 1914, just as the Great War begins. It traces the fate of four friends—Zoya, Natasha, Asya, the boy Senka—and their adult mentor, the worker-communist Andrei. The children, although adorable, are ragamuffins from the underbelly of czarist society. They early demonstrate their revolutionary sympathies; their stirring renditions of revolutionary songs arouse drunken, striking workers lounging in a seedy tavern.

This prologue is followed by a wipe to 1919, the second year of the Civil War. Senka is a Red Army soldier; the girls are frontline nurses. The female characters, foregrounded without condescension, are steadfast, resourceful, and brave. Oblivious to their own safety, they drag the wounded to shelter under gunfire. Although they are not soldiers, they do not shrink from battle when necessary, as we see when Zoya feeds bullets to a machine gunner.

Yet these young women are more than selfless handmaidens of the Revolution. In many respects, they represent the values of the Stalin era more than those of the Civil War. Yes, they are hardworking and courageous, but they also are pretty and charming, very feminine. Zoya has fallen in love with Senka, "boyfriend" to all the girls. Unlike the chaste romances that generally characterized Soviet cinema of this period (including Petka and

Anka's in *Chapaev*), Zoya and Senka sleep together, in a brief soft-focus scene where we see them lying in each other's arms in a shed. "We'll have a son," sighs Senka. (Premarital sex was officially frowned upon at this time of increasing patriarchalism, but parenthood was not.)[53]

Duty intervenes for both men and women. Disaster strikes at an unexpected moment: the hungry girls are boiling a chicken they have caught when two White soldiers, likely deserters, stumble upon them. Natasha slips away unnoticed, but after the White thugs have devoured the chicken, they prepare to execute Asya and Zoya. The girls refuse to die without a fight, and little Asya is mortally wounded in the struggle. Zoya manages to shoot one of the Whites before Natasha returns with help: Andrei, now a Red commander, and Senka. Given that men have come to the rescue, the second White soldier is quickly dispatched. Before angelic Asya expires, she looks straight at the camera and intones melodramatically: "Dear girlfriends of the future, don't forget your 'mothers.' Be ready for the final, decisive battle." The film ends with Zoya and Natasha riding alongside the men straight into battle.

Stalin loved *Girlfriends* and watched it at least three times.[54] This charming picture must have been inspirational to Soviet girls and young women: it reassures them that they can be stereotypically feminine in appearance, find true love, and fight the "final decisive battle" at the same time. When *Girlfriends* was released, this battle was as likely to be against internal "enemies of the people" as against fascism. Regardless, it reminded girls of the key role their "mothers" had played in wars past.

Another War on the Horizon

The USSR had been preparing for another war since the manufactured war scare against Britain in 1927. With the exception of *Shchors*, it is highly questionable that the major war films of the 1930s supported that effort to any degree. True, they did a good job bringing the heroism and sacrifices of the period 1914–1921 to life, but despite their overt adherence to patriotic values, they did not provide a consistent picture of the role of the Party and the ideology in the Red victory. Given the political pressures toward conformity, it is doubtful that this was accidental.

In theory, one of socialist realism's major goals is to demonstrate the spontaneity of the people harnessed for the use of the Party. Yet at the end of *Chapaev*, Chapaev's unit is only marginally better disciplined than it was in the beginning. It is, in fact, decimated, and Chapaev is killed. *Kronstadt's* Commissar Martynov is more successful than Chapaev at whipping his men into shape, but they are captured and executed (with the exception of Artyom). In *Riders*, Chubenko is not under anyone's control, and his partisans fall apart when he is not with them. The girls in *Girlfriends* also exemplify spontaneity over consciousness. As ineffective as these films might have been in buttressing Stalinism's drive toward a highly disciplined military and citizenry, they did unwittingly foreshadow the country's needs in the Great Patriotic War. Women, partisans, and spontaneous action would prove exceptionally important in the coming war effort.

We will never know how Civil War films might have evolved had there not been another, even more terrible, conflict on the horizon. Two Civil War films were released during World War II—the Vasilevs' *The Defense of Tsaritsyn* (Oborona Tsaritsyna, 1942) and an adaptation of Nikolai Ostrovsky's novel *How the Steel Was Tempered* (Kak zakalialas stal') that was directed by Mark Donskoi and released in 1942. But as we shall see in the next chapter, during the war, Soviet cinema focused almost exclusively on promoting the war effort by making movies about the conflict itself. The results were interesting indeed.

3 The Great Patriotic War, 1941–1945

At the beginning of the summer of 1941, just as schoolchildren are heading off to camp, the German army invades the Soviet Union in a sneak attack. Filmmakers have two goals: to record the history of the war as it unfolds and to inspire the people to victory. The historiophoty of this period is uncontested. Pillaging, torturing, raping, destroying, the Germans also recruit "enemies of the people" from both inside and outside the USSR to aid them. The Soviet people, however, rally to save their motherland, led by partisans, with women fighting alongside men. Red soldiers, pilots, and sailors finish the job.

On 22 June 1941, disregarding its 1939 nonaggression treaty and without declaration of war, Germany invaded the USSR. It is impossible to overstate the impact of the Russo-German war on Soviet society. In sharp contrast to World War I, which the newborn Soviet state denigrated as an imperialist, czarist conflict, World War II—called the Great Patriotic War in the USSR—was in all respects truly Soviet. The Soviet Union fought for its very survival. Much of the USSR west of the Urals was devastated by the German advance and subsequent retreat, with loss of life so massive that estimates of 20 to 28 million dead may be too low.[1]

The Great Patriotic War quickly supplanted the Civil War as the "war remembered." With the exception of the period 1946–1953, it occupied pride of place in Soviet public culture for the next fifty years, to the very end of the state in 1991.[2] This chapter explores the role of cinema during the war and the evolution of the war film from 1941 to 1945. World War I had served as a catalyst to native Russian film production; as we shall see, World War II also had a beneficial impact on cinema—not in terms of boosting production but, paradoxically, in terms of increased artistic freedom as filmmakers contributed to the war effort without reservations.

The Film Industry during the Great Patriotic War

With this war, the Soviet "war film" truly takes shape. Movies were a significant aspect of the Soviet war effort from the very beginning of the conflict.
It is well known that key Soviet industries were dismantled and removed to
safe zones east of the Urals. Less well known (except, perhaps, to special-
ists) is the fact that film studios were also part of this targeted evacuation,
indicating the centrality of movies to the wartime propaganda effort.

The important Kiev studio was lost when the city fell to the invaders on
13 July 1941. In September 1941, with the German army rapidly closing in,
the Moscow and Leningrad studios were relocated to Alma-Ata (now Al-
maty, Kazakhstan), although facilities for newsreel production remained in
Moscow. Although other cities in Soviet Central Asia also hosted relocated
film studios, Alma-Ata became the USSR's Hollywood during the war. With
director Ivan Pyrev at its head, Mosfilm dominated production.[3]

All studios were placed under the aegis of a new governing body, TsOKS,
the Central Union of Cinema Studios.[4] Censorship was dramatically stream-
lined; under these emergency conditions, the country could not afford the
time-consuming process of endless script revisions, an extreme example of
which is *Shchors*.[5] (Valery Fomin's recent research has indicated, however,
that bureaucratic interference in artistic decisions continued to plague directors.)[6] Planning for the production of projectors and generators necessary for traveling exhibition once again became quite important—not only
to bring movies to the soldiers at the front but also to show them to civilians
where theaters had been destroyed by bombing.

As discussed in the previous chapter, Soviet film production had never
recovered its 1928 record due to a combination of economic, technological,
and political reasons. Given the exigencies of wartime and the difficulties
of working in makeshift studios, production fell even further and remained
low during the war itself. Until summer 1942, production consisted mainly
of newsreels, documentary compilations, and short fiction films very much
like the *agitki* of the Civil War. The most important of these early documentaries was *The Defeat of the German Fascist Troops near Moscow* (Razgrom
nemetskikh fashistskikh voiskakh pod Moskvoi, 1942).

A full-length compilation documentary on the Battle of Moscow directed
by Leonid Varlamov (1907–1962) and Ilya Kopalin (1900–1976), this powerful film is based on the footage shot by a number of frontline camera-

men. It opens in October 1941 and ends in January 1942; it was released in February 1942 to great acclaim. *The Defeat* features four major themes that are deeply rooted in Russian culture. First, the war with Germany is a holy war to save the motherland, so it is natural to draw inspiration from traditional Russia's heroes: Dmitry Donskoy, Aleksandr Nevsky, Kuzma Minin and Dmitry Pozharsky, Aleksandr Suvorov, and Mikhail Kutuzov. Second, this is a people's war in which everyone must participate: soldiers, civilians, partisans, women, children, old people, and so on. Third, this is a battle to the death, because the Germans show no mercy to anyone, regardless of age, infirmity, or gender. Finally, this is a war to save Russian civilization; the Germans are bent on destroying Russia's religious and cultural monuments, including churches and the homes of Peter Tchaikovsky and Leo Tolstoy.

The depiction of German atrocities is especially interesting because it presented a challenging and delicate task for the filmmakers. Varlamov and Kopalin needed to select images that were graphic enough to outrage but not so graphic as to terrify. They draw very close to this line, showing a smoking pyre of Red soldiers who were dragged from an infirmary and torched, corpses of executed peasants, including a mother and child, and hanged partisans. Most striking among these terrible images are the shots of women who have been raped and killed, the shape of their frozen corpses telegraphing their horrific fates. This heavy dose of reality was possible only because Moscow had been successfully defended, but it contrasts markedly to Western censorship of images of the dead.

By mid-1942, the newly relocated studios began releasing films, and by the end of the war, Soviet filmmakers had completed 102 fiction films, an impressive number given the dire circumstances.[7] Of the 70 titles that can be counted as full-length feature films, 48 (nearly 70 percent) focused on subjects directly related to the war.[8] This single-minded concentration on the war reflects the fact that the USSR did not have the luxury of fighting the war in other countries as did its allies. By way of contrast, less than one-third of Hollywood's feature film production in the three-year period 1942–1945 concerned the war. In Britain, American entertainment films accounted for 75 percent of the titles screened, with a mix of British entertainment and war films constituting the rest.[9]

War films enjoyed great prestige during the war. Pyrev's *The Regional Party Secretary*, which will be discussed below, won the Stalin Prize, the USSR's highest cultural honor, in 1942.[10] War films dominated the 1943 and 1944 Stalin Prizes (which were not awarded until 1946). Of the nine Stalin Prizes awarded to movies, six went to World War II films: *Zoya* and *The Rainbow* received first-class prizes; second-class prizes went to *The Invasion, Six o' Clock in the Evening after the War, Person No. 217*, and *She Defends the Motherland.*[11]

In many respects Soviet wartime war films were similar to the war films of their American and British allies, but there were also key differences. Movies about the war made in the United States and Great Britain came in two basic types: war front (the combat film) and home front (wives, mothers, sisters, lovers dutifully waiting and/or working).[12] In the first two years of the war, however, Soviet combat films ignored the regular army. Even though early newsreels were heavily doctored with stock footage, the calamity was so all-encompassing that no amount of propaganda could hide the extent of the catastrophe from the citizens.[13] With the Red Army decimated, its remnants in retreat, a socialist realist view of the situation beggared the imagination of even the most stalwart Stalinists. As we shall see, directors who wanted to make combat movies about soldiers at the front were strongly discouraged until later in the war, when the Red Army took the offensive.

Likewise, even a British-style home front was a luxury most people living in the European USSR did not have. Forty percent of the population lived under the occupation for at least part of the war.[14] The terrors of the German occupation could scarcely be exaggerated.[15] Soviet citizens who were fortunate enough to be designated essential personnel were evacuated from European Russia to settlements and camps far from home. Those left behind struggled for survival.

Filmmakers faced the conundrum of conveying the brutal war and occupation in a believable yet inspirational fashion. Realistic depictions of the carnage at the front and in the occupied territories were out of the question, for they would be far too demoralizing to an already demoralized population, especially given the defeatism evident in the western borderlands. Pride of place was, therefore, given to the exploits of the partisans, and especially the role of *women* in the partisan movement.[16] Women were foregrounded in many of the important war films made from 1942 through 1944, and in most of the memorable ones.[17] The stage was set even before feature film production was fully under way, as we can see in the "fighting cinema anthologies" (*boevye kino-sborniki*), compilations of quickly made short films, that were rushed to the screens.

These short and simple stories, made quickly under unbelievably difficult conditions, stress the cruelty of the Germans and the resourcefulness of ordinary Soviet citizens in fighting back. The best-known example, directed by Vsevolod Pudovkin, tells the tale of a peasant woman who poisons the food she cooks for the occupiers, offering herself up as "taster" to prove that the meal is safe.[18] Given the formulaic nature of the kino-sborniki, it is hard to imagine that directors could find themselves in difficulty with the censors, especially at a time of relaxed censorship. But at least one kino-sbornik was banned, Our Girls (Nashi devushki, 1942), which consisted of two stories, Abram Room's "Tonya" and Grigory Kozintsev's "Once at Night" (Odnazhdy nochiu).

At first glance, the reasons behind the decision to ban are far from obvious, especially for "Tonya." Like many other wartime war films, it is purportedly based on a true story, in this case of Tonya Pavlova, a nineteen-year-old telephone operator who died heroically at her post. The opening title informing viewers that the picture is dedicated to "women fighters" is superimposed over a photomontage of newspaper articles commemorating various heroines. We initially see Tonya as a stereotypical "girl" who, unlike her girlfriends and her boyfriend, is content to remain at home and therefore does not volunteer to go to the front. But staying behind as the German army advances proves to be the greatest test of courage. She matures overnight and keeps one telephone line open so that she can report on German maneuvers to the Red Army. Inevitably (since she is standing in a window), a German soldier spots her, and just as inevitably, she is executed. Even though Tonya is redeemed by her sacrifice, the censors believed that she was too passive and too distanced from real-life concerns in a frontline town to serve as a viable role model for Soviet girls in wartime.[19]

It is, however, possible that "Tonya" might have passed censorship scrutiny had it not been paired with "Once at Night." This picture, which is odd enough to give pause to latter-day viewers, attracted the attention of censors. A farm girl tending her sick pig is faced with two paratroopers seeking shelter. One is a German spy (who speaks perfect Russian), the other, a Red airman. Each denounces the other. Although the girl would like to poison the German, she is more concerned about her pig's health than with determining which man is the spy. (And why not? The pig means food for survival.) The overall tone is lightly satirical, but the censorship concluded that "Once at Night" was "pathological."[20] When defeat seemed almost certain, as it did in 1942, war could not be a joking matter.

This persistent privileging of women as heroes stands in jarring contrast to the pervasive patriarchalism of Soviet society under Stalin, but it is not as paradoxical as it might seem. During the war, Stalin found that defining the conflict as a Russian (rather than Soviet) enterprise was a useful tool to rally and mobilize the population. Appeal to selected czarist traditions and Russian heroes of yore had been part of Stalin's reconstruction of tradition in the 1930s, and it continued full tilt during World War II, influencing all aspects of culture and entertainment.[21] Particularly notable was the return of the word *motherland* (*rodina*) to public discourse, frequently replacing *fatherland* (*otechestvo*). This change was epitomized by the most famous of Soviet wartime posters, the ubiquitous recruiting poster that proclaimed "The Motherland Mother Calls" (*Rodina Mat' Zovët*). A powerful, red-garbed woman, with a stern and hypnotic stare, beckons. A mother's call cannot be resisted. The new cinematic focus on heroines can, therefore, be considered part of the "mother's call."

But the other part is purely practical. Women were *necessary* in combat roles. On the eve of World War II, approximately 80 percent of the adult female population was already employed, often at hard industrial or agricultural labor in a militarized economy. They were factory and farm laborers, engineers, and physicians—as well as secretaries, nurses, and teachers. The one sector of Soviet life in which women were called upon to increase their numbers due to the war was the Red Army. The precedents for Russian women in combat had already been established during the Civil War. Women soldiers like *Chapaev*'s Anka were a reality of the Civil War, not to mention World War I.[22]

Women served the Red Army in many capacities. They were cooks and nurses. They were surgeons in frontline hospitals. They were soldiers and pilots—and not "merely" supply plane pilots but also bomber and fighter pilots.[23] More than 800,000 women served in combat roles during the war, not counting the number of women who fought with the partisans for whom we have no accurate record. The contributions of Soviet women to the war effort were real, as was their heroism.

Women Warriors

The canonical movie of the war years was Fridrikh Ermler's *She Defends the Motherland* (*Ona zashchishchaet rodinu*, 1943, released in the United States as *No Greater Love*).[24] This film represents the prototypical narrative for the heroine films. Films of this type spun some variation of this plot: halcyon days on the eve of war turn to terrible tragedy as bestial Germans kill husband/children/parents while the mother/wife/lover survives to be transformed into an avenging angel.

The "she" of the title is a lovely young wife, mother, and champion tractor driver, Praskovia Lukianova, also known by her diminutive Pasha and, later, as "Comrade P." Her idyllic rural life in a model village will soon be destroyed. Pasha's husband is immediately drafted after the invasion, but she remains confident and calm. She organizes the evacuation of her village and soothes the anxieties of frightened elders and confused children. Characteristically self-sacrificing, Pasha gives up her place on the evacuation trucks to someone more helpless than she, because she can wait for the next convoy. Too late. She discovers her husband's corpse on a truck carting dead and wounded soldiers. As she grieves over his loss, the Germans enter the town. A demonic German soldier seizes Pasha's baby son, shoots him, and then runs over him with a tank. As this horror unfolds, Pasha is dragged away and apparently raped. She is next seen wandering through the forest, her clothing tattered, her expression blank, eventually meeting up with some refugees from her village. The pretty, vibrant young woman has been transformed overnight into the stone-faced icon of the Motherland Mother poster.[25]

Pasha quickly emerges from her nearly catatonic state to reassume her leadership role among the survivors. When German soldiers approach to finish them off, she picks up an ax and commands her neighbors to follow her into the fray. "Don't run!" she shouts. "Kill them! Kill the beasts!" In a wonderfully staged scene of hand-to-hand combat, Pasha and her peasant comrades rout the German convoy. It is a remarkable moment, unimaginable in Allied war films: a "normal" woman rushes into battle hacking away at Germans with an ax, without a sign of revulsion or remorse. This scene marks the birth of Comrade P. and her band of partisans. Under her leadership, the partisans become the scourge of the occupying army, attacking convoys, burning buildings, even kidnapping a German general. In fine melodramatic fashion, Comrade P. eventually comes across the German soldier who killed her baby. She exacts poetic justice by running him down with his own tank.

Pasha, like all the woman warriors in films of this type, must remain pure and focused. Finding another man to replace her husband is, for her, absolutely out of the question. Yet there is room for romance between secondary characters. As we have seen, this tradition was begun in *Chapaev*, with the Vasilevs' introduction of the Anka-Petka subplot. The young lovers in *She Defends the Motherland* are a winsome pair, with endearingly human, if clichéd, traits reminiscent of Anka and Petka or Zoya and Senka in *Girlfriends*.

There are, however, important differences that reflect the increasingly patriarchal attitudes toward family and sex that were part of developed Stalinism. The girl Fenka is more stereotypically feminized than Anka: a silly chatterbox, she talks and giggles while she and her boyfriend are out on reconnaissance. But when her lover, Senka, presses her for sex, she wants marriage first, which would have been unthinkably "bourgeois" in revolutionary Russia. Comrade P. solemnly acknowledges the importance of marriage by performing a wedding ceremony with the rights given her as their "captain"; without a trace of irony, she offers the happy couple the captured German general as a "wedding present." As in *Chapaev*, war puts young lovers in peril; the woman lives and the man dies. Just as Petka was killed by the Whites, so is Senka coldly executed by the Germans.

By the midthirties Ermler, once a trenchant social critic, seemed to have been co-opted by the Stalinist regime, as exemplified by his films *Peasants* (Krestiane, 1935) and *The Great Citizen* (Velikii grazhdanin, 1939).[26] This film is by no means the equal of any of his early work. Pasha displays little depth of character apart from what Vera Maretskaya, a gifted film actress, can impose on the stilted dialogue.[27] The Germans are vicious and hysterical cartoon characters (but it would be unfair to expect otherwise under the circumstances).

Yet signs of Ermler's considerable talent are obvious throughout. Pasha's ferocity and physical courage make her a far cry from the demure, wholesome cheerleaders for Soviet power who dominated Soviet screens in the late thirties. There are other important, if subtle, deviations from the prewar conventions. During the war, religious symbols, references, and allusions reentered public life, and we see a number of examples in this movie. Pasha helps an old woman carefully place her icon onto an evacuation vehicle. When one of the partisans is murdered by a captured German soldier, his last words are "May the Lord forgive you"; a cross is erected over his grave. Fenka refuses to have sex with Senka not only because she believes in marriage first but also because it is Lent, and she needs to sacrifice a pleasure of the flesh. In the context of Stalinist society, even such

She Defends the Motherland: Comrade P. at the gallows. The sign reads "I am a partisan. I killed German soldiers." Courtesy BFI Stills.

fleeting references to religion represent a major change from the repressive antireligious policies and practices of the previous decade.

Another important deviation from prior conventions is that ordinary citizens express negative ideas. In the cinema of the 1930s, "wreckers" and saboteurs attempt to undermine Soviet authority, but their actions are motivated and governed by the international anticommunist conspiracy, not by the shortcomings of Soviet society. The defeatists in *She Defends the Motherland* are not collaborators, spies, or returned émigrés; they are Soviet citizens demoralized by fear and deprivation. In an extraordinary scene shortly after the ragtag survivors from the village decide that they have been forced by circumstance (rather than by patriotism or ideology) to become partisans, they sit around their campfire to decide what to do next. One man grumbles: "Oh, sure, at a time like this, we call a conference [twitting the endless meetings that characterized the "democracy" of Soviet communism] . . . [but there is] no bread, no food." When some attempt to remonstrate with him, he counters sharply: "I don't say it will be pleasant under the Nazis, *but we're accustomed to that* [emphasis added]. . . . Don't try to scare us. . . . Did you see them hang *everyone*? . . . Oh, sure, maybe the

The Rainbow: A serene Olena comes to terms with her fate. Courtesy BFI Stills.

Communists and the Jews. . . . Enough of this rotten Red paradise!" Pasha shoots him point-blank. As she walks away from his body, she impassively intones: "While we live, we fight."

Just as it would be a mistake to ignore this acknowledgment that not all Soviet citizens were rallying to the cause, so would it be a mistake to overstate its importance. After all, Comrade P. quickly and decisively dispatches the defeatist. And in the end, despite the heavy losses the little partisan band suffers, positive and activist thinking dominates. Comrade P.'s loyal followers rescue her in a dramatic raid just as the hangman's noose tightens around her neck. In socialist realist fashion—completely contrary to what was truly realistic—Pasha lives to fight another day.[28] Painted with broad strokes, the message was clear and inspirational: ordinary citizens, especially women, had an essential role to play in the resistance against the fascist invaders. Years later, Vera Maretskaya recalled her role as Praskovia Lukianova: "I would say that in this picture, she won the War."[29]

Unlike Pasha, two other cinematic partisan heroines were not lucky enough to survive. Olena Kostiukh in *The Rainbow* (Raduga, 1943, released January 1944) and Zoya Kosmodemianskaya in *Zoya* (Zoia, 1944) are both executed. A realistic depiction of their fates was possible in 1944, given that the Red Army was definitely on the offensive.

Mark Donskoy's *The Rainbow* is the more cinematically interesting of the two films. Based on a novella by Wanda Wasiłewska, *The Rainbow* is set in wintry Ukraine (although it was actually filmed in Ashkhabad in brutally hot conditions).[30] It traces the intertwined fates of two women: Olena, a partisan fighter who has turned herself in to give birth, and her opposite, the corrupt and self-centered Pusya, who has betrayed her partisan husband by becoming the "camp wife" of a sniveling German officer. Despite Olena's advanced pregnancy, the Germans torture her by depriving her of sleep and forcing her to walk back and forth in the snow. They execute a boy in the village who tries to sneak a piece of bread to her. As the sun rises and a new day dawns, surrounded by Germans, the Madonna-like Olena gives birth to a boy, on whom she bestows the everyman name Ivan. The Germans, ever cruel, kill him before her very eyes. Afterward, she is interrogated incessantly, without food or water, before being marched up a hill (Golgotha) to be shot. The religious allusions are mixed but pointed.

More interesting than the saintly Olena is her opportunist counterpart, Pusya, the wayward wife of the partisan commander. Pusya is perhaps the most extravagant villainess in Soviet cinema. Surrounded by luxury in the midst of death and unspeakable cruelty, Pusya lounges in her lingerie, eats chocolates, and in a time of starvation, brags about how fat her legs are. Her stuffed monkey dangles over her canopied bed like a mockery of the gibbeted partisans outside. When Pusya attempts to share her largesse with her sister, the schoolteacher Olga, Olga understands that Pusya's real purpose is to gain information, not to feed Olga's sick child. Olga spurns her: "I can't believe we had the same mother. You didn't have a *Russian mother* [emphasis added]."[31]

At the end, the camp is liberated by both the partisans and the Red Army, an alliance that indicates the regular army's changing fortunes, and the need to gain control over the partisans. They are aided by prisoners and peasants, including women wielding shovels and pitchforks as weapons. Pusya cowers under her bed, calling out for her despicable German lover, Kurt, to save her. Kurt, however, has already fled, and so Pusya is shot in the head, point-blank—*by her own husband*. A rainbow fills the horizon.

The Rainbow's brutality is more graphic than that in She Defends the Motherland. The scene in which a child who attempts to bring bread to Olena is shot is particularly wrenching. Dying, he crawls back to his family's hut, crying, "Mama! Mama!" Indiscriminate slaughter of the collective—elderly, children, and women with babes-in-arms—is also emphasized. Again, the message is obvious: there can be no middle ground. Each person had a black-and-white choice to make. Olena makes the right choice, Pusya the wrong one. Despite the heroine's death, The Rainbow ends on a positive note, with the camp liberated and justice meted out to the villainess Pusya. Franklin Roosevelt was said to have admired the film's pathos and "understood [it] without translation," which added to its luster at home and was a source of great pride for director Donskoy.[32]

Leo Arnshtam's first independent feature film was Girlfriends, the lively Civil War story discussed in chapter 2. With Zoya (1944), he turned to a highly publicized, heavily mythologized true story that provides an interesting comparison to The Rainbow and She Defends the Motherland. Zoya Kosmodemianskaya was a partisan girl hanged by the Germans and memorialized in a famously beautiful photograph of her frozen, bare-breasted corpse.[33] The film, which features a score by Dmitry Shostakovich, opens with Zoya's capture and torture, with most of the film a flashback, showing how she became a Soviet heroine.

The cultural markers in the one-hour flashback are fascinating. Born on the day of Lenin's funeral, the day that marks Stalin's accession to power in the public consciousness, Zoya grew up in a happy family that worshiped Stalin and Maxim Gorky. She finds inspiration in the Pioneers ("always prepared!"), the Spanish civil war, the aviation pioneer Valery Chkalov, and Nikolai Ostrovsky's Civil War novel How the Steel Was Tempered. She even has time for a romance, with her fellow komsomolets Boris. Given that the Komsomol members are called to defend Moscow ("For the Motherland! For Stalin!" [Za rodinu! Za Stalinu!]), Boris joins a tank division and Zoya, the partisans. In a ten-minute montage of Zoya's wartime activities, we see this "daughter of the people" (doch' naroda) planting bombs, blowing up tanks, manning machine guns. With heroines like Zoya, how could the Soviet people possibly lose?

Even her death is inspiring. Although she has been badly tortured (whipped and burned), she walks confidently to the gallows. To the villagers who have been forced to watch her execution, she declares in a clear, steady voice: "I'm not afraid to die. I'm glad to die for my motherland

[rodina], for my people [narod]" (both words have the same root, emphasized). The viewer never sees her die; the movie ends with a close-up of
her face, newsreel battle footage superimposed over it. She is no longer
a person but an icon. Indeed, Vadim Kozhevnikov stressed in his Pravda
review that Zoya's life "is typical for millions of youth and girls who grew
up after October," concluding that the film was a fitting "memorial" to the
"immortal" Zoya.[34] Nearly 22 million viewers saw the film, which earned
third place at the box office in 1944.[35]

Apart from Olena and Zoya, none of the other female protagonists in
the "heroine" films was killed off. They were subjected to great privation
and suffering, but they survived, however tormented and traumatized. A
particularly dark example is Mikhail Romm's 1944 movie Person No. 217
(Chelovek no. 217, also known in English as Girl No. 217 and Prisoner No.
217). A film that concerns the fate of Soviet women transported to Germany
for forced labor, Person No. 217 tells the story of Tanya (no. 217), a young
woman captured in 1942. Virtually the entire film takes place in Germany, a
sign that Romm could be confident that the Red Army would soon take the
war to the enemy. Romm's depiction of his "ordinary Germans" is highly
negative and clichéd, but certainly plausible in the context of a wartime
film.

Tanya, played by Yelena Kuzmina (Manka in Borderlands), is selected by
unsavory "ordinary Germans" to work as a household drudge. She labors
from day to night, compelled to perform demeaning tasks like washing her
master's feet. She collapses from hunger and fatigue. These people have
also enslaved a Soviet mathematician, Sergei Ivanovich, who is being used
as a subject in a medical experiment until the Germans learn that he is a
world famous specialist in optics. They try to recruit him to work for the
German war effort, but he refuses. Before they can retaliate against him,
Tanya finds him dead in the room they were forced to share.

Sergei Ivanovich and Tanya (joined by her friend, Klara, another Soviet
slave laborer) had planned to escape Germany. How they dreamed of seeing Russia's cranes and birch trees once again! Sergei Ivanovich's death upset
their plans. Another obstacle to Tanya's escape is the sudden arrival of the
family's son Max, an SS officer from the death head battalion, with his sadis-
tic friend Kurt. Both men appear to be more psychotic than most German
villains of this era, to the extent that they frighten even Max's own family.

The film climaxes when the drunken, vile Kurt decides to humiliate
Tanya by forcing her to her knees, so that he can pretend to execute her with

Person No. 217: "Ordinary Germans": Max and his sister enjoy a sumptuous meal.
Courtesy BFI Stills.

a realistic-looking water gun. He squirts her in the face, laughing uproari-
ously. She has had enough. After everyone is asleep, she takes a butcher
knife and makes her rounds, killing first Kurt and then Max. She stands
in the parents' bedroom with her bloody knife, contemplating them impassively. Startled awake, as always more concerned with possessions than
people, they think she must have stolen something. As Max's mother discovers his body, air-raid sirens sound, and the house of evil is immediately
(and conveniently) hit by a bomb. In the ensuing chaos, Tanya and Klara escape. Klara dies on the improbable trek, but Tanya survives to view German
prisoners of war being marched through the streets of Moscow (which is
crosscut with newsreel footage of the actual event). Her face contorted with
bitterness, Tanya delivers an impromptu speech to the crowd about the vengeance the Soviet people will wreak on the Germans (a grim foreshadowing
of what actually happened a few months later, as the Red Army crossed into
German territory).

Romm's oeuvre is characterized by its deep humanism, so *Person No. 217*
is an atypical Romm picture. One can argue, of course, that Tanya's actions

are morally justifiable. Max and Kurt are the "enemy" even if they are not on the battlefield. But in this case, despite the film's high moral tone, it is hard to see Tanya as anything other than a murderer.

There is, however, one extraordinary sequence in which Romm's talent as a filmmaker shines. When Tanya attempts to prevent Sergei Ivanovich from being beaten, she is arrested and held in solitary confinement in a stand-up cell for three days. Extreme close-ups of Kuzmina's expressive face behind the bars of the tiny window of her cell are crosscut with hallucinatory flashbacks of her former life, her father, her school graduation, a dance. In this powerful scene, she becomes, however briefly, a person rather than a "type."

Heroines on the Home Front

As memorable as these fighting women were in Soviet wartime cinema, it would be a mistake to overemphasize their significance. A number of heroine films closely resembled their counterparts in American and British cinema, depicting women who support the war effort in more traditional ways. These girls and women are more conventionally pretty than a Comrade P. or a Tanya. Their personalities are also more conventionally feminine: softer, less assertive, even when dealing with the tribulations of wartime. Since they adhere closely to the melodramatic conventions of Hollywood-style filmmaking, these pictures are much less noteworthy than those discussed previously.

Yuly Raizman's *Mashenka* (Mashen'ka, 1942), which takes place during the 1939 "Winter War" with Finland, rather than the Great Patriotic War, is the most cinematically interesting of the lot. Its prewar halcyon days are therefore set in spring 1939, rather than spring 1941. Indeed, so much of the movie takes place prior to the outbreak of the war that it is only tenuously a "war film." Conceived before the German invasion, it was among the first fiction films released during the war.

The story is a sweet one. Mashenka falls in love with Alyosha, a good-looking and gallant student whom she first met driving a cab. Their romance falters when Alyosha finds himself attracted to Mashenka's vivacious, buxom friend Vera, who flirts with him shamelessly. By the time Mashenka and Alyosha cross paths again, he is a wounded soldier, and she is a frontline nurse. After a few other conventional mishaps, including a misplaced letter, the young lovers, reunited, warmly embrace. The message is simple and appealingly human, promising hope for the future: wars end, and lovers may be reunited.[36] Mashenka is no Comrade P., but she is a believable young woman whose character received praise from a Russian feminist film critic decades later.[37] Although it is often difficult to trace which films were shown where during the war, *Mashenka* was widely seen at the front, in hospitals, and in military encampments behind the lines.[38]

Wait for Me (Zhdi menia, 1943, directed by Aleksandr Stolper and Boris Ivanov) was inspired by the enormous popularity of Konstantin Simonov's famous poem and based on Simonov's play of the same title. The poem's words, both moving and maudlin—"Wait for me, and I'll come back. . . . Wait when others cease to wait, forgetting yesterday"—were also set to music.[39] The unapologetic sentimentality of the poem became an overly complicated plot-driven narrative that gives little hint of Stolper's true talents as a director of war films.

Wait for Me is a stereotypical home front melodrama, contrasting Liza, the good woman who waits, with Sonya, the "bad" woman who does not. Early in the war, Liza learns that her pilot-husband's plane has crashed; he is missing and presumed dead. (We know that Kolya initially survived the crash, but it seems that he was shot by Germans tracking him.) Even when Liza hears the news from their friend Misha, the sole surviving member of Kolya's crew, she refuses to believe that her husband is gone. She continues her work on labor details, digging trenches with other wives and mothers.

In the meantime, Sonya has found a lover, never seen, presumably a high-ranking officer or other official. As a result of this liaison, Sonya dresses lavishly and no longer joins the work detail. When Sonya's unwitting husband returns on leave, Liza intercepts him and tries, unsuccessfully, to shield him from the truth about his wife. Sonya eventually realizes her error in moral judgment, but her husband has been killed in action. (Before his death, however, he fell in love with the saintly Liza, although she did not reciprocate his feelings.)

The plot twists continue. Kolya's comrade Misha finds him alive in a partisan camp, but Misha is killed in battle before he can deliver the good news to Liza. We suspect that Kolya may not have been as faithful to Liza as she has been to him; there is obvious tension when the good-looking woman in his partisan unit overhears Misha talking about Liza. Then we see Kolya shot, this time for certain—but he survives to return to Liza in the final scene. Her fidelity has been rewarded. The best parts of this shallow picture, and its only believable moments, are the brief scenes showing the camaraderie of women in the labor details.

A cinematically more effective variation of the home front melodrama can be found in Viktor Eisymont's *Once There Was a Girl* (Zhila-byla devochka, 1944), from a screenplay by Vladimir Nedobrovo. Unlike *Wait for Me*, this film is specifically Soviet in content, if not in form. Eisymont's fairy tale of Nastenka, a little girl who survives the siege of Leningrad after the death of her mother, is signaled by its title: *zhila-byla*, "once upon a time," which prefaces the stories Nastenka loves to tell the other children in the orphanage. The 900 days of the Leningrad blockade and the famine that accompanied it is one of the most heroic and tragic episodes of the war. The majority of the victims were women and children.[40]

Nastenka, like the other children of the siege, is adult beyond her years. She wanders besieged Leningrad without supervision, gravely observing the city's slow death. Her mother, laboring long hours for the war effort, does what she can to shield her daughter from the heartbreak around them. They receive no letters from the father. Mama, like most mothers, gives her child the majority of her bread rations. Eventually she is too weak to leave her bed, and Nastenka must go alone to the river, in the driving snow, to get water. She cares for her mother on her own until Mama expires from hunger and cold. The film's second half shows Nastenka's life in the orphanage. The little girl, grievously wounded in the Soviet offensive that marked the breaking of the siege, lies comatose in a hospital, awakening only when her beloved father arrives to greet her. Nastenka's fairy tale has a happy ending.

Once There Was a Girl was made in haste to commemorate the lifting of the blockade, and at only sixty minutes' running time, its plot and characters are underdeveloped. Although there is much that is unbelievable in the film—such as the clean, well-lit conditions in the children's home in the depths of the siege—there is also a good measure of honesty, especially in the first half of the film, which is reinforced by Eisymont's quasi-documentary style. Its humanity and its neorealist style foreshadow the war films of the Khrushchev era's Thaw.[41]

The Hero Films

Not all war films centered on women, of course. By 1944, women were being displaced. Of the major wartime films featuring men as protagonists, only two focused on the partisans, rather than the Red Army: Ivan Pyrev's *The Regional Party Secretary* (Sekretar raikoma, 1942) and Abram Room's *The Invasion* (Nashestvie, 1944). Pyrev's film has the distinction of being the first full-length fiction film to be conceived and produced after the USSR entered the war.[42] It borrows some elements of its plot and characterization from Savchenko's *Riders*, which was in turn a film on the *Chapaev* model.

The Regional Party Secretary is a rousing and entertaining movie from a director who could easily have made a Hollywood career for himself. The Party functionary of the title is one Stepan Gavrilovich. A great positive hero, he is more polished than *Riders'* Chubenko, with a little of the ideological correctness of *Chapaev's* commissar thrown in, but none of the prissiness. A man's man, he inspires respect for his strength of character rather than his status as a Party official.[43]

The film opens with a "little Soviet town" in flames. The Red Army is pulling out; refugees are on the march. Stepan stays behind to destroy important Party documents, aided by Natasha (played by Marina Ladynina, Pyrev's leading lady both on and off the screen).[44] Escaping to the forest, they join a partisan unit. They have already witnessed enough of the Germans burning, pillaging, and executing for Stepan to promise: "Blood for blood. Death for death."

Under Stepan's leadership, the partisans are spectacularly successful. They blow up bridges, set fires to oil tanks, and ambush German troops regularly. The Germans know that they will not be able to defeat these partisans without subterfuge, and so they send Orlov, a Russian officer who is serving with them, to infiltrate the band, as had Gurkovsky in *Riders*. Like Gurkovsky, Orlov is good-looking in an aristocratic way—blonde, slim, fine-featured. Orlov easily insinuates himself with the partisans, who have "saved" him from being executed by the Germans, and charms Natasha, Stepan's right-hand woman.

Much more than a "romantic interest," Natasha fits the woman warrior model and often initiates action. However, in contrast to a film like *She Defends the Motherland*, a man, Stepan Gavrilovich, is in charge from beginning to end. Natasha in fact imperils the partisans by teaching the traitor Orlov how to operate their radio and telegraph; based on Orlov's information, the Germans encircle them and take over the encampment.

Natasha redeems herself by unmasking Orlov as a spy, despite his rather absurd attempt to allay her growing suspicions by proposing marriage to her. The Party secretary, who remains under Orlov's spell, initially refuses

The Invasion: Fyodor assumes Kolesnikov's identity. Courtesy BFI Stills.

to act on Natasha's concerns. In the exciting finale, the partisans fight the Germans from a church, while Natasha and Orlov engage in a shoot-out in the bell-tower. The craven traitor begs for his life, but Natasha coldly executes him.

The Regional Party Secretary is action-packed, with three large-scale combat scenes. It is a more effective combat film than *She Defends the Motherland* because these Germans present a realistic threat and occasionally win skirmishes with the partisans. But realism vies with unreality. For instance, the Germans have placed a 50,000-mark reward on Stepan Gavrilovich's head, but when he is captured, they seem unprepared to hold him, and he easily escapes.

The Regional Party Secretary was intended as popular entertainment as well as "propaganda," and it succeeds at both. *Pravda* no longer devoted the same attention to promoting key films as it had in the 1930s, but Pyrev's movie received a long, generally laudatory review. (Concerns were expressed that Orlov had managed to foil the partisans for so long.)[45] Soviet film historian Rostislav Yurenev, who saw the film while serving at the front, recalls that he and his fellow soldiers enjoyed the movie, especially its comic and adventure elements.[46]

Abram Room's The Invasion, based on the play by Leonid Leonov, is a more complex film, character-driven rather than plot-driven.[47] Room follows Leonov's play very closely; it is a vivid and often superb cinematic adaptation, in large part due to the excellence of the ensemble cast. The film is set in 1941 in occupied territory and follows the fortunes of the Talanov family: the town's respected doctor, Ivan Tikhonovich; his wife, Anna; their daughter, Olga, a teacher who has joined the partisans; and their ne'er-do-well son, Fyodor, a drunk who has just been released from prison after serving a sentence for a crime that is never explained but that Soviet audiences assumed was "political."[48]

The German occupation offers Fyodor an opportunity for redemption. At first, his participation in the resistance is accidental, as when he spontaneously helps a wounded partisan escape from the Germans early in the film. Later, the sight of their housekeeper's little granddaughter, who has been raped by the Germans, jolts Fyodor out of his complacent cynicism, and inspires him to conscious action. He assassinates a German general outside his parents' house and assumes the identity of Kolesnikov, the partisan leader who is his sister's lover. Fyodor is hanged before he can be rescued, but his grieving mother is at last able to say, "He is ours."

The Invasion is richly populated with characters that the director and the actors quickly bring to life. Fyodor is not the only one transformed, in believable ways, by wartime. His very "bourgeois" parents are as well. Ivan Tikhonovich learns to respect his daughter's working-class lover, the ruggedly handsome communist Kolesnikov, and to recognize the primacy of the cause over the safety of his family. Likewise, his wife, Anna, stops believing Olga's feeble explanations for her nocturnal absences and accepts the fact that her daughter is indeed a partisan.

Anna's truly transformative moment marks the film's climax. Their reputations for probity well known, Anna and Ivan Tikhonovich have been dragged before the Germans to confirm that Fyodor is, as he claims to be, Kolesnikov. Anna hesitates for a second, struggling to master her emotions. But when Fyodor says: "I am a Russian. This is my homeland," she realizes that his sacrifice will also be his salvation. "Now I know him," she says quietly.

It is as important to The Invasion as to The Regional Party Secretary that a native collaborator is the villain. In this case the collaborator is not a handsome young man like Orlov but a wretched old one, the émigré Faiunin, who has returned to reclaim his house, which the Talanovs now occupy. Faiunin, suspecting that Olga is a partisan, tries unsuccessfully to recruit her brother Fyodor to inform on her. On the other hand, unlike the cunning Faiunin, the German occupiers are shown as being rather stupid; a pointed message of the film is that the occupation could not have succeeded without native collaborators. Of course, when the Germans are driven out, they leave their friend Faiunin behind to his fate.

The only stock characters in the film (apart from the mainly anonymous Germans) are Olga and Kolesnikov. Positive heroes, they display no fear or doubts as they successfully engage in sabotage and assassination. Here the partisans are shown as playing an absolutely essential role in the war effort, so that by film's end, the Red Army can quickly and easily retake the town. The film received an excellent and very thoughtful review in Pravda and certainly marked a high point in Abram Room's troubled career.[49]

By mid-1943, after the Soviet victories at Stalingrad and Kursk, the cinematic focus shifted from the partisans to the Red Army. Like the home front heroine movies, these soldier-centered combat films closely conformed to the Hollywood style. Leonid Lukov's *Two Warriors* (Dva boitsa, 1943), which screenwriter Yevgeny Gabrilovich adapted from a story by Lev Slavin, was among the first of the Red Army combat films. It enjoyed enormous popularity, in part because of its catchy theme song, "A Dark Night" (Tëmnaia noch'). It is also important as the paradigm for the comrades type of combat film, focusing on the bonding that occurs between frontline soldiers. It draws its inspiration, whether consciously or unconsciously, from *Girlfriends*, Arnshtam's Civil War film of 1935, although unlike the girls, who have been friends since childhood, Sasha and Arkasha are new friends, drawn together only by war.

Shy Sasha and charming Arkasha (played by the popular singer and actor Mark Bernes) are infantry soldiers on the Leningrad front—at the end of the tram line. Between attacks, they travel into the city to visit Tasha, a female engineer whom Sasha has met, but who falls for Arkasha as soon as she meets him. In a spin borrowed from *Cyrano de Bergerac*, Arkasha manages to redirect Tasha's affections by writing eloquent love letters to her, signing Sasha's name. (Unlike Cyrano, however, Arkasha does not really love "Roxanne.") After several scenes of heavy fighting, Arkasha is eventually killed, although Sasha tries desperately to save him. (This is a reversal of a previous scene in which Arkasha drags Sasha, wounded while "grandstanding," to safety.)

Two Warriors remains an appealing film because of its unaffected warmth and Mark Bernes's screen presence as Arkasha. A featured war film, *Two*

Warriors was praised in the press even before its release, and the prominent director Vsevolod Pudovkin was commissioned to write a glowing review.[50] An important part of the picture's message—and one that was stressed in the reviews—is that Soviets from different regions and ethnicities can be friends as well as comrades. (Sasha is a Russian blacksmith from the Urals, Arkasha a Jewish welder from Odessa.) Its relatively honest depiction of the soldier's life is also noteworthy; unlike generic, action-packed combat films, *Two Warriors* also shows the waiting and the boredom of wartime.[51]

Many years later, one veteran of the Leningrad front recalled that within days of its release in December 1943, soldiers were humming or singing its songs. The film, he poignantly observed, reminded him and his comrades that *"We were not living waiting for death, but waiting for life* [emphasis in the original]."[52] More than any other wartime war film, *Two Warriors* figures in the reminiscences of veterans.[53]

The final films to be discussed under this rubric—*Moscow Skies* (Nebo Moskvy, 1944), directed by Yuly Raizman from a screenplay by Mikhail Bleiman, and *Malakhov Hill* (Malakhov Kurgan, 1944, also titled in English *The Last Hill*), directed by Aleksandr Zarkhi and Iosif Kheifits—also broke new ground in the development of the Soviet war film genre. *Moscow Skies*, which centers on the exploits of fighter pilots (especially the arrogant young ace Ilya Streltsov), is based on the adventures of the real-life pilot-hero Viktor Tomalikhin.[54] Like *The Invasion*, *Moscow Skies* is an unusually complex work for a wartime war film. The story is familiar enough in other cinematic contexts: the closed fraternity of fighter pilots, the brash newcomer struggling to break into the circle, eventually winning their trust. But in the Soviet context of positive pilot-heroes like Valery Chkalov (whom John Haynes has characterized as the "classic resolute Soviet positive hero, outwardly stern and proud"),[55] the markedly imperfect Streltsov is a daring character.

Not only is he arrogant and foolhardy, he is also downright childish. When Ilya reports to his unit, he is instantly distracted by the sight of a girl he knows, Zoya, a nurse with the company. Zoya tries to maintain a professional distance from him; Ilya expects her to act like his girlfriend and picks an argument with her. He frowns petulantly at the good-natured snubbing by the other pilots and whines to his sergeant that nobody likes him. Despite his own successes in the air (he has lots of kills), he remains jealous of his comrades, especially the regiment's best pilot, Sergei Nikolaevich. Near the end of the film, when both young men are lying wounded in the hospital, the self-centered Streltsov babbles away, not waiting for comment or response. Not until he stops talking long enough to wonder why Sergei Nikolaevich is so silent does Ilya turn to see that his roommate has died.

The representation of Streltsov's upper-middle-class family (his father is a professor) is also interesting because it is believable, rather than picture perfect. When Ilya returns home for a brief visit between flying school and assuming his assignment, his younger sister Natashka (far from a model Soviet child) squeals and pouts for attention; unlike the starving children of Leningrad, she is distinctly chubby. Later on, in a hilarious scene, his family learns that he has been named a Hero of the Soviet Union (the equivalent of receiving the Medal of Honor in the United States). First, his parents are sure this is a mistake. Their son is no hero. Then, they cannot awake him from his deep slumber so that *Pravda* can take his picture. All the while Natashka is jumping up and down, screaming with delight thinking about the attention this will bring *her*.

This is not a psychological drama (or comedy) by any means. After a half dozen well-staged action scenes, Streltsov eventually grows up (to be twenty), is promoted to captain, and wins over Zoya by saving her life during an air raid on the air base. *Moscow Skies* was praised for its realistic depiction of the role aviators played in the defense of Moscow in fall 1941.[56] It ranked seventh at the box office in 1946, with more than 15 million viewers.[57] Many of the motifs of *Moscow Skies* reappeared in a number of postwar movies, and in the post-Soviet era, there has been renewed interest in this intriguing film.[58]

Another comrades' film, *Malakhov Hill*, updates the concept of the collective hero that the cinema avant-garde had embraced in the 1920s. It is unusual in two key respects: its focus on the Red Navy, rather than land forces, and the fact that virtually everyone dies. The sole survivor is the captain.

Malakhov Hill's story is set during the last days of the defense of Sevastopol before the city fell on 4 July 1942; Malakhov Hill is the name of the promontory and Crimean War battlefield. The plot is bare-bones: a woman, Maria Pervintseva, comes to Sevastopol trying to find her husband, a naval officer, during the chaos of the evacuation of the city. She befriends a number of the sailors, including their captain, Captain Third Class Likhachov, who have become marines after the sinking of their ship at the beginning of the film. The sailors, on a suicide mission to defend the promontory, are all killed, save the gravely wounded Likhachov, who is promoted to captain second class. He and Maria bid each other farewell.

Malakhov Hill unfolds in a matter-of-fact fashion. This is war. Everything is in flux. Husbands and wives are separated, friends are made, heroes are born, people are killed, life goes on. Maria Vladimirovna is neither hysterical nor vengeful in the face of adversity. She helps out as best she can, whether to dance with the sailors or take up a gun. The men, in their turn, enjoy a gentle flirtation with her; it reminds them of their humanity. The romance between Maria Pervintseva and Captain Likhachov that one would expect in a more conventional movie never materializes.

Malakhov Hill does not, however, lack drama and action. There is plenty of both, from the beginning—the sinking of the battleship *Ivan Groznyi* (Ivan the Terrible)—to the end, the suicide mission. The six sailors attempt to halt the advance of German tanks by throwing themselves under them with Molotov cocktails. This film could not, of course, have been made prior to the liberation of Sevastopol, but its bleak finale, lacking any note of uplift, brought added scrutiny. TsOKS chairman Ivan Bolshakov, who became minister of cinema affairs after the war, considered this movie to be "not entirely successful," niggardly praise under any circumstances.[59]

Transitions

As already noted, with the Red Army on the offensive after Stalingrad, the formulas for war films changed. Heroines could be killed (*Zoya*, *The Rainbow*); Red Army soldiers, sailors, and pilots could displace the partisans as heroes (*Two Warriors*, *Moscow Skies*, *Malakhov Hill*); directors could imagine taking the war to the enemy in Germany (*Person No. 217*). By mid-1944, the changes in tone were even more pronounced. With benefit of hindsight, these changes denote important, if subtle, shifts in cinematic direction. Not surprisingly, the head of the Mosfilm studio, director Ivan Pyrev, led the way.

In the late thirties, Ivan Pyrev became famous as a maker of musical comedies. His 1944 film *Six o' Clock in the Evening after the War* (V shest' chasov vechera posle voiny) represents a return to his patented style, after his conventional war film *The Regional Party Secretary*, discussed above. *Six o' Clock in the Evening* is a musical comedy–drama concerning the on-again, off-again romance between Vasya Kuleshov and the schoolteacher Varya (as always, Marina Ladynina) and the friendship between Vasya and his friend Pasha Demidov, who works to broker his friends' up-and-down affair.

The first half of the film is amazingly upbeat, despite long tracking shots of burning tanks. Moscow schoolchildren have sent the "hero–artillery men" quite a care package: chocolates, cognac, cigarettes—and a photo of their pretty teacher. When Vasya and Pasha are on leave in Moscow, they decide to visit the school, the walls of which are beautifully decorated with fanciful paintings of tanks and Comrade Stalin. The teachers and staff prepare a feast and have a dance. The party continues at Varya's idyllic dacha, to which she has invited Vasya and Pasha. They sing around the campfire and enjoy a walk in the woods. Except for an occasional air-raid siren or a shot of a women's work detail, one would be hard put to guess that their country is fighting for its survival. Vasya and Varya pledge their love for one another and promise to meet on the bridge over the Moscow River near the Kremlin "at six o'clock in the evening after the war."

The picture abruptly turns serious, as Vasya is critically wounded in battle and loses a leg. Here it becomes interesting. To this point, Vasya has been a model socialist realist hero, brave but upbeat. Now he is not only despondent but also wallowing in self-pity. "Everything's finished," he tells his ever-faithful comrade Pasha. Certain that Varya cannot love a cripple, Vasya wants to break his engagement and sends Pasha to the school to inform her that he has been killed. Happily, he is wrong, and with Pasha's help, Varya manages to find him at the front and reassure him of her love (providing the occasion for another song). As Varya leaves for home, the train on which she is traveling is bombed. We last see her, with a gun and a smile, merrily firing away. She actually takes down a German plane on her first try!

We know nothing of the lovers' fate until the final scene, on the bridge in Moscow, at six o'clock in the evening after the war. Vasya and Pasha are there, waiting. The hours pass. Still Vasya waits for Varya. His hopes are rewarded, as she appears, and they embrace to fireworks, a scene that was actually filmed on location in Moscow.[60] Soviet soldiers watching the film in Berlin in June 1945 reacted to the happy ending with understandable appreciation.[61]

Of course, such an optimistic picture could not have been made before victory was close at hand. Its message—the first cinematic recognition of the large number of disabled veterans that society would need to embrace— would be an important one in the transitional period between war and peace. For Soviet critics, it also signaled that humor was once again permissible.[62]

A second transitional picture that is less successful cinematically than Six o' Clock in the Evening, but equally important in terms of its implications, is Igor Savchenko's Ivan Nikulin, Russian Sailor (Ivan Nikulin, russkii matros, 1944). The first Soviet war film to be shot entirely in color, it was based on a purportedly true story, reported in the newspaper Red Navy (Krasnyi flot) in 1942, about sailors heading south to join the Black Sea Fleet when their train is ambushed.[63] Twenty-two survivors, commanded by an ordinary sailor, Ivan Nikulin, continue on foot, fighting Germans all the way, to join in the defense of Sevastopol. What is alarming about this variant of the comrades' film is that it represents a regression to the hackneyed stereotypes of Stalinist filmmaking in the 1930s, from the director of the delightful Civil War movie *Riders*.

All the characters are drawn from the playbook of socialist realist typage: the feminine, sympathetic girlfriend; the blustering, bearded grandfather; the skinny, inept civilian; the slightly scared sidekick; and so on, until we get to Ivan Nikulin, socialist realist hero extraordinaire, tall, muscled, square-jawed. Savchenko develops the men's camaraderie in clichéd ways: singing, card playing, storytelling. The genuine warmth and humanity of *Two Warriors* is entirely absent. Whether having a conversation or addressing his men, Nikulin shouts, even when he should be concerned about attracting the attention of the Germans.

The girl who tags along, Mariussya (played by Zoya Fyodorova, a rising starlet who was to spend many years in prison because of her affair with an American soldier), bears no resemblance to Comrade P., Zoya, or Tanya—or even to Mashenka or Varya. For most of the film Mariussya is crying prettily when one of the men is killed or wounded or gazing admiringly at Nikulin. When one of the men wonders why Nikulin is not asleep (ignoring the fact that no one is sleeping), Mariussya sighs, "The commander walks and thinks. I don't believe he ever sleeps." This theme is reprised at the very end. Mariussya, now unaccountably in a uniform, kneels by Nikulin's body. He has been mortally wounded in battle; uncharacteristically pessimistic, he announces to Mariussya, "I'm dying." "You're not dying," she soothes him. "You just want to sleep." "Yes, I want to sleep," he says, and dies. There are a number of ways to interpret this emphasis on wakefulness, of course, but it definitely harkens back to *Chapaev*, whose division is decimated because everyone is asleep when the Whites launch their surprise attack.

In addition to the return of a Shchors-like hero and a conventional heroine, *Ivan Nikulin*'s depiction of the enemy foreshadows yet another shift in tone. Even though Nikulin and most of his comrades die in the final battle, for most of the movie, the Germans are rather inept and not at all fearsome and bestial. They always seem surprised at the appearance of armed Soviets, even though they are deep in Soviet territory. They prefer to run or be captured rather than fight. One German prisoner constantly chirps, "Hitler *kaput*, Hitler *kaput*," which is very anachronistic for 1942, when the movie is set. The truest sign of the trouble the Germans face is the unreliability of their Italian allies, dubbed "macaroni," who care more about grooming their moustaches than fighting a war.

Between War and Peace

Peter Kenez's characterization of the impact of the Great Patriotic War on Soviet cinema is worth quoting at length. Although the Soviet characters in the war films were far from "uniformly clever and heroic," as he asserts, Kenez is right to characterize the war as a "liberating experience." As he writes, "Films once again expressed genuine feeling and real pathos: the hatred for the enemy, the call for sacrifice and heroism, and the sorrow for the abused Soviet people were heartfelt. The directors believed in what they were saying. The period of the war was a small oasis of freedom in the film history of the Stalinist years."[64]

This "small oasis of freedom" was about to disappear, but only temporarily. The legacy of the wartime war films, as art and entertainment, was substantial and long-lasting. The stories told were authentic, if not strictly factual. Heroism derived from character, not ideology. Bonds of family and friendship did not weaken resistance; they strengthened the resolve to resist. Citizens and soldiers did not need to be disciplined or threatened to do what is right. At the same time, human imperfection did not vanish in time of war; it may in fact have been exacerbated. Just as there were heroes and heroines, so there were the weak and selfish, people who were unfaithful to their spouses and, much worse, to their motherland. All these issues would reappear in Soviet war films after Stalin's death.

At war's end, the true victors of the eastern campaign—the Soviet people—received no rewards at all. That life would continue to be hard came as no surprise to them. The most productive regions of their country had been destroyed, and they were accustomed to deprivation. That the state would quickly resume its war against its own population—that was a shock. As we shall see in the next chapter, the film industry was also shocked, into a state of near paralysis. The calamitous decline in production lasted to the death of Stalin in 1953, and the few war films that appeared were very different from their predecessors.

4 From War to the Thaw, 1946–1955

Even before the victory, women and partisans disappear from the film annals of the Great Patriotic War. Red Army soldiers recede into the background. According to the historiophoty of the first postwar decade, the war was won by the generals, following the detailed instructions and wise counsel of Comrade Stalin. Soon the generals vanish as well, and the victory becomes Stalin's alone. The Russian Civil War reemerges as a topic for war films, but only to enshrine Stalin as the leading Bolshevik military strategist in 1919.

Many Soviet citizens who lived through the terrible war with Germany paradoxically remembered it as the best time of their lives. The heavy hand of the state lifted a little, and nowhere was this more evident than in the cultural sphere. Although a few films were banned during the war, directors worked more freely than they had since the advent of socialist realism. The wartime war films were authentic and deeply felt.

After the war, however, the cultural climate chilled rapidly. By the late 1940s, it was in a deep freeze, not only because of the cold war but also because of the stresses of economic recovery, exacerbated by an expanded and reinvigorated Stalin cult. Few films were made at this time, and war films were particularly difficult for directors to make. As we shall see in this chapter, the few postwar war films that did appear differed significantly from the wartime war films—and were deeply rooted in the realities of late Stalinist society. Despite all this, filmmakers were still able to find ways to humanize their material.

The Great Turning Point

In the last chapter, we saw that Pyrev's 1944 film *Six o' Clock in the Evening after the War* predicted the victory. By 1945, even before the war ended, the foundations for Stalinist postwar society were being laid. In the cinema world, this process can be illustrated by turning to two war films that were in the planning stages well before the end of the war. Their production began in early 1945, and they became two of the "big" films of 1946. These two movies—*Celestial Sloth* and *The Great Turning Point*—can hardly be more different in terms of style and content. But like *Six o' Clock in the Evening after the War*, they carry a subtext that soon proved prophetic.

Celestial Sloth (Nebesnyi tikhokhod, 1945, also translated as "Heavenly Slow-Mover") was directed by Semyon Timoshenko (1899–1958), a second-tier Soviet director. The film is marked by unflagging good cheer that masks a dispiriting message, at least for the women soldiers who were being demobilized when the film was released in January 1946.[1] Unlike *Six o' Clock in the Evening*, which vacillated between fantasy and melodrama, *Celestial Sloth* is a high-spirited musical comedy from beginning to end. Major Bulochkin manages to survive a plane crash with little harm to himself, even though his parachute has been shot out, by landing in a pond. Quickly discharged from the hospital, to his dismay he is assigned to demeaning convalescence duty at an all-female air squadron. "Planes come first; girls after," according to a song Bulochkin and his friends have sung earlier in the film. Although Bulochkin has not been cleared to fly, he displaces from the controls an experienced woman pilot, Senior Lieutenant Kutuzova, who has been flying for three years, because he needs a "brave, intelligent pilot," namely, himself.

Major Bulochkin's "girls" (*devochki* and even the pejorative *baby* are the Russian words used to refer to the women in the film) are not the women warriors of earlier films. They are pretty, well-coiffed, giggling females in neatly starched uniforms. We first see them not flying their planes but engaged in homemaking tasks such as sewing and cooking. The girls prepare an elaborate feast for Bulochkin and his two flying buddies, who have come to visit. "Look, it's International Women's Day!" they joke, ogling the women through a window. During dinner, when the women begin singing at the table, the men enthusiastically join in. Then the after-dinner entertainment begins: the "girls" put on an elaborate song-and-dance show for the admiring trio of "real" pilots.

Bulochkin's two pals pair off with female aviators. We quickly learn that one couple is secretly married, which legitimizes their ardent, but covert, hugs and kisses. The hero does not, however, fall in love with one of "his" girls. Rather, the screenplay contrives to introduce a civilian woman, a journalist, to serve as Bulochkin's romantic interest. This journalist, Varya, arrives at the front dressed in skirt and heels, carrying a purse. To be fair, she is as spunky as she is pretty. Despite her impractical attire, she sprints across a field and nimbly leaps over a fence as she runs to escape the strafing of the airfield.

Varya and Bulochkin banter smartly and flirt in the best Hollywood style. But when Varya accompanies Bulochkin on a flying mission, they are attacked by the Germans, and their plane is forced down. We then learn that Varya's bravery is mere bravado, and Bulochkin sweetly sings the frightened girl to sleep. Despite this promising start, they part on a misunderstanding that is a classic convention of romantic comedy: she believes he is interested in one of his women pilots, not in her. Happily, however, she eventually learns the truth. Bulochkin is awarded another medal, providing an excuse for a celebration at which all the lovers are reunited. Best yet, as a sign that Bulochkin has chosen the right woman with whom to fall in love, Varya's father turns out to be a general. We expect Bulochkin's career prospects to soar even higher through such an influential connection; the kind of careerism formerly denounced as "petty bourgeois" would become a hallmark of the late forties.

Celestial Sloth contrasts sharply with all the pictures examined in the previous chapter, whether female-centered or not. However gently and amusingly, the film mocks the contributions of fighting women to the war and foreshadows their removal from war cinema as it evolved in the last years of the Stalin era. This movie reinforces what became public practice after the war: ignoring or even denigrating the contributions of the women veterans. Although retrograde in terms of its gender politics, *Celestial Sloth* is an amusing romantic comedy that compares favorably with its Western counterparts. It is not surprising, therefore, that the film earned second place at the box office in 1946, with more than 21 million viewers.[2] Given that the USSR was only beginning its long process of economic recovery and that movies were once again a cultural commodity mainly for city dwellers (due to the destruction of movie theaters during the war and the perennial lack of projectors for the countryside), this respectable box office reflects the film's strong entertainment and production values.

Fridrikh Ermler's *The Great Turning Point* (Velikii perelom, 1945, released January 1946) is a very different type of picture, but it too marks "the great turning point" in Soviet war films.[3] *The Great Turning Point*'s production history is quite interesting. Ermler and the screenplay's coauthor, Boris Chirskov, initially discussed making a film about a Soviet general in 1942. Their early efforts were stymied not only by the logistics of making a frontline war film during the war but equally importantly by the politics, given the less than stellar performance of the Red Army at that time.[4] Both men turned their attention to other films, Ermler to *She Defends the Motherland* and Chirskov to *Zoya*.

After the Soviet victory at Stalingrad in 1943, Ermler and Chirskov felt the time was right to return to their generals project with renewed vigor. The Battle of Stalingrad provided them with a concrete subject, a great victory to celebrate. Surely now the Red Army could be the subject of a major film. In order to better understand the travails of the high command, Ermler and Chirskov traveled to the front, interviewed officers, and showed them the script, which the soldiers criticized as too melodramatic.

The final version of the script, or so Ermler and Chirskov claimed, reflected what they learned from the officers they had met at the front. They excised all story elements (like romance) that would have introduced some life and lightness to the picture. In the end, Ermler and Chirskov achieved enough realism to satisfy at least one high-ranking officer: Major General Galaktionov praised the picture in a review in *Pravda*.[5] Sadly, however, the finished picture is as boring as its creators feared it would be. Ermler and Chirskov admitted their failure in 1946: "How could we portray the drama of personal human passions through the medium of the professional conversations of generals? How could we express the invisible mental strain of the general bending over a dry map? . . . The vision of a map, as a *symbol of boredom* [emphasis added], dogged us to the very end of our work on this film."[6]

The Great Turning Point tracks the activities of a fictional general, Kiril Muravev, rather than an actual hero-general of Stalingrad—indicating a shift away from the military leaders responsible for the victory. Only about 20 minutes out of more than 100 show any aspect of the titanic struggle on the field. Most of the film features Muravev poring over maps and talking to other generals. They wait and talk, talk and wait. Time passes through numerous close-ups of clocks and watches. And all those maps! Maps on the tables, maps on the walls.

There are, however, three brief moments in which Ermler and Chirskov manage to insert some semblance of dramatic interest into *The Great Turning Point*. The first is the only famous scene in the film: the purportedly true incident when a Soviet soldier (here Muravev's driver) reconnects a vital

The Great Turning Point: Muravev and his generals study the maps. Courtesy BFI Stills.

telephone line by clenching the two ends in his teeth. He has been shot and killed, but his corpse continues to serve as the conductor for the line. The second episode concerns Muravev's relationship with his wife, Liza, who also serves at the Stalingrad front. When Muravev arrives from Moscow, in a homely touch, he brings Liza the latest news of their daughter, along with her photograph. Yet when Liza is killed, he refuses to allow his sorrow to interfere with his public duties. He shrugs off condolences and continues working; we discern his emotional distress only from his tense posture. The final effort to enliven the film with some humanity concerns the conflict between Muravev's official duties and his close friendship with one of his generals, Krivenko. When Krivenko takes advantage of their relationship by openly questioning Muravev's judgment, Muravev does not hesitate to replace him. Krivenko eventually acknowledges that not only was Muravev's strategy correct, as the commander, he was owed unconditional obedience.

The Great Turning Point is exceptionally important because it marks a sharp shift in the focus away from ordinary people. It resembles *Shchors* more than it does Ermler's wartime film *She Defends the Motherland*, Pyrev's *The Regional Party Secretary*, or Raizman's *Moscow Skies. The Great Turning Point* celebrates conformity over individuality, discipline over spontaneity, public duty over private life. Muravev is not even allowed to grieve his wife's death, much less avenge her (as Comrade P. avenges her son in *She Defends the Motherland*). Muravev is a perfectly correct and almost lifeless symbol of the cultural desert that lay ahead. Even without much competition (fewer than twenty new Soviet films were released for the 1946 season), *The Great Turning Point* was not a box office success.

Late Stalinist Society and the Film Famine

When the war in Europe ended on 9 May 1945, the exhausted Soviet people had every reason to expect that their struggles and sacrifices would be rewarded.[7] *Celestial Sloth* and *The Great Turning Point* suggested otherwise (although one might argue that the abundance of food in *Celestial Sloth* was a sign of hope). There were many other telltale signals that the state intended to execute another about-face. Stalin moved quickly against the Red Army, epitomized by the brilliant but high-handed and arrogant Marshal Zhukov, architect of the Victory. The Red Army, symbol of the Revolution, victor in the Great Patriotic War, was renamed the Soviet Army, and the commissariats, another symbol of the Revolution, became "ministries." Zhukov was soon dispatched to a series of progressively more insulting minor commands. Returning prisoners of war and other repatriated peoples were arrested as traitors and sent off to the prison camps. "Cosmopolitans"—soldiers who had seen the West (with its astonishingly high standard of living, even in wartime), people who knew foreign languages (in demand during the war), Jews (staunch supporters of the Revolution but soon to have another homeland in the state of Israel)—were all suspect. How could they possibly be patriots? By 1947, Victory Day was no longer an official state holiday.[8]

With the war over, the motherland faded away, while the Stalin cult revived with vigor and became more exaggerated than ever before.[9] Stalin's image, words, accomplishments, and ideas—whether they were actually his or not—were everywhere, as ubiquitous as the omnipresent slogan "Stalin is always with us." Because the arts were so central to the cult, it was necessary to remind artists, swiftly and decisively, that they were once again in the service of the state—not the motherland.

The shortage of postwar movies was so severe that calling this period a film famine is not an exaggeration. As the USSR struggled to rebuild economically after the catastrophic war, without the Marshall Plan money that saved Western Europe, film production collapsed. In the eight-year period spanning 1946–1953, only 165 feature films were made; 124 of these were full-length fiction films.[10] In 1951, astonishingly, only 9 Soviet feature films were released.[11]

Political issues were also a factor. The state no longer needed the persuasive powers of cinema to the extent that it had during the Great Patriotic War; scarce resources were therefore diverted to more pressing needs. Nevertheless, production, which was centrally planned, fell so far below projections that each of the few films made was released in 1,500 to 2,000 copies, just to keep movie theaters supplied with something to screen.[12]

The revival of heavy-handed censorship also played a role.[13] Sergei Eisenstein's travails over the second part of Ivan the Terrible are a perfect case in point. Stalin himself had commissioned the film—and yet it was banned. Stalin's wrath over his hero's unfavorable portrayal caused Eisenstein to fear for his future. The stress certainly contributed to the renowned director's rapidly declining health and untimely death in 1948 at the age of only fifty.[14]

This was not a time for experimentation. A significant percentage of the films released were not really cinema but, rather, filmed productions of plays and concerts. In such cases, authorship did not reside with the film's director; in case of trouble, responsibility lay elsewhere. The two other leading types of films were biopics and cold war melodramas, both of which were intimately intertwined with the Stalinist political scene. The biopics, which featured composers, scientists, and historic military figures, showed the majesty of the Russian people and fueled the fires of the Great Russian chauvinism that was integral to late Stalinist society. Cold war melodramas—which of course had their direct counterparts in the United States—reminded the Soviet people of the perfidy of the once-friendly Americans.[15]

There were also a few musical comedies, most notably Ivan Pyrev's The Kuban Cossacks (Kubanskie kazaki, 1949, released 1950), but also Grigory Aleksandrov's Spring (Vesna, 1947). Both films were popular, especially The Kuban Cossacks, which attracted more than twice as many viewers as Spring,

40.6 million to 16.2 million.[16] War films were in particularly short supply: in 1946, nine were produced; in 1949, five; in 1951, none.[17]

Filmmakers paid little heed to exhortations from the cultural bureaucrats for more films. In 1948–1949, a number of directors who "happened" to be Jewish—Sergei Yutkevich, Leonid Trauberg, and Dziga Vertov—were publicly excoriated in the campaign against "cosmopolitanism" that was being waged by Stalin's culture czar, Andrei Zhdanov.[18] These filmmakers were lambasted in the press as "miserable tramps of humanity" and "base spokesmen of reactionary aestheticism."[19]

What did people watch? The hunger for entertainment was greater than ever in these hard times, when even the most basic goods were still rationed. Since the 1930s, Soviet moviegoers had become accustomed to watching the same movies again and again because there was nothing else to see and few other leisure activities. This pattern continued. Popular entertainment films from the 1930s, like Aleksandrov's and Pyrev's musical comedies were rereleased, to be sure, but the single most important source of cinematic entertainment was, ironically, the films captured from the Germans, as well as other foreign pictures. As a result, Marika Rökk, the Hungarian actress who became a German film star, enjoyed enormous popularity with postwar Soviet viewers, especially in The Girl of My Dreams (Die Frau meiner Traüme, 1944).[20]

State-sanctioned conformity also destroyed the last vestiges of authentic public film criticism. As we have seen, serious debates about the merits of one film or style over another had ended by 1930, but even in the 1930s, not all "objectionable" films were immediately banned. Critics still discussed a film's weaknesses as well as its strengths. Although cultural journals suspended production during World War II, leaving film criticism to newspaper critics, Pravda's reviewers occasionally wrote thoughtful, rather than formulaic, critiques of movies. But after the war, the Art of the Cinema (Iskusstvo kino, sometimes translated as Film Art) resumed publication as the sole source of scholarly film criticism, and reasoned debate about films in the press ended. With each passing year, the space devoted to movies in the Art of the Cinema shrank while the photo spreads of Comrade Stalin expanded. Film critics and film scholars were also swept up in the "anti-cosmopolitan" campaign of the late 1940s; Mikhail Bleiman (the hard-line critic and scenarist who had attacked Barnet's Borderlands) and Nikolai Lebedev (who was never allowed to finish his history of Soviet cinema) were among the most prominent to fall.[21]

The New War Heroes

Only a handful of war movies appeared in the decade following the war. Given the fraught cultural scene, this is not surprising. Nor is it surprising, given Stalin's newly exclusive role in the victory, that cinematic war heroes fell into two basic categories: the dead (or maimed)—and Stalin.

The major exception to this generalization was Boris Barnet's *The Exploits of an Intelligence Officer* (Podvig razvedchika), which led the box office in 1947 with 22.7 million viewers and received a Stalin Prize, second class, the following year.[22] An army intelligence officer, Major Fedotov (played by Pavel Kadochnikov, a popular leading man), parachutes into German-occupied Vinnitsa to infiltrate the German army as "Major Eckert." Fedotov's chief obstacles come not from the Germans but, tellingly, from the local collaborators who spy on their neighbors and betray them to the Gestapo. Fedotov skillfully exposes the traitor, saves the city's underground organization, and returns to Moscow to embrace the loving wife who waits. This is not among Barnet's best films; the jerky pacing reflects his discomfort with this kind of overtly political material. Nevertheless, the lighting and shot composition make a powerful statement. *The Exploits of an Intelligence Officer* is a Soviet film noir. The action takes place almost entirely at night, and although Fedotov is presented as a hero, watching him curry favor with the Germans and scurry from one shadow to another to avoid the light suggests another interpretation.

The two most important "war hero" films of the dead or maimed variety both appeared in 1948: Aleksandr Stolper's *The Story of a Real Man* (Povest' o nastoiashchem cheloveke) and Sergei Gerasimov's *The Young Guard* (Molodaia gvardiia). Both were true stories that had already been popularized in postwar novels by Boris Polevoi and Aleksandr Fadeev, respectively.[23] These tales were presumably safer subjects than original screenplays because they had already passed through the literary censorship in order to be published. Sergei Gerasimov, however, had an unpleasant shock when Fadeev's novel *The Young Guard*, which had won a Stalin Prize in 1946, was suddenly castigated for emphasizing spontaneity over consciousness and for alleged inaccuracies that deeply divided the citizens of Krasnodon.[24]

The living hero Aleksei Maresev, a "real-life" Soviet pilot who took to the skies again after losing both legs to gangrene, could hardly pose a threat to Stalin. Maresev's dramatic story had already been celebrated in rather dry fashion by Boris Polevoi, who rendered his name "Meresev," leading to endless confusion in the sources.[25] Aleksandr Stolper, the director of *Wait for Me* whose career had taken off during the war, understood the dramatic potential of the story and undoubtedly considered it a foolproof subject.[26]

In Polevoi's narrative, the fictionalized "Meresev" is a socialist realist hero much like the ascetic martyr Pavel Korchagin in Ostrovsky's *How the Steel Was Tempered*. Indeed, lying in his hospital bed, Alyosha meditates on the lessons of Ostrovsky's classic socialist realist novel. Although Stolper followed the novel's plot closely, he and Pavel Kadochnikov, who played Alyosha, tweak conventions just enough to make the film interesting.

The first third of *Real Man* shows the accident and Alyosha's agonizing eighteen-day crawl through the snowy forest before he is rescued by partisans. Eluding the Germans, as well as a bear, the young pilot has nearly succumbed to pain, hunger, cold, and despair when some little boys find him. The rest of the picture focuses on his salvation rather than on his suffering. Alyosha's life is saved by the physicians at the magnificent military hospital, an immaculate palace with large, well-lit rooms. Although the Soviet medical profession had been feminized for quite some time, all the doctors at this hospital are men, not just the chief surgeon.[27] Alyosha's soul, however, is saved by the Party, and this is the real story.

The Party is represented by the most grievously wounded member of the ward: the saintly Comrade Colonel Commissar, Semyon Petrovich (played by Nikolai Okhlopkov, an important theater director and a fine character actor). Alyosha languishes in his bed, rarely speaking to anyone, bemoaning his bad luck to be a pilot without legs. Semyon Petrovich, by contrast, is still very much alive. He chats and jokes, reads and teaches himself German. He even sneaks a smoke under the covers when he can avoid the watchful eye of their beautiful nurse, the "Soviet angel" Varvara Mikhailovna. Semyon Petrovich shows Alyosha a newspaper article about a prerevolutionary pilot who lost one leg but managed to fly again. Alyosha points out that he has lost two, not one, to which the commissar replies insistently, "But you are a Soviet person [*sovetskii chelovek*], Soviet, Soviet . . . !" Alyosha is at last inspired by this "real man, a Bolshevik." His earthly task accomplished, Semyon Petrovich has another medical crisis and soon dies.

Alyosha does not let his savior down. In fifteen days he will face a medical review board. On state-of-the-art, Soviet-made artificial legs (a grim irony given the shortage of prostheses), Alyosha is in endless motion: walking, running, jumping—he even learns to dance! In the end, his dancing ability

The Story of a Real Man: Alyosha sublimates his pain. Courtesy BFI Stills.

persuades the medical board. Returning to the front, Alyosha quickly earns everyone's respect with his flying skills and his bravery. Our hero inspires another wounded young pilot to believe that he, too, will fly again.

This film was seen by 34.4 million viewers (making it the third most popular film in 1948). Like *The Exploits of an Intelligence Officer, The Story of a Real Man* received a Stalin Prize, second class, in 1949. The "real man" himself was reportedly pleased with the results.[28] *Pravda* hailed *Story of a Real Man* as a "poem" and a "truthful and moving story about the people of the Stalin epoch."[29] Despite the movie's obvious tendentiousness, its production values are high, it is well acted, and the first half hour of the film (Meresev's struggle to survive the elements) is beautifully shot and edited in a style reminiscent of the best Soviet silent films. The handsome, soulful actor Pavel Kadochnikov also worked hard to inject humanity and authenticity into his underwritten and cliché-filled role.[30] Kadochnikov was sensitive to impersonating a living hero and met with the real Maresev to study his mannerisms and learn more about his experiences.[31]

As hard as Stolper and Kadochnikov strained for greatness, top box office honors in 1948 went to Sergei Gerasimov's two-part epic, The Young
Guard, which was seen by 42.4 million viewers in the first part and 36.7 million in the second.[32] The film is a rousing tale of komsomoltsy in Krasnodon.
They form an underground partisan unit called the "Young Guard" (after
the name of the Komsomol newspaper) and are eventually captured and executed. Gerasimov, who had begun his film career as an actor in Kozintsev
and Trauberg's FEKS collective in the 1920s, made the picture for Moscow's
Gorky Studio (formerly Soiuzdetfilm), which focused on pictures intended
for children and youth. For his cast of teenage heroes, Gerasimov drew on
acting students from VGIK. The Young Guard stars many actors who were
soon to become major players in Soviet cinema, most notably the two female leads—Inna Makarova as Liuba and Nonna Mordiukova as Yuliana.
(Sergei Bondarchuk, later a leading director, also made his debut in this
film.)

The Young Guard opens in July 1942, with the German advance on Krasnodon. The camera work in the opening scenes—long takes and traveling
shots—is unusual in Soviet cinema at this stage, but well suited to depicting the scale of the invasion and evacuation. (Later directors of combat
films emulated this style.) Gerasimov's sound direction is also effective; the
noise—shouting, shooting, motorcycles, music—is overwhelming.

The occupation's first days are terrifying: most of the refugees are forced
to turn back. Their homes have been commandeered by the Germans, who
are as rude and drunk as they could be. The men of the town are rounded
up and executed after they have dug the pit that serves as their mass grave.
However, death is implied rather than seen, probably because this film
was intended for younger audiences. There is no hint of sexual assault, although one of the characters, Liuba, aggressively flirts with the Germans as
a diversionary tactic.

The teenagers are an appealing collection of heroes: attractive, slim,
mainly blonde—definitely more Aryan in appearance than the Aryans themselves. As komsomoltsy, they know all the revolutionary songs, poems, and
traditions, but they rarely discuss communism or Stalin. Like the partisans
in the wartime war films, the members of the Young Guard are motivated by
love of the motherland and hatred of the enemy.

The film's first half, which sets up the action, tends to bog down. Gerasimov (who also wrote the screenplay) labors hard to differentiate the characters in his large cast, which includes not only the children but also their

mothers and grandmothers. He must establish the villainy of the Germans as well as the relationship between the local partisans (who are all male) and the Young Guard. As a result, there is little action after the Germans have taken the town; the Young Guard's first attempts at sabotage and provocation are relatively minor. Again, their assassinations of Germans are implied rather than shown, by contrast to the adult partisans who take obvious pleasure in killing Germans.

The Young Guard lost 6 million viewers between the first and second parts, which is unfortunate because part 2 is quite satisfying in building dramatic tension (an especially noteworthy achievement given that everyone knew the film must end with the execution of the entire collective). The Young Guard stages a concert for the Germans, which provides a diversion that draws most of the enemy soldiers into the hall for the show and a cover for the Young Guardists who torch German headquarters and then appear on-stage shortly thereafter. The fact that it takes the Germans so long to realize that the town is on fire means that we can enjoy more of the performance, which is as entertaining for us as it is for the Germans. Their variety show features lots of folk and gypsy song and dance, which the young men and women deliver with energy and spirit.

The Germans finally realize what has happened, and they track down the members of the Young Guard, who have dispersed. Eventually they are all arrested and interrogated, giving up nothing. They are only slightly roughed up, in deference to audience sensibilities but in sharp contrast to the gruesome fortune they really suffered.[33] This execution, like the one in Zoya, occurs off-screen; Gerasimov superimposes newsreel footage of Soviet planes, tanks, and artillery over the faces of the defiant teens. Unlike 1944, the year Zoya was released, the Great Patriotic War's victorious outcome is known, so Gerasimov can construct a montage of the Red Army triumphant in Berlin from newsreel footage. The film's finale depicts the postwar commemoration of the fallen heroes. Their names are read aloud to the beat of a military salute, as their mothers stand nearby, grieving but proud.

Like Stolper, Gerasimov manages to invigorate a turgid socialist realist novel and transform it into a reasonably entertaining popular film. In terms of its stylistic legacy, The Young Guard is a very influential film. As we have seen, Gerasimov builds on the conventions of the wartime partisan films, but he also resolves some of the stylistic weaknesses of those films through

The Young Guard: The interrogation begins. Courtesy BFI Stills.

his use of long tracking and panning shots, as well as deep-focus shots in the interior scenes.

His characters are reasonably believable; during the filming, the actors lived with the families of the people they played in order to add authenticity to their roles.[34] Over the course of the film, the characters evolve from awkward adolescents to young men and women. The youth are not uniformly brave; some shake and cry and cling to their mothers, even the boys. The Soviet press praised the film with the canned bombast reserved for all "important films."[35] Years later, Gerasimov's efforts to bring some much-needed humanity to the screen at a very difficult time were recognized.[36]

Stalin as War-Hero-in-Chief

Despite the success of *The Story of a Real Man* and *The Young Guard*, Soviet directors understood all too well that the one true war hero was Stalin. The absence of war films at this time might, therefore, be interpreted as passive resistance from directors: it was better to make a biopic or a cold war picture, or even nothing at all, than to heroicize Stalin. Of the four major films depicting Stalin as war-hero-in-chief, three of them were World War II pictures. The first, Savchenko's The Third Blow (Tretii udar', 1948), may be considered a "warm-up," with a running time just under two hours. The second two, The Battle of Stalingrad (Stalingradskaia bitva, 1949) and The Fall of Berlin (Padenie Berlina, 1949), were conceived as "blockbusters" to be released in two parts. All three films were costly, large-scale motion pictures, employing "casts of thousands." The Fall of Berlin is in color, then a great rarity in Soviet cinema. The fourth movie to be discussed in this section, The Unforgettable Year 1919 (Nezabyvaemyi god 1919, 1951), "revisions" Stalin as a Civil War hero.

The Third Blow centers on the Soviet counteroffensive to drive the German army out of the Crimea and liberate Sevastopol, reversing the loss of the city depicted in Malakhov Hill. Like The Great Turning Point, The Third Blow is an excruciatingly dull war film with few combat scenes. It presents the war as a battle of minds: Stalin versus the entire German General Staff. Most of the film shows Soviet generals standing and talking, waiting for Stalin to enlighten them.

The Third Blow constructs the typical Stalin of the postwar war films: soft-spoken, thoughtful, very much in charge of every detail, no matter how small. Savchenko's Stalin (played by Aleksandr Diky, a frequent Stalin impersonator) is often alone, sitting at his simple desk, reflecting on a small map, before he goes to tell his generals what to do. There is some truth to this representation. As John Erickson writes, "It was apparently always Stalin who had the last word."[37] Once Stalin has made a decision, he is smiling and quietly confident. Puffing on his pipe, he glances at his watch from time to time but displays no nervousness.

While Stalin works alone in his austere office, German commanders are living it up in a palace in Simferopol, where they have staged themselves in preparation to defend Sevastopol.[38] They learn Leningrad has been retaken, and by now they are so accustomed to defeat that one of the generals confuses "Stalingrad" with "Sevastopol." The German rank and file are little better. A hapless lot, they cower in their trenches and surrender screaming.

Savchenko does what he can within the limitations of the "Stalin war film." Although it would be hard to imagine that Riders and The Third Blow came from the same director, evidence of Savchenko's artistic sensibilities can still be found. For example, he often uses panning shots to give viewers a sense of the vast spaces that need to be traversed and conquered. He intercuts his played footage with much newsreel footage in the battle scenes. In a small effort to subvert the attention from the "top" to the ranks, Savchenko personalizes the film by focusing on a unit of several dozen men. Although none of them receives enough screen time to become truly individualized, by the end they have all been killed, an authentic note. *Pravda* praised the documentary realism and authenticity of this film, which was labeled an "artistic documentary," or what we would now call a docudrama.[39]

Vladimir Petrov's *The Battle of Stalingrad* was produced on an even larger scale, but its only noteworthy element is the score composed by Aram Khachaturian.[40] As in some Hollywood productions of this period, the epic nature of this film is signaled from the very beginning by a shot of a thick book, with pages turning. The film's structure is quite mechanistic: Stalin/ fighting/Soviet generals/fighting/Germans/fighting/Stalin, and so forth.[41] Stalin (again played by Aleksandr Diky) is alone more often even than in *The Third Blow*. He mainly looks at maps and talks to his generals on the telephone, not face-to-face. Information is delivered through intertitles rather than through the visuals or the dialogue.

The Battle of Stalingrad was accorded a much more overblown official reception than *The Third Blow*, although as cinema, it is even less interesting. One article described the film's unbelievably enthusiastic reception when it was shown to an overflow crowd in Stalingrad on Victory Day, 1949, by quoting viewers formulaically praising the authenticity of the movie's depiction of "our beloved leader Iosif Vissarionovich Stalin" and urging all Soviet citizens to see the film.[42] *Pravda*'s critic concurred: "The viewer leaves the hall deeply moved, with feelings of profound gratitude to the leader [vozhd'] who led our people [narod] to the great victory and saved humankind from the menace of fascist enslavement."[43]

Mikhail Chiaureli's *The Fall of Berlin* is the most famous cinematic artifact of the Stalin cult.[44] Chiaureli, like Stalin a native son of Georgia, was among the dictator's favorite directors and conceived this film as a present for Stalin's seventieth birthday in 1949. What a gift it was! Its novelty lay not in placing Stalin front and center at every stage in the Great Patriotic War; that had already been made abundantly clear to the Soviet people. Chiaureli created the first true epic about the war, with Stalin as epic hero.

The Fall of Berlin was released in two parts, each running approximately seventy-five minutes. Part 1 provides a macrocosmic view of the prelude to the war and moves quickly through to 1945, ending with the Yalta Conference. Part 2 is a combat film, ending, as the title promises, with the fall of Berlin.

Chiaureli constructed his elaborate film with three narratives that occasionally intersect. The least interesting is the purely fictional romantic tale of Natasha (a teacher) and Alyosha (a shock worker). Pretty and girlish, Natasha loves poetry (especially Pushkin's) and classical music. In contrast, stocky and strong Alyosha, with an open, boyish face, is a true man of the people. Alyosha was born on 25 October 1917 (Old Style), the day the Bolshevik Revolution began. He comes from generations of steelworkers and holds the world record in steel production: eleven tons per square meter! Classical music bores him, as does poetry. When Natasha recites poetry to him, the only verses he recognizes are those by the revolutionary poet Vladimir Mayakovsky, whereas Pushkin's immortal words strike no chord.

This clichéd romance is disrupted by the German invasion. Alyosha is seriously wounded in the initial onslaught and suffers from temporary amnesia. When he recovers his memory, he learns that Nastasha's pupils were executed and that she has been deported to German as a slave laborer. Although Alyosha's expertise as a steelworker is invaluable for the war effort, he gives up the factory for the front in order to avenge Nastasha. ("My production will be making dead Fritzes," he somberly intones.) Alyosha becomes a decorated soldier and a confidant of General Chuikov and is eventually reunited with Natasha in Berlin.

The second, and most important, narrative thread is the Stalin story. Fittingly, we first see Stalin as an icon, in a gigantic portrait dominating the hall where Natasha has been asked to give an address honoring Alyosha's record-breaking achievement. Her speech is well received, especially her closing line, delivered with a catch in her throat and tears welling in her eyes: "Long live Stalin, who has given us such a happy life!" (Forty years later, one Soviet critic used this scene as an example to attack Natasha as a "zombie.")[45]

We see Stalin (played by Mikhail Gelovani, Stalin's favorite "Stalin") in person when Alyosha has been called to Moscow to meet him. Stalin, shot in soft focus, is carefully tending saplings in his garden. Alyosha confides to Stalin his concerns that Natasha is too intellectual for him. Stalin's advice reassures him: "Don't worry about poetry. Love her and she'll love you."

The Fall of Berlin: Alyosha, "simple and proud." Courtesy BFI Stills.

Besides being a confidant to the common man, Stalin is also a teacher and adviser to his generals. He makes all strategic decisions, advising them, rather than the other way around. At the beginning, he scoffs at their concerns about the lack of equipment. Stalin argues that it really does not matter that the army lacks tanks and artillery and offers his generals merely 20 percent of what they have requested. According to Stalin, as long as they do not "panic" and continue with their holidays and celebrations (like the 7 November holiday that commemorates the October Revolution—and Alyosha's birthday), all will be well. Near the end of the war, Stalin graciously provides the cowed generals *more* war matériel than they ask for. As Khrushchev wrote about *The Fall of Berlin* in his Secret Speech of 1956, "Stalin acts for everybody. . . . Why? In order to surround Stalin with glory, contrary to the facts and contrary to historical truth."[46]

Chiaureli underscores Stalin's preferences among his generals. When Alyosha meets General Chuikov after the Battle of Stalingrad, Chuikov has the honor of telling him that "Stalin is always with us." Marshal Zhukov, on the other hand, is portrayed as a fool who believes the disinformation delivered by German POWs. Zhukov needs to be supervised by General Konev, whom Stalin sagely advises in a telephone conversation, "Zhukov's having trouble."

In terms of his stature within the Big Three, Stalin can more than hold his own with his chief rival, Churchill, and the perfidious British. The British delay opening of the second front in order to destroy the Soviet Union; they are also in a secret alliance with Nazi industrialists. But even the British know that "Stalin is a great general," as the collaborator Bedstone informs Göring in a secret meeting.

In Chiaureli's depiction of the Yalta Conference, Stalin is portrayed as the only true statesman. Churchill, on the other hand, scowls petulantly and sinks down in his chair like a child thwarted, whereas Stalin refuses to respond to his provocations. Roosevelt, a "fifth wheel," receives little screen time; in a different scene American air raids over Germany are labeled "publicity stunts." Whether dealing with his generals, world leaders, or a steelworker, Stalin presents an appealing image: well-informed, wise, thoughtful, calm, but strong nonetheless.

Hitler stands in sharp contrast to Stalin, of course, and his story provides the third narrative thread. The Fall of Berlin is unique among Soviet war films in the amount of screen time given the enemy. Chiaureli's portrait of Hitler and his coterie is extravagant and amusing. Hitler is Stalin's opposite: egotistical rather than selfless, hysterical rather than calm, prone to snap judgments rather than thoughtful reflection. Hitler's private life diverts his attention and saps his strength; a tarted-up Eva Braun sashays around the bunker. (Stalin, on the other hand, has no personal distractions and is thus totally focused on the cause.) Hitler's military advisers, unlike Stalin's, actually try to give him advice—usually about how great Stalin is—which the führer willfully ignores. The scenes of Hitler's final hours—his wedding in the bunker as Berlin collapses above him—are particularly entertaining. Berlin falls to the strains of Mendelssohn's "Wedding March." Shortly before he takes his life, Hitler curses: "Stalin! He brought everyone to their knees."

The Fall of Berlin presents an unusually upbeat view of the Great Patriotic War. Nothing that happens over the course of the four terrible years presents a crisis or dilemma for Stalin. Until the Battle of Berlin, the Germans do not even appear to be particularly formidable foes; the twenty-seven months between the victory at Stalingrad and the end of the war are elided in one triumphant procession of Soviet tanks and artillery. Combat scenes lack emotion and tension until the scenes of hand-to-hand combat storming the Reichstag, which are drawn straight from Yuly Raizman's brilliant compilation documentary about the city's conquest, *Berlin* (Berlin, 1945). In the fighting in the Reichstag, Alyosha's two closest comrades-in-arms, Kostya and Yusupov, are killed, the only two deaths we see of recognizable fighting men. (Before they reach Berlin, the trio seems to be immune from bullets and shells.)

At the end of *The Fall of Berlin*, the heavens open to allow the plane carrying the Prince of Peace, Comrade Stalin, to the city. Dressed in white, with a beatific smile on his face, he is met by smiling Soviet soldiers of every nationality. The chorus swells.

The real Stalin enjoyed his birthday tribute, and the film garnered various prizes. Its box office was 38.4 million, presumably for each part, ranking third, which is certainly believable.[47] Of course, the film faced little competition—not to mention the fact that workers and schoolchildren were compelled to attend organized screenings.[48] Nevertheless, after the tedious and didactic exposition of the Alyosha story in part 1, *The Fall of Berlin* is quite entertaining.

As was the case with *The Battle of Stalingrad*, viewers' opinions were sought, but here the stakes were much higher. Spectator commentary was now signed, not anonymous, and ranged from the famous (the sculptor Vera Mukhina and Hero of the Soviet Union Aleksei Maresev) to ordinary veterans. Regardless of their stature in Soviet society, their views on *The Fall of Berlin* were uniformly, unqualifiedly enthusiastic (at least for attribution in *Pravda*).[49] *Pravda*'s reviewer proclaimed that the film's main theme was Stalin's "genius" and "wisdom." The victory in the Russo-German War was flatly declared to be "Stalin's victory."[50] The *Art of the Cinema* also lavished the film with praise in these essays stressing Stalin's extraordinary genius. Equally significant was the emphasis placed on Alyosha as the "type" to which the Soviet working man should aspire: "simple and proud, kind and manly."[51] Richard Taylor puts it best: *The Fall of Berlin* is "the apotheosis of Stalin's Cult of Stalin."[52]

Chiaureli directed a "prequel" to *The Fall of Berlin* entitled *The Unforgettable Year 1919*, which was made in 1951 and released in 1952, the year before Stalin's death. The film was based on the play by Vsevolod Vishnevsky. Less well known outside the USSR than *The Fall of Berlin*, *The Unforgettable Year 1919* is a more amazing falsification of the historical record. Neya Zorkaya, the doyenne of Soviet film historians, describes it as "the 'swan song' of the film cycle soon to be called the 'personality cult in art.'"[53]

As absurd as Stalin's role is in *The Fall of Berlin*, there is a grain of truth to it. Stalin *was*, after all, the leader of the Soviet Union during the Great Patriotic War. He was *not* the head of the Party in 1919, the year that the Bolsheviks almost lost the Revolution. Nor was he a Civil War hero. Another big-budget, officially sanctioned production, with a score by Dmitry Shostakovich, the movie was trumpeted in all the press organs well in advance of its release.

Like *The Fall of Berlin*, *The Unforgettable Year 1919* offers a tripartite narrative structure: the tale of "ordinary" young lovers, this time named Volodya and Katya; the schemes of assorted "enemies": Whites, émigrés, the British, the French, and Woodrow Wilson; and the relationship between Lenin and Stalin in managing the military crisis. This last strand quickly becomes paramount. After the disaster for the Reds of the film's first battle scene, Volodya manages to find his way to Moscow to tell the Party's leadership how desperate the situation is in the hinterland. Lenin is portrayed as an out-of-touch bourgeois; he attends a voluntary working Saturday (*subbotnik*), wearing a *suit* to engage in heavy labor. He realizes that only Stalin can save the Revolution, noting gratefully that "Stalin could be found everywhere on the front where he was needed." And Stalin *is* everywhere, even at the wedding of Volodya and Katya at film's end. As Khrushchev wrote in his Secret Speech: "Stalin loved to see the film *The Unforgettable Year 1919* in which he was shown on the steps of an armoured train and where he practically vanquished the foe with his own sabre."[54]

The Unforgettable Year 1919 finished in fifth place in 1952; four American *Tarzan* pictures from the 1930s led the box office in that "unforgettable" year preceding Stalin's death.[55] The press for this mediocre tribute to Stalin was colossally overblown; viewers were being prepared for its release in the pages of the *Art of the Cinema* a year in advance of its opening, and coverage continued for months after its premiere in May 1952.[56]

Transitions: War as Adventure

By the late forties, it seemed highly unlikely that there was any hope for "revisioning" either the Civil War or the Great Patriotic War on film. But even before Stalin's death, new life was breathed into what seemed to be a moribund genre. The most entertaining film of the late Stalin era may well have been Konstantin Yudin's *Brave People* (Smelye liudi, 1950), a spirited wartime adventure tale.[57] It took first place at the box office in 1950, with 41.2 million viewers, just edging out Pyrev's very popular *The Kuban Cossacks*.[58] *Pravda* called *Brave People* a "good gift to the Soviet viewer and especially, to the young."[59] Yudin's directorial career was a modest one, but his talent for action and warmhearted humor is evident in *Brave People*, a jolly story film.

Brave People takes place over nearly a decade, from 1937 to 1946, and traces the fates of horsemen and horses in the North Caucasus. The halcyon prewar days are very nice indeed. The protagonists live in a spectacular mountain valley that is far from Moscow and Soviet power. In sharp contrast to *The Fall of Berlin*, signs of Stalin, the Party, and Communist rhetoric are few. Yudin was clearly conversant with the conventions of the American Western genre, as well as with the way Ivan Perestiani nearly thirty years earlier had transformed the Civil War into a fine adventure suitable for children's viewing in *Little Red Devils*. The result is a plot-driven, action-packed film.

The first part of *Brave People* might be titled "National Velvet in the Caucasus," with Velvet masculinized as Vasya Govorukhin, a lad who loves horses. With the help of the kindly old breeder and trainer Konstantin Sergeevich, Vasya has raised an orphan colt, Bulian, to become a champion race horse. By 1939, Vasya and Bulian are winning all the races; Bulian is named Horse of the Year for two years running, 1939 and 1940.

Konstantin Sergeevich's spunky teenage granddaughter, Nadya, provides the romantic interest. Like Natasha in *The Fall of Berlin*, Nadya loves poetry, but unlike Natasha, she quotes the revolutionary poet Mayakovsky rather than the classical Pushkin (indeed, the portrait over her bed is not Stalin but Mayakovsky). Like Semyon Konstantinovich in *The Story of a Real Man*, Nadya is teaching herself German, which becomes an integral part of the film's plot. The one sour note in this prewar mountain idyll comes in the person of Vadim, a slick, blond gentleman who flirts with Nadya and, most tellingly, *is cruel to horses*, whipping Bulian in an unsuccessful attempt to ride him.

When war breaks out in 1941, we soon learn that our suspicions of Vadim are justified. He is a Nazi spy who has infiltrated the close-knit horse world. In cinematic terms, the Great Patriotic War becomes a pretense for a string of chases that require fast horses and hard riding. After the Germans

Brave People: Vadim has been unmasked as an enemy. Courtesy BFI Stills.

incinerate the farm's stables, the horsemen drive the surviving horses over the mountains for the Red Army's cavalry. Vasya unmasks Vadim when he catches the traitor setting signal fires for German paratroopers. Instead, the horsemen build pyres in a lake, so that the paratroopers drown (or are easily shot) when they land. Vadim, however, manages to escape after shooting Vasya in the chest.

In the style of a Hollywood Western, Vasya is saved by his horse, Bulian, who *kneels* to pick up his wounded, barely conscious master and carry him to an elderly peasant couple. The old couple successfully dissembles when the Germans come to search their hut looking for partisans, but they cannot prevent the Germans from confiscating Bulian. Vasya, refusing to be separated from his steed, tracks him to the German encampment, where the Germans are foolishly relaxing and bathing in the river without any apparent concern for partisans. Boy and horse easily escape, and Vasya decides the best way to avoid being recaptured will be to don a German uniform. Naturally, he immediately falls into partisan hands, but fortunately, this partisan band is headed by Comrade Kozhin, who recognizes Vasya and believes his tale. (In real life, Vasya would likely have been arrested, if not immediately shot.)

Time for one more chase. Nadya and her grandfather have been serving as partisan couriers in town. Because she speaks German, Nadya is able to avoid detection by flirting and joking with the enemy; Konstantin Sergeevich transports Germans in his "taxi," a horse-drawn cart. Nadya has, however, run into Vadim accidentally at the German officers' club; he orders her arrest.

With the Red Army advancing, the Germans evacuate but load the women prisoners into a boxcar, to take with them as slaves. Unaware of this development, the partisans have already mined the tunnel to blow up the train. How to save the Soviet women?! Only Bulian and Vasya could be fast enough for the rescue. Just before the train enters the tunnel, Vasya unhooks the prisoner car (conveniently the last one). The Germans die (including Vadim); the women live; Vasya and Nadya are reunited.

The film closes at the racetrack, with a victory celebration of a parade and races. The spectators in the grandstand are beautifully dressed and coiffed. Vasya and Bulian win, as always. The war has had no impact on them or their way of life.

Brave People is an entertaining fairy tale, a film as sunny as Aleksandrov's and Pyrev's musical comedies. This is not to say that the movie lacks a message. One wonders how the German army, as depicted in *Brave People*, could have wreaked such devastation on the USSR for so many years. In this movie, like others in the Stalin cult, the Germans are pompous bumblers, cowards, and drunkards. The only really dangerous person in the film is the enemy within, Vadim, a plot device that mirrors the foreboding in Soviet society at the time the film was made. When Stalin succumbed to a stroke in early 1953, many in the Politburo and the military feared another major purge was just around the corner.

Brave People does not merit even a footnote in the history of Soviet cinema as art. But in the history of Soviet cinema as *entertainment*, it was an important step forward because it was a step back, a return to the spirit of the war-as-adventure films from the 1930s, like *Chapaev*, *The Girlfriends*, and *Riders*. Likewise, *The Story of a Real Man* and *The Young Guard* broke new ground by building on the achievements of the past, the spirit of the *personal* heroism and sacrifice of the wartime war films.

In this transitional period between the end of the Great Patriotic War and the death of Stalin, all three of these films, but especially *Brave People*, signaled the possibilities for a return to a more humane Soviet war cinema. These possibilities were realized in the cultural Thaw of the Khrushchev era, in part because during de-Stalinization, the Stalin cult was replaced by a cult of the Great Patriotic War. The war films of the Thaw, several of which brought Soviet cinema back into the international spotlight, are the subject of the next chapter.

5 The Thaw, 1956–1966

Two points of emphasis emerge in the historiophoty of the Civil War in the late 1950s: the terrible hardships suffered by both citizens and soldiers and the conflict's destructive impact on personal life and individual relationships. The Great Patriotic War is likewise viewed through the eyes of individuals, whether combatants or civilians. The contributions (and tribulations) of noncombatants and quiet heroes to the war effort come to the forefront for the first time.

When Stalin died on 5 March 1953, he left a nation rudderless. The first order of business was to find a successor, and Nikita Khrushchev, Lavrenty Beria, and Georgy Malenkov engaged in a struggle for sole power. As we know, Khrushchev won. Beria was executed at the end of 1953, and Malenkov resigned as prime minister in 1955 (but continued to battle Khrushchev for two more years). The cultural thaw that is inextricably linked with the name of Nikita Khrushchev did not begin with the death of Stalin, nor did it end with Khrushchev's ouster by Leonid Brezhnev in 1964. The Thaw was a quiet cultural revolution, but its impact on Soviet society was at least as important as that of the Cultural Revolution of 1928–1932. Indeed, one might well argue that cultural production during the Thaw planted the seeds of doubt that gradually undermined the Soviet regime during the next four decades.

The cinema of the Thaw marked the first time since Soviet cinema's golden age in the 1920s that cineastes outside the USSR took serious notice of Soviet movies and their makers.[1] The cinematic Thaw was part of the European transformation in film art known as Neorealism in Italy and the New Wave in France. However, because of Soviet cinema's centrality to the state's political project, one might argue that this transformation had even greater social impact here than it did elsewhere. As we shall see, Thaw cinema was marked first and foremost by its humanism (with the individual, not the group, placed front and center) and, second, by its reflective questioning of received canons.

Although war films did not dominate the cinematic discourse during the Thaw, they contributed to the cultural dialogue in significant ways, as many younger directors were veterans who attended VGIK after the war. The war film's stock rose as Khrushchev began slowly to dismantle the Stalin cult and replace it, just as slowly, with the sanctification of the Great Patriotic War. As Nina Tumarkin describes the process, "[A] cult of the Great Patriotic War—an organized system of symbols and rituals driven by political imperatives determined by its managers—was in its formative stage. Some aspects of the symbolic matrix—like the basic plot of the war and the Victory Banner as the cult's central symbol—had been fixed. Others—such as Stalin's role in the war—were in flux."[2] This chapter will examine the changes that occurred in the war film genre, the resistance to those changes, and the extent to which the Thaw films truly supported the incipient war cult.

Developments in the Soviet Film Industry

As discussed in the previous chapter, at the time of Stalin's death, Soviet film production was so low as to be nearly nonexistent. Of the dozen studios, only Mosfilm, Lenfilm, and Soiuzdetfilm/Gorky Studio were producing with any regularity. The number of movie theaters was on the rise, but nearly a decade after war's end, there were few new Soviet movies to be seen. Although the literary debate about socialist realism's efficacy as the state's aesthetic doctrine had begun, very cautiously, by late 1953, the new thinking did not trickle down to the studios until the end of 1954.

In 1954, the influential director Ivan Pyrev (*The Regional Party Secretary*, *Six o' Clock in the Evening after the War*), who had been at Mosfilm's helm during the war, regained that position. Unpredictable and autocratic, but a good judge of authentic talent, Pyrev brought new energy and initiative to the filmmaking enterprise. When the new Five Year Plan was unveiled in 1955, it called for substantial investment in all aspects of cinema, with a target of seventy-five new titles to be produced in 1956.[3]

As is well known, the Twentieth Party Congress in February 1956 culminated in Khrushchev's Secret Speech denouncing Stalin. This was followed by Khrushchev's efforts to remove Party hard-liners from their positions.

As the attempted coup in 1957 demonstrated all too clearly, this purge was only partially successful. "De-Stalinization" placed the Party's imprimatur on the process of gradual cultural relaxation that was already under way. This period became known as the Thaw (*ottepel'*), after the title of Ilya Ehrenburg's 1954 novel.[4]

Movie production did indeed expand, and for the first time in over twenty years, people who loved movies had real choices in the repertory. Cinema surged in popularity. Studios began organizing film festivals that encouraged genuine public discussion of the pictures screened. The *Art of the Cinema*, which had been transformed in the late 1940s into an organ of the "cult of personality," once again published film criticism of genuine merit, and the long-defunct fan magazine *Soviet Screen* was brought back in 1957. The reborn *Soviet Screen* was mainly a pictorial devoted to developing a star culture, but it also translated some of the critical debates for its readership, the nonprofessional moviegoing public. The same could not be said of *Pravda*, where film reviews remained as formulaic as they had been in the previous two decades.[5] Censorship began to decentralize, with more emphasis placed on the studios governing themselves than on central oversight.[6]

As exciting as these changes were, the Thaw was only partial, and it would be a mistake to overstate the extent of the cultural liberalization. Khrushchev had no real cultural policy, but he did not hesitate to rebuke artists personally when he felt they were taking the new emphasis on truthfulness to extremes, as he did in 1957.[7] Within the film industry, many whose careers had flourished under the Stalin regime resisted change, believing that the liberalization of the film industry was going too far. For the reform-minded, Khrushchev's erratic policies and uncertain political position could not inspire confidence that the regime change was permanent.

The Russian Civil War's Return to the Screen

As we have seen in the previous chapter, by the late 1940s, the Great Patriotic War had been put in "deep freeze," whether as a topic for art or as a rationale for public celebration. Apart from Mikhail Chiaureli, who occupied an unusually secure position as one of Stalin's "favorites," few seasoned directors undertook assignments that required them to glorify Stalin. Artistic scruples aside, there was too much room for error in interpreting the late leader's role in winning the war. Even after the Secret Speech, some directors preferred to move cautiously, especially those who had experienced the Party line's twists and turns under Stalin.

For these reasons, the Civil War seemed a safer war to reinterpret, despite Chiaureli's efforts in *The Unforgettable Year 1919* to turn Stalin into a Civil War hero. The year 1957 marked the fortieth anniversary of the Russian Revolution; movies about the revolutionary era were, therefore, specifically encouraged as part of the film industry's production plan. The Russian Civil War's dramatic contradictions and tensions provided stories that were tailor-made for the kinds of movies the Thaw directors wanted to make. Directors continued to prefer literary adaptations over untested story lines and drew from the vast fictional literature of the 1920s for screenplays.

Of the four major Civil War films made during the Thaw—*The Communist, Pavel Korchagin, The Forty-first,* and *The Quiet Don*—only one, *The Communist,* was based on an original screenplay, by Yevgeny Gabrilovich. The others not only were adapted from well-known novels but also were "remakes" of older movies. These four movies naturally fit into thematic pairs: *Pavel Korchagin* with *The Communist, The Forty-first* with *The Quiet Don.*

The first to appear was *Pavel Korchagin* (1956, released 1957), an adaptation of Nikolai Ostrovsky's *How the Steel Was Tempered*.[8] Aleksandr Alov (1923–1983) and Vladimir Naumov (b. 1927) represented the new generation of Soviet film directors. Born and raised in the USSR rather than in czarist Russia, they were children of the Stalin era, "forged" in the crucible of the Great Patriotic War, where Alov had served, rather than the Civil War.[9] For Alov and Naumov, the Civil War was not lived experience, but someone else's memory.

Like most major directors, Alov and Naumov learned their art at VGIK, where they had trained with Igor Savchenko (director of *Riders, Ivan Nikulin,* and *The Third Blow*). Savchenko died late in 1950, while filming *Taras Shevchenko,* a "biopic" about the Ukrainian national hero.[10] To honor their mentor's memory, Alov and Naumov finished this film in 1951, the year they graduated from the institute.

The young directors' approach to *How the Steel Was Tempered* is evident in the title they chose, *Pavel Korchagin,* the name of Ostrovsky's protagonist, rather than the original title, with its unpleasant reminders of the jargon of the 1930s. *How the Steel Was Tempered,* an inspirational story of sacrifice, was loosely based on Ostrovsky's own life story. The novel's "Ostrovsky" is Pavel Korchagin, a young proletarian who is grievously wounded during the Civil

War. Korchagin's struggles for the cause permanently ruin his health; eventually he becomes totally blind and semiparalyzed. He consciously gives up his chances for love and happiness to devote what little time he has left to building the revolutionary society. Ostrovsky's novel, written like a saint's life, inspired Soviet youth in the 1930s—or so we are to believe. (Recall that in The Story of a Real Man, Alyosha Meresev, in the throes of desperation after his double amputation, seeks to model his life after Pavel Korchagin, to find the courage to overcome his disability.)

Konstantin Isaev's screenplay retained the outlines of Ostrovsky's plot, although he substantially condensed the postwar sections. By emphasizing the costs of Pavel's sacrifice, the filmmakers avoided the tendentiousness of the novel while deepening its meaning. Alov and Naumov's Pavel Korchagin is a real person, not a plaster saint. Through their interpretation and Vasily Lanovoy's acting ability in the title role, Pavel Korchagin at last became an authentic hero—to borrow from the title of Lermontov's classic novel, "a hero of our time."

Pavel Korchagin is constructed as a protracted flashback. Pavel's "prewar" is his prerevolutionary youth, beginning in 1913. Because Pavel is a poor boy growing up in czarist times, this "prewar," like that in Arnshtam's Girlfriends, illustrates the many injustices of late imperial Russia. But Pavel's class consciousness is not fully raised until the Revolution (the Great War is never mentioned). Inspired at a Bolshevik meeting, he volunteers for the Red Army and joins Semyon Budyonnyi's legendary First Cavalry. When Pavel is wounded too seriously to rejoin his unit, he devotes himself to supporting the Reds' military efforts in a different way, by repairing railroad track under terrible conditions of filth, disease, cold, and deprivation. His health ruined, the love of his life lost to another, Pavel goes home to his mother for the last time and begins to write his memoir.

Pavel Korchagin's Civil War is not an adventure. In battle, on his steed, swinging his saber, Pavel looks more alive than he ever does again, and we believe for a minute in the possibility of swashbuckling derring-do in the style of Chapaev. That moment quickly passes; when he and his horse are felled by an artillery charge, Pavel's combat days are over, but the struggle is not. Alov and Naumov's home front is postapocalyptic; revolutionary Russia is a nation of beggars, orphans, and the starving on the move. Pavel's first and only embrace with Frida, the Communist girl he loves, occurs as a death cart loaded with corpses rattles by. "Famine," says Frida, simply. The romantic mood broken, they shake hands and go their separate ways.

For a near invalid like Pavel, the squalor of the railroad work camp renders it almost as dangerous as the front. The men labor in cold, driving rain, and, as winter falls, in the snow. There is little food and poor shelter. Overcrowding and filthy conditions lead to a typhus epidemic. Defeatism is rampant. The camp is attacked by brigands. In these powerfully filmed scenes, Alov and Naumov boldly equate the Civil War with the end of civilization, an idea once expressed by long-suppressed writers like Yevgeny Zamiatin and Boris Pilniak.

Pavel Korchagin's Civil War also signifies the end of traditional personal relations. War constantly separates Pavel from the only two people he loves: his mother and Frida. Mothers always wait; lovers may not. Frida waits in spirit but not in body. Like Pavel, she is constantly on the move in the service of the Revolution, which makes their reunion problematic. Their many separations engender misunderstanding: Pavel rushes out of Frida's room when he finds a man in her bed; he does not stay to learn that this man is her brother, a soldier on leave who needs a place to sleep. When Frida eventually finds Pavel at the labor camp, he is too exhausted to hear her confession of love. They are far apart when Pavel collapses from typhus and is evacuated from the camp. Rumors fly in wartime; solid sources of information are few. Frida is devastated when she hears from a seemingly authoritative source that Pavel has died.

Postwar brings no happy ending for Pavel. This is not *Wait for Me*. He and Frida meet again at a Komsomol conference, but Frida has married and has a child. Losing his sight, and any hope that he and Frida will be reunited, Pavel contemplates suicide, but he rejects this selfish idea when he recalls the sacrifices of his dead comrades. Instead, he decides to memorialize his generation by writing about their experiences.

Yuly Raizman's *The Communist* (Kommunist) resembles *Pavel Korchagin* in many respects. Like *Pavel Korchagin*, *The Communist* is constructed as a flashback but as a remembered, rather than experienced, tale. It is also a home front Civil War story, focusing on the heroism of a wounded soldier, Vasily Gubanov, who is reassigned to an electrification project during his convalescence. Although Raizman also shows the anarchy and despair of 1918–1919, *The Communist's* tone is much brighter than that of *Pavel Korchagin*. Raizman (1903–1994) came from the "father's generation." A filmmaker since 1924, he was adept at constructing the positive hero of socialist realism with a human touch. *The Communist* is, like its protagonist Vasily Gubanov, caught between two worlds, the "old" and the "new."

Unlike the melancholy Pavel, Vasily Gubanov bursts with energy and a "can-do" spirit. Played by the tall, ruggedly handsome young actor Yevgeny Urbansky, Gubanov could serve as a poster boy for socialist realist art. Gubanov deals with two crises over the course of the film: one personal, one public. His personal crisis is a romantic one. He has fallen in love with an "unreconstructed" peasant woman, Aniuta, whose husband, Stepan, is a drunken batterer and a speculator. Stepan leaves home to barter food to starving refugees, then fails to return (a common occurrence during these chaotic times), which drives Aniuta to the factory to support herself. Although she does not experience a political awakening, she discovers that she can survive independently. Stepan eventually tries to reclaim Aniuta, but with Gubanov's help, she finds the courage to escape her old life for good. She goes to live with Gubanov and gives birth to their son. For his part, Gubanov suffers some fleeting moral qualms—"What's Marxist theory about love with a married woman?" he muses—but surely rescuing a woman from a wife beater cannot be wrong. (At least one reviewer felt that this love triangle weakened the picture.)[11]

Gubanov's public, political struggle ends with his death. He is "the Communist," the representative of the new order in this backwoods. He leads the battle to build a new society (to transform peasants into workers) while a war rages. Besieged by enemies within (bureaucrats in Moscow, suspicious peasants at home) and enemies without (brigands, counterrevolutionary Greens), he overcomes them all with Lenin's help and through his personal fortitude. When supplies run short, Gubanov heads immediately to Moscow to seek help directly from Comrade Lenin. Lenin picks up the phone, and all Gubanov's problems are solved, at least for the moment. (Stalin has vanished from the scene, since de-Stalinization was well under way by this time.)

This is not to suggest that Raizman glosses over the difficulties of life during those years, which he and scenarist Gabrilovich had survived. By 1919, Gubanov's village is threatened by White forces. Typhus is rampant. There is no food, no fuel. The climax of the film is a desperate moment: the village is starving. Gubanov needs to find bread, but the supply train sits motionless for lack of fuel. Gubanov, though himself weak from hunger, maniacally begins chopping trees for fuel. Counterrevolutionary forces arrive and torch the town. Gubanov is surrounded; he attempts to fight them single-handed. He is shot, again and again, until finally he is downed for good, lying dead in the thick mud. This is a shocking scene for Soviet cinema in the midfifties.

The Communist: Gubanov is mortally wounded. Courtesy BFI Stills.

The denouement, however, is strictly old school, right out of the pages of socialist realism. When Lenin calls to find out what has happened, he hears the "good news" from the regional Party secretary that only one person has been killed, "only" Gubanov. Lenin admonishes him in true Leninist fashion: "This is also a front. Every technical success is a strike against capitalism." At his funeral, Gubanov is eulogized as a man "from a working family," who has "worked since the age of thirteen." Aniuta, garbed in black, stands like a statue with her baby, as her repentant husband begs her to return to him. She refuses. The final shot shows her walking down one path, her husband, another.

The critical response to these two films was predictable. *Pavel Korchagin* aroused more debate than *The Communist*. For some critics, Alov and Naumov's picture was too negative, disturbing, *different*, although indubitably the work of talented filmmakers.[12] For others, it breathed new life into a badly aging socialist realist classic.[13] On the other hand, *The Communist*, which had been commissioned for the fortieth anniversary of the beginning of the Civil War, was built on a familiar model, even though Raizman incorporated some elements from the new thinking.[14] Viewers responded well to both films, although they gave a slight edge to *Pavel Korchagin*, which recorded 25.3 million viewers (fifteenth place in 1957) to *The Communist*'s 22.3 million.[15] In 1959, however, the readers of *Soviet Screen* ranked *The Communist* as the "third best" film of the year in the magazine's annual readers' poll.[16]

The romantic melodramas *The Forty-first* (1956) and *The Quiet Don* (1957–1958) are as different from *Pavel Korchagin* and *The Communist* as movies set in the same time period could be. These two films and their receptions provide another way to illustrate the tensions between the old and the new in Thaw war cinema. *The Forty-first*'s Grigory Chukhrai (1921–2001) was one of the most interesting filmmakers to emerge during the Thaw. A decorated veteran, Chukhrai served during the Winter War with Finland (although he did not see action due to frostbite), as well as the Great Patriotic War (where he was wounded twice, the second time critically). Chukhrai had been preparing to enter VGIK in 1939, when he was drafted; after a long recovery from his war wounds and a bout with tuberculosis, he finally was able to enroll and graduated in 1953. Chukhrai's independent streak led to his dismissal from his first position at the Kiev Studio. Fortunately, one of his mentors at VGIK, director Mikhail Romm, persuaded the Mosfilm Studio to offer him a second chance. There Chukhrai found a patron in the studio's head, Ivan Pyrev, who enjoyed the power to sponsor politically unpopular directors without harming himself.[17] To his credit, he often did so.

Chukhrai's idea of remaking *The Forty-first* (*Sorok pervyi*) met with resistance. Yakov Protazanov's 1927 silent adaptation of Boris Lavrenev's novella about the love affair between the Red sharpshooter and the White lieutenant (discussed in chapter 1) held an enduring place in Soviet film history. Chukhrai was certainly aware that Protazanov's version had sparked a firestorm of criticism in the late 1920s for its sympathetic portrayal of the class enemy. How much had Soviet society changed in the thirty years that separated the films?[18]

Chukhrai closely follows the basic outline of Lavrenev's work and Protazanov's previous adaptation. Red soldiers trudging through the Kara-Kum Desert capture a handsome White officer, Lieutenant Govorukhin, who is on a secret mission to carry a message from Admiral Kolchak to General Denikin. The sharpshooter Mariutka is among those Reds designated to accompany the prisoner to headquarters, which requires that they cross the raging Caspian in a tiny boat. Only Mariutka and Govorukhin survive, as castaways on an island. They fall in love, but when they are about to be rescued by the Whites, Mariutka claims her forty-first victim.

The same source produced two very different movies. Chukhrai's film is a romantic melodrama filmed in gauzy Technicolor. Pathbreaking, often brilliant, it is a love story with war as a backdrop. Protazanov's *Forty-first* is all sharp edges; Chukhrai's are rounded. For Chukhrai, nature, even at its harshest, is beautiful, as is Mariutka, even at her most "common." Unlike Ada Voitsik, who played Mariutka in Protazanov's version, Izolda Izvitskaya is unconvincing as a working-class girl, despite the advantage of being able to develop her character through occasionally coarse speech. Mariutka's transformation from soldier to lover is far more complete than it was in Protazanov's film. As a result, her final action strains credulity, whereas in Protazanov's version, it is firmly grounded in revolutionary reality. But does it matter? The lush romanticism and overt sensuousness of the picture are also revolutionary, but in a very different way.[19]

Veteran director Sergei Gerasimov (1906–1985) had long wanted to make a screen adaptation of Mikhail Sholokhov's epic novel *The Quiet Don* (Tikhii Don, also known in English as *And Quiet Flows the Don*),[20] about a village of Don Cossacks during World War I, the Revolution, and the Civil War. Although the film was celebrated as a classic of socialist realism, *The Quiet Don*'s Cossack milieu was as problematic as its ambiguous protagonist, Grigory Melekhov, who had been pejoratively labeled by critics a "Don Hamlet [*donskoi Gamlet*]."[21] The violent, impetuous, unreliable Melekhov might in fact be considered among the first antiheroes of Soviet fiction.

The novel's first screen adaptation was a 1931 silent version directed by Olga Preobrazhenskaya and Ivan Pravov. This early effort had not, however, attracted much attention, so Gerasimov only competed with the novel's considerable grip on the imagination. As a novel, *The Quiet Don* had the epic scale and large cast of characters that attracted Gerasimov to *The Young Guard*, and the Gorky Studio gave him the budget necessary to do it justice, including color film stock. The 350-minute film was released in three parts: the first two in 1957, the third in 1958.

As with *The Young Guard*, Gerasimov wrote the screenplay himself, adhering closely to *The Quiet Don*'s complicated plots and large cast of characters. Gerasimov, who always strove for historical verisimilitude in his work, lovingly re-created the Cossack way of life, particularly its patriarchal and military aspects. His battle scenes are drawn on the grand scale of Savchenko's in *The Third Blow*, but with the romantic heroism unique to the screen's clichés of cavalry warfare.

Gerasimov's interpretation of Cossack participation in both the Great War and the Civil War is not ideologically driven. His Cossacks fight with the czars and their successors because they have always done so. As a relatively privileged military caste, they have no natural inclination or obvious motivation to join the Reds. Grigory Melekhov himself is buffeted from one side to the other, mainly through happenstance. Both sides, Red and White, are equally violent—this is war, after all, war never-ending.

The romance between Grigory and his married neighbor Aksinya is arguably the only great love story in Soviet (as distinct from Russian) literature. Their love is as tumultuous as the times they live in; they change sexual partners as frequently as they change sides. But their passion for each other remains constant. Aksinya's death, when the couple has finally come together for good, jolts Grigory as have none of the other tragedies of wartime. Aksinya's death symbolizes the end of Grigory's life as he knew it. Never redeemed, Grigory Melekhov is more truly a "fragment of the empire" than was Filimonov, the protagonist of Ermler's 1929 film by that title. But by the end of The Quiet Don, this shallow man of action achieves a degree of self-awareness and resigns himself to the triumph of Soviet power.

In the context of Hollywood cinema, The Quiet Don is a competent but conventional costume drama. But in the context of Soviet cinema, The Quiet Don set a new standard for the historical blockbuster, greatly influencing Sergei Bondarchuk's monumental (and Oscar-winning) adaptation of War and Peace a decade later. The preferences of the moviegoers were clear. Chukhrai's lyrical, sensitive film Forty-first drew 25.1 million viewers, a very respectable audience for an art film, on the order of Pavel Korchagin and The Communist.[22] By contrast, each part of The Quiet Don was seen by 47 million people. It led the box office and was named best picture in 1957 and 1958 by Soviet Screen's readers, as well as best picture in 1958 by Soviet Screen's survey of film critics.[23] It certainly did not hurt that the Art of the Cinema heavily promoted the picture.[24]

The Great Patriotic War as Art

Khrushchev's Secret Speech had an enormous impact on the development of the Soviet World War II film. The last serious movies about the war had appeared in 1944 (e.g., The Invasion). The postwar war films had celebrated the "Great Patriotic" as national triumph, but the war as national tragedy remained virgin territory for directors.

It is not a coincidence, therefore, that the movies for which the Thaw is best known outside Russia are four pictures about World War II: Mikhail

Kalatozov's *The Cranes Are Flying* (Letiat zhuravli, 1957); Grigory Chukhrai's *The Ballad of a Soldier* (Ballada o soldate, 1959); Sergei Bondarchuk's *The Fate of a Man* (Sud'ba cheloveka, 1959, also known in English as *The Destiny of a Man*); and Andrei Tarkovsky's *Ivan's Childhood* (Ivanovo detstvo, 1962, also known in English as *My Name Is Ivan*). Each of these films is an original; what ties them together is their humanism.

For the first time, Soviet filmmakers were able to show the emotional costs of the war, without the need for heroics to offset the suffering. In the Secret Speech, Khrushchev had revealed that because of Stalin's arrogance and egoism, the USSR had faced the German invasion unprepared, leading to the unnecessary deaths of millions. As Josephine Woll writes: "Film-makers seized on the theme of the Second World War as a meaningful context within which to elaborate heroic potential and celebrate heroic deeds and to recouch their definitions of heroism."[25]

Kalatozov's *The Cranes Are Flying*, which Viktor Rozov adapted from his play *Forever Alive* (Vechno zhivye), is arguably the most innovative of the four great World War II films of the Thaw, and it is certainly the most analyzed.[26] Like the Civil War films of this period, World War II films were generally inspired by literary sources. The ties between Soviet literature and Soviet cinema, always strong, became stronger yet during the Thaw.[27] Two World War II films that sought to humanize the conflict—Zakhar Agranenko's *The Immortal Garrison* (Bessmertnyi garnizon, 1956), about the defense of Brest, and Aleksandr Ivanov's *Soldiers* (Soldaty, 1957), based on Viktor Nekrasov's play *In the Trenches of Stalingrad*—preceded Kalatozov's movie. Neither film prepared Soviet viewers for the originality of *Cranes*.[28] Although Mikhail Kalatozov (b. Kalatozishvili, 1903–1973), like Sergei Gerasimov and Yuly Raizman, was indubitably a member of the older generation of directors, no one who had seen his 1930 avant-garde masterpiece *The Salt of Svanetia* (Sol' svanetii) could have been completely surprised by *Cranes*. In the words of Soviet critic Lev Anninsky, "It [the Thaw in cinema] all started with *Cranes*."[29]

The story upends the tropes of *Wait for Me*. The film's protagonist, Veronika (wonderfully played by Tatiana Samoilova), is the girl who does not wait. In love with Boris Borozdin, a young engineer who quickly volunteers when war breaks out in summer 1941, she marries Boris's sleazy cousin Mark after he rapes her. Veronika is evacuated from Moscow to western Siberia with her husband and Boris's father and sister, who are both surgeons. Boris is killed early in the war, near Smolensk, around the time that Veronika and Mark wed, although the family does not learn the terrible news until late in the film, from one of Boris's comrades. By film's end, Veronika adopts an orphan, separates from Mark, and waits vainly at the train station for Boris at war's end.

Compared with any of the films we have discussed so far, Veronika is a remarkable protagonist. She certainly cannot be called a heroine. For most of the film, she is completely passive, lacking in independence and initiative, a victim of circumstances. Due to a miscommunication, she does not even arrive in time to see Boris off at the train station (which makes for a memorable scene of sorrow and confusion). After her parents are killed when their apartment building is bombed (they have refused to go to the bomb shelter), Veronika runs to the Borozdins for living space. Depressed by Boris's silence (there are no letters), Veronika ignores the air-raid siren and stays in the Borozdin's apartment. This lapse in judgment does not lead to her physical death, like her parents, but to something worse, her spiritual death. Mark finds her alone in the flat and forces himself on her. Although she does attempt to get away, and strikes him several times, when she realizes it is hopeless, she faints before he rapes her. Completely benumbed by the experience, she is as stiff as a mannequin during the scene of her wedding to Mark.

Working as a nurse's aide in the evacuation camp's hospital, tending to the wounded from the Battle of Stalingrad, Veronika always appears to be in a trance. She witnesses the heartbreak of men who have been betrayed. When a young soldier receives a "Dear Ivan" letter, Veronika listens despondently as the other men, including Fyodor Borozdin, commiserate with him, saying: "Girls like that are worse than fascists"; "women like her, we men despise them, there can be no pardon for her." Her depression ever-deepening, Veronika intends to commit suicide by throwing herself under a train like Anna Karenina. Her salvation comes through saving another: she rescues an orphan boy who is about to be run over by a truck. Learning that the child is also a Boris, "Borka from Voroshilovgrad," she takes this as a sign from her true love and adopts him. At last Veronika comes to her senses and decides to change her empty life. When Fyodor Borozdin evicts Mark because he has obtained his military exemption fraudulently, Veronika does not follow her husband. She will no longer tolerate Mark's deceits.

Although Boris (played by the popular young actor Aleksei Batalov) has little screen time, the contrasts between him and Mark are stark. Boris is a humanized version of "Homo sovieticus." He works in a factory. He does

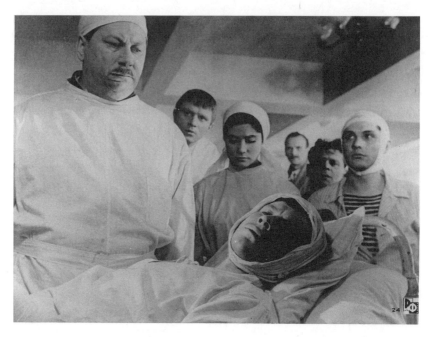

The Cranes Are Flying: Veronika and Dr. Borozdin at the hospital. Courtesy BFI Stills.

not hesitate to volunteer, but he is sleeping too soundly to awake when others are trying to tell him about the invasion. He sacrifices his own safety to carry a wounded comrade. In his dying moments, his last thoughts are of Veronika as he imagines their wedding.

The other Borozdins are also full-fledged human beings. Father Fyodor, who often displays a sarcastic streak, is far from pleased that his son has rushed to volunteer. On the surface sister Irina models Soviet self-sacrifice, but we sense the pain beneath her chilly exterior. Although many Soviet women were physicians, few were surgeons; the film implies that Irina's pursuit of this male-dominated field in medicine has forced her to give up a personal life.

Cousin Mark, on the other hand, is a shirker, a pianist, who hopes for an exemption from the draft, which "all the clever ones" will get. Obtaining a deferment is, in fact, his very first thought when he learns that his country has been invaded by the Germans. He lies to get his exemption, using his uncle's name and connections without the older man's knowledge. Even with an exemption, Mark finds the war a great inconvenience that interrupts his career plans, though it does not interfere with his social life. (He takes up with a dubious group of evacuees and spends most of his time drinking with them.) Finally, Mark is also a faithless husband who steals Veronika's most precious possession, a toy squirrel from Boris, to give to his girlfriend as a present.

The intelligentsia rushed to see this film. It startled a public that was starved for challenging art. Its style was controversial, especially the flashy rape scene, with its skewed camera angles and extreme close-ups. An exciting and stormy public debate over its morality reminded older viewers of the intellectual vitality of the 1920s, before the Cultural Revolution.[30] It dislodged critics from their usual polemical positions: the liberal critic Maya Turovskaya thought it deeply flawed, while the conservative Rostislav Yurenev loved it.[31] Why was the imperfect Veronika portrayed so sympathetically? Why was Mark not punished? Where is the vaunted Soviet courage and selflessness that supposedly lay at the heart of the victory? The cranes of the title, which we see flying overhead at the end, symbolize rebirth and hope, but how will Veronika be able to achieve this? For too long, Soviet critics and viewers had been accustomed to films that provided answers to the questions they raised.

The Cranes Are Flying brought international recognition to Mikhail Kalatozov—and, perhaps more important, to the dramatic changes under way in Soviet cinema. The film won the Palme d'Or, the grand prize at the Cannes Film Festival, in 1957 and was seen by 5.4 million people in France, a record for a Soviet film. At home, the audience was a very solid 28.3 million, earning tenth place at the box office,[32] but well behind The Quiet Don.

A comparison between the two most important World War II films of 1959 offers another basis for understanding the preferences of the Soviet mass audience. The first to open was The Fate of a Man, which was adapted from a story by Mikhail Sholokhov that had been suppressed by censorship in 1946 for its inflammatory subject matter; its "hero" was an escaped prisoner of war.[33] Sergei Bondarchuk (1920–1994), a popular actor and World War II veteran, both directed and starred in the film, his first as a director. Trained at VGIK by Sergei Gerasimov, Bondarchuk had appeared in Gerasimov's film The Young Guard. The style of The Fate of a Man did not, however, reveal much of Gerasimov's influence; that would come in Bondarchuk's later work.

The plot is retrospectively narrated: an ordinary Soviet soldier is captured by the Germans, escapes, survives the war, and (like Veronika in The Cranes Are Flying) adopts a war orphan. His entire family—wife and three

The Fate of a Man: Sokolov, a new kind of hero. Courtesy of BFI Stills.

children—have been killed by war's end. The success of the film, which is so much better than its literary source, hinges to a great extent on Sokolov's portrayal. As an actor and a director, Bondarchuk does a masterly job of depicting an ordinary man in extraordinary times. Returning to the main theme of the wartime war films, Sokolov fights not for state and Party but for family and Russia—and for his own survival.

The two most famous episodes in the film illustrate its power. The first takes place in a church where the Germans have temporarily placed the Russian prisoners. Bondarchuk shows the rapid breakdown of prisoner solidarity, as one man discusses his plans to betray a Party member to the Germans. Although not himself a Party member, Sokolov does not hesitate to strangle the traitor, but he takes no pleasure in doing so. (This is a far cry from the exultation shown in *Person No. 217,* when the slave laborer Tanya murders the SS officers Kurt and Max while they sleep in their beds.) The second episode features a drinking challenge. The German officers at the camp attempt to humiliate Sokolov by forcing him to toast the German offensive at Stalingrad. He drinks three large tumblers of vodka quickly and smoothly, takes the food he is offered as a reward for his "prowess," and walks away, his dignity intact until he is out of their sight. Only then does he collapse, from fear as well as from the overdose of alcohol.[34]

After his success with The Forty-first, Grigory Chukhrai turned to the Great Patriotic War for The Ballad of a Soldier, with an original screenplay coauthored with Valentin Yezhov. Like The Forty-first, The Ballad of a Soldier is also a lyrical tale, a poem in black-and-white about a young soldier, Alyosha. Nineteen-year-old Alyosha's odyssey begins at the front, when he requests a six-day home leave to help his mother, instead of a medal for his bravery. "To tell the truth, I get scared," the reluctant hero admits; in fact, we see that his first instinct is to flee from the oncoming tank, before turning and firing.

At each phase of Alyosha's journey behind the lines, he faces delays, usually of his own making, as he seeks to help people whom he meets along the way. When he finally reaches his village, he has only time enough to kiss his mother before returning to the front. She never sees him again. This iconic mother revisions the image of the woman-who-waits. Ten years after the end of the war, she still waits by the road where she last saw him. Her vigil shapes the opening and closing shots of the movie.

The Ballad of a Soldier is a series of incidents that are vignettes more than events. Each reveals a key aspect of life in wartime. The first person Alyosha helps on his journey is a crippled veteran (a cameo role played by Yevgeny Urbansky, star of The Communist) who is ashamed of his disability and afraid to face his wife's imagined rejection. All is well: the man's wife embraces him joyously. Next Alyosha meets a young girl, Shura, when they both hitch a ride on a hay train. With false bravado, Shura tells Alyosha that she is traveling to meet her "future husband," a gravely wounded pilot. When the train stops in Voronezh, Alyosha disembarks to search for water for them both, but when he returns, the train is gone. He hitches a ride with an old woman to the next station, where Shura has disembarked and waits for him. His next mission is to deliver soap to the wife of one of his comrades. Although the couple's apartment building has been destroyed, Alyosha keeps searching. When he finds the woman, she is with a lover. Another train. This one is bombed and burns, but oblivious to his own safety, Alyosha rescues passengers from the fire. Time running out, worried, he asks a trucker for a ride. Although the trucker initially refuses and drives off, he

The Ballad of a Soldier: Alyosha and Shura at a stop. Courtesy BFI Stills.

turns back, and so, through the kindness of another the boy finally reaches his mother. "I'll come back, Mama," he assures her, but like millions of others, he cannot keep his promise.

In the hands of a lesser director, this picture could have been overwhelmed by sentimentality. Chukhrai keeps the tone matter-of-fact: Alyosha is an ordinary Russian boy doing what ordinary Russians do. What is equally important to the success of the movie is that everyone Alyosha meets—the disabled veteran, the faithless wife, the trucker who initially refuses to give him a ride—is normal, too, in both their virtues and their vices. *The Ballad of a Soldier* is a very quiet, very moving film that reveals not only the sorrows but also the fleeting happiness that was possible behind the front lines in wartime.[35]

The Fate of a Man and *The Ballad of a Soldier* framed the year 1959. Critics and other filmmakers praised them both.[36] Both were popular with filmgoers, *The Fate of a Man* enormously so, with 39.25 million viewers (ranked fifth) and named the best film of the year by *Soviet Screen's* readers.[37] *The Ballad of a Soldier* was seen by 30.1 million.[38] Both contributed in important ways to the de-heroicization of the war, but *The Fate of a Man* was more overtly dramatic and optimistic, qualities that viewers evidently prized. Not only is Chukhrai's film low-key, but the mother loses her son, a sad and truthful reminder to the millions of mothers whose sons never returned. Bondarchuk's Sokolov is a much showier protagonist; it is a riveting performance of despair. Although he loses his family, he survives physically. We sense that he will, by bonding with a war orphan, survive emotionally as well. But most important, he does not suffer the fate that beset many other returning Soviet POWs: he was not arrested. (This subject would be tackled again, more directly, by Grigorii Chukhrai in *Clear Skies*, to be discussed below.)

The final film in this quartet marked another directorial debut, by Andrei Tarkovsky (1932–1986), with his first feature film, *Ivan's Childhood* (1962). Tarkovsky had just graduated from VGIK, where he had studied with Mikhail Romm; his diploma film took first place at a student film competition in New York.[39] *Ivan's Childhood* launched his brilliant but troubled career. Based on Vladimir Bogomolov's short story, "Ivan," this film tells the story of the last days of Ivan Bondarev, a twelve-year-old orphan boy who becomes a scout for a Red Army reconnaissance unit. The child is eventually captured and executed by the Germans.

By 1962, Khrushchev was in serious political trouble, and the cultural climate was cooling rapidly. It was not a propitious moment to launch the harshest, most morally complex vision of the war to appear on the Soviet screen. The story idea had run into trouble for its "negativism" even before Tarkovsky joined the project.[40] The preternaturally mature Ivan, so thin that he is almost skeletal, is alternately coddled and exploited by the unit's officers. Avuncular Lieutenant Colonel Griaznov is determined to send the child away to a military boarding school (which Ivan vehemently opposes), while pragmatic Captain Kholin would not mind using Ivan for "one last mission." The child, who is a "bundle of nerves," is tormented by recurring dreams of his mother laughing in the sunshine, moments before she is blown up before his eyes. His waking hours are haunted by recurring images of the eight young partisans who were tortured and executed in the cellar where he sleeps. "Avenge us!" is scrawled on the walls.

But Ivan's true nightmare is the waking world, the ruined landscape of the villages, the muck of the murky swamps that he patrols. This is a world populated by a deranged old man who hides in the rubble of his ruined home waiting for his dead wife to return, and by the corpses of Ivan's comrades, hanging on the trees as warning signs from the Germans. It is

Ivan's Childhood: Ivan on a mission. Courtesy BFI Stills.

also populated by soldiers (particularly Kholin) who are torn between their desire to love Ivan and to protect him and by their need to exploit him for their cause. The nurse Masha is likewise vulnerable to Kholin. In the justly famous scene in the birch forest, a scene that is both beautiful and terrible, Kholin almost succeeds in seducing Masha, then draws back as she seems about to faint into his arms. The sexual tension is suffocating.

On the periphery of the film stands Lieutenant Galtsev. Little older than a boy himself, Galtsev serves as the picture's moral center. He strongly disapproves of the way Ivan is being used as a scout. He seeks to foil the worldly, cynical Kholin by protecting both Ivan and Masha from Kholin's schemes and desires. But while Galtsev succeeds in transferring Masha out of harm's way to a hospital behind the lines, he cannot save Ivan, who disappears during "one last" reconnaissance mission.

At war's end, the weary, battle-hardened Galtsev is the unit's only survivor. In Berlin, sifting through the debris at Gestapo headquarters, Galtsev comes across Ivan's dossier among prisoner files strewn over the floor. The child was hanged as a partisan. The boy-man stares, hollow eyed and defiant, from the photograph. The film closes by cutting to scenes from Ivan's idyllic prewar childhood, the childhood ended by war. He runs along the beach, away from the camera, into the sun-dappled water. Is this a sign of optimism? Or that, in death, Ivan has gone home?

Of all the Thaw's war films, *Ivan's Childhood* is probably the most disturbing. Ivan is the unredeemed child. In earlier movies—*The Cranes Are Flying*, *The Fate of a Man*, *The Two Fyodors*[41]—children served to provide hope to war-scarred adults, but Tarkovsky's child symbolizes not only the death of innocence, but also the finality of corporeal death. Although this film won many international prizes and garnered favorable notices from Soviet film critics, it was too pessimistic for audiences, drawing considerably fewer viewers—16.7 million—than the other war films we have discussed.[42]

Two other art films from the Thaw deserve to be better known outside Russia: Chukhrai's *Clear Skies* (Chistoe nebo, 1961) and Alov and Naumov's *Peace to Him Who Enters* (Mir vkhodiashchemu, 1960, released 1961). *Clear Skies* was a major box office success; *Peace* was subjected to severely restricted distribution. Their histories illustrate the vagaries of cultural politics in the late Khrushchev era.

Clear Skies is a harsh study of the impact of war on its survivors, a startlingly frank story tracing the fate of a pilot, once a hero, who had the misfortune to be captured by the Germans. With its awkward mixture of prewar romance and postwar decline, the film is deeply flawed but also very moving, due in large part to a riveting performance by Yevgeny Urbansky, in one of the last roles in his tragically short career. (He was killed in an auto accident in 1965.)[43] Chukhrai's mischievous manipulation of the tropes of socialist realism, especially the positive hero, is fascinating. His protagonist Aleksei Astakhov is a hero, then he isn't, then he is. . . . Casting *The Communist*'s Urbansky in this role was brilliant, since the actor was already identified as the paradigmatic positive hero of the post-Stalin period.

The young pilot Astakhov briefly becomes a hero at the end of 1941 before he is lost in action. Dashing and a bit arrogant, this aviator-hero falls for an unlikely girl, the childlike factory worker Sasha, while he is on a five-day leave. She becomes pregnant after their one night together (like sex, pregnancy outside marriage was not a subject ordinarily treated in Soviet films). Missing in action, Astakhov is reported as dead (rather than as a deserter, which was more common) and is posthumously decorated. The faithful Sasha gives birth to her baby and waits for Astakhov, even though her prewar boyfriend, who has survived the war, wants to marry her.

Against the odds, Astakhov eventually returns, but in disgrace, since he had been a prisoner of the Germans all these years. His handsome face is

Clear Skies: Astakhov rages at his fate. Courtesy BFI Stills.

deeply disfigured from his war wounds, and his soul is likewise scarred. Stripped of his Party card, barred from flying, regarded with suspicion, he becomes a bitter, shiftless drunk. Yet Sasha stays. Now a Party member and a celebrated factory worker, she supports him and their son. After Stalin's death and the coming of the Thaw, however, Astakhov's life and career are restored.

   Clear Skies is an atypical twist on the theme of the woman-who-waits. In the brief prewar minutes of the film, Sasha is shown as a silly, not very "Soviet," girl from a bourgeois family. Obsessed with her appearance, Sasha wants to be tall and pretty like her sister. Sasha has entertained romantic fantasies about Astakhov since he tried to crash her sister's New Year's party. After she accidentally runs into him on the streets of Moscow in late November 1941, she telephones him to set up a date. Intrigued, he agrees; we see him ogling the prettier, more mature young women passing by, hoping that one is Sasha. Taken aback by her obvious youth, he wants to be reassured that she has actually finished school. Such scruples do not, however, prevent him from assuming (on the basis of her aggressiveness in phoning him) that she will have sex with him in an abandoned building, where they are playing hide-and-seek.

Their short romance is a bit creepy, combining childish activities—cavorting, shrieking, snowball fights—with rising sexual tension. In one "playful" scene, a group of women soldiers are the voyeurs. We can imagine their thoughts: they have volunteered to defend their country, but this giggling child is the one who "gets" the man.

War and a baby force Sasha to grow up quickly. Her sister and brother evacuated, her father called up, Sasha is left entirely alone to raise her son. Although she is serving the war effort by working in a factory, she barely scrapes by; since she and Astakhov were not married, she does not receive a widow's pension. Poverty forces her to put pride aside and reluctantly accept a cash handout from her former boyfriend.

By the time Astakhov returns, however, Sasha has a well-established life. She is a Party member, featured in the press as a model worker. Yet she remains stubbornly loyal to this man, now branded a traitor, whom she really does not know. The surviving members of her family, especially her new brother-in-law, are not particularly happy to have this suspect individual living with them. (Sasha's father was killed at the front, but her sister and brother have returned, along with the sister's rather nasty, older husband; the six live together in the three-room family apartment.) Sasha has to explain to her son that his father is really "good," not the abusive drunk he appears to be. She believes in her husband's innocence yet continues to trust in the system that brands a soldier a traitor for having been taken prisoner and surviving. (When Sasha attempts to plead for Astakhov to a Party committee after they have refused to reinstate him, the secretary explains that it is well known that the Germans immediately executed POWs who were Party members, so . . .)

This is an uncomfortable film on many levels, but the thoroughness of Astakhov's eventual rehabilitation must have reassured viewers. Astakhov's restored Party card is the talisman that abruptly transforms him, ending years of alcoholism and abusive behavior. Not only is Astakhov trusted to become a pilot again, he is made a test pilot! *Clear Skies* was Chukhrai's biggest hit yet. With 41.3 million viewers, it ranked second at the box office in 1961, and the film buffs who responded to *Soviet Screen*'s annual survey voted it the best movie of the year.[44] Reviewers criticized the film's formal flaws, but their critiques were thoughtful and balanced, a sign of the growing self-confidence of the post-Stalin generation of Soviet film critics.[45]

While there was still room for original filmmaking in the early sixties, as we have seen with *Ivan's Childhood* and *Clear Skies*, the harsh critical reception of Alov and Naumov's *Peace to Him Who Enters* provides evidence that war films could push the limits only so far. After *Pavel Korchagin*, Alov and Naumov made another film set during the Civil War and its aftermath: *Wind* (Veter, 1959). Now they turned to the last day of World War II in Europe, 8 May 1945. The plot is deceptively simple: three Soviet soldiers are assigned a good deed, ordered to take a heavily pregnant (and terrified) German woman to a hospital. Although cheerful music blares everywhere to signal that the war is almost over, the landscape is joyless. Exhausted soldiers and hopeless refugees pack the muddy, debris-cluttered roads. Since everything has been bombed out, shelter is nonexistent.

This odyssey is very different from Alyosha's in *The Ballad of a Soldier*. The three men—the wet-behind-the-ears Junior Lieutenant Ivlev, the garrulous driver Pasha, and the soldier Yamshchikov, traumatized and deaf from a concussion—have no idea how to get where they are going because most road signs have been sabotaged. Moreover, they cannot communicate, either with the German woman or with each other. Yamshchikov, of course, cannot hear. Pasha talks so much that he cannot listen. Young Ivlev is fresh out of training; he spouts the textbook rules, which might as well be a foreign language at the front. The German woman does not speak their language, nor they hers. She tries to flee, doubtless assuming the worst from them. They pass other lost souls on the way.

This is a pointless, quixotic mission, no more so when the small company is ambushed in town. Pasha is killed. Is the war over or not? The three survivors are picked up by a friendly American soldier driving a truck full of wine to God knows where (he cannot understand them either). More fighting. Yamshchikov disappears and reappears. They make it to the hospital, where the woman gives birth to a son, who promptly urinates over a pile of weapons. It is Victory Day, 9 May 1945.

The film was excoriated when it was shown to officials at the Ministry of Culture. They were outraged at what they perceived as the negative depiction of Soviet soldiers. (Actually, all three are decent men, but they do not seem to have any idea what they are doing and why.) Minister of Culture Yekaterina Furtseva, who was Alov and Naumov's patron, rescued the picture from oblivion. Even though Furtseva did not like the movie, she took it to the Venice Film Festival, where it won a prize. As a result of the international recognition, it was eventually released, but in curtailed distribution.[46]

Peace to Him Who Enters: Yamshchikov alone with his thoughts. Courtesy BFI Stills.

Its restricted release (only 370 copies were made) certainly limited its audience (11.1 million viewers).[47] At the same time, it is hard to imagine that this movie's "abstract humanism" would have appealed to the mass spectator even if it had been more widely seen.[48] As one outraged critic claimed, in language reminiscent of the rhetoric of the Cultural Revolution, *Peace to Him Who Enters* was no more than "a film-symbol from the first to the last scenes"; he believed that its acclaim abroad should not immunize it from criticism.[49] The picture was, however, "rehabilitated" in the glasnost era, recognized as a war film far ahead of its time.[50]

The Great Patriotic War as Entertainment

It is always tempting to privilege prize-winning films, especially if they have won international prizes, over the purely domestic product. It is even more tempting when cinema is as politicized as Soviet cinema. But a central premise of this book is the importance of the typical and the ordinary. Not every film about the war was a work of art, of course; indeed, most were far from it. Many "typical" war movies were very widely seen, and we shall now turn to some of the most popular. The revival of a genuine entertainment cinema was an important, but often overlooked, achievement of the Thaw. Popular war films fell into two basic categories: home front melodramas taking place from the 1930s to the 1950s, and the first full-fledged combat films.

Home front melodramas came first. *The House I Live In* (Dom v ktorom ia zhivu, 1957) was intended by the Gorky Studio to compete with *The Cranes Are Flying* as a more viewer-friendly depiction of the travails of the home front.[51] The strategy worked: *House* drew 600,000 more viewers than *Cranes*, coming in at ninth place in the box office.[52] The film was directed by Lev Kulidzhanov (1924–2002) and Yakov Segel (1923–1995) from an original screenplay by Iosif Olshansky and Nina Rudneva that won a script competition in 1956.[53] Both Kulidzhanov and Segel had recently graduated from VGIK under the tutelage of Sergei Gerasimov.[54] *The House I Live In* is a family melodrama tracing the lives and fates of four families, each representing a different class in the classless society, who move into a new apartment building in 1935. The prewar section of the film is so long (half the film's running time) that *The House I Live In* can only partially be considered a war film.

War interrupts the families' lives, of course, as well as their interrelationships. Seryozha, an intelligent young man from a working-class background, has fallen in love with Galya, from a "bourgeois" family, but Galya eschews her class privileges and returns to Moscow even though she has been evacuated. She eventually enlists and is killed during the war. Seryozha, who has volunteered despite his mother's objections, survives, but his father does not, and his older brother, Kostya, who has been seriously wounded, returns home disabled and embittered. The geologist Dmitry, whose shallow wife, Lida, slept with Kostya before the war, is missing in action. But Lida, shamed by the sacrifice of her fellow citizens, expiates her infidelity by refusing to live with Kostya on his return. Finally, in 1948, she relents, and so the film has its happy ending.

The melodramatic elements of the story threaten to crush it more than once; for example, Lida decides to leave her husband on 22 June 1941, the day the Germans invade the USSR (but changes her mind). There are more fairy-tale elements in this picture than in the best of Thaw cinema: the happy intermingling of various social groups was not terribly realistic nor was the putative standard of living in 1935. However, there is just enough

The House I Live In: Lida and Dmitry part, in front of the Motherland Calls recruiting poster. Courtesy BFI Stills.

authenticity to redeem the film. It was refreshing, for example, to see the Soviet class system acknowledged on the screen, even if it was not treated critically.

The Lida-Kostya-Dmitry triangle serves to illustrate the tensions wrought by overcrowding (the bane of Soviet domestic life), although they are fortunate to live in a brand-new apartment building. Lida and her husband, who are childless, live in one claustrophobic room, even though Dmitry is a geologist, a high-status profession in the USSR. Kostya, Seryozha, their parents, their sister, her husband, and eventually the sister's baby reside in what appears to be a three-room apartment. The unemployed Lida has little housekeeping to do in such a small space. Bored, she invites Kostya in when she sees him loitering in the hall to escape the crowd at home. Of course, when everyone lives in such close proximity, Lida's marital transgression immediately becomes the talk of the building and, notably, it is Lida, not Kostya, who bears the brunt of the nasty gossip.

Kulidzhanov and Segel also honestly depict the human costs of the war. Three important characters—Dmitry, Galya, and Seryozha's father—have been killed. Kostya has been critically wounded. Unlike Aleksei Meresev in *The Story of a Real Man*, Kostya will not be dancing any time soon—nor, it seems, will he be reintegrated as a happy, productive member of Soviet society.

This is not a great film, but it is a good one, humane and lacking in bombast. Its realistic style and skillful interweaving of multiple story lines set the standard for other films of the "prewar, wartime, postwar" type, like Iosif Kheifits's *My Dear Man* (Dorogoi moi chelovek) and Yury Yegorov's *Volunteers* (Dobrovol'tsy), both from 1958. *My Dear Man*, a romanticized adaptation of the second installment in Yury Gherman's epic war novel *The Cause You Serve* (Delo, kotoremu ty sluzhilish), softens the harrowing conditions faced by frontline army medical personnel.[55] One of the most popular films of 1958, *My Dear Man* starred Aleksei Batalov as a frontline surgeon who marries a wartime comrade, a social-climbing, philistine physician, instead of his prewar girlfriend.[56] *Volunteers*, released after *My Dear Man*, suffered by comparison; rather than focusing on the trials of one individual, it diluted its potential dramatic impact with too many protagonists. It is also likely that audiences were tiring of the multigenerational saga, at least for war films.[57]

Combat films promised more excitement to mainstream viewers. One popular and completely uncontroversial entertainment film was *Baltic Skies* (Baltiiskoe nebo, part 1, 1960; part 2, 1961), adapted by Nikolai Chukovsky from his mammoth novel[58] and directed by Vladimir Vengerov (b. 1920). This two-part Lenfilm production was emphatically a war film. A story about the air defense of Leningrad during the siege, *Baltic Skies* was the first important film about the air war since *Moscow Skies* in 1944. Although Vengerov had been Sergei Eisenstein's student at VGIK,[59] there is no trace of the master's influence in this picture. Clearly Vengerov was counting on the fact that most spectators had already read Chukovsky's elaborately plotted novel and were, therefore, able to fill in the many blanks in the sketchy film narrative.

The film takes place from the beginning of the blockade in the terrible winter of 1941 and continues through May Day 1943, when the Soviet offensive to retake the city shows some signs of success. The film alternates between life in the dying city, focusing on the survival story of Sonya and her little brother, Slava, and life on the air base, centering on the fate of Major Lunin, a good pilot and a decent man. The two tales eventually intersect, and the boy Slava is taken in by the airmen and allowed to live on the base (a variation of the war orphan theme in *The Fate of a Man* and other pictures of this period).

Baltic Skies was not the first Thaw movie to treat the Leningrad blockade. In 1957, Lenfilm released The Leningrad Symphony (Leningradskaia simfoniia), directed by Zakhar Agranenko (1912–1960), which romanticizes the true story about the Leningrad musicians who stage a public performance of Dmitry Shostakovich's Seventh Symphony. (Agranenko also includes a subplot about the air base.) The Leningrad Symphony is a heroic story that celebrates the power of art, but the travails of the musicians and others left behind in the city are softened so much that the film lacks the punch that it should have had. Indeed, reviewers strongly criticized the film for trivializing its subject.[60] Everyone looks too sturdy to be starving, including the mother, who is the only character to die. Agranenko was undoubtedly uncertain as to how far he could go in depicting the awful reality of Leningrad in 1942, but he did slip in a startling and unexpected bit of newsreel footage, showing starving Leningraders pulling sleds with corpses on them.

By comparison with The Leningrad Symphony, the first half of Vengerov's movie is quite effective at conveying the rapidly deteriorating conditions in the city. The people left behind are mainly women and children who look convincingly hungry and haggard. Their fatigue and despair are palpable, especially as the winter deepens. The city is dying, of starvation and cold.

The contrast between conditions on the air base and in the city underscores the despair of Leningrad's citizens. As dangerous as their missions are (and this is not downplayed), the airmen are not only free to move, unlike the people trapped in the city, they are visibly well fed. This startling contrast is reinforced when Major Lunin goes into the city to look for his ex-wife's mother, to bring her food. Instead, he saves a dying family, a mother and two small children. Eventually, he is able to evacuate them by claiming that they are his wife and children.

The second part of Baltic Skies is lighter, more optimistic, but even sketchier in its narrative development. The city has survived into spring 1942. An operating streetcar is a cause for celebration; some women are strong enough to join work details clearing the streets from the rubble of the bombing. Combat occupies more screen time than in part 1, as Soviet planes bomb German tanks and supply lines. Major Lunin is shot down, but, happily, his men rescue him, and he survives his injuries. By May Day 1943, conditions have improved enough for Sonya to visit her brother Slava at the base, where she meets a young pilot at a dance and falls in love. With two years left in the war, it was too soon for a definitive happy ending, but audiences flocked to the film, 38.6 million for part 1 and 33 million for part 2 (ranked fifth in 1961).[61]

Even more successful was Aleksandr Stolper's *The Living and the Dead* (Zhivye i mërtvye, 1963, released 1964), which Stolper himself adapted from Konstantin Simonov's beloved novel about the collapse of the Red Army in the summer of 1941.[62] The canonical combat film of the Thaw, *The Living and the Dead*'s influence was long-lasting; fifteen years later the important director Aleksei Gherman (b. 1938), whose work will be discussed in the next chapter, recalled it as his inspiration.[63] *The Living and the Dead* led the box office in 1964; 41.5 million people saw the first part, 40.3 million, the second.[64] One critic reported long lines at the theaters, which is quite plausible.[65] More than four decades later, it remains a compelling movie.

The Living and the Dead follows the intertwined fates of two men, Ivan Sintsov, a Red Army political officer (*politruk*), who manages to break out of the encirclement, losing his Party card in the process. The second is Fyodor Serpilin, a Civil War brigade commander (*kombrig*) who was swept up in the purge of the Red Army in 1937 and has just been released after four years in prison to save his country from the invasion. Stolper faithfully follows Simonov's novel, too faithfully for at least one critic, who criticized both Stolper and Simonov for emphasizing the "horror" of the encirclement.[66] Indeed, Simonov's novel is replete with authentic details from Simonov's own experiences as one of the leading Soviet frontline war correspondents for the army newspaper the *Red Star* (Krasnaia zvezda).[67]

Part 1 of *The Living and the Dead* is arguably the best combat film in Soviet cinema. From beginning to end, Stolper brilliantly stages what Simonov describes: the absolute chaos and confusion of the German invasion and the encirclement of the Red Army. There is no "prewar." The film opens with a brief scene of Sintsov and his wife, Masha, bidding each other farewell at a train station crowded with soldiers heading for the front. Their baby daughter and Masha's mother have been trapped in Grodno. Then there is a cut to a triage station for the wounded; bodies are everywhere, and the fear and disorganization are obvious. Nobody knows what is going on; no one is "in charge." The enormity of the disaster is portrayed through long traveling shots showing the constant strafing, crowds of refugees, soldiers running in small groups, air battles overhead, soldiers falling right and left under German bombardment. Sintsov narrowly escapes death when the truck he was running to catch is bombed before he reaches it.

Shortly thereafter he is shot by a Soviet pilot who has ejected from his aircraft. Confusing Sintsov and other Red soldiers who are running to rescue him as Germans, the pilot opens fire; terrified of being captured, he shoots himself.

Sintsov eventually finds his way to Serpilin's unit and convinces the commander to let him stay and fight. Serpilin is one of the few high-ranking officers with battle experience, and he quickly takes charge to try to save his men by breaking out of the encirclement. They fight hard, with occasional success, but few survive for long. In addition to showing the inability of the mainly inexperienced field officers to take command, the film stresses the devastating impact of arrogant central decision making that bore no relevance to the circumstances in the encirclement as well as the army's lack of weapons and other necessary equipment. The climax of part 1 illustrates this with heartbreaking force: Sintsov and his comrades are forced to give up the weapons they have taken from German dead, the only weapons they have, because they are supposedly going to be safely escorted out of harm's way in order to regroup. This unarmed convoy is quickly attacked by a line of German tanks. Desperate soldiers try to outrun the tanks, throwing stones, scattering everywhere. . . . The message is clear: the rank and file perished as much from the total failure of leadership as from the brilliance of the German strategy. According to one critic, Stolper's picture provided Soviet viewers with what they had "long wanted to see: an artistic explanation of what happened in the summer and fall of 1941."[68]

Part 2 of *The Living and the Dead* is less powerful cinematographically, although the story continues to carry political weight. Carrying the "little doctor" Tanya, who is ill with pneumonia, Sintsov and the driver Zolotarev have managed to make it to the woods before being cut down by tanks. (Tanya admits when she is assigned to Serpilin's unit that she is a medical student, not really a doctor, a common occurrence during the war.) They leave Tanya with an old man and his granddaughter who have not evacuated because they believed so strongly that they would be defended and not abandoned to the Germans—and move on, to try to find their way to their own troops. Sintsov is hit, concussed rather than badly wounded, but Zolotarev does not know that. In an attempt to save Sintsov's life if the Germans find him, Zolotarev takes his documents, including his Party card, and strips off his tunic. (As a *politruk*, Sintsov would have been shot immediately under the infamous German Commissar Order.)

The Living and the Dead: Sintsov carries the "little doctor." Courtesy BFI Stills.

In Simonov's novel, Sintsov is next briefly captured by the Germans but quickly escapes. Stolper cut that episode—the only substantive cut from the book—possibly because it makes Sintsov's survival even more unrealistic. We next see Sintsov on the road to Moscow. Given these circumstances (lack of papers and tunic), Sintsov should have been arrested and either executed as a deserter or sent to a penal battalion. (In *The Fate of a Man*, Sokolov traded a captured German officer for his freedom, but Sintsov has nothing of value to barter.)

Sintsov faces a problematic situation. It strains credulity that Sintsov is so outraged by the suspicion with which he is greeted, even by people he knows, like fellow political instructor Liusin, who gives him a lift part of the way back to Moscow. Sintsov is, after all, not only a Party member but a *politruk*, a sign of his absolute conformity to Party orthodoxy. If anyone should understand the signal importance of preserving his Party card, he should—and feel very lucky that he avoided the fate of so many others separated from their uniforms and documents.

Even if we were to believe that somehow Sintsov had missed such a key aspect of his own political education, part 1 emphasizes it in an important scene. Serpilin demotes Colonel Baranov to a private because Baranov took off his uniform and left his Party card and other documents in it. For Serpilin, this indicated Baranov's cowardice: expecting capture by the Germans, he did not want to be identified as either an officer or a Party member. Sintsov has witnessed Baranov's public humiliation, but unlike Sintsov, Baranov is truly a coward. He commits suicide rather than fight, and we later learn that Baranov had denounced Serpilin in 1937, leading to Serpilin's arrest and imprisonment.

Nevertheless, Sintsov is not satisfied with all the lucky breaks he gets in Moscow. First, his wife happens to arrive in their apartment at the same time he does, but he is too sick, tired, and shy to have sex with her. Next, when Sintsov goes to Party headquarters, the functionary with whom he speaks, Malinin, happens to remember signing his Party paperwork. Malinin takes the ungrateful Sintsov under his wing, into a Communist battalion that Malinin is forming. Completely untrained, this battalion goes to the front to fill in for the losses in a regular rifle unit. There, Sintsov continues to complain about the bureaucratic emphasis on the piece of paper, rather than on the stalwart citizen he is. Fortunately (and Sintsov is nothing if not fortunate), Serpilin, now a general and the new division commander, reappears at just the right moment to save Sintsov from the indignity of serving as a lowly sergeant. The column of soldiers trudges off in the snow, away from the camera, an image that will be repeated in many subsequent war films.

The Living and the Dead set the standard for the combat film in the so-called era of stagnation between the ouster of Khrushchev and the beginnings of glasnost: a male-dominated story without significant female characters or romance subplots; a flawed but likable male protagonist in his late twenties, usually a junior officer, with an older, wiser secondary male protagonist (usually a senior officer); realistic, well-staged battle scenes; death of most of the secondary characters; inconclusive or tragic ending.

By the early 1960s, cultural hard-liners were once again gaining ascendancy. More and more war films were badly made variations on the themes developed by *Baltic Skies* and *The Living and the Dead*, but they still appealed to audiences. A good example of the Great Patriotic War's transformation from popular entertainment into pulp fiction can be seen in the first Soviet television miniseries, *We Draw Fire on Ourselves* (Vyzyvaem ogon' na sebia),[69] which was released in four parts, 311 minutes, in 1963–1964. (Television was only just beginning to pose competition to the movies, because relatively few Soviet citizens could afford to buy TV sets.)

Directed and written by Sergei Kolosov (b. 1921), based on a story by Ovidy Gorchakov and Janusz Przymanowski, this is an expensive, large-scale production featuring a star-studded cast whose talents are mainly wasted. It borrows themes from the occupation, which received serious treatment in Room's The Invasion and even Gerasimov's The Young Guard, and trivializes them by depicting the German army as idiotically inept: evil, yes, but spending much more time drinking, smoking, and card playing than attending to the war. This is not the first time we have seen a Soviet director use the war as an excuse to make an adventure film—Brave People is an example from the end of the Stalin era.

One key difference between Brave People and We Draw Fire on Ourselves is the latter's pretentiousness and self-importance, compared with the former's simplicity and good humor. Heavily relying on documentary footage, Kolosov's miniseries seems to be much more authentic than it actually is. Half-truths (and outright falsehoods) masquerading as truth had been the hallmark of the Stalin era; the return of the half-truth, epitomized by We Draw Fire on Ourselves, was one sign among many that harder times were on the horizon for filmmakers with independent inclinations.

From Thaw to Stagnation

By 1964, therefore, even before Khrushchev was ousted, there were signs that the novelty of the Thaw had worn off. Wonderful and innovative war films, rich in genuine humanity and pathos, had graced the screens for a number of years. Soviet directors had, however, learned that they could take their newfound creative freedoms only so far, and by the midsixties, many of them had exhausted the ideas they could express with the means available to them. Some, like Aleksandr Stolper, seemed satisfied with the gains that had been made. Others, like Andrei Tarkovsky, wanted to push harder. Audiences appeared to prefer those films that conformed more closely to the classic Hollywood style. Yes, they wanted "humanity," but they also wanted a rousing, well-told story that made them feel good about past sacrifices.

For those in the government, the military, and the Party who may have expected war films to contribute to patriotic culture and to the growing War Cult, the Thaw's revolution in cinema could not have been very satisfying. The classic art films of the Thaw, like The Cranes Are Flying or Ivan's Childhood, were not intended to inspire patriotism, nor did they. Even a great combat film like *The Living and the Dead* was problematic. Its depiction of the Red Army and its leadership hardly promoted confidence in the Soviet military, not to mention the Party and its policies.

Leonid Brezhnev loved military pomp and parades, and the cult of the Great Patriotic War reached its zenith during his eighteen-year reign. His era came to be known as the Stagnation (*zastoi*) for good reasons, but it would be a mistake to overemphasize the impact of the "stagnation" on cinema. As we shall see in the next two chapters, it was still possible, though more difficult, for interesting films to be made, especially war films. Indeed, it may be argued that the best war films appeared, paradoxically, during this period of stagnation.

6 The Stagnation, 1967–1971

Two schools of thought emerge in the historiophoty of the Russian Civil War. For some filmmakers, the Civil War becomes an existential conflict without closure. For others, it is a grand adventure, with heroes and villains whose status is defined more by moral virtues (or lack thereof) than by ideological commitments. Interpretations of the Great Patriotic War likewise diverge. Some directors continue to develop the quiet heroism and low-key questioning that characterized the Thaw, while others return to patterns established during the Stalin era: large-scale combat films and lighthearted high jinks. Soviet spies are introduced as a new type of World War II hero.

By the time Khrushchev was ousted from power in fall 1964, the cultural climate had been cooling for some time. Although Leonid Brezhnev was not a known quantity to filmmakers, politically astute directors understood that a return to greater cultural control was likely. Like Stalin, whom Brezhnev admired in many ways, Brezhnev preferred straightforward, representational art, and he sought to harness the arts in pursuit of the state's goals. This shift in direction was confirmed in mid-1965, when Goskino (as Gosfilm was renamed in 1963) turned down a number of scripts intended to explore the late Stalin era critically.[1] The first years of the Stagnation were particularly difficult for filmmakers, especially after a number of films about the Russian Civil War were banned.

Brezhnev wanted to promote patriotic culture in the USSR and raise the military's profile. He understood the importance of past cults, like Lenin's and Stalin's, in building support for state and Party. He did not intend to revive the Stalin cult, but his government devoted much effort to expanding the nascent cult of the Great Patriotic War into a massive state enterprise, with Victory Day as a major national holiday.[2] As we shall see in this chapter, war films were an important, but not necessarily effective, part of the program.

In the Brezhnev era, filmmakers also faced increasing pressure to make movies with mass appeal. By this time, more Soviet citizens owned televisions, and television began to compete seriously with cinema for the first time. Movie ticket sales declined some 20 percent from the midsixties to the midseventies, which forced Goskino to pay more careful attention to audience preferences.[3] As a result, it vigorously promoted the work of directors who catered to the public's taste for lighter popular genres like comedies, science fiction, detective films, and, if well-made, contemporary melodramas.[4] Since war is not an inherently "light" subject, this requirement placed directors of war films in a bind.

This chapter examines the first, most challenging years of the Brezhnev era, as filmmakers struggled to understand the new "rules" and the extent to which they could be accommodated or resisted. When Yury Ozerov's monumental tribute to the twenty-fifth anniversary of the victory hit the screen in 1970, it seemed that Brezhnevian thinking had succeeded in taming the film industry and marshaling war film directors into the service of his war cult. This proved to be a transitory moment.

The War Cult and Patriotic Culture

Although Brezhnev-era cultural politics discouraged directors interested in treating serious subjects seriously, there was a place for World War II movies in the repertory. Brezhnev realized that the cult of the Great Patriotic War that took shape under Khrushchev could buttress his own power if managed carefully. Brezhnev therefore insisted not only on maintaining the cult but, indeed, on expanding it. As Nina Tumarkin writes, "From 1965 on, the Great Patriotic War continued its transformation from a national trauma of monumental proportions into a sacrosanct cluster of heroic exploits that had once and for all proven the superiority of communism over capitalism."[5] In addition, rites celebrating the war were no longer confined to Victory Day. For Westerners the most bizarre of them was the custom of the bridal couple, in full regalia, solemnly delivering the bride's bouquet to the local war memorial, right after the wedding ceremony.

In this period, the Soviet film community began a remarkable conversation about the role of films, particularly war films, in the creation of Soviet patriotic culture. This subject had first been broached in 1959 in the newly revived Soviet Screen, as part of a series of articles commemorating the fortieth anniversary of the nationalization of the Russian film industry. The dialogue was revived in the midsixties because of the impending twentieth anniversary of Victory Day in 1965—and the plethora of forgettable, mass-produced war films appearing on Soviet screens.

In a 1959 article titled "The Army and Cinema," none other than Marshal Konstantin Rokossovsky (survivor of both world wars, the Civil War, and the Gulag) praised Soviet cinema and its film heroes for modeling patriotism for viewers, particularly youth.[6] Over the next several years, *Soviet Screen* continued to publish retrospectives as film historians struggled to construct a usable past from the Stalin era. Four Civil War films from the 1930s—*The Twenty-six Commissars, Chapaev, Girlfriends,* and *We Are from Kronstadt* (but not *Shchors*)—were singled out for renewed attention.[7]

The year 1964 marked *Chapaev*'s thirtieth anniversary, and the movie was rereleased with great fanfare. If Vasily Chapaev was, as Rostislav Yurenev claimed, the "hero for a generation," who would be the cinematic hero(es) for the 1960s?[8] Another conservative critic, Vladimir Baskakov, argued that none of the important war films of the late 1940s—*The Great Turning Point, The Story of a Real Man, The Young Guard,* and *The Fall of Berlin*—provided a good role model for contemporary directors. Indeed, in his view, these films were so tainted by the "cult of personality" that they needed to be shelved. Yet Baskakov also expressed concern about the kinds of heroes Thaw war films had produced. In Baskakov's opinion, *The Fate of a Man* and *The Ballad of a Soldier* might offer acceptable heroes for Soviet audiences to emulate, but others—*The Cranes Are Flying, The House I Live In,* and, especially, *Peace to Him Who Enters*—did not. Rather, these latter pictures represented the "deheroicization" of Soviet cinema.[9]

But what about the wartime war films? The most thorough and insightful reassessment of their value came from the pen of Yury Khaniutin (1929–1978), an astute liberal critic with a great interest in the role of war films in Soviet society. While Khaniutin acknowledged the "enormous popularity" of *Two Warriors*, as well as the persuasive power of *The Regional Party Secretary* and *She Defends the Motherland* in the context of the war, he argued that none of these films broke any new ground in stylistic terms.[10] Khaniutin did, however, believe that Mark Donskoy's *The Rainbow* and Mikhail Romm's *Person No. 217 were* pathbreaking, creating a Soviet version of Neorealism. For Khaniutin, *The Rainbow* was unarguably the war's most significant war film,[11] a sentiment echoed a few years later when Semyon Freilikh asserted that *The Rainbow* had *influenced* Italian Neorealism.[12]

Their importance notwithstanding, *The Rainbow* and *Person No. 217* were the most emotionally extravagant cinematic artifacts of the war and, as such, alien to the spirit of the Thaw. (Recall the images of Pusya cowering in her flouncy bed or Tanya murdering the SS men.) As an antecedent to the important war movies of the Thaw, Khaniutin singled out Abram Room's *The Invasion*, as the first film to hint at the existence of unjustly imprisoned political prisoners, through the character of Fyodor Talankin. Although both the film and the play are silent on this point, Khaniutin says that it was clear "to everyone" that Fyodor was a "political."[13]

Soviet Screen began to run feature articles and photo layouts on the favored wartime war films, especially *The Rainbow*, but also *Two Warriors*, *Person No. 217*, *The Invasion*, and *Zoya*.[14] A new canon was being established. There was growing consensus about which wartime war films would enter it, but little consensus about which Thaw films belonged. *The Fate of a Man* and *The Ballad of a Soldier* seemed to be acceptable to just about everyone, regardless of position on the cultural spectrum, but others, like *Peace to Him Who Enters* and *The Living and the Dead*, were more problematic. As the Great Patriotic War assumed an increasingly privileged position in the rites of the Soviet state, articulating and revising the canon became an important preoccupation among critics.[15]

Combat and Comedy for Brezhnev

The film industry's bureaucrats had no clear idea of how to motivate filmmakers to serve the war cult effectively. The movies released in the mid-sixties to commemorate the twentieth anniversary of Victory Day were an undistinguished lot that reflected the malaise surrounding the war film and the uncertainty over the direction that film censorship would take under Brezhnev. Given that Victory Day was reinstated as a national holiday in 1965 after nearly two decades, the absence of blockbusters indicates cinema's disarray.[16]

The late sixties were dominated by big, loud war films. Typical examples are Aleksandr Stolper's *Retribution* (Vozmedie, 1967), a lackluster two-part sequel to *The Living and the Dead* that follows Sintsov and Serpilin to Stalingrad, and, especially, Vladimir Basov's *Shield and Sword* (Shchit i mech, 1967–1968), the title of which refers to the NKVD's emblem. *Shield and Sword*, adapted by Vladimir Kozhevnikov from his popular novel, featured the slickly handsome matinee idol Stanislav Liubshin as a Soviet spy who infiltrates the SS. This film is most important for reintroducing the spy thriller variant of the war film to Soviet audiences, a subtype that had been largely dormant in the twenty years following Barnet's *The Exploits of an Intelligence Officer* but which proved increasingly workable as a surefire formula for successful entertainment.[17]

The phenomenal popularity of this gargantuan film (325 minutes, four parts) indicates that most Soviet spectators were tiring of serious war films, preferring well-made adventure/suspense films. *Shield and Sword* led the box office in 1968: 68.3 million viewers saw part 1, 66.3 million, part 2; with parts 3 and 4 trailing off at a still extraordinary 46.9 million.[18] *Soviet Screen's* readers selected *Shield and Sword* as best film of 1968 and Liubshin as best actor.[19] The trend of long, loud war movies culminated in Yury Ozerov's massive five-part film *Liberation* (Osvobozhdenie), released 1968–1971, which will be discussed in some detail at chapter's end.

Given the Soviet return to a monumental portrayal of World War II, reminiscent of the late Stalin era, it is not surprising that there was a return to the lighthearted approach to the war that was also popular in the 1940s (recall *Six o' Clock in the Evening after the War* and *Celestial Sloth*). Vladimir Motyl's *Zhenya, Zhenechka and "Katiusha"* (Zhenia, Zhenechka i "Katiusha," 1967) was reminiscent of Ivan Pyrev's romantic comedy–drama *Six o' Clock in the Evening after the War*. Red Army soldiers, especially the charming youth Zhenya (a diminutive for Yevgeny), vie for the attention of Zhenechka (a diminutive for Yevgenia), a glamorous, somewhat older, platinum-haired female soldier in their unit. Zhenya plays a dashing gallant for the amused Zhenechka; eventually she decides to favor him over the other rivals for her affection. Although Zhenechka is killed in action at the end, Zhenya and her other admirers take it in stride. Apparently Zhenya loved the idea of a wartime romance more than he loved Zhenechka.

Teodor Vulfovich (who had studied with Lev Kuleshov at VGIK)[20] pays direct homage to *Celestial Sloth* in his eccentric comedy *A Hard Little Nut* (Krepkii oreshëk, 1967). Like Major Bulochkin in *Celestial Sloth*, *A Hard Little Nut* features an officer assigned to command a women's unit as "light duty" during his convalescence. The young lieutenant's duties prove unexpectedly challenging, not because of the Germans, but because of the antics of the giddy Oreshkina (her surname is derived from the Russian for "nut"). She could lose the war all by herself. This is a comedy of errors: Oreshkina and the lieutenant have lost control of their reconnaissance blimp. Oreshkina accidentally shoots down a Russian plane, sets the haystack in which they are hiding from the Germans on fire, and so on. The lieutenant soon contributes to the fun: after disguising himself as a woman, he derails a train for the sole purpose of obtaining a straight razor in order to shave and thereby maintain his disguise. Next they discover a top secret German chemical weapons factory disguised as a Red Cross hospital. Resourceful Oreshkina drugs the Germans with their own chemicals (she pours the powder into their soup, sparking a food fight at lunch), and the entire SS unit is captured. These goofy German soldiers are no more frightening than those in *Hogan's Heroes*, a popular American television series from the 1960s. *Zhenya, Zhenochka*, and "*Katiusha*" and especially *A Hard Little Nut*, which drew 32.5 million viewers, were both popular with audiences.[21]

The final film to be discussed in this section, Aleksei Saltykov's *A Woman's Kingdom* (Bab'e tsarstvo, 1967, released 1968), evoked even earlier traditions. An intense melodrama reminiscent of *The Rainbow*, *A Woman's Kingdom* depicted the horrors of the occupation on a collective farm and their impact on the women left behind. Highly romanticized and sentimental, *A Woman's Kingdom* celebrated the soul of Mother Russia. Although retrograde, it served as an antidote to the hard-driving masculinity of the year's blockbuster hit, *Shield and Sword*.[22]

Resistance to the War Cult

The dominance of old-style moviemaking notwithstanding, there was still room for small, quiet films about the war, and a cohort of moviegoers who wanted to see them. All reprise the themes of the Thaw war films. *The Father of a Soldier* (Otets soldata, 1964, released 1965), exemplifies the revival of Georgian cinema, and the wider distribution for the best ethnic films that was possible in the sixties. Its director, Rezo (Revaz) Chkheidze (b. 1926), trained with Sergei Iutkevich and Mikhail Romm at VGIK and was well known in Georgia.[23] *The Father of a Soldier* is a Georgian reversal of *The Ballad of a Soldier*'s odyssey: instead of a son traveling to his mother, a father journeys to his soldier son, who is wounded in a hospital. The father of the title, wonderfully played by the Georgian character actor Sergo Zakhariadze, is the romanticized peasant: simple, but upright and kindly.

Given that the war rages and the old man speaks Russian poorly, he faces many difficulties finding his way, but none are insurmountable. By the time he reaches the hospital, however, his son has already returned to the front.

He decides to join the war effort and signs up. Father and son meet briefly during the Battle of Berlin, but the son is killed on the last day of the war. Like *The Ballad of a Soldier*, the film restrains its obvious sentimentality and serves as a moving testament to the human costs of war. *The Father of a Soldier* was shown at international film festivals and seen at home by 23.8 million, a highly successful box office for a Georgian picture.[24]

Naum Birman's *The Chronicle of a Dive Bomber* (Khronika pikiruiushchego bombardirovshchika, 1967) revises some of the motifs of the comrades films. This curious little film, only seventy-eight minutes long, is oddly compelling. It tells the story of the last three days in the lives of a three-man bomber crew. The young men at the base are all good friends, with the exception of one obnoxious captain, who is quickly ejected from the mess hall. They lack the ego and competitiveness of pilots in most aviator movies (recall *Moscow Skies*) and rarely observe military rank and hierarchy. One of the main characters is obviously Jewish, a rarity. Indeed, this air base appears to model the classless society.

In recognition of the importance of the ground war, most Soviet World War II films focus on the army, rather than the navy or air force. The few movies about the aerial war serve to remind viewers what a different war it was. *The Chronicle*'s first two days evoke summer camp: the aviators play cards, table foosball, and kick-the-can. They joke, smoke, and drink. (Unlike in earlier war films, heavy vodka consumption is presented matter-of-factly.) They sing, draw, and practice their musical instruments. They dine at tables covered with white cloths, served by pretty waitresses. Day 3 sends them off on a major mission. When their bombardier is killed during the raid, the pilot and copilot know they are doomed; indeed, a German pilot flies up close to give them the "thumbs-down" sign. The survivors spontaneously carry out a suicide mission, crashing their plane into a line of Fokkers at a German airfield. The film closes with a shot of the Soviet senior mechanic, waiting as darkness falls, hoping against hope that his airmen will return. Shoulders sagging, he turns slowly and disappears in the fog. More than 24 million people saw this affecting picture about three unassuming heroes.[25]

Vladimir Chebotaryov's *Wild Honey* (Dikii mëd, 1966), based on Leonid Pervomaisky's novel, depicts the unrealized romance between Varvara, a war photographer, and the colonel of the regiment to which she is assigned. The movie consists of a series of finely observed moments about

wartime. Unlike the perky female journalist who provides Major Bulochkin's romantic interest in *Celestial Sloth*, Varvara is a sober-minded woman
whose war experiences are neither lighthearted nor thrilling. For example,
she has to crawl through the mud on her belly to snap a picture of a German
tank and drag a wounded soldier to safety. Yet not everything is grim. The
viewer is also reminded of the Russia for which the soldiers were fighting
in a beautiful scene in which Varvara and the colonel take a moonlight stroll
through the birch forest.

The best and most interesting scenes, however, focus on the NKVD major attached to the unit, a man with a great deal of power but no combat
experience. Varvara stumbles across a military tribunal, in which the major
sentences a soldier to death for desertion. To the major's fury, the general
refuses to sign the order or to carry it out, declaring: "I will only fight fascists." Later, in battle for the first time, the major learns how difficult it is to
determine who is a coward and who is a hero. *Wild Honey* was a modest box
office success, reaching 21.5 million viewers.[26]

Another female-centered war film, *Gold* (Zoloto, 1969), was based on
Boris Polevoi's novel and directed by Damir Viatich-Berezhnykh (b. 1925).
Viatich-Berezhnykh, a member of Igor Savchenko's last class of directing
students, specialized in war films based on Polevoi's work.[27] In this story,
a young typist, Mashenka, and her boss, Mitrofan Ilich (the bank's senior
cashier), flee their occupied town with a sack of jewelry and gold that they
plan to deliver to the Red Army. The old man does not last long on this
arduous trek and soon dies of an apparent heart attack. With the help of
some partisans, and after several close calls, including a brief capture by the
Germans, Mashenka succeeds in delivering the booty.

Gold is conventionally plotted; its beauty lies in Viatich-Berezhnykh's
visualization of Polevoi's famously dry prose. The point of view is unusual;
in the picture's first half, Mashenka is a spectator to the German victimiza-
tion of her countrymen, rather than a victim herself. Hidden in the forest
she watches refugees being herded into trucks, being robbed, and so on,
amid the detritus of the occupation: abandoned tanks, clothes, books, etc.
She and two partisans whom she encounters find a farmhouse and eat the
food the peasants had prepared for the Germans. The fare is simple—soup,
potatoes, milk—but the dining scene is sensuous, reminding viewers how
famished these refugees were. In such circumstances, Mashenka becomes
an adult very quickly.[28]

The most unusual of these four films was, however, Mikhail Yershov's *On the Road to Berlin* (Na puti v Berlin, 1969). On the surface it seems to reprise the themes of *Peace to Him Who Enters*. The war is almost over, but death is around every corner, whether by friendly fire or a scared German soldier who wants to surrender. *On the Road to Berlin* gives the viewer a palpable sense of the malaise and weariness of the Red Army's soldiers, some of whom have been fighting for four years. The film's second half focuses on the efforts of an ordinary soldier, Ivan Grigorevich, to establish an occupation government in a German town on the outskirts of Berlin. To his great discomfiture, he has temporarily been named commandant because he speaks a little German. In contrast to Alov and Naumov in *Peace to Him Who Enters*, however, Yershov mines the situation for its dark humor, rather than existential angst.

Ivan Grigorevich's primary task is to feed people: children, prisoners, the performers in the variety theater. He also has to figure out how to move an elephant, stolen from Kiev's zoo, which is wreaking havoc on trucks in the yard. All the while the theater director is hovering, begging for permission to put on a show so that his actors can earn a little money to survive. The beautiful junior lieutenant serving as his interpreter, who does speak German, is alarmed at his ineptitude. (Why was she not given the command?) But the real commandant arrives before too long, and suddenly, the shooting stops. The silence is heavy.

Hope is soon overturned: Hitler is dead, but Germany has not yet capitulated. *On the Road to Berlin* ends with newsreel footage of the capitulation, accompanied by the song "It Will Be Difficult to Die on the Last Day of the War." This wonderful film did not attract much attention at the time.[29] Sadly, Yershov (b. 1924) later turned to conventional war epics, the most notable of which was a four-part film about the siege of Leningrad, *The Blockade* (Blokada, 1974 and 1977), which earned him the accolade of People's Artist of the USSR.[30]

The Fiftieth Anniversary of the Russian Civil War

The years 1967–1970 marked the fiftieth anniversary of the Russian Revolution and the Civil War—and the "last hurrah" for serious films about the Civil War. Of the six important Civil War films, three were banned and not released until the Gorbachev era. Most of the Civil War movies that appeared at this time were, however, far from important in artistic terms. Nevertheless, they reveal a great deal about the tastes of the moviegoing public and provide strong hints that the state regarded the Civil War as an aspect of Soviet history that was best forgotten, unless treated humorously or sensationally.

The market was saturated with lighthearted Civil War films. One particularly entertaining series came from a new director, Edmond Keosaian (b. 1936), a 1965 graduate of Yefim Dzigan's directing workshop at VGIK.[31] Keosaian's first major independent production was his 1967 remake of Ivan Perestiani's 1923 film *Little Red Devils*, retitled *The Elusive Avengers* (Neulovimye mstiteli), with a Gypsy boy replacing the black child in the original movie. *The Elusive Avengers* earned fourth place at the box office with 54.5 million viewers. Keosaian followed it with two sequels: *The New Adventures of the Elusive* (Novye prikliucheniia neulovimykh, 1969, 66.2 million viewers), and the two-part extravaganza *The Crown of the Russian Empire, or the Elusive Once Again* (Korona rossiiskoi imperii, ili snova neulovimye, 1970–1971, 60.8 million).[32]

Other popular comic adventures about the Civil War era and its immediate aftermath were *The Chief of Chukchi* (Nachal'nik Chukotki, dir. Vitaly Melnikov, 1966), a comedy of mistaken identities and culture clash; *The Wedding in Malinovka* (Svad'ba v Malinovke, 1967, dir. Andrei Tytyshkin), a musical comedy set in a Cossack village; *The White Sun of the Desert* (Beloe solntse pustyni, 1969, dir. Vladimir Motyl), an "Eastern" in which the dashing hero attempts to liberate the wives of a sheikh; and *The Property of the Republic* (Dostoianie respubliki, 1971, dir. Vladimir Bychkov), in which a homeless war orphan helps save a stolen art collection.[33] These movies drew huge audiences, indicating the public's appetite for escapist entertainment that was only superficially Soviet in content. For example, *The Wedding in Malinovka* ranked second at the box office in 1967, drawing a sensational 74.64 million spectators.[34]

The trend was also apparent on television. The nearly seven-hour-long television miniseries *His Excellency's Adjutant* (Adiutant ego prevoskhoditel'stva, dir. Yevgeny Tashkov, 1969) was so popular that it was later released on the big screen. Dedicated to the "first Chekisty," the film glamorizes the exploits of Soviet intelligence officers operating in Ukraine. The hero, who has infiltrated the general staff of Denikin's army, successfully smashes a large counterrevolutionary organization and blows up a train, but before he is caught and executed, he finds time to fall in love with the daughter of a White colonel and to convert to socialism the orphaned son of a another White officer.

In sharp contrast to these comedies and adventures, *Two Comrades Served* (Sluzhili dva tovarishcha, 1968) was seen by "only" 22.5 million, a number that a decade earlier would have signaled quite a popular movie.[35] Directed by Yevgeny Karelov (1931–1977), *Two Comrades Served* is an unusual, mainly successful mix of the humorous and the deadly serious. It featured two major Soviet stars: Oleg Yankovsky as Nekrasov, a university student turned Red Army cameraman, and Rolan Bykov as Kariakin, his mechanic.

The film opens on 1 November 1920, at Red Army headquarters in the Crimea as the Civil War is coming to its bloody finale. Sevastopol is about to fall to the Reds. The Red commander, who has acquired a movie camera, orders Nekrasov to figure out how to operate it in order to record the heroism of these last days. The older, working-class soldier Kariakin does not hesitate to express his doubts about everything; he is a reluctant "comrade" to the educated Nekrasov. Frustrated by Kariakin's jibes, Nekrasov retorts that Comrade Lenin also hails from the gentry (*dvorianstvo*).

This odd couple embarks on their tragicomic adventure, becoming true comrades in the process. Their first effort to take some aerial photographs ends in disaster. The plane crashes, their pilot is killed, and they are "captured" by their own side. Because they lack the all-important identity papers, they must escape for their lives, pursued by Cossacks, until they reach another Red encampment. Still no luck. The commander, a woman, mistakes Nekrasov for a White officer she knows, so she orders their execution. At the last minute, another Red officer recognizes them, and they are saved. But when Nekrasov develops the film, all he has to show for their labors is a shot of the Cossacks chasing them.

Two Comrades Served has a curious, entirely serious subplot featuring two White "Sashas," one a lieutenant (Aleksandr), the other a nurse (Aleksandra), who join together in the chaos of the evacuation from Sevastopol. Nurse Sasha remains an enigma throughout the movie. Lieutenant Sasha (played by the beloved pop culture icon Vladimir Vysotsky) is a cynical brute who coldly shoots a fellow officer who accidentally interrupts his lovemaking. What does such a man have to lose?

The two narratives come together on 8 November 1920, as the Red Army begins its night attack on Sevastopol. The fighting is fierce. Nekrasov has finally figured out how to use the camera, but he has to fight as well as film. The female commander who had earlier ordered his execution is killed storming the fortress. Hard fighting continues, and on the battle's final day Lieutenant Sasha commits his last evil deed, mortally wounding Nekrasov.

The panicky evacuation of Sevastopol has a real poignancy, even though the Whites are clearly the enemy. The two Sashas have pushed their way to the pier as the last boat is pulling away but soon become separated in the mob of desperate refugees. Lieutenant Sasha starts shooting to force the gangplank down again. As he and others rush on, the authorities refuse to let him take his horse. The boat moves away from shore, leaving a horde of screaming and crying people behind on the dock. Sasha stands on the deck, watching his horse desperately swimming, trying to follow the boat (a scene straight from newsreel footage of the evacuation). He shoots himself.

This wonderfully strange film has a strange denouement. On 17 November, we see Kariakin sadly returning his dead comrade's movie camera to their commander. Not surprisingly, given the response to *Peace to Him Who Enters*, some critics did not know what to make of it.[36] In the most charitable reading, *Two Comrades Served* was seen as an "intelligent film," but one that did not provide a model for the new hero.[37]

For all its idiosyncrasies, *Two Comrades Served* featured some terrific battle scenes, the best of any Civil War film to date. These combat scenes were soon to be surpassed in Alov and Naumov's *The Flight* (Beg, 1970), a two-part adaptation of Mikhail Bulgakov's play. Like *Two Comrades Served*, part 1 of *The Flight* is set during the evacuation of Sevastopol in November 1920. The combat scenes are brilliantly filmed, and although one might argue that Alov and Naumov have aestheticized the carnage, these scenes show the absurdity as well as the grandeur of battle. Like Karelov in *Two Comrades Served*, Alov and Naumov also focus on the pathos as well as the chaos of the evacuation from Sevastopol. The White commander responsible for organizing the withdrawal sits alone in his office, catatonic; his face and body are emotionless, expressionless in sharp contrast to the frenetic motion on the streets outside his door. His officers draw straws to determine who will shoot the others before committing suicide himself. The directors allow us to pity them.

Unfortunately, part 2 of *The Flight*, which is set in the emigration to Istanbul and Paris, lacks the humanity of part 1. In emigration the Whites are no longer people but are degraded to "types" filmed in an exaggerated comic-grotesque manner. Although stylistically more abstract than *Peace to Him Who Enters*, *The Flight* was not criticized for its formalism, which was seen as appropriate to its subject.[38] *The Flight* was, however, less successful with audiences than *Two Comrades Served*.[39]

Another sign of the vagaries of Brezhnevian cultural politics can be seen in the release of *No Crossing under Fire* (V ogne broda net, 1967). Yevgeny Gabrilovich adapted the screenplay from his short story by the same title, and Gleb Panfilov (b. 1936), who became one of the most accomplished Soviet filmmakers of the 1970s and 1980s, directed. *No Crossing under Fire* is a very bleak visualization of the Civil War. Set in a field hospital, the movie tells the "true story" of Tanya Tyotkina, a peasant girl who has been recruited as a nurse. Played by Panfilov's wife, Inna Churikova, who starred in all his films, Tanya behaves so oddly that it is hard to tell whether the girl is simpleminded—or badly traumatized by her wartime experiences. Tanya begins painting as therapy, composing naive scenes of the horrors she has encountered.

The "brave new world" she inhabits is alien, even grotesque. The war takes place outside the compound's walls. Only the endless stream of wounded soldiers provides physical proof of its existence. We do not know why they are fighting; Panfilov makes no appeals either to ideology or to patriotism. *No Crossing under Fire*'s extreme naturalism and enigmatic characters hardly fit the style and themes of Brezhnev's return to Soviet traditionalism. As post-Soviet critic Liudviga Zakrzhevskaya notes in her reevaluation of the movie, the failure of the Soviet censors to ban it is almost as extraordinary as the picture itself.[40] Its distribution was, however, restricted.

The three Civil War movies that *were* banned until glasnost were *The Angel* (Angel, 1967), *The Intervention* (Interventsiia, 1967), and *The Commissar* (Kommissar, 1968). The suppression of *The Intervention* is not surprising; that it was ever approved for production is. Based on the play by Lev Slavin and directed by Gennady Poloka, the film is set in Odessa during its occupation by the counterrevolutionary forces of the entente. Poloka (b. 1930) trained at VGIK in Lev Kuleshov's workshop and was obviously influenced by Kuleshov's silent film aesthetics.[41] *The Intervention* is probably the zaniest motion picture ever made in the Soviet Union, filmed in "buffo" style from beginning to end. It is most certainly *not* a movie "for the masses," even though, like *Two Comrades Served*, it starred the popular singer and actor Vladimir Vysotsky. Although it openly mocks all the "ists" who opposed the Soviet regime—Zionists, anarchists, nationalists, and so on—it becomes clear all too soon that the military pomp and circumstance so dear to Brezhnev is also being mercilessly skewered.[42]

The Angel, directed by Andrei Smirnov (b. 1941), was part of a three-part "cinema almanac" titled *The Beginning of an Unknown Century* (Nachalo nevedemogo veka) and produced in Mosfilm's Experimental Creative Studio, founded in 1963 by Grigory Chukhrai. The second short film in the series, Genrikh Gabai's *Motria*, was eventually released, although only for television, in 1969.[43] Larissa Shepitko's *The Motherland of Electricity* (Rodina elektrichestva) was, like *The Angel*, banned for its alienated style and desacralization of the sacred subject of electrification.

The Angel was suppressed for different reasons. Based on a novella by Yury Olesha, set in 1920, Smirnov's short film is a harsh, realistic look at the fate of a number of refugees—a non-Party intellectual, a commissar, a soldier, a student, a peasant, a teenage girl, and a pregnant woman—captured from their stalled train by a Cossack bandit, an ataman ironically nicknamed "Angel." He is an angel, the angel of death. (Little is known about the real Ataman Angel, whose gang roamed the Chernigov region in 1919, carrying out pogroms.)

The Angel is uncompromisingly dark. The girl is raped. The intellectual hesitates when Angel asks him if he believes in God. He knows his life depends on his answer. Finally, he answers that he does. That turns out to be what Angel wanted to hear, but we do not know who is fooling whom. The commissar, on the other hand, resolutely refuses to renounce his faith and is savagely murdered, his head smashed in with a sledgehammer (symbol of the workers' revolution). The survivors wander out of the woods. This bleak film was far too pessimistic for the times. A hero's death could not go unavenged.

The film was first screened for Mosfilm's bureaucrats on 29 October 1967. According to Vladimir Ognev, who was present for the screening and discussion, the young girl's rape caused particular shock. The film was seen as too grim, to which Ognev recalls retorting, "Was the revolution a holiday?"[44] Smirnov was only willing to make a few cosmetic changes; when *The Angel* was shown again on 14 November, it was shelved as "defective" (brak).[45]

Smirnov, Poloka, and Shepitko continued their careers in the USSR; Gabai emigrated to Western Europe. Smirnov directed a critically well-received film about the reunion of wartime comrades at a funeral, *The Belorussian Station* (Belorusskii vokzal, 1972), and became the head of the filmmakers' union during glasnost; Poloka turned to conventional comedies; Shepitko's work will figure in the next chapter. Aleksandr Askoldov, who had been a student in Leonid Trauberg's directing workshop at VGIK, was not so lucky; *The Commissar* was his first and last film. It not only ended his career but also led to his expulsion from the Party in 1969.[46]

The Commissar (1967, released 1988) became the most celebrated of the many banned films that "came off the shelf" during glasnost not because of its quality—although it is very good—but because of Askoldov's sad fate and, more important, the reasons behind the ban. *The Commissar* is a reasonably faithful adaptation of Vasily Grossman's short story "In the Town of Berdichev" ("V gorode Berdicheve"), which was set like much of Grossman's fiction in the predominantly Jewish Ukrainian village of his birth.[47] Askoldov was unaware that Grossman had been unable to publish his magnum opus about World War II, *Life and Fate* (Zhizn' i sud'ba), or, as Yelena Stishova wryly stated, that the book had been "arrested."[48]

The commissar of the title is not a self-satisfied intellectual like *Chapaev*'s Furmanov but a tall, strong, and fierce amazon, Klavdia Vavilova (played by Nonna Mordiukova). One of Klavdia's first acts in the film is to order the execution of a deserter. Klavdia has an embarrassing secret that cannot be kept secret much longer. She is very pregnant; the baby's father, another Red Army officer, has been killed in action. For her confinement, she is bivouacked in the home of the Magazanniks, a poor Jewish family headed by the tinker Yefim (the incomparable Rolan Bykov).

Klavdia's relationship with her new "family" is initially awkward; she has taken their best room, after all. Yefim is openly resentful, but his wife, Maria, soon realizes that the commissar is pregnant and is determined to help her, woman to woman. Klavdia blossoms in this homely environment and loves her little son, Kiril, named for his father. But soon Berdichev will change hands once again. The Reds are leaving, and the Whites are coming. Klavdia knows that she too must go, not only for the sake of her baby but also for the sake of Yefim's family, who would surely be executed by the Whites if they were discovered harboring a Red commissar. This heartbreaking moment is a testament, not to the power of ideology, but to the strength of a mother's love.

It was one thing to read this story, one of Grossman's earliest (originally published in 1934), and quite another to see it on the big screen. This was the first Russian film in which Jewish characters had major, extremely sympathetic roles. Maria and Yefim teach Klavdia how to be human. But Askoldov went further, much further than Grossman.

In the film's most famous scene, as the children are playing "kill the Jew," a game they have witnessed all too often during the Civil War, one of

The Commissar: Vavilova confronts the deserter. Courtesy BFI Stills.

the youngest, a little girl, is very nearly hanged by her brothers. Askoldov
then cuts to newsreel footage of Nazi pogroms against the Jews. With
this, Askoldov commits the unforgivable sin, breaking the cinematic silence about the Holocaust. Of course he was aware of the scandal that had
erupted over Yevgeny Yevtushenko's poem "Babi Yar."[49] But even without
that, the trial of the writers Yuly Daniel and Andrei Siniavsky (aka Abram
Tertz), with its strongly anti-Semitic overtones, had just begun, and the Six
Day War between Israel and Egypt had just ended.[50] This was definitely not
the time to bring Jewish characters to the Soviet screen.

That this was a main reason behind the ban became clear when documents concerning film censorship were made public in the late eighties.[51]
"Why," it was asked during one closed session, "do Jews even need to be
in the film at all?"[52] Jewish filmmakers were trotted out to denounce it; Leonid Trauberg, himself a victim of Soviet anti-Semitism in the anticosmopolitan
campaign of the late 1940s, led the attack against his former student, Askoldov,
saying, "I want to see a picture about a commissar; I don't need a picture
about the sad fate of the Jewish people!"[53] Klavdia's characterization was also

criticized. She was seen as "rude" and "harsh," a primitive woman who lived in a "poor and narrow" ideological universe.[54] Like The Angel, The Commissar presented a drastic, unacceptable revision to the new canonical interpretation of the Civil War as "a romantic, almost bloodless break [proryv]—illusion, self-deception, anti-historicism."[55] With the "Jewish element" added in, the film was considered so incendiary that it was the last one taken off the shelf, and Askoldov had to do public battle with Elem Klimov in 1987 to get it released.[56]

The Turning Point: *Liberation*

Yury Ozerov's eight-hour, five-part epic Liberation (Osvobozhdenie, 1968–1971; released 1970–1972) was intended to be the Great Patriotic War's War and Peace and was commissioned for the twenty-fifth anniversary of Victory Day in 1970. Mosfilm and its coproducers Dino de Laurentis (Italy), DEFA (GDR), and PSFZF (Poland) spared no expense. Liberation's first and second installments led the box office in 1970 with 56.1 million viewers, some of whom were "encouraged" to attend by their Party organizations.[57] Despite the strong box office, it ranked as fourth best picture of 1970 among those who responded to Soviet Screen's annual survey, but only 15 percent gave it their highest rating.[58]

After the first two installments, attendance dropped precipitously, 35.8 million viewers for part 3 in 1971 to 28 million for parts 4 and 5 in 1972.[59] (Soviet Screen's readers did, however, rank part 3 the best picture of 1971.)[60] Although Ozerov tried hard to develop recognizable characters, and the film is competently made, it would have been difficult for any director, however skilled, to sustain interest in a movie composed on such a grandiose scale. Liberation is, however, notable for returning Stalin to the war film after a long absence. Stalin did not occupy center stage, but Ozerov's interpretation of the war was heavily influenced by Savchenko's The Third Blow and Chiaureli's The Fall of Berlin. (Ozerov, born in 1921, was one of Savchenko's directing students at VGIK and was certainly very familiar with both movies.)[61]

Liberation provides an excellent overview of the prevailing official interpretation of the Great Patriotic War. It adds detail to what Nina Tumarkin calls the war cult's "master plot" as it developed in the Brezhnev era: "Collectivization and rapid industrialization . . . prepared our country for war, and despite an overpowering surprise attack by the fascist beast and its inhuman wartime practices, despite the loss of twenty million valiant martyrs to the cause, our country, under the leadership of the Communist Party headed by Comrade Stalin, arose as one united front and expelled the enemy from our own territory and that of Eastern Europe, thus saving Europe—and the world—from fascist enslavement."[62]

Importantly, *Liberation* begins on 12 April 1943, *after* the victory at Stalingrad, which allowed Ozerov to avoid the disagreeable subject of the encirclement and subsequent annihilation of the Red Army. Part 1, titled *The Flaming Arc* (Ognënnaia duga), opens with Stalin advising his generals about how to retake Kursk. The generals study maps and listen attentively. The Germans are shown recruiting Soviet POWs to join the Vlasovites; prisoners who want to live step forward to fight with Vlasov. The Germans also try to persuade POW Yakov Dzhugashvili, Stalin's elder son, to write to his father to beg for a prisoner exchange with Field Marshal Paulus, taken prisoner at Stalingrad. Dzhugashvili refuses. On to London, where Churchill insists, against military advisers' counsel, that the Allies delay opening a second front as long as possible in order to destroy the Red Army. Next, on to Yugoslavia, where Tito tells his partisans that he has opened the second front, in the Balkans. Part 1 ends on 12 July 1943, as the Battle of Kursk begins.

The Breakthrough (Proryv) picks up the story on 19 July 1943, in Italy. Hitler has arrived to straighten out the mess Mussolini left behind when he fled Rome. Subsequent episodes show partisan activity in Warsaw and the German rescue of Mussolini. As the Red Army advances on Kiev in autumn 1943, the battle scenes are particularly effective, especially when the Soviet soldiers cross the Dnieper River on log rafts under heavy German fire. A mortally wounded colonel somberly hands a young captain his Party card but pointedly keeps his pistol. (Unlike Sintsov in *The Living and the Dead*, this officer will not be found alive without his Party card.) On to Tehran: Churchill's scheming against the USSR provokes bickering; Stalin understands him all too well. *The Breakthrough* ends on New Year's Day, 1944.

Part 3, *Directing the Main Blow* (Napravlenie glavnogo udara), begins with a flashback to Tehran and a reminder that Churchill and Roosevelt had sworn to open the second front in May 1944. The twenty-ninth of February 1944, finds Zhukov on the Ukrainian front. Although *Liberation* does rehabilitate Stalin, it is important to note that it also rehabilitates Zhukov. Furthermore, it depicts the dissent in the high command and the generals' shameless jockeying for position around Stalin. D-Day appears briefly: an

Liberation: War as combat epic. Courtesy BFI Stills.

assault as easy as fording a river, accompanied by cheerful, stirring mar-
tial music. (Why, therefore, did it take so long to open the second front?)
Meanwhile, Churchill busily manipulates Roosevelt. (According to *Liberation*, the American president is Churchill's dupe, even though Roosevelt
expresses his own suspicions of Stalin's "Asiatic cunning.") The Germans
believe the next Soviet offensive will be a drive south through Ukraine to the
Balkans. Instead, it is west through Belorussia, where partisans sabotage
the Germans under the careful direction of the underground Party organization (thereby handily dismissing the notion of the partisan initiative and
autonomy in defending the motherland). Bobriusk is liberated on 29 June
1944, and the partisans join the tanks on their way to Minsk. On 20 July, the
plot against Hitler fails, which pleases Churchill because he wants the war
to continue in order to destroy the Red Army. Part 3 ends as the Red Army
crosses into Poland.

The *Battle for Berlin* (*Bitva za Berlin*) shows little of the battle. Although
this installment opens on 12 January 1945, the first important episode is
the Yalta Conference in February, where Churchill agitates an obviously

weakened Roosevelt with concerns about the ramifications of the Red Army reaching Berlin first. In the meantime, Stalin grows increasingly suspicious of America's motivations and fears the Americans will negotiate separate terms of surrender with the German army. Generals Zhukov and Konev engage in prolonged consultations with Stalin about strategy. On 21 April, the Belorussian divisions enter Berlin.

Finally, The Last Storm (Poslednii shturm): Hitler orders the flooding of Berlin's subway system, which is filled with screaming civilians who have taken refuge there. "If the German people can't defeat the Slavs," Hitler shrieks, "they must disappear from the earth!" Like Chiaureli's The Fall of Berlin, Liberation treats the taking of the Reichstag and the raising of the Soviet flag in detail. Too cowardly to shoot himself, Hitler orders an aide to shoot him. The surrender marks the end of the film; Zhukov magnanimously declares that "everyone is guaranteed life." The final credits announce the roll call of death:

What did fascism bring? [Death to the]

French	520,000
Italians	400,000
English	320,000
Americans	325,000
Czechs/Slovaks	364,000
Yugoslavs	1.6 million
Poles	6 million[63]
Germans	9.7 million
Soviets	20 million

Liberation is more tiresome than "bad" and illustrates the limited efficacy of a gargantuan historical movie epic. There are a few splendid combat scenes and a few imaginative moments. Especially noteworthy is the scene at the end of part 4, when a Soviet tankist is fascinated by the animals in the Berlin zoo. Because he lets down his guard to take a closer look, and thereby experience a split second of joy, he is killed by a sniper.

The romance between the soldier Sergei and the nurse Zoya, which punctuates each part, also serves to remind viewers of the people among the machinery of war. Particularly poignant is the scene in part 3 when Zoya decides with some embarrassment to become Sergei's lover. "You're my wife," he attempts to reassure her. "I'm your camp wife," she replies wryly.

At the end of the film, Zoya and Sergei are separated, and Ozerov wisely leaves their futures a question mark. It is too little, too late, because by then Ozerov had already lost more than half his initial audience.

The press promoted *Liberation* energetically.[64] Aging veterans were trotted out to praise its authenticity.[65] This campaign clearly indicated that the film was intended to be the canonical movie for the twenty-fifth anniversary of Victory Day. The director himself contributed an article to the *Art of the Cinema* in which he immodestly asserted that *Liberation* deserved to be listed among the best movies about World War II, in the same company as *The Fate of a Man*, *The Ballad of a Soldier*, *The Cranes Are Flying*, and *The Father of a Soldier*.[66]

After *Liberation*

In fact, Ozerov's film bears no resemblance at all to any of these pictures. Given the relentless hype surrounding *Liberation*, it cannot be coincidental that only two months after Ozerov's self-congratulatory essay appeared, Semyon Freilikh reopened the discussion about the archetypal war film hero, whom he found in *The Living and the Dead*'s General Serpilin, rather than the flawed politruk Sintsov.[67] Not surprisingly, Freilikh also argued that Stolper's film should be the paradigm for the historical epic.[68] He did not mention *Liberation*.

The silence was deafening. Just as the fate of *The Commissar* and the efflorescence of trivial war films sent signals to the filmmaking community, so did the failure of *Liberation*. Given the film's massive production budget, the unparalleled advertising campaign, and the thinly veiled coercion to boost attendance, the film's final attendance figures of 28 million are almost pitiable. The relative failure of *Liberation* with viewers indicates that although the state could channel resources to a favored director, it could not control the audience. Unlike in the Stalin era, moviegoers now had choices, with an average of 150 new domestic titles annually and an additional 100 imported films, mainly from the socialist countries but also some from Western Europe and the United States.

As we have seen in this chapter, Brezhnev's regime exerted effort to regain control over the film industry with limited success. Although a mass-market cinema flourished, the emphasis on entertainment undermined the revival of a patriotic film culture. Audiences clearly enjoyed *A Hard Little Nut* and *The Elusive Avengers*, but neither film inspired reverence for the sacrifices of past heroes, nor for the goals of state and Party. The same is true of *Shield and Sword*, where the Great Patriotic War is portrayed as a grand adventure and an opportunity to see the world, images in stark contrast to the monuments to the dead dotting the countryside.

The serious war films of the early Brezhnev years—*The Chronicle of a Dive Bomber, Wild Honey, Two Comrades Served*—indicated that the themes and artistic sensibilities of the Thaw continued, as long as directors respected certain limitations. In the 1970s, as we shall see in the next chapter, a number of directors were able to navigate the constraints under which they worked to produce very good films. Indeed, it is arguable that this period of the Stagnation is as important as the Thaw in the history of the Soviet war film.

7 Challenges to Stagnation, 1972–1979

The historiophoty of the Great Patriotic War shifts focus during the 1970s. Now Soviet citizens are seen fighting as much against their own human frailties as against the enemy fascists. Teenage soldiers fall prey to their inexperience, hubris, fear, and hormones. Battle-hardened veterans struggle to hold on to a shred of their humanity; they have been fighting so long that they scarcely remember why. Collaborators may be the natural by-products of war rather than perfidious traitors. Not all mothers willingly sacrifice their sons to the cause.

By the early seventies, filmmakers were having a hard time finding new and different ways to tell the story of men in the Great Patriotic War. It is not surprising, therefore, that the most popular war film of the 1970s was the one that least resembled *Liberation* and the other male-dominated combat films that were being churned out with some regularity. Stanislav Rostotsky's blockbuster *And the Dawns Are Quiet Here* (A zori zdes' tikhie, 1972, two parts), was adapted by Rostotsky and Boris Vasilev from the latter's eponymous story. Released late in 1972, *And the Dawns Are Quiet Here* was named best picture of 1972 in *Soviet Screen*'s readers' survey and led the box office in 1973 with 66 million viewers for each of its two parts.[1] Critic Lev Anninsky hoped the picture would revitalize the war film genre.[2]

As we shall see in this chapter, the genre was indeed revitalized. The most important of the war films of the 1970s bore little resemblance to *Dawns*, but Rostotsky's film whetted the viewers' appetites for war films that were large-scale but not monumental, that centered on people without forgoing action. Even the World War II spy thriller could be humanized, as convincingly demonstrated by Tatiana Lioznova's twelve-part television miniseries *Seventeen Moments of Spring* (Semnadtsat' mgnovenii vesny, 1979), with its achingly lonely hero, the Soviet intelligence officer "Stirlitz," who has lived his double life in Nazi Germany for too many years.

Goskino continued to promote the production of movies about the Great Patriotic War, especially because the war cult reached its apogee at this time. In the 1970s, this eagerness for war films sometimes led to the approval of projects that ended up challenging the cult's truisms by raising more questions about the war than they answered. During this period important Thaw directors like Sergei Bondarchuk and Grigory Chukhrai returned to the topic of the Great Patriotic War, joined by substantial new talents, like Aleksei Gherman and Larissa Shepitko.

Combat and Comrades

And the Dawns Are Quiet Here is, like The Living and the Dead, an accomplished piece of popular filmmaking that has withstood time's test. The story is simplicity itself. A women's corps, overseen by a sergeant major (starshina), is stationed in a small northern village to defend a region that is unlikely to need defending. But the Germans do come, and the sergeant major and five of the young women must head out on a scouting party. The women are all killed, but the sergeant major survives to remember their heroic deeds.

In its opening scenes, it seems that the film will be another of those lighthearted romps mocking the contributions of women to the war effort. These women are scarcely out of girlhood, and Rostotsky takes care to emphasize their innocence. Their service is like summer camp. The village is beautiful and unspoiled, nestled in the forest near a lake. They spend their time giggling and gossiping about their love lives (real and imagined), reciting sentimental verse, and comparing their figures. Two of them are more experienced sexually; one was briefly married but lost her husband in the war, the other has had an affair with a married officer (which both shocks and titillates her friends). Their kindly middle-aged sergeant, Fyodor Ivanovich, is like an indulgent uncle; he does not mind being teased by these girls, and he tolerates their silliness.

The tone quickly changes. Germans are spotted in the forest, and Fyodor Ivanovich forms his scouting party, which heads into the forest to find the German camp. They are picked off, one by one. Each death is individualized because Rostotsky wants the viewer to understand that each death matters, countering the oft-recited aphorism, attributed to Stalin, that "a single death is a tragedy, a thousand is a statistic."

Fyodor Ivanovich survives not only to kill the Germans but, more important, to remember these women. As they feared, they left no husbands or children behind. Nothing remains but the memory of the old man who witnessed them fight and die for their country. The subtitle of the second part underscores that this was a battle of purely "local significance." It will never appear in history books. At the end, we see an aged Fyodor Ivanovich somberly watching a soldier affix a commemorative plaque to a rock by the lake where the women perished.

Rostotsky successfully blends elements from the best Thaw films as well as from the best combat films, without a trace of irony or cynicism. The women are real people—some are frightened, some are brave. One even vomits after she kills a German. Yet they *are* heroines nevertheless.

Although dated in some of its techniques, *Dawns* retains its emotional power. Vadim Sokolov opened his *Soviet Screen* review with these words: "The war again? Yes, again. And not only about the war, about Russia. About the depth and beauty of her soul . . . about the good kids of the Siberian taiga . . . about the people [*narod*] . . . And about the Victory . . . [ellipses in the original]."[3]

And the Dawns Are Quiet Here provided the postwar generation, sick of the war cult's shrill grandiosity, with a usable past on a human scale. In the straightforward narrative style of the classical Hollywood cinema, with few artistic flourishes and no intellectual pretensions, Rostotsky infused the various types of the comrades' films with genuine individuality. And by making the comrades women, he paid tribute to an important but long diminished aspect of the victory.

None of the other combat films of this period celebrated the contributions of Soviet women and girls in war, but like the heroines in *Dawns*, heroes were allowed to have doubts and discernible flaws. There are two good examples of the small-scale combat film that continued Thaw traditions. The first is *Burning Snow* (Gorchiachii sneg, 1972), directed by Gavriil Yegiazarov (b. 1916) from Yury Bondarev's novel, set in the Battle of Stalingrad. Reminiscent of *Peace to Him Who Enters*, one of the main characters is a fresh young lieutenant, Kolya Kuznetsov, placed in a battle-hardened unit. Kolya is clearly from another world. He indignantly informs a startled general that the men need to rest because they are tired, cold, and hungry; he vomits on the eve of combat; he cries when he discovers one of his men severely wounded.

The battalion commander, Volodya, is as hard as Kolya is soft, although they are about the same age. The difference is battle experience. When one of the soldiers refuses an order to shoot an injured horse, Volodya does it himself, as Kolya cringes in horror. Needless to say, Volodya does not see Kolya as an asset to the company, especially since Kolya is drawn to the nurse Tanya, Volodya's camp wife.

The relationship between Volodya and Tanya is less discreet and more complex than the usual portrayal of the wartime field marriage in Soviet fiction and film. Tanya clings to Volodya and publicly expresses her affection; he, in contrast, tries to maintain a professional distance in front of the men who all adore the flirtatious Tanya. At several key moments, Volodya is distracted by her, and his men are afraid to interrupt their trysts, even when they need to speak to him. Nurse-as-sister is a cliché of war films, but the innocently flirtatious Tanya is a disruptive presence. When she visits the men in their bunker, her smiles and jokes encourage their romantic fantasies, whether or not she intends it. Love-struck Kolya thinks about her constantly and takes foolish risks trying to protect her. When she is killed because she rushes into the field against direct orders, everyone breaks down in tears, even the stern Volodya. Volodya and Kolya become unhinged. Volodya keeps muttering to himself: "Fire! Not one step back!" Kolya cries: "I hate you! I hate you!" as he shoots aimlessly in the direction of the Germans, wasting precious ammunition. (Not surprisingly, this aspect of the film was criticized.)[4]

In sharp contrast, when the general learns that his twenty-year-old son has been killed in battle, he pauses for less than a moment before ordering one of his colonels to deliver his report. Volodya's and Kolya's behavior is childishly irritating by comparison. Why are they quarreling over a girl in these life-and-death circumstances? The answer is painfully obvious: because they are adolescents. They may not have lost their childhoods like Tarkovsky's Ivan, but they have lost their youth. Not only is the Stalingrad front no place for teenage rivalry over a girl, it is no place for teenagers. They do not belong in the hell that is war.

Burning Snow struck a chord with viewers. It was not a major box office hit, but the movie buffs who responded to Soviet Screen's annual survey nevertheless ranked it among the top ten films of the year.[5] Although a journeyman director, Yegiazarov was largely successful in refining the tropes of the midlevel combat film. These boys seem to have no idea what they are fighting for—except to stay alive themselves.

Another interesting variation on the comrades theme—the ironically titled *Only the Old Go to Battle* (V boi idut odni stariki, 1973)—dealt with the air war. Like *Moscow Skies* (now thirty years old) and the more recent *The Chronicle of a Dive Bomber*, it emphasized the short lives of combat pilots and the intensity of their relationships, whether friendly or competitive. Leonid Bykov (1928–1979) wrote, directed, and starred in *Only the Old*, a slice-of-life (and death) picture about a few days in a "musical" air squadron. The pilot-musicians find that their music-making lightens their spiritual load as they deal with the inevitable deaths of their comrades. Life is ephemeral, but art (music) is eternal. They socialize with a women's air squadron, but as equals, a refreshing change from the treatment of women pilots in *Celestial Sloth*. Yet women pilots die, too; one of the men no sooner falls in love with a young woman than she is killed. Bykov ends the film with a panning shot of graves, including a monument to an unknown soldier. The superimposed legend dedicates the film to "those pilots who did not return."

Only the Old Go to Battle combined the lighthearted and the melodramatic in a way Soviet moviegoers found very appealing; it ranked fifth at the box office in 1974, with 44.3 million viewers.[6] Although clearly conceived for the mass spectator, this film, like *Burning Snow*, demonstrated that a small-budget combat film could appeal to viewers' hearts and simultaneously question the meaning of war. Camaraderie and unit cohesion are more important than anything else.

The move away from the grandiosity of combat films like *Liberation* was confirmed by *They Fought for the Motherland* (Oni srazhalis' za rodinu), the blockbuster film commissioned to commemorate the thirtieth anniversary of Victory Day in 1975. The title is a pointed wordplay on *She Defends the Motherland*. "They" are the male collective, the Red Army, and "fought" connotes an offensive rather than defensive action. The two-part movie was directed by the estimable Sergei Bondarchuk, who demonstrated in his adaptation of *War and Peace* (1966) that he could make an epic with recognizable, believable characters (not to mention one that won Soviet cinema's first Oscar for Best Foreign Film).[7]

They Fought for the Motherland differs in scale from Bondarchuk's directorial debut, *The Fate of a Man*, but it also differs in humanity from *Liberation*, the twenty-fifth-anniversary film. Bondarchuk found inspiration in Sholokhov and wrote his own screenplay. His large, star-studded cast included many important actors, including himself, but he wisely cast Vasily Shukshin (1929–1974) in the lead role of Petya Lopakin. Shukshin was an enormously popular writer, film director, and actor, and his considerable charisma sustains this last film before his early death.

They Fought for the Motherland is set in July 1942, as the Red Army heads for Stalingrad. It is both a combat film and a comrades film, although on a much larger scale than most. Yet the focus is resolutely grassroots, at the platoon level. Lopakin initially appears to be an antihero: a womanizer, a jokester, and, most important, a fixer. He forages for food to supplement their rations at every village they come across. He prefers to "charm" peasant women for food (as he would call his leering and groping behavior), and he enjoys regaling his buddies with tales of his conquests. Underneath this vulgar facade, however, is a more complex individual. When charm fails, Lopakin works for food and works hard. The effort is all his, yet he never hesitates to share the fruits of his labors with his comrades.

For all his braggadocio, Lopakin is not very successful with the women he meets. These peasant women are tough (one gives Lopakin a black eye), as they must be in order to save their families with all the men at the front. But they realize, as does the viewer, that Lopakin is putting on an act as much for himself as for everyone else around him. His devil-may-care insouciance in the face of death sustains him. If he pretends that life is normal, it might become so.

Other noteworthy characters are a severely depressed man whose wife left him on the day war broke out (a plot device recalling the Thaw film *The House I Live In*). Even the irrepressible Lopakin cannot draw him out of his shell. Shot, believed killed, and mourned by his unit as a "serious" man, he later turns up, deaf, palsied, stuttering, but now happy, happy to be alive (recalling Yamshchikov in *Peace to Him Who Enters*). "I'm so glad to be with you again," he tells a stunned Lopakin, who is amazed by the man's courage.

Bondarchuk assigned himself a small, gritty role as a seriously wounded soldier. As the Germans appear, he begins crossing himself, whispering, "Lord save me" (*gospodi spasi*) over and over. Soaked in blood, moaning, he is too heavy for the terrified nurse to move him. This is the first reasonably realistic depiction of the blood and gore of World War II combat in Soviet cinema. Bondarchuk's character is operated on in a tent, without anesthesia. It beggars belief that he is able to talk all the way through the operation, but this conceit permits him a small, ironic joke. He complains that the weary surgeon is an "enemy of the people" (*vrag naroda*), a reminder that the film is, after all, set in Stalin's time (although Stalin's name is never mentioned).

Bondarchuk clearly had substantial resources at his disposal. Vadim Yusov's camera work successfully captures the vast expanses of the steppe, as well as the intimate spaces of the battlefield's hastily dug trenches. The special effects, especially the fiery conflagrations, are unusually good for a Soviet film of this era.

The picture ends before this unit reaches Stalingrad. Exhausted and battered, they know that the worst is to come. Will they have the strength and stamina to survive Stalingrad? The film ends with a long aerial shot of their column winding across the steppe. With its emphasis on the rhythms of the soldier's life, punctuated by occasional combat, They Fought for the Motherland depicts a self-contained heroism that is much more moving than the bombast of Liberation.[8] They Fought for the Motherland, which drew an audience of 40.6 million, was named best picture of the year in Soviet Screen's survey, and readers also selected Vasily Shukshin as best actor.[9] Given that 1975 marked the high-water point of the war cult,[10] the popularity of this movie's not-very-heroic heroes is noteworthy.

Making the War Relevant

There are signs, however, of an effort to expand the genre by making a different kind of war film designed to appeal specifically to the postwar generation. A pair of World War II movies released around the time of the thirtieth-anniversary celebrations attempted to draw connections between the past and the present by showing the continuing impact of this long-ago conflict on present-day Soviet citizens. The first of these was Remember Your Name (Pomni imia svoë, 1974). Only tenuously a war film, this Soviet-Polish coproduction, directed by Sergei Kolosov (Sword and Shield), must be mentioned because of its depiction of the camps at Auschwitz.

The film's protagonist, Zinaida Grigorevna, is transported to Auschwitz with her baby son. Later, mother and child are separated, and she is moved to a different camp. After the war, she learns that her husband was killed on the first day of the war and that her son is likely dead as well. Although she initially suffers from hysterical blindness at the news, she eventually recovers to lead a productive, though lonely, life as a technician at a television factory. Thirty years later, she is reunited with her son, who was raised by a Polish family.

The rather strained story is told through multiple flashbacks. It is notable not only for showing life in Auschwitz but also for its silence regarding Auschwitz's main purpose. There are no Jews to be seen, and only the concentration camp is depicted, with no reference to the extermination camp. Based on the film alone, one would believe Auschwitz was built as a laboratory for Josef Mengele's medical experimentation on cute, blond, Russian children. Nevertheless, *Remember Your Name* put another tiny chink in the public wall of silence, first broken by Yevtushenko's poem "Babi Yar." *Remember Your Name* drew a large audience for a woman's picture, ranking eighth at the box office in 1975, with 35.7 million viewers.[11]

Leonid Bykov also tried his hand at directing a film of this type. *There the Soldiers Went* (Aty-baty shli soldaty, 1976, released 1977) is a more somber and more melodramatic story than his airmen's film *Only the Old Go to Battle*; tellingly, *Soldiers* did not do quite as well at the box office, attracting an audience of 35.8 million.[12] Bykov recounts the tale of eighteen members of a Komsomol brigade who are killed in a skirmish on 18 March 1944. Most of these are students and other novices, with a few seasoned soldiers mixed in. (Bykov cast himself as one of the latter.) On the thirtieth anniversary of their deaths, their children gather together at the memorial to the event to share their few memories. Building and visiting war memorials was an important cult rite.[13] The constant crosscutting between past and present is more confusing than illuminating, but a familiar plot emerges.

A cadre of Komsomol members, led by Junior Lieutenant Susin, is charged with holding the line against an incipient German advance. Susin, inherently decent but very scared, attempts to lead by fear in order to mask his own inexperience. He cannot maintain his tough guy image for long; he breaks down in front of his men, begging them to support him: "I'm a bad commander, but you're *komsomoltsy*," he implores them. "You're my comrades. I'm ashamed of myself, guys." Susin soon faces a test in which he must choose between mercy and discipline: he learns that one of his soldiers has stolen and hidden some bread. "You've never been hungry, comrade junior lieutenant, you've never been hungry," the man pleads. Susin chooses mercy over punishment, even for a transgression as serious as this.

Thoroughly unprepared for any kind of combat, the young men are charged with keeping the Germans at bay until reinforcements arrive. They are cut down, one by one. "We face death in the name of life," reads the inscription on their memorial.

Because the majority of these men are very young, little more than boys, the notion that they all had children to survive them and gather on the anniversary of their deaths beggars belief. Bykov does, however, provide a plausible explanation for Susin's heir. On the night before the massacre, some nurses join them for dinner. One of them is Kima, a girl Susin knows from home. They sleep together, the advance initiated by Kima (whose unusual name, we learn, is an acronym derived from the Russian for Communist Youth International, KIM). Bykov's strenuous effort to make the war relevant to the 1970s is one indication that the postwar generation was experiencing its own kind of battle fatigue. Nevertheless, like *Burning Snow* and *Only the Old Go to Battle*, *There the Soldiers Went* shows very young men cut down "in the name of life," not for Party or motherland.

Art and War under Brezhnev

As we have seen, war lends itself well to popular filmmaking because of its intrinsic pathos and action. But the "commercial" films just discussed are far from the mindless political hackwork that supposedly characterized the war films of the late Brezhnev era. Art films are, of course, a different matter. Given that art films by definition privilege interiority over action, war is a difficult subject to treat. Artistically important war films tend, therefore, to carry an antiwar message. As we know, the Brezhnev regime sought to build patriotism by exalting the memory of the Great Patriotic War to the extent that it reached cultlike proportions by the midseventies. As a result, it was more difficult than ever to make war movies that stressed reflection and introspection over action. The best Soviet directors were extremely resourceful, however, and four important art films about the Great Patriotic War, as well as two interesting ones about the Russian Civil War, made it to the screen in the seventies.

Two of these films came from directors who rose to prominence during the Thaw. The first, *It Was the Month of May* (Byl' mesiats mai, 1970), was directed by Marlen Khutsiev (b. 1925). Khutsiev, who like other prominent war film directors had studied at VGIK with Igor Savchenko, made his mark in the fifties with films like *The House on Zarechnaya Street* and *The Two Fyodors*. In *Month of May*, Khutsiev takes a microscope to the sixth and seventh days after the end of the war in a German village, where four Soviet scouts and their lieutenant are billeted with a wealthy German farmer, his much younger wife, and their son. The first two-thirds of the film are deceptively quiet, with the language barrier serving as the main focus. (The Germans speak German without voice-overs or subtitles.) The soldiers attempt to flirt with the pretty wife as she works in the barn. They speculate among themselves as to why she married the older man, whether she is the mother of the teenage boy, whether she is a second wife, and so on. Inside the well-kept farmhouse, the lieutenant drinks with his host, toasting the peace. Despite the nods and smiles on all sides, the atmosphere is tense.

In the middle third of the film, the lieutenant has been called away to meet his superiors. He takes off on a motorcycle his men have requisitioned and refurbished; it is a sunny day, the countryside is pretty, the war is over, his mood is lighthearted. But he is going too fast and wipes out, landing in the yard of a house occupied by more Red Army soldiers. They talk and drink, and sing and drink, and drink and drink and drink—to oblivion. The few who can still walk take an unsteady stroll in the moonlight. They pile into an abandoned car and drive it to the end of the road, to a compound surrounded by barbed wire. They have discovered a death camp with crematoriums.

In the final, increasingly surrealistic third of the film, the lieutenant returns to his "home" to find that the German family is very angry with his men over some incomprehensible matter, which appears to be the killing of a pig. In the evening, as he is having dinner, an emaciated, filthy Pole stumbles in, looking for the farmer. Two other camp inmates wander into the yard. The Soviets learn to their horror that their kindly host had also "hosted" slave laborers from the camp and was deeply complicit in the war effort, despite his toasts of "Hitler kaput!" and "Krieg kaput!"

This movie was filmed in a cinema verité style unusual for Soviet cinema, especially for a war film. The impromptu house party that occupies the middle of the picture is rather extraordinary. Its overlapping dialogue and improvisational air are deeply subversive to the official "script"—especially considering that It Was the Month of May appeared the same year as Liberation. Khutsiev cannot openly discuss the Holocaust; it would appear from the last part of his film that the victims were mainly Poles and German communists. But at the very end, he shows (without comment) newsreel footage of Jews being herded into the Warsaw ghetto, interwoven with faux-newsreel footage showing the happy life of Berliners in the GDR.

Grigory Chukhrai, who directed the important Thaw films The Forty-first, The Ballad of a Soldier, and Clear Skies, resurfaced at his time. In the

1960s, Chukhrai devoted much of his professional energy to supervising Mosfilm's Experimental Creative Studio as its artistic director. The Experimental Creative Studio was permitted to work outside the established paradigms as long as its films paid for themselves and were not so radical as to be banned. The studio survived the debacle of the banning of *The Angel* and *The Motherland of Electricity*, but just barely. Mosfilm terminated the experiment in 1972; among the studio's last films was the not-very-experimental World War II submarine melodrama *The Commander of the Lucky "Pike"* (Komandir schastlivoi "Shchuki," dir. Vladimir Volchek, 1972), which featured an amazingly spacious submarine manned by a picturesque, good-hearted crew.

Chukhrai did not make a film between 1971 and *The Quagmire* (Triasina) in 1977. Despite his previous troubles, *The Quagmire* certainly indicated that Chukhrai had not changed much. He was a born rebel.

The Quagmire, a psychological drama about a woman who hides her deserter son throughout the war, broke new ground for Chukhrai and for Soviet cinema. The idea was suggested to Chukhrai by Georgian actress Leila Abashidze from a newspaper story. Chukhrai recalled that as a veteran, he was completely uninterested in making a film about a deserter until he realized the dramatic possibilities inherent in shifting the story's focus from the son to the mother.[14] Casting Nonna Mordiukova in the lead role of Matryona was a stroke of genius. Now in her fifties, Mordiukova (*The Young Guard*, *The Commissar*) could have served as a model for the Great Patriotic War's "The Motherland Mother Calls" recruiting poster.

This peasant mother puts her desire to preserve her younger son's corporeal being over his soul. Matryona's husband has been killed, and her older son Styopa is reported missing in action when her remaining child, Mitya, is called up. Before Mitya can even get to the front, the front comes to him. The Germans bomb the railway depot where the new recruits are gathered. Mitya is reported dead, but in reality he finds his way home, where his mother hides him in the attic. She later urges him to flee, but as he reminds her, his lack of "Documents! Documents!" prohibits a life on the lam.

Thus begins Matryona's life of deceit. She avoids her neighbors; she pretends grief when she is informed that Mitya has been killed. She is at Mitya's mercy; in his own despair, he has become increasingly brutish. As difficult as it is for Matryona to hide Mitya when he first returns, keeping her terrible secret becomes much harder. Her other son is in fact alive and reappears, repatriated from German captivity. Now her double life becomes impossible to manage. She must choose between her sons, and in a heart-breaking scene, she decides to throw out her "good" son, the bewildered Styopa, in order to keep him from learning the truth about the "bad" son, Mitya.

At war's end, both Matryona and Mitya are in steep mental, emotional, and physical decline. Mitya pretends to hang himself for a little excitement; Matryona confesses to her priest, who refuses to absolve her. Finally, Mitya breaks down, admitting his cowardice and telling his mother that he will give himself up. She dies of a heart attack, her hand gripping his wrist to prevent him from leaving.

Mitya leaves the dark cabin for the light of the real world for the first time in years. He attempts to surrender himself at the police station. The denouement is startling and deeply ironic. The police officer is extremely annoyed at the trouble it would cause him to arrest a deserter now that the war is over. He waves Mitya away. The young man is now stripped of all identification—he cannot even claim "deserter" as a status.

Mordiukova's performance is a riveting portrayal of psychological decline and misplaced motherly love. Keeping Mitya "safe" becomes the sole reason for her existence. When Styopa returns home, she is completely unable to tend to his psychological needs and orders him to leave. Her obsession orphans him. He has no brother, no father, and now no mother. His girlfriend, who believed he was dead, has married. He has to deal with the stigma of having been a prisoner. Yet he does rebuild his life. Styopa goes back to school, marries, and has a son (whom he names Mitya, after his brother). He is in fact on his way to introduce his wife and baby to his mother as Matryona collapses and dies.

The message of this original film is far from clear. One might assume that Matryona is guilty of privileging her role as a mother over her role as a Soviet citizen. The Quagmire does not, however, provide any compelling evidence that this is what Chukhrai intended. Perhaps Matryona is guilty of having betrayed herself through her "selflessness." She has certainly betrayed the trust of her older son by cutting the last family ties that he has. And perhaps she has betrayed her younger son by supporting his failure to take responsibility for his actions.

Not surprisingly, this bleak and difficult picture did not set any box-office records. However, given its darkness and ambiguity, its audience of 19.7 million was quite respectable, larger than that for other movies of this type.[15] It received a thoughtful review in Soviet Screen and ranked tenth in its annual poll;[16] as always, one must keep in mind that *Soviet Screen*'s read-ers were hard-core film fans and therefore do not necessarily represent the views of the average citizen.

As Chukhrai was making the final films of his career, a popular young actor turned director, Nikita Mikhalkov (b. 1945), began experimenting with the adventure and melodrama genres using the Civil War as his back-drop. The politically well-connected Mikhalkov (his father, Sergei, wrote the lyrics to the Soviet national anthem) was certainly aware of the banned films from the sixties—*The Intervention, The Angel,* and *The Commissar*—and took care to avoid them in his maiden efforts as a director. Mikhalkov's first and second feature films—*At Home among Strangers, a Stranger at Home* (Svoi sredi chuzhikh, chuzhoi sredi svoikh, 1974)[17] and *The Slave of Love* (Raba liubvi, 1975)—are both set in the Civil War, but they are only tangentially *about* the Civil War.

At Home among Strangers, an adult-oriented riff on *The Elusive Avengers* and its sequels, was the more popular of the two films, with 23.7 million view-ers. Although more than 20 million is a very good box office for an art film, Keosaian's *Avengers* films drew 40 million more.[18] Mikhalkov's hero, Yegor Shilov (played by the director himself), is charged by the Cheka to protect a shipment of gold, but the train is robbed by counterrevolutionary ban-dits, who are in turn robbed by Cossack bandits. Shilov, whose brother is a known White confederate, is suspected of being a double or triple agent. There is lots of action, much of it confusing.

Like Keosaian in the *Avenger* films, Mikhalkov saw the Civil War as an opportunity to adapt the Hollywood Western genre to Soviet cinema. Mikhalkov's conflicted Shilov is, however, an ambiguous hero (in contrast to Keosaian's brave urchins), and the tone of *At Home among Strangers* is arch and detached. For Mikhalkov, the Civil War is an object for nostalgic reflection and artistic experimentation rather than a subject for critical examination.

In his next film, *The Slave of Love,* Mikhalkov pays homage to the last days of Russian filmmaking in the Crimea, before the remnants of the industry fled the Bolsheviks for the West.[19] As in *At Home among Strangers,* we see a young director luxuriating in his opportunities for genre experimentation, in this case with the melodrama. A movie company has set up in White-occupied territory. Russia is wracked by war and revolution, but it is mak-ing one of the sensational, apolitical melodramas that characterized late imperial cinema. The star of the movie-within-the-movie is the diva, Olga, reputedly modeled after Vera Kholodnaya, a queen of the prerevolutionary Russian screen. However, the blonde, girlishly pretty Olga (played by Yelena Solovei in a highly mannered performance) does not at all resemble the svelte, dark-haired, glamorous Kholodnaya. The apolitical, self-absorbed Olga falls in love with the handsome cameraman Viktor, an undercover Bolshevik agent. After Viktor is found out and killed, Olga, "converted" to the cause through love (hardly a very Marxist idea), attempts to carry on. Given Mikhalkov's stylized rendition of this arcane subject, *The Slave of Love*'s audience of 11.2 million indicated public recognition of his talent, if not open embrace of his emotional detachment.

A few years older than Mikhalkov, Aleksei Gherman (b. 1938) came into his own in the 1970s, even though his second movie, *The Trial on the Road* (Proverka na dorogakh, 1971), was banned and not released until 1987. *The Trial on the Road* is loosely based on stories by the director's father, the famous war writer Yury Gherman, with the screenplay by Eduard Volodarsky. Like the protagonists of *The Fate of a Man* and *Clear Skies*, Lazarev has been a prisoner of the Germans, a subject avoided over the past decade. But unlike Sokolov and Astakhov, Lazarev has actually been fighting with the Germans and surrenders to the partisans wearing a German uniform.

The dramatic conflict centers on what to do with him—arrest him? Or allow him to rise from the dead like Lazarus (whom his surname recalls) and prove himself as a Soviet soldier? In the meantime, there are Germans to kill and bridges to blow up, and Lazarev offers another hand in the fight.

The picture's daring lies in large part in its ambiguity: we do not know whether Lazarev sincerely hopes to reclaim his Soviet identity or is merely an opportunist trying to survive. Like their commander (played by Anatoly Solonitsyn), the partisans are reluctant to trust his intentions. Finally, they decide to put Lazarev's experience with the Germans to good use. He is sent into the German encampment to take the watchtower by the tracks and bomb the German supply train. His success results in his death. He will not rise again. The high degree of uncertainty in *The Trial on the Road* would make it a difficult film for viewers anywhere; in the Soviet context, it was intolerable and unacceptable. How could a "Lazarev" be allowed this heroic death?[20]

Gherman's great abilities as a director were, however, obvious, and he was eventually given another chance. His third movie (the second to be released) was *Twenty Days without War* (Dvadtsat' dnei bez voiny, 1976, released 1977). Konstantin Simonov wrote the screenplay, based on his loosely autobiographical "Loptin Stories," ("Lopatinskie povesty") about a war correspondent on leave, on his way to Tashkent to visit the movie studio where one of his works is being filmed. This was the first time Simonov himself had adapted one of his works for the screen;[21] he also read the film's voice-over narration.

Like *The Ballad of a Soldier*, *Twenty Days without War* is an odyssey film. Unlike Alyosha Skvortsov, however, Lopatin is a spectator, not an activist. Particularly in the film's first half, Lopatin is a detached outsider who sits and waits, watching and listening. His passivity is exemplified in the movie's most famous scene: a ten-minute monologue delivered by a mentally disturbed soldier on the train, which is shot in close-up in a single take. Lopatin does not even try to respond to his seatmate's complicated story of matrimonial betrayal.

There is more "action" in the second half of the film, but not much. Lopatin delivers the personal effects of a dead soldier to his widow; she throws him out, screaming hysterically. He runs into a woman he met on the train; they have a brief affair. He is asked to deliver a morale-raising speech at a factory. Tongue-tied, he resorts to stock phrases, stuttering almost incoherently: "Comrades, comrades, comrades. . . . Our soldiers at Stalingrad. They're relying on your production. Fighting for you. All for the front!" Regardless of whether or not he has made any sense, the workers respond with stormy applause.

His visit to the set of his film is particularly interesting. True to the style of the wartime war films, the action is brisk, sharp, clear. But this provides a marked contrast to the "reality" that Gherman has painted for the viewers of *his* film. In *Twenty Days without War*, people are confused and sad; the mood is desultory.

Back at the front, enemy shelling immediately forces Lopatin to dive into a trench. Given that he has been in slow motion for most of the film, we are surprised that he can move so quickly, but this is clearly a reflexive action. A sudden happy smile crosses his face: he is home; his real life is here, at the front. The film ends with Lopatin and a scared novice lieutenant crossing the scarred and muddy plain. Their figures slowly disappear, shrouded in the mist.

Yury Khaniutin wrote an incisive analysis of this picture and its contributions to the Soviet war film genre. He saw its cinematic antecedents in *Two Warriors* and *The Ballad of a Soldier*, in that it depicts a localized and individualized view of the war. Anticipating criticism of Lopatin's perpetual air of resignation, Khaniutin argued that it was a mistake to label Lopatin an

Twenty Days without War: Lopatin is an unwelcome visitor. Courtesy BFI Stills.

antihero; rather, he was "not-a-hero" (*negeroi*), in other words, an ordinary person in extraordinary times.[22]

The third important director of the generation that came to adulthood after the war was Larissa Shepitko (1938–1979), whose oeuvre is limited not only because her artistic daring slowed down approval of her projects, but also by her early death in an automobile accident.[23] Shepitko garnered an unusual amount of attention in a film press that usually resisted star-making. Besides being a gifted director, she was a beautiful young woman working in a male-dominated field. (Studio publicity shots of Shepitko frequently appeared in *Soviet Screen*, which was highly unusual for a director.) Her diploma film at VGIK (where she studied in Romm's directing workshop) won a prize; her next movie, *Wings* (Krylia, 1966), generated both controversy and praise.[24]

Wings told the story of the unhappy postwar life of a stern school principal (wonderfully played by Maya Bulgakova), who was a World War II veteran and a decorated pilot. Like other women war pilots, she had been compelled to give up flying, her one joy in life, after the war. Unlike male veterans, her heroic deeds were pushed to the background, meriting only a placard in the local museum. A war widow who has built an outwardly successful postwar life as a professional woman with an adopted daughter, she has not really adapted to the postwar world. At the end of the film, she impulsively drives a plane out of the hangar and flies off. Whether or not she intended to commit suicide was one source of controversy concerning the film.[25] Regardless of her intentions, she is beaming with happiness as she ascends into the clouds (heavens?).

Shepitko returned to the topic of the war in her fourth film, *The Ascent* (Voskhozhdenie, 1976), the last completed before her death.[26] In contrast to *Wings*, where we see the war only in memory (flashbacks), *The Ascent* places the war front and center. It is a harsh and uncompromising look at wartime collaboration and betrayal. Unlike Lazarev in *Trial on the Road*, Shepitko's collaborators are beyond redemption. *The Ascent* did, however, have a strike against it from the start, given that it was based on a 1970 novella by Belorussian writer Vasyl Bykaǔ that had already been criticized as "too gloomy and hopeless."[27] It is certainly gloomy, but perhaps not completely without hope.

The film opens with a German punitive force chasing a band of partisans and refugees across the bleak and frozen landscape. Sotnikov (Boris Plotnikov), a haggard former teacher who brings to mind the prototypical tubercular intellectual from a nineteenth-century Russian novel, volunteers to join Rybak (Vladimir Gostiukhin), a sergeant in the regular army and a man of the people, in a quest for food. Struggling through the deep snow, they eventually find what appears to be an abandoned homestead. Breaking in, they discover an elderly couple. The old woman is frightened (who knows who the enemies are these days?), but her husband continues reading his Bible. When Rybak sees their cow, he is quick to denounce them as collaborators: "Only someone who collaborated would still have a cow. You've sinned by turning traitor. Put down your Bible."

Sotnikov and Rybak decide to requisition a sheep instead of the cow, but the shot that kills it draws the attention of German patrols. The duo's attempt to flee is a particularly desperate one. Not only is Sotnikov weakened by his hacking cough, he has also been shot in the leg. Literally frozen to the tree that he rests against, Sotnikov wants to shoot himself, but Rybak insists he will not leave him behind. Alternately crawling and being dragged by Rybak, ice crystals forming on his bearded face, Sotnikov makes it to another cottage Rybak has found. Sotnikov has had his epiphany; he has accepted the certainty of his death, telling Rybak, "I'm not scared anymore. The main thing is to get used to the idea." Rybak, on the other hand, wants to live, regardless of the cost. In retrospect, this is the viewer's first sign that Rybak may not be as brave and selfless as he seems, despite his quick accusation of the old man.

This next refuge belongs to a widowed mother, who is terrified by their presence and rightly so. She understands what will happen to her three young children if the Germans track Rybak and Sotnikov to her cabin, which will be easy to do in the snow. Sure enough, the Germans are not far behind. Sotnikov's inability to suppress his cough leads to their quick discovery in the attic. The widow is also arrested, sobbing and screaming that they are sentencing her babies to certain death. Sotnikov pleads with the Germans to leave her behind, since she was not in fact allied with the partisans. Rybak, however, is silent.

At the German camp, Sotnikov and Rybak are questioned by a native collaborator, Pavlo Portnov. This character has a much larger role in the movie than he had in Bykaŭ's story, where the dramatic and moral tension centered on the relationship between Rybak and Sotnikov. Portnov (played by Anatoly Solonitsyn) is one of the most memorable villains in the Soviet war film. Once a model Soviet citizen—a Party propagandist, community organizer, director of the village choir, and perhaps an NKVD informer—Portnov has become a model fascist.

Portnov decides to deal with Sotnikov first, certain that the sick man is the weaker of the two comrades. Portnov is wrong. He calls for the gigantic brute "Redbeard" to torture Sotnikov, hissing before Sotnikov is dragged away: "Terror will replace everything. You'll finally become your true self, an ordinary human, full of shit. I know what a human is really like." But Portnov recoils when Sotnikov retorts, "And what did you do before the war?"

As Sotnikov is branded in the chest with the "Red Star," a large branding iron shaped like a star that the Germans used to torture captured partisans, Portnov begins to work on Rybak. It is not hard to soften Rybak, who is scared enough already. (Notably, Portnov immediately addresses Rybak with the familiar second-person pronoun ty, rather than the formal vy that he used with Sotnikov.)

Back in the cellar with the widow and Rybak, Sotnikov is semiconscious, rats crawling across his burned chest. Even in this state, he can sense Rybak's fear and begs him not to capitulate. Two more people join them—the Bible-reading elder from their first stop (who turns out to be a partisan) and a young Jewish girl who had been hidden by a local family. The five await their execution. Sotnikov is determined to stay alive until morning so that he can attempt to convince their captors that he alone is responsible for their "terrorist" activities.

By this point in the picture, Sotnikov is openly portrayed as Christlike, through the staging, editing, and especially the lighting of the extreme close-up shots of his suffering face, lit with a holy glow. The five begin their ascent, up the hill to the gallows. Sotnikov is now ready to speak. He identifies himself in politically resonant terms: "I am Sotnikov, Boris Andreevich. I was born in 1917. I joined the Party in 1935. I am a teacher and a Red Army commander. I have a father, a mother, and a motherland." (In Bykaŭ's original story, Sotnikov never reveals his real name, calling himself the generic "Ivanov.") Portnov flinches at Sotnikov's speech, but when the German officers who have come to watch the execution ask him what Sotnikov said, Portnov replies, "It was nothing of importance."

The end is near. The widow is on the verge of revealing which family hid the little Jewish girl, but the old man stops her. Rybak's offer to join the local police is accepted, and he steps out of the line (although he guiltily tries to help the faltering Sotnikov walk upright as he ascends Golgotha). The villagers have been forced out of their cottages to watch the execution and stand stone-faced. Meanwhile, the Germans are chatting and joking among themselves, pointedly excluding Portnov, who stands on the sidelines. The execution scene is protracted—with crosscutting from gallows to the hero-victims to the frozen landscape to the crowd (focusing particularly on the face of a little boy wearing a Budyonnyi hat, a reference to the Civil War leader).

After the hanging, an old village woman hisses at Rybak, "Judas. Judas." The significance of his actions suddenly sinks in. Rybak imagines himself running away, past the sentries, and being shot. He cannot do it. Like the biblical Judas, he then tries to hang himself in the outhouse. He is in all respects a pathetic failure. The film closes with Rybak standing at the gate, looking over the landscape of the motherland, from which he is cut off forever.

With *The Ascent* Shepitko returned to the overt heroism of the wartime war films—to Comrade P., Olena Kostiukh, Zoya, and Fyodor Talankin. Sotnikov is a child of the Revolution, a Party member, born in 1917. For whom does he fight? His father, his mother, and his motherland. But the film is deeply subversive as well, with its heavy religious overtones that suggest

The Ascent: Rybak accompanies Sotnikov to the gallows. Courtesy BFI Stills.

that the two faiths—communism and Orthodoxy—may not be so antagonistic after all.[28] And then there is the expanded version of Portnov—the Red fascist, superbly portrayed by Solonitsyn in one of his last roles.[29] It should come as no surprise that *The Ascent* breathed new life into cinematic debates in this quiet decade.

The picture was extensively discussed in the *Art of the Cinema*.[30] A particularly perceptive review came from Yelena Stishova, who argued that the main point of the film was not to condemn Rybak but to help viewers understand that the "inhuman conditions of war put people in a place where they must choose between life and conscience."[31] She and Yury Khaniutin both saw Tarkovsky's *Ivan's Childhood* as the aesthetic and moral antecedent of *The Ascent*.[32] Khaniutin expressed his hope that *Twenty Days without War* and *The Ascent* would serve as new paradigms for the Soviet war film, but the political upheaval of the 1980s made that hope impossible to achieve.[33]

Somewhat surprisingly, *The Ascent* was also covered extensively in the popular film magazine *Soviet Screen*. Like Stishova and Khaniutin, *Soviet Screen*'s critic Vadim Sokolov praised *The Ascent* for raising moral questions but refusing to make moral judgments.[34] *Soviet Screen* also reported on a discussion of the film that Shepitko herself held with viewers at a film club, which centered on the tensions between Sotnikov and Rybak, on the one hand, and Sotnikov and Portnov, on the other.[35] In the annual *Soviet Screen* survey, *The Ascent* ranked sixth among all respondents, and *second* among viewers aged thirty-one to forty.[36] However, its audience was quite a bit lower than that for Chukhrai's *The Quagmire*, only by 10.7 million, perhaps due to restricted distribution.[37]

The Apogee of the Soviet War Film

When *The Quagmire*, *Twenty Days without War*, and *The Ascent* reached screens in the late seventies, Leonid Brezhnev was in the last years of his rule and his life. By this time, Soviet society was not just in Stagnation but also in a "quagmire." More important than the low standard of living was the loss of faith in the system and its ideology. Few any longer believed that "communism will conquer."

The Soviet war film genre was emphatically *not* in stagnation. This is not as paradoxical as it might seem. As we have seen in this chapter, the thematic gap between the war films intended for a popular audience and those for the intelligentsia narrowed significantly. None of these films was heroic in a conventional sense. All emphasized ordinary people stumbling blindly through the waking nightmare of war. The dark pessimism of *The Quagmire* and *The Ascent* make Gherman's films *Twenty Days without War* and even *The Trial on the Road* appear light by comparison. Indeed, one might well argue that *Trial on the Road*, which was banned, is more positive than *The Ascent*, which was not. In the former, the collaborator Lazarev is redeemed through the sacrifice of his life for his motherland, whereas in the latter, Rybak is consigned to purgatory.

As remarkable as Shepitko's and Gherman's pictures are, the transformation of the popular war film is even more noteworthy. Unlike the World War II films of the late sixties, post-*Liberation* war films intended for the mass audience emphasized the way youth were thrust into horrific situations without training and without leadership. Their tone is one of futility and resignation. Directors like Rostotsky and Bykov do not lay blame, but they do not have to. The absence of state, Party, and military high command from their films speaks volumes. None of these movies remotely supports the master plot of the war cult as described in the previous chapter. Instead, they elicit tears of bitterness and regret that so many young lives were squandered.

By 1980, the foundations for the second Thaw were being laid, a thaw in which cinema would play a central role. With one notable exception, none of these important glasnost-era films concerned the war. The genre was about to enter a long period of quiescence.

8 To Glasnost and Beyond, 1980–1991

Interest in the war film falters during the USSR's final decade. The last important film about the Great Patriotic War presents a dystopian vision that draws on important themes from the canon. A child wanders alone through the postapocalyptic landscape and disappears into the darkness.

The war films of the 1970s bore almost no resemblance to what Nina Tumarkin has called the "tragic splendor" of the war cult.[1] There was tragedy galore, but not a bit of splendor. Filmmakers peeled away the shiny surface of the "war cult's war" to reveal the blood, grit, fear, and desperation that lay below. After *And the Dawns Are Quiet Here* and *They Fought for the Motherland*, however, hits were few, and the most serious and original war movies, like *The Ascent* and *Twenty Days without War*, drew relatively small audiences.

The postwar generation had heard quite enough about the sacrifices of their elders—and in 1979 young men had a new war to face in Afghanistan. Like Nicholas II, Brezhnev did not live to see the end of the war in which he embroiled Russia. Like World War I, the Afghan War generated little patriotic fervor among a population that no longer believed in the promises of the state.

The social, political, and economic malaise was palpable by 1980. In times of trouble, the public often desires escapist entertainment, but escapism takes different forms in different times. During the Great War, Russians loved sensational murder/suicide/sex melodramas. During the Great Terror, the lighthearted Aleksandrov and Pyrev musicals were seen again and again. On the eve of Brezhnev's death, along came the fairy tale that was the biggest box office success in Soviet film history: Vladimir Menshov's *Moscow Does Not Believe in Tears* (Moskva slezam ne verit, 1979). No film better illustrates the turn away from serious entertainment toward the dewy sentimentality that characterized Soviet popular cinema in the early 1980s.

Tears might well be considered the apogee of Soviet socialist realism. It tells the story of a working-class girl from the provinces who is seduced to the strains of "Bésame mucho" by a lothario improbably named Rudolf. She raises her baby daughter alone, becomes the director of a factory, *and* lands a good-looking guy (played by the Thaw heartthrob Aleksei Batalov, now gracefully middle-aged) who cooks for her. More than 80 million Soviet viewers saw the film in its first year. The voters of the American Academy of Motion Picture Arts and Sciences understood *Moscow Does Not Believe in Tears* for what it is, a classical Hollywood film made in the USSR, and awarded it the Oscar for Best Foreign Picture in 1981, the second time a Soviet film was so honored.[2]

The ongoing war in Afghanistan, coupled with the desire of the Soviet public for more escapist fare, meant that gritty war films of the type discussed in the last chapter held little appeal. No important films commemorated the thirty-fifth anniversary of Victory Day in 1980. The downward trajectory of the Soviet war film, especially during glasnost, is the subject of this chapter.

War Films before Glasnost

In preparation for the thirty-fifth anniversary of Victory Day in 1980, the *Art of the Cinema* critic Yevgeny Matveev reflected on the Soviet war film canon, revising it to add films from the sixties and seventies. Matveev's list of the best wartime war films included the long-established standards: *The Rainbow, She Defends the Motherland, The Regional Party Secretary, Two Warriors, Zoya*, and *The Invasion*. From the period 1945–1955, he chose only one, *The Young Guard*. From the Thaw, he selected the long-canonical *The Cranes Are Flying, The Ballad of a Soldier, The Fate of a Man*, and Matveev's personal favorite, *Ivan's Childhood*. From the movies made since 1962, he picked five: *The Living and the Dead, They Fought for the Motherland, And the Dawns Are Quiet Here* (his favorite), *Burning Snow*, and *The Chronicle of a Dive Bomber*.[3] This list is notable in that Matveev excluded both aesthetic extremes. There are no films that pander to the war cult (like *Liberation*), but also none that openly attempt to subvert it (like *Peace to Him Who Enters*).

It is doubtful that Matveev would have made any selections from the war films made in the period 1980 to 1985. With few exceptions, these fell into two categories: slick, soulless adventures or their opposite, sentimental exercises in nostalgia. The most popular war film of this period, *Tehran-43* (Tegeran-43, 1980), belonged to the first type, a political adventure, with the emphasis on "adventure." The Germans are preparing to derail the Big Three meeting at Tehran in 1943, through a major terrorist plot, which is foiled by Soviet intelligence. The story provides the excuse for flashy cars and glamorous clothes, a relative rarity in Soviet films. *Tehran-43* led the box office in 1981, with 47.5 million spectators, and came in fifth in *Soviet Screen*'s annual readers' survey.[4] The film's only noteworthy aspect was its directorial team: Alov and Naumov, who had made important Thaw war movies like *Pavel Korchagin* and *Peace to Him Who Enters.* Sadly, Alov and Naumov had by this time been co-opted by the commercial imperatives of the Brezhnev era.

The box office success of *Tehran-43* spawned a number of imitators. The best of these was probably Viktor Georgiev's *At a Dangerous Boundary Line* (U opasnoi cherty, 1983), which features Soviet saboteurs, evil Nazis, and chemical weapons. Like *Tehran-43*, *At a Dangerous Boundary* is a reasonably entertaining adventure-suspense film that has no intentions of taxing its audience with any burning moral questions about war or wartime.[5]

The other "big" war film of the early eighties, written and directed by the popular poet Yevgeny Yevtushenko (b. 1933), was *Tehran-43*'s emotional opposite. *Kindergarten* (Detskii sad, 1984), a semiautobiographical account of Yevtushenko's perilous evacuation to Siberia in 1941, bursts with Russian soul. *Kindergarten* draws on the form of *The Ballad of a Soldier* to express some of the ideas behind *Ivan's Childhood* but with a precious sentimentality absent from Chukhrai's and Tarkovsky's films. Yevtushenko also adds a dose of "Fellini-esque" surrealism to the mix.

Kindergarten is an idiosyncratic contribution to the genre. In October 1941, with the German army on the outskirts of Moscow, nine-year-old Zhenya is put on a train by his mother to travel alone to his grandmother, who lives in a village in Siberia.[6] He has a little money, but no food. Much depends on the kindness of strangers, which is also in short supply. There is no Alyosha Skvortsov to help him, but only Lila, the girlfriend of a gangster. Along the way, Zhenya is exploited by two Fagins, a fake blind man and Lila's deranged, drink-addled boyfriend, a burglar who leads a band of pickpockets and thieves. Zhenya is a reluctant accomplice to their scams and thievery. After Lila murders her lover, she helps Zhenya find his way to his grandmother. But when Lila decides that she cannot lead a straight life,

Zhenya heads out after her. We last see him on the roof of a train, playing his violin with a Gypsy family.

An expansive, self-indulgent film, Kindergarten contains many interesting themes, too many for comfort. Yevtushenko has quite a lot to say about the war, and he does not seem to care about integrating his ideas into the film's aesthetic fabric. The beginning of the picture highlights strange and absurd aspects of the evacuation of Moscow: people running around wearing gas masks; a disoriented man (portrayed by Yevtushenko himself) looking for someone with whom to play chess; little Zhenya carrying his aquarium; the building superintendent practicing a Hitler salute, "just in case," and so on. Later, on the refugee train, Yevtushenko introduces the Jewish question by focusing sympathetically on an old Jew, who is forced to sit on top of the train, rather than inside. He is the one who covers the sleeping Zhenya with a blanket, when Zhenya is forced out of the car by the sailor and barmaid who want to use his precious inside space for sex.

Although Zhenya does not know it, his father has been captured by the Germans almost immediately, in the Red Army's unsuccessful defense of Leo Tolstoy's ancestral estate, Yasnaya Poliana. In this scene we witness a lengthy, philosophical-political exchange between the father and his captor (played by famous German actor Klaus Maria Brandauer). The German officer tells his captive that since he will be labeled a traitor for being taken prisoner, he might as well supply some information. Zhenya's father responds patriotically: "It's better to be called a traitor than to be one." (We never learn whether the father survived the war.) Other key episodes concern children who are "manning" a munitions factory; a mass wedding of soldiers about to leave for the front; and a teacher asking her class to define "motherland" (rodina). The teacher smiles indulgently when a girl announces that rodina is "Comrade Stalin." In Yevtushenko's world, the correct answer appears to be "everyone": "You, all of you, are the motherland," the teacher responds. Finally, the closing scene with the Gypsies is important in that Yevtushenko explicitly acknowledges Gypsies, along with Jews, as a target of the Nazis. ("Russians, Jews, and Gypsies are being killed by the Nazis.")

The two major motifs in Kindergarten are the power of art and the vulnerability of children in wartime. Zhenya's most precious possession, indeed his only possession after he has become separated from his train, is his violin. He refuses to barter the violin for a jar of honey even when he is starving. When he is beaten up by food speculators for stealing a potato, their final and most terrible punishment is to smash his violin to bits. Near the end of the film, Zhenya's friend Tolya (also an artist, a folk dancer) finds him another violin, a gift from a dying violinmaker who was evacuated from Leningrad. The violin also provides a point of commonality between Zhenya's father and the German officer. The German examines a photograph of Zhenya with his violin and then shows Zhenya's father a similar photo of his son with violin, musing that the two boys have undoubtedly played the same music. In *Kindergarten*'s final scene, children playing violins fill Red Square. Zhenya and the German boy from the photo march at the forefront.

The motif of children and war, with war as the "kindergarten" for this generation, is endlessly repeated, not only in the dialogue and situations but also in the songs and poems that punctuate the picture. ("The war is their kindergarten," "You can forget everything, but not the children," and so on.) *Kindergarten* is not a subtle film, and Zhenya is not Tarkovsky's Ivan. Even at his most bedraggled, he is clean and cute, with big, dark, mournful eyes.[7]

Although less grandiose than *Kindergarten*, *The Fourth Year of the War Came* (Shël chetvërtyi god voiny, 1983) is also a highly sentimentalized variation on a familiar theme, this time, Soviet women in combat. Directed by Georgy Nikolaenko, the film stars the popular actress Liudmila Saveleva as Captain Nadezhda Moroz ("Hope Frost"), who leads an army intelligence unit to infiltrate a German encampment hidden in the forest and report their location. She and her men are all killed, but not before they have seized a German reconnaissance vehicle and broadcast a message to their own troops.

This picture is not as gritty as it sounds. The tone is set by soft-focus cinematography and a soaring, anachronistic orchestral score. Captain Moroz is established first as the perfectly coiffed camp wife of another officer, and only later as the highly trained specialist that she is. When her lover is stabbed to death by a Russian collaborator, she breaks down in sobs as her men stand around looking at their feet, unsure what to do next. Only when they suggest that she is too upset to continue the mission does she stiffen up. From this point on, however, she is collected and in charge; not only does she personally broadcast the message, she efficiently dispatches a number of Germans.

Unlike those of the Germans, the deaths of Moroz and company occur off-screen, heard rather than seen. The film's point of view cuts back to the base, where the commander and the radio operator listen to Moroz's message. We, like their comrades, hear the shots. The transmission stops. The final scene shows their colonel slowly walking away from the base, tears glistening in his reddened eyes. His driver follows him in his car, convulsively sobbing. Sentimental music swells.[8]

By this time it is very difficult to find a war film with a harder edge. *Torpedo Bombers* (Torpedonostsy, 1983), adapted by Semyon Aranovich (b. 1934) from stories by Yury Gherman, the well-known writer of war fiction, is a bleak and concise exception that examines the many relationships disrupted by war: friends, family, romantic love. The film's protagonist is the melancholy Belobrov, who is returning to active duty after a three-month convalescence from battle injuries. At the base, he must face his former girlfriend Nastya, who left him to marry another pilot. Shortly after Belobrov's return, Nastya's husband is killed in combat, which presents Belobrov with a moral dilemma. Is their relationship really over? It is, regardless of Nastya's marital status. Belobrov's good friend, the pilot Gavrilov, suffers from his own personal issues. Although he believed that his wife and child had both been killed, a little boy from the orphanage is delivered to him as his son. He is not sure that the child is really his because the boy has no memory of his mother. Moreover, Gavrilov is disgusted that the boy steals and hoards food, which arouses Belobrov's pity, not condemnation. Finally, there is Belobrov's friend Shura, a pilot's wife, who leaves the base with her mother and baby after her husband is killed. When Belobrov learns that the Germans have sunk the transport ship carrying Shura and other evacuees, he is determined to avenge them. We last see him aflame in his burning plane.

There are no positive heroes in this character-driven film. Belobrov is deeply depressed; his final action is purely personal revenge. Unlike the characters in so many other war films who willingly, lovingly adopt war orphans, Gavrilov is obsessed with determining whether the little boy is "really" his. Shura is not a stalwart war widow. In the film's most perfectly realized scene, as her forlorn little family prepares to leave the base, she viciously lashes out at her mother, who is simply trying to be helpful and sympathetic. This is a stunningly authentic emotional moment, one that every mother and daughter would recognize. Despite a two-page spread promoting the film in *Soviet Screen*, its audience numbers (11.5 million) put it squarely in the "art film" category.[9] Although *Torpedo Bombers* was too downbeat to attract a mass audience, its box office indicates that an audience for serious films persisted.

More evidence for the persistence of the art film audience can be found in the success of Pyotr Todorovsky's A Wartime Romance (Voenno-polevoi roman, 1983), which attracted favorable critical notice and 14.7 million viewers.[10] Although only marginally a war film, its examination of the poverty and dislocation faced by some veterans of the Great Patriotic War is unusual and therefore noteworthy. There had been surprisingly few movies on any aspect of the adjustment to postwar life, among them Vsevolod Pudovkin's The Return of Vasily Bortnikov, Marlen Khutsiev's The Two Fyodors, Grigory Chukhrai's Clear Skies, and Larissa Shepitko's Wings.

Examples from the 1970s include Everyone Knows Kadkin (Kadkina vsiakii znaet, 1976, dir. Anatoly Vekhotko and Natalia Trishchenko), a lighthearted spin on The Two Fyodors' theme of a veteran returning home with a child.[11] Kadkin has found a baby girl whom he believes to have been abandoned, but his neighbors and his wife assume she is his wartime love child, although he is entirely innocent of any marital transgressions. (All ends happily when the baby's distraught mother turns up.) There was also Nikolai Gubenko's Wounded Birds (Podranki, 1977, also known in English as War Orphans), a serious and touching acknowledgment that most war orphans grew up in orphanages, with long-term emotional consequences.[12] This film was exported and achieved critical success both at home and abroad.

A Wartime Romance recounts the story of two wartime romances, one real and the other imagined. Nikolai Burliaev (best known as Ivan in Ivan's Childhood) here stars as Sasha, an unprepossessing veteran living a normal, prosaic life with his wife, Vera. In his memory, the war has become exciting, glamorous, the best time of his life. In the opening scene (which presents his gauzy memories of his experiences rather than the experiences themselves), we see that he was infatuated with Liuba, a beautiful soldier who was the camp wife of the handsome kombat.[13] (Liuba is the diminutive for Liubov, meaning "love.") Observing their romance fueled Sasha's unrealistic fantasies of love. Liuba never even noticed Sasha in those days; he was neither manly nor powerful. A decade after the war, he runs into her on the street. Their relative positions in society are reversed. Liuba is now a blowsy street vendor, coarsened by her postwar life. Her lover was killed and left her with a child to raise alone. Although Sasha is eager to abandon his loving and unbelievably patient wife, Liuba wisely chooses to marry a man with better prospects for success in life, both materially and emotionally.[14] Soviet Screen's viewers ranked it the seventh best film of 1984.[15]

This grab bag of war films provides yet another sign of the ineffectiveness of the bureaucracy in persuading directors to make patriotic war films that might actually support the war cult. The master plot and message (exemplified by *Liberation*) had totally disintegrated.

The Fortieth-Anniversary Films, 1985

When Mikhail Gorbachev became the First Secretary of the Communist Party of the Soviet Union in March 1985, the USSR was not so much in stagnation as in stasis. The fortieth anniversary of Victory Day was celebrated with the usual pomp, but without genuine enthusiasm. With one significant exception, the movies released in 1985 to commemorate the Great Patriotic War broke no new ground.

Fifteen years after *Liberation*, Yury Ozerov again celebrated a major Victory Day anniversary with an epic, titled *The Battle for Moscow* (Bitva za Moskvu), which ran just over seven hours. Unlike *Liberation*, no one was forced to see it, and it set no box office records.[16] In a feature article in the *Art of the Cinema*, conservative critic and bureaucrat Vladimir Baskakov praised the picture in formulaic terms.[17] *The Battle for Moscow's* polar opposite was Albert Mkrtchian's *Legal Marriage* (Zakonnyi brak), a small and humane film about a theater actor who enters into a fictitious marriage with a homeless war refugee so that she can live in his Moscow apartment.[18] Although the accidental husband and wife are attracted to each other, shyness and old-fashioned good manners inhibit the odd intimacy of their situation from developing further. The actor decides to give up his deferment and enlist. He is killed, leaving her a widow from a marriage that never was, except by law. The contrast between these two movies—*The Battle for Moscow* a war film of the Brezhnev-Stalinist type, *Legal Marriage* straight from the Thaw—could not have been more sharply drawn. *Soviet Screen's* readers underscored their preference by naming *Legal Marriage* the best film of the year in the magazine's annual survey.[19]

Artistically speaking, the only important anniversary film is an original work that sought to bridge the divide between the grand and the intimate views of the war. This was Elem Klimov's *Come and See*, from a screenplay by the outspoken Belorussian writer Ales Adamovich, who adapted his short story about the annihilation of the village of Khatyn. Adamovich and Klimov had been thinking about collaborating on a film on this topic since the late seventies, but the project was put aside when Klimov's wife, director Larissa Shepitko, died in 1979.[20]

Come and See took a long look at a large subject—the genocide in Belorussia—but showed it to viewers through the eyes of one individual, an adolescent boy named Florian Gainush.[21] Set in war-ravaged Belorussia as the German army was in retreat in 1943, *Come and See* drew on some of the established tropes of the Soviet war film but also subverted them. It is a relentlessly grim movie; the great victory that it ostensibly intends to celebrate is completely absent.

Come and See opens to a scene of children playing, romping on a beach. But this is not "prewar," and their play is not innocent. They are robbing graves, looking for guns. "Dig harder! Can't join the partisans without a gun!" a grimy urchin growls at Flor, a boy of about thirteen or fourteen. The children jeer at a village elder who tries to stop them—no respect for their elders here. Flor finally retrieves a weapon and runs home to face his mother, who is hysterical at the thought of his leaving home for the partisans. As his younger brothers and sisters watch, she weeps, screams, clutches at him. "Then kill yourself now! And the other children too! I won't let you go! I won't!" The partisans who have come to fetch new recruits are a press gang;[22] crude and disrespectful, they are nothing like the partisans in earlier films.

The next scene takes place in a large partisan encampment, swarming with battle-weary and hardened men who are, on a closer look, not much older than Flor. They drink and carouse with the desperate conviviality of people who know they do not have long to live. Despite the swarm of humanity, the noise, the activity, Flor is very much alone. Unlike them, he is still an innocent. As the unit prepares to move out for an operation, the impassive young commander, Kosach, takes pity on Flor at the last minute and leaves him behind. Pity goes only so far, however, and he orders Flor to exchange his good boots for another partisan's worn ones.

Flor is furious and insulted; he is no child to sit "at home." He sobs as he slogs through a swamp. He is startled to hear someone else crying bitterly; it is Glasha, Kosach's camp wife, a girl only a year or two older than Flor. Kosach has also left her. Although she attempts to act grown-up around Flor, flaunting her intimacy with the commander, she too is no more than a frightened child. German strafing of their camp starts. Amid the convulsive whistling and explosive sounds of war, the disoriented and terrified kids try to find their way out of the nightmare, back to Flor's village.

The village is deserted, and his family's house is empty, although a pot of soup still hangs in the fireplace. They hear distant screaming; Flor knows where his neighbors have sought refuge. As Flor and Glasha run along the overgrown path away from the village, Glasha looks back. She sees a heap of nude corpses stacked high against the cottage. As Flor frantically drags Glasha through the wetlands, she resists, screaming: "They aren't here! They're murdered!" Demented with rage and grief, Flor begins choking her to prevent her from speaking the unspeakable words: "His family! Killed! All of them! He's deaf! Crazy! His whole family murdered!" Joined by a stray Soviet soldier, they stumble on until they meet up with a small group of refugees who confirm Glasha's terrible news. Flor's visage, formerly so open and innocent, is transformed into a death mask. As he breaks blindly through the crowd of keening and wailing peasant women, he comes upon the old man whom he and the other boys had tormented on the beach only days before. Near death, the man is a mass of charred flesh; "I was set on fire," he gasps. "I warned you not to dig. I begged them to kill me. They laughed. I said not to dig."

Flor continues his journey through hell. Nearly catatonic, he joins several other men on a trek to forage for food. They are carrying a Hitler effigy used as a scarecrow across open fields as German bombers strafe them. Leaflets flutter from the sky: "Make a stew of the Bolshevik yids." The cow they steal from a local farmer is killed by the bombers, as are the men. The sole survivor of the foursome, Flor is rescued by a peasant and taken to his village, called Perekhody in the film.

Although the Germans have already occupied the village, the man is confident that he can pass Flor off as his nephew. Shortly after Flor's arrival, the villagers are rounded up and forced into the town hall, where they are told to await their deportation to Germany. No one listens to Flor, helplessly shouting to warn them, crushed by the weight of his lost innocence: "Where are you rushing off to?! They'll kill everybody!" He manages to escape the building through an open window. The German soldiers—drunk, boisterous—ignore him. Cowering on the ground, Flor becomes survivor and witness to what may well be the most brilliantly choreographed massacre in film history. Through long takes and panoramic shots, we are forced to watch as the entire village goes up in flames. Those who initially escape are beaten, raped, humiliated, killed, their corpses desecrated. As terrible

Come and See: Flor rests on the dead cow. Courtesy BFI Stills.

as are the visual images of the carnage, even more remarkable is the racket: screaming, barking, laughing, shouting, motor noise, music, gunshots, the whistling of flamethrowers. When it is all over, the quiet is both affecting and startling. The Germans pile in their vehicles and continue their westward retreat.

Kosach's forces arrive, too late to save Perekhody's inhabitants, but not too late to ambush some of the perpetrators and capture a German major, a Russian collaborator, and a few other Germans. The major begs for mercy, pleading that he is "old, sick." The collaborator attempts to rationalize his aid to the enemy. Only the young, blond German lieutenant faces death with the courage of his convictions intact: "Your nation has no right to exist. Inferior races spread the microbe of communism. Some nations must be exterminated." As Kosach listens impassively, the partisans shout for vengeance and douse their prisoners with gasoline, to be set aflame. Before the fire can be lit, however, Kosach opens fire, executing them quickly and humanely. This is his answer to the German lieutenant; barbarians are indeed at the gates, but they are the Germans, not the Soviets.

As the partisans move slowly away from the carnage, Flor rejoins them. Suddenly, in the detritus, he sees a photograph of Hitler floating in a puddle. Enraged, he begins shooting at it. As he fires, we see a montage of images, Hitler's life in reverse: World War I, Hitler in school, and then, Hitler as a baby in his mother's arms. Flor cocks his rifle, aims, but cannot shoot. Unlike the Germans, he will not kill a child, no matter who he will grow up to be. Slavic humanism triumphs.

Flor runs up the hill to catch up to the ragged partisan line. As they disappear into the birch forest, a title informs us: "628 Belorussian villages were destroyed, along with all their inhabitants." The film's closing shot is of the partisans, backs to the camera, shoulders slumped, gait weary. They vanish into the trees.

Come and See is the most powerful antiwar war film in Soviet cinema; in the words of one Soviet critic, it is a "tocsin" (nabat) calling for "eternal peace in the entire world."[23] It stands in defiant contrast to traditional anniversary films like Liberation and The Battle for Moscow. There is not a single hero to be found—nor any glory. It drew 28.9 million viewers, ranking sixth at the box office in 1986. It was named best film at the Moscow Film Festival in 1985, and best film of 1986 in the Soviet Screen poll.[24]

In retrospect, Come and See foreshadows the second thaw on the horizon. Both Elem Klimov and Ales Adamovich figured prominently in the glasnost era. Klimov was elected head of the Filmmakers' Union in May 1986, replacing the conservative director Lev Kulidzhanov.[25] Adamovich became the head of VNIIK, the film research institute, in 1987 and in 1989 was elected to the new People's Congress.[26]

Another cinematic event prefiguring the impact that glasnost would have on the war film was much quieter than Come and See, but in its own way, no less important. This was Lev Anninsky's aptly titled "Quiet Explosions: Polemical Notes," published in the May 1985 issue of the Art of the Cinema. Anninsky declared that the Great Patriotic War had at last passed into memory, that what appears on the screen "isn't what was [emphasis in the original], but what is remembered."[27] He argued that since postwar artists could only understand the war as "legend," they not only had the right but the duty to break with the old paradigms.[28] Anninsky greatly admired Nikolai Gubenko's Wounded Birds, arguing that it was the first Soviet movie to deal with the war and its aftermath as no more (and no less) than memory. He urged artists of Gubenko's generation—Gubenko was born in 1941—to "sing their own songs about the war."[29] Observations like these signaled the incipient cultural and political rebellion. As we know, there was much more to come.

Perestroika, Glasnost, and the War Film

Like the Twentieth Party Congress in February 1956, when Khrushchev first denounced Stalin, the Twenty-seventh Party Congress in March 1986 was a revolutionary moment. This time, however, there was no turning back as Gorbachev announced his plans to introduce sweeping reforms. Indeed, it can easily be argued that Gorbachev's policies picked up where Khrushchev's had left off.

Gorbachev understood the power of art and the media to persuade and to mobilize, and so he quickly recruited like-minded artists and journalists to his reform program. This was not new, of course; Gorbachev was following the path that Lenin and Stalin had blazed.[30] Elem Klimov's election that spring as First Secretary of the Filmmakers' Union was engineered by one of Gorbachev's closest political allies, Aleksandr Yakovlev, who headed the Party Central Committee's propaganda department. As union secretary, Klimov presided over an extensive restructuring of the Soviet film industry, which reversed the power relationship between the union, the studios, and Goskino.

The industry radically decentralized. After the reforms, Goskino's primary remaining function was to coordinate distribution. The studios were now under the titular control of the Ministry of Culture, with the republic studios reporting to their regional ministries. In 1988 film actor and director Nikolai Gubenko was appointed minister of culture, yet another sign of cinema's leading position in the cultural hierarchy. The studios were completely responsible for their own operations, including self-financing production. Censorship ended de facto, although it was not legally abolished until 1990. The film industry's rapid decentralization and democratization quickly led not only to feuding and infighting within the union but also to the desire for further decentralization from the republic studios.[31] Cinema was moving in directions that Gorbachev never expected.

With the end of censorship, the banned films came "off the shelf," and film critics were free to debate them openly. Although there were relatively few war films among these, *The Angel, Trial on the Road*, and especially *The Commissar* received particular attention in the press. The formerly banned films attracted the intelligentsia and hard-core cineastes but were generally too serious (and in some cases too dated) to interest ordinary viewers.

Classic war films were also reexamined at this time. Gerasimov's *The Young Guard* was rehabilitated, and the late Yury Khaniutin was criticized for unfairly comparing *The Young Guard* to Stalin cult films such as Mikhail Chiaureli's *The Vow* (Kliatva, 1946).[32] Long-forgotten silent films like Protazanov's *The Forty-first* and Pudovkin's *The Heir to Genghis Khan* were revived as part of a series on neglected masterpieces from the silent era. Miron Chernenko argued that *The Forty-first* demonstrated Protazanov's awareness that the real tragedy of "class struggle" lay in "the conflict between duty and feeling, the personal and the social."[33] For Valentin Mikhailovich, *The Heir to Genghis Khan*'s aesthetic formalism was not a weakness but, rather, essential to its "mythic" elements.[34] Sanctified classics from the Thaw—*The Fate of a Man, The Ballad of a Soldier*—were also reevaluated, but now seen as outdated reflections of a particular zeitgeist.[35]

These concrete discussions of particular movies are rather tame when compared with the theoretical debates that scorched the pages of the film press. An example of the no-holds-barred approach of the new film criticism can be found in Mikhail Yampolsky's essay "Cinema without Cinema" ("Kino bez kino"), which appeared in the *Art of the Cinema* in 1988. In this wide-ranging attack on the state of Soviet cinema, Yampolsky turned to the problem of "screaming" that he finds common in war (and factory) films. "Hysterical acting," in his view, stems from the lack of "erotica" (which he defines broadly as sensuality) in Soviet cinema. "A strange syndrome has developed," Yampolsky writes, "characterized by hysterical acting, which is nothing short of the actors' sublimation of the screen's lack of erotica. We are all well acquainted with the standard scenes of yelling and hysterics in our films. . . . Battle-fatigued officers in war movies scream . . . into field telephones when demanding ammunition . . . the hysterical scream seems to announce the absence of normal human relations."[36] Soviet film criticism had certainly changed.

The types of films being made also changed dramatically; the less like their socialist realist predecessors, the better. Documentaries, made both for television and for theatrical release, came to the forefront, mainly journalistic exposés of the USSR's many burning social problems—alcoholism, juvenile delinquency, the prison system, treatment of the elderly, and so on. The wall of silence was rapidly being dismantled.

There were also historical documentaries. Just as historians were encour-

aged to revisit the cover-ups in Soviet history, so were documentary filmmakers to investigate the gaps in Soviet history, particularly in the Stalin era.[37]
What they did not explore to any significant extent, however, were the USSR's
wars. That would come later, after the breakup of the Soviet Union.

For forty years, images of war were force-fed to the Soviet public, and
they were quite sated. Some of the newly revealed truths of glasnost—like
Soviet responsibility for the massacre of thousands of Polish army officers
in the Katyn Forest near Smolensk—were too difficult to bear.[38] Two documentaries about the war in Afghanistan—Tatiana Chubakova's The Homecoming (Vozvrashchenie, 1987) and S. Lukianchikov's Pain (Bol', 1988)—and
Lev Danilov's 1990 exposé about the penal battalions in World War II were
among the very few glasnost-era documentaries to deal with Soviet wars.

Both The Homecoming and Pain contain interviews with veterans and
family members of soldiers who did not return. In the style of American
antiwar documentaries about Vietnam, both films emphasize the horror,
waste, and alienation wrought by a meaningless war in a far-off land. As
Anna Lawton has noted, unlike the celebratory tone of the typical Soviet war
documentary, these films evoke "the sense of futility" that many citizens
felt.[39] The Homecoming, for example, opens with an exhortation: "Hear me,
motherland!" and ends with a question posed by a veteran: "What are we to
do with our memories of this war?"

Fiction films, on the other hand, focused on the sensational. In the context of late Soviet society, this meant explicit sex and gory violence, so far
absent from the screen. The biggest box office hit of the glasnost era, Vasily
Pichul's Little Vera (Malenkaia Vera, 1988), was seen by almost 55 million
viewers.[40] Pichul exposed the seamy underside of Soviet life—underem-
ployment, alienation, alcoholism—but its big draw was that it was the first
Soviet film to depict graphic sexual intercourse on screen. Other "sensational" hits were Yury Kara's organized crime thriller Thieves in the Law (Vory
v zakone, 1988, also known in English as Kings of Crime), inspired by some
of Fazil Iskander's stories, and Pyotr Todorovsky's Intergirl (Interdevochka,
1989), the tale of a hard currency prostitute who marries a Swedish businessman. Thieves in the Law drew an audience of 39.4 million for fifth place
at the box office in 1988; Intergirl ranked second in 1989, with 41.3 million
viewers.[41]

War films could hardly compete with such titillating new fare, and few
directors tried. Vladimir Chebotaryov, maker of the quiet and thoughtful
Wild Honey more than two decades earlier, tried a war film in the "new style"

with Unknown Pages from the Life of a Scout (Neizvestnye stranitsy iz zhizni raz-vedchika, 1990).[42] But this slick adventure film about a Soviet scout operating behind the lines was not new at all. As we have seen, Alov and Naumov had had no problem making Tehran-43 during the Stagnation and had done it with more skill and verve.

Aleksandr Muratov's Moonzund (Moonzund, 1987) was better suited to glasnost's emerging themes because it was set during an "unknown war," World War I. Based on Vasily Pikul's novel, the film follows the fortunes of a young officer with the Baltic Fleet, which is defending Petrograd from the Germans in the Moonzund Archipelago. Despite the relative novelty of its 1915–1917 setting, this is a conventionally plotted Soviet war film. In neo–socialist realist fashion, the officer evolves politically over the course of the film, converted by his aide, who is a Bolshevik.[43]

The best war film of the glasnost era was Stanislav Govorukhin's Sprays of Champagne (Bryzgi shampanskogo, 1988), adapted by Govorukhin and V. Kondratev from Kondratev's story about a wounded lieutenant who returns to Moscow in May 1942 for a short leave with his mother and sister. Sprays of Champagne, an updated version of The Ballad of a Soldier, reveals the disillusionment about the Soviet past that was ubiquitous by this time. Volodya's homecoming is not particularly happy. His mother complains bitterly about food shortages and inflation; his little sister has taken up smoking. Volodya also finds the atmosphere outside the apartment uncongenial. Citizens waiting in a long queue for vodka berate him when he uses his service privilege to go straight to the head of the line. The hotel where he is meeting his old friend Sergei wants to eject him because he is wearing a uniform instead of civilian clothes. Volodya seethes with anger in this elegant environment; he picks a fight with one of the guests, brandishes his service revolver, and ends up having to flee the police.

Volodya spends his leave wandering the streets and drinking. He suffers from flashbacks and nightmares. He cannot readjust to civilian life in this short period of time and rebuffs his old girlfriend. His moodiness attracts a much more glamorous girlfriend, Tonya, the daughter of a general, who persuades her father to transfer Volodya away from the front. In the end, to the horror of his mother and Tonya, Volodya decides that his comrades are more important than mother, love, or life and returns to the front.

Govorukhin's best-known glasnost film was the documentary We Cannot Live Like This (Tak zhit nel'zia, 1990; also known in English as This Is No Way to Live), a devastating critique of the country's ruin and desperation after seventy years of Soviet power. More subtle in its social criticism than *We Cannot Live*, *Sprays of Champagne* nevertheless puts the duplicity and double standards of Soviet life on trial. Volodya is shocked to see Moscow's citizens so divorced from the realities of war, now that the imminent danger to the city has passed. More important, he is angry when he realizes how unevenly the burden of military service has been spread. The socialites at the hotel do not want to be reminded that there is a war going on, hence the "no uniforms" rule. The general's family does not worry about food shortages or vodka lines; Tonya's table is abundantly set.

Volodya's misgivings notwithstanding, the invitation to join the protected class is seductive, and he seriously considers accepting. Why should he suffer when others do not? But he has witnessed the grief of the widow of a comrade he has visited; he has run into his sergeant, also on leave. He knows where he belongs: at the front. Although *Sprays of Champagne* was too dark and disturbing to draw much of an audience,[44] the film explored new territory in the home front film, undercutting old paradigms.

Another glasnost-era war film worth noting is Vladimir Khotinenko's *In the Dangerous Backwoods* (*V streliaiushchei glushi*, 1986), a rare return to the Russian Civil War.[45] Although promoted as an "adventure drama," *In the Dangerous Backwoods* reprises the themes of *The Communist*. Its tone is, however, much harsher, befitting the jaundiced outlook of the mideighties, as opposed to the hope of the midfifties.

Khotinenko sets his film in a deeply impoverished village in August 1918, the first year of the Civil War. Fyodor, a naive, young Red Army soldier, has been assigned the task of requisitioning grain from poor peasants who barely have enough to feed themselves. He hopes to persuade them to give up their grain voluntarily; in reality, the Reds would have sent troops, not one man, and they would have taken what they wanted, with as much force as necessary. The peasants hate everything this young worker-soldier represents, feelings encouraged by their kulak, the village elder who is marginally better off than the rest. Like Vasily Gubanov in *The Communist*, Fyodor is attracted to another man's wife. Unlike *The Communist*'s Aniuta, however, this woman, Anna, refuses to go away with Fyodor, even after her husband, whom the kulak has denounced as a Red collaborator, is brutally murdered by the Whites.

This plot sounds like the outline for an agit-film; the differences can only be seen on the screen. Three decades earlier, Yuly Raizman had aestheticized rural poverty in *The Communist*, but Khotinenko takes a different tack in In the Dangerous Backwoods. Poverty does not ennoble; it degrades. The villagers do not support the Whites, but they cannot see one good reason why they should support something called the "proletariat" either. Neither, we suspect, does Khotinenko.

Another "Great Turning Point"

By May 1990, the forty-fifth anniversary of Victory Day, the surviving veterans of the Great Patriotic War had little left to celebrate. The war in Afghanistan had ended in defeat masquerading as victory. The empire in Eastern Europe was gone; the non-Russian peoples of the USSR were restive; hazing scandals rocked the military; the list goes on and on. Glasnost had destroyed most, if not all, illusions about Soviet grandeur. To quote Tumarkin: "Almost fifty years after the invasion, the winds of glasnost and perestroika had demolished that sonorous combination of self-pity and self-congratulation that for so long had characterized the official memorialization of the war. The bronzed saga of the Great Patriotic War was being replaced with raw human memory."[46]

The traditional parade in Red Square was subdued.[47] Gorbachev raised the official estimate of the dead to 27 million in his speech at the "celebration," a figure supported by the most recent research.[48] The movie that best reflected the overall mood was Lev Danilov's documentary, Penal Soldiers (Shtrafniki, 1990).[49] The use of Soviet prisoners as suicide troops was one of the uglier secrets of the war and one that would continue to be explored cinematically in the post-Soviet period.

The great and terrible social experiment that began on 7 November 1917 came to a formal end on 25 December 1991. The Soviet Union might have been able to survive perestroika, but it could not survive glasnost. Khrushchev's Thaw had dismantled the Stalin cult; glasnost dismantled its remaining foundational myths, the cults of Lenin and the Great Patriotic War.

Although filmmakers had benefited from the freedoms of glasnost, the economic reforms of perestroika brought them to their knees. With the advent of the cost-accounting (khozraschët) system in 1988, Soviet cinema was supposed to be self-supporting, as it had been during the New Economic Policy period of the 1920s. Commercial films now needed to generate sufficient profits to subsidize the production of art films. An alternative would be to raise money from investors, organize international coproductions, and so on. As we have seen, Soviet directors were quite adept in dealing with political censorship, but they had no idea how to operate in a market system. "Commercial censorship" quickly seemed more difficult to navigate than political censorship, especially for the older generation of filmmakers.[50]

But there was more. Not only did directors now need to make more audience-friendly films in order to earn profits, the state's protection from the American cinematic juggernaut abruptly ended. In April 1991, of the 313 films showing in Moscow, only 22 were Soviet; the vast majority of the 291 foreign films were cheap imports—mostly very bad American films that had never found a U.S. distributor.[51]

From Soviet to Russian Cinema

With the collapse of the Soviet Union, the Russian film industry had to create a new identity. Russian cinema was about to experience its third incarnation, as a mass medium in a democratizing society with a quasi-capitalist market. The economic free-for-all devastated the film industry. The understandable backlash against all things Soviet meant that the Great Patriotic War was relegated to history's trash bin. This was, however, only temporary. As we shall see in the next chapter, the quest to define a new national identity and a new patriotic culture has sparked a renewed interest in an old war.

9 After the Fall, 1992–2005

Two competing trends emerge in the historiophoty of the Afghan and Chechen conflicts. Conservative filmmakers see these wars as necessary to preserve Russian civilization (under attack from encroaching "barbarians") and as a means to shore up the post-Soviet Russian state. Liberals, on the other hand, view the conflicts as postcolonial remnants of the old imperial thinking, whether czarist or Soviet.[1] Cinematic interpretations of World War II are likewise bifurcated, between critical examination of the hidden tragedies of Stalin's war and romanticization of a heroic Russian past epitomized by the Great Patriotic.

The first post-Soviet years were as bleak as the last years of the Stalin era for Russian cinema and even worse for the cinemas of the newly independent states. The nearly total collapse in production was a cultural calamity. Trashy foreign films flooded the screens; foreign soap operas and domestic soft porn dominated television. Although Moscow's mayor ordered a concerted effort to clean up the city center in preparation for President Bill Clinton's visit to Moscow for the fiftieth anniversary of Victory Day in 1995, there were no anniversary films in the theaters.[2]

Since 1995, the road to rebuilding Russian cinema has been a rough one, with several turning points behind it and undoubtedly more to come. The first turning point came in 1996, when the Russian government once again allocated a small subsidy to Goskino, which enabled it to produce twenty-one feature films. Two private television studios—NTV-Profit and STV—had raised enough capital to begin to produce high-quality films that made profits.[3] Since then, Russian television has continued its substantial underwriting of feature film production.

The international success of Nikita Mikhalkov's *Burnt by the Sun* (Utomlënnye sol'ntsem, 1994), an exposé of the Great Terror's beginnings, raised the profile of the new Russian cinema at home as well as abroad.[4] It won Russian/Soviet cinema's third Oscar for Best Foreign Picture and raised filmmakers' confidence that Russian-themed movies could attract investors and audiences. Film production has continued to increase since 2000. As the Russian film industry begins to find its way again, directors are returning to established genres and themes: social melodramas, comedies, literary adaptations, historical dramas, adventures, and, of course, war films.[5]

As we shall see in this chapter, the war films of the last decade focus on the Chechen wars and most recently on World War II, in which there has been a great resurgence in interest. World War II and the Chechen wars present as clear a contrast for most Russians as did World War II and the Vietnam War for most Americans. The war against fascist aggression was a good war, whereas the Chechen (and Afghan) conflicts were, if not "bad," painfully ambiguous. Complicating the picture of the good war, however, was the continuing investigation into that war's unsavory aspects: the omnipresence of the NKVD and SMERSH, the penal battalions, the arrest and imprisonment of *frontoviki*, and so on. As a result, the trajectory of the Russian war film is not obvious, and directors are exploring interesting possibilities.

Afghanistan and the Chechen Wars

Although the Chechen conflict has deep roots in the Russian past, both czarist and Soviet, the Chechen separatist movement did not begin in earnest until the collapse of the Soviet Union in 1991, which led to independence for Chechnya's neighbors to the south, Georgia, Armenia, and Azerbaijan. Because this conflict is truly Russian (as opposed to Soviet), fought on federation territory, with civilian populations specifically targeted, it has captured the Russian imagination in a way that the war in Afghanistan had not—at least, not until the release of Fyodor Bondarchuk's *Company 9* (Deviataia rota, also translated as *9th Company*) in fall 2005.

As discussed in the previous chapter, a few documentaries showing the Afghan conflict's impact on soldiers and their families appeared in the late eighties. In 1991, two full-length films appeared: the four-part television serial *Afghan Break* (Afganskii izlom, dir. Vladimir Bortko), which was set near the end of the war, and the crime thriller *The Afghan* (Afganets, dir. Vladimir Mauer), about a Soviet veteran of the Afghan war who joins a criminal gang upon his return to civilian life.[6] The first years of the Russian Federation saw two feature films, both about Soviet prisoners of war. Timur Bekmambetov's The Peshawar Waltz (Peshavarskii val's, 1994) is a combat film, while Vladimir Khotinenko's The Muslim (Musulmanin, 1995) deals with the postwar return of a Russian POW to his village.

The Peshawar Waltz, a horrifically violent action thriller about an abortive prison escape, closely adheres to Hollywood B movie conventions. Although it was shown at the 1994 Moscow Film Festival, it did not find a distributor. This was an ironic career opener for Bekmanbetov, whose recent films like the science fiction horror movie Night Watch (Nochnoi dozor, 2004) have enjoyed phenomenal popularity globally, as well as in Russia. In 2002, nearly a decade after its completion, Peshawar Waltz was purchased by an American company and released as Escape from Afghanistan in a badly dubbed DVD version that bowdlerized the story to change the nationality of two main characters from French and British to American. As Anna Lawton observes, this reediting was likely intended to exploit the U.S. invasion of Afghanistan.[7] The images do not, however, inspire patriotism: the Soviet soldiers have become as dehumanized by this conflict as have the Afghans. With the exception of the French doctor and the British journalist who have inadvertently gotten caught up in the escape attempt, everyone in The Peshawar Waltz is a savage, not just the "enemy."

The Muslim sets quite a different tone from The Peshawar Waltz. The protagonist is a Soviet soldier, Kolya, converted to Islam while he was a prisoner in Afghanistan. He is reluctantly repatriated to a Russia that he no longer considers his home. After spending seven years living in Afghanistan, Kolya finds the new Russia impossibly corrupt and debauched. Indeed, Khotinenko's film is more a critique of the effects of post-Soviet capitalism on Russian society than it is an indictment of Soviet involvement in Afghanistan.

Kolya's brother is a savage, out-of-work drunk who beats him senseless; his former girlfriend has become a prostitute; his mother is a cynical battle-ax, a far cry from the typically warmhearted Russian mother in films of yore. Kolya's neighbors hate and distrust him; as a Muslim, he abstains from pork and vodka, two staples of their diet. Clearly, he is no longer one of them. This relentlessly nasty film ends in predictable tragedy: Kolya is murdered as he prays. The Muslim won prizes at the Sochi and Montreal film festivals and sold well in its video release.[8]

The war in Afghanistan seemed a dead topic in Russian cinema until Company 9 hit the screens at the end of September 2005, earning back its entire production costs in its first week.[9] Its extensive prerelease publicity predicted a blockbuster.[10] Director Fyodor Bondarchuk dedicated the film to the memory of his father, Sergei Bondarchuk, but there is little evidence of the elder Bondarchuk's influence in it. *Company 9* is a comrades film for the age of disillusionment; it lacks the careful character development that distinguished Bondarchuk Sr.'s films like *The Fate of a Man* and *They Fought for the Motherland*. Bondarchuk Jr.'s cynicism is so heavy-handed that it renders his film as unrealistic as anything from the Stalin era.

Company 9 shares its zeitgeist with Sam Mendes's *Jarhead* (released in the United States a month after *Company 9*). It takes a group of young draftees from training to death in two hours' time. The first half is their "prewar": five months of training camp under the control of a cruel drill sergeant, who immediately informs the boys that their past lives and personalities no longer matter, because they are "nobody." Most of the new recruits are thugs from the Soviet underclass: brutish, vulgar, ignorant, physically marked by their broken noses, bad teeth, and lanky bodies. The two heroes, on the other hand, are handsome, sensitive young men from the intelligentsia: one an artist, the other an aspiring doctor.

As miserable as the training camp is—and near the end of training, their sergeant expresses his fears that he has not been tough enough—it cannot possibly prepare them for Afghanistan. The dehumanized veterans whose ranks they join in Company 9 are initially more frightening than the *mujahidin*. Veterans and rookies alike are massacred in a horrific battle, save the one who survives to tell the tale (a cynical nod to *And the Dawns Are Quiet Here*). Gunfire and explosions compete with the sonorous orchestral score. The bloodied corpses of the fair-skinned and light-haired Russian boys are contrasted to those of hook-nosed swarthy Afghans swathed in black and to the aestheticized, high art Afghan landscape filmed in gauzy soft pinks and taupes. Although the setting is Soviet, in the last months of the war, no viewer could possibly miss the implicit comparison to Chechnya; indeed, according to a Russian television producer, the project was initially conceived as one about the war in Chechnya.[11]

The Chechen conflict has allowed Russian directors to deal with issues of the "other" in war in a direct and immediate way. Since 1994, when the first Chechen war broke out, the inhabitants of Chechnya, whether ethnically Chechen or Russian, have lived in a state of fear, even though the second Chechen war theoretically ended in 2000. This is the kind of peace that redefines the concept of "postwar": chronic terrorist activity and continuous military occupation. The Chechen wars introduce interesting complexities to the concept of "othering," because the Chechen conflict is a civil war—citizens of the Russian Federation in rebellion against the federation. It differs from the Russian Civil War, however, in that its origins are ethnic and religious rather than class-based and ideological.

At the time of this writing, there have been five important Russian films about the Chechen wars: Sergei Bodrov's 1996 *The Prisoner of the Caucasus* (Kavkazkii plennik; also known in English as *The Prisoner of the Mountains*); two films from 1998: Aleksandr Rogozhkin's *Checkpoint* (Blokpost) and Aleksandr Nevzorov's *Purgatory* (Chistilishche); Aleksei Balabanov's 2002 *War* (Voina), and Andrei Konchalovsky's 2003 *The House of Fools* (Dom durakov). These films can be divided into two categories: those that romanticize the conflict by presenting the Chechens as the orientalized other: a proud, noble people, close to nature; and those that present the conflict as a sign that "barbarians are at the gates"—at both sides of the gates.

The most important film of the orientalizing type is *The Prisoner of the Caucasus*. Its director, Sergei Bodrov (b. 1948), is among the leading director-writers working in Russian cinema today. *The Prisoner of the Caucasus* drew its inspiration and title from Leo Tolstoy's story, which was based on his experiences serving in the imperial Russian army in the Caucasus in the 1850s. Filmed in Dagestan, Bodrov's movie was in the works prior to the outbreak of the first Chechen war. It was, however, widely interpreted as a commentary on the Chechen war by audiences, including Chechens (some of whom objected to its romanticization of Chechen backwardness).

This is the kind of war film that humanists love to love: an antiwar war film. Two Russian soldiers, the innocent young draftee Vanya Zhilin and the cynical Sasha Kostylin, are taken captive by the Chechen village elder Abdul, who hopes to exchange them for his son, a captured rebel. The first attempt at an exchange fails due to Russian double-dealing. Vanya's mother has almost arranged another exchange when the deal is inadvertently upset by an unrelated revenge killing. Abdul's daughter Dina persuades her father to release young Vanya; by this time Kostylin has been executed for killing a shepherd in an escape attempt. To save face with his people, Abdul takes Vanya off for a sham execution but releases him. Too late. Russian helicopters destroy the village in retaliation.

Not only is the war meaningless, but the so-called enemy, the Chechens, are obviously noble people—backward, yes, but people whose word stands for something, unlike the perfidious Russians. Vanya and Kostylin are prisoners, of course, but prisoners for a reason: to obtain the release of Abdul's

The Prisoner of the Caucasus: Kostylin and Vanya await their fates. Courtesy BFI Stills.

son, about whom we know nothing, except that the Russian authorities suspect him to be a terrorist. The two prisoners are kept in a shed, but they are fed and not overtly mistreated. Unlike the embittered Kostylin, Vanya has not yet been corrupted by military service to think of the Chechen as the other. He is, therefore, able to establish the vital human connection with the Chechens that saves his life. Vanya's mother, on the other hand, has to work ever so much harder to establish that kind of connection with her own people, as she struggles to press her son's cause with the soulless Russian military bureaucrats.

This film is beautifully made and well acted by Sergei Sergeevich Bodrov, the director's son, as Vanya, and Oleg Menshikov as Kostylin. It was nominated for many filmmaking awards, including best foreign picture at the Academy Awards and the Golden Globe Awards. It won the top prizes at all the Russian film festivals and at Karlovy Vary in 1996, as well as the Critics' Prize at Cannes, but it did not do particularly well at the domestic box office.[12] Elite Russian film critics attacked *Prisoner* as a "politically correct ballad" reflecting the Americanization of Sergei Bodrov Sr., who by this time was married to an American woman and living in Santa Monica, California.[13] Several years later, Bodrov Sr. admitted that *Prisoner* does not reflect the Russian war film tradition.[14]

In *The House of Fools*, Andrei Konchalovsky, another director with long-standing American ties,[15] presented the Chechen war as a parable. Like *The Prisoner of the Caucasus*, *The House of Fools* garnered favorable international attention, winning the Jury Grand Prize at the Venice Film Festival and earning a nomination for Best Foreign Film at the Academy Awards.

In this film, when Chechen rebels draw near a mental hospital ("Russia"), the staff ("government") evacuates, leaving the patients to fend for themselves. One of the more "normal" among them, a young woman who fantasizes about marrying the British pop singer Brian Adams, takes charge of the hospital and its inmates. The patients are happier and healthier without the doctors in attendance. The Chechens, though loud and gruff, are bemused by the bizarre situation and do not harm their "hostages." Nor are the Chechens harmed in the end; it seems that the Russian troops sent to roust them are not keen for a fight. Both sides withdraw. Again, this is the kind of antiwar war film that tends to appeal to liberals, but conservative Russian critics complained about its "abstract humanism," reprising a lament from the late Soviet period.[16]

Most films about the Chechen conflict emphasize hatred and violence, rather than possibilities for reconciliation and understanding. The most extreme example, the aptly titled television film *Purgatory*, is extreme by any standards. Its director, Vladimir Nevzorov, is known for his support of ultranationalist policies and causes.[17] Considerably more nihilistic than *The Peshawar Waltz* (which of course had not even been distributed, let alone shown on television), *Purgatory* recounts the story of Russian troops trapped by Chechen forces in a hospital in Grozny. It wields its violence like a cudgel. With ninety minutes of little more than mutilated bodies and bloodied body parts, *Purgatory*'s violence is pornographic even by the standards of American shock filmmaking. Nevzorov's sole purpose is to whip up race hatred against the Chechen rebels and their alleged collaborators, which (according to *Purgatory*) include not only Afghans but also Lithuanian, African, and African American mercenaries.

The main dramatic conflict concerns the relationship between the two adversaries, Colonel Suvorov (reminding viewers of the eighteenth-century Russian military hero General Aleksandr Suvorov)[18] and the rebel commander Dr. Israpilov (a photogenic "barbarian" who had been a surgeon at the hospital before the conflict). The battle is punctuated by the two adversaries screaming at each other over their field telephones, as when Israpilov yells at Suvorov, "I will operate on you!" Unlike his men, who are ugly ethnic stereotypes, Israpilov is a charismatic Prince of Darkness. With his hip combat gear (including earrings and a beautiful pair of boots), slicked-back hair gathered in a ponytail, and vivid green eyes, Israpilov contrasts sharply with the solid, stolid, and very Russian-looking Suvorov, whose bloodied, empty eye socket makes him anything but chic (even when he dons a black eye patch near the film's end).

The film spends a great deal of time building up Israpilov as an amoral monster, with two brief interludes. The first occurs when Israpilov tells Suvorov in one of their shouted phone conversations, "This is my home, my land [zemlia], my skies. Why are you here?" The second, very fleeting moment occurs near the end of the film, when the Afghans are nailing to a makeshift cross the mutilated body of the *tankist* Lieutenant Grigorashchenko, whose legs and one arm have just been blown off. As the Afghans and Chechens laugh and shout, a shadow of regret crosses Israpilov's face, as though he is remembering his former life, when he took his Hippocratic oath to do no harm. He quickly turns away.

Distinguishing between the secondary characters, whether Russian or rebels, is difficult. The film's emphasis is on body parts, not people. The exceptions, therefore, are telling. Among the mercenaries fighting with the Chechens are two blonde women sharpshooters (one with a twisted, scarred face) who are identified as Lithuanians. They enjoy blowing the genitals off Russian soldiers, and they die shot in their crotches, the director's idea of poetic justice. There are also a number of black mercenaries. It is hard to hear the dialogue over the endless explosions, but two of the black soldiers who appear early in the film speak distinctly American English. They admire an Afghan who fits a wire contraption over the head of a young Russian soldier and then beheads the terrified boy. "Yeah, cool, cool," they laugh. They then attempt to flirt with the two mannish-looking women sharpshooters. Later, black soldiers who speak English with African accents are seen giggling over the women's corpses. They stab them for sport and rifle their pockets, which are stuffed with U.S. dollars. Racism and xenophobia are rampant throughout the picture.

The Russian soldiers are primarily young, blond draftees, who are also hard to tell apart. One exception is the *tankist* Grigorashchenko, who has two major, shocking scenes. Late in the film's first half, Grigorashchenko is ordered to obliterate the corpses of the Russian dead with his tank because the army brass wants to underplay the number of casualties. For five endless minutes, we watch the tank squashing bodies, mainly in extreme close-ups of the wheels, spattered with brains, blood, and guts. From time to time, the film cuts back to a close-up of Grigorashchenko's tormented face. Near film's end, Grigorashchenko has been captured, and Israpilov attempts to persuade him to defect, luring him with a "5,000-dollar Rolex watch." Grigorashchenko refuses and goes back into his tank to await his death. After the Chechens have thrown a grenade in the tank, they drag him out horribly mutilated but still alive, to be crucified. The rebels erect the cross in the entry of one of the hospital's buildings, positioned so that the Russians can easily see their countryman. Grigorashchenko's "time on the cross" is excruciatingly long; he slowly expires as the camera lovingly explores his mangled extremities and fading blue eyes.

Spurred on by this monstrous atrocity and sacrilege, the Russians kill all the Chechens. The ending title notes, however, that the Chechen rebels soon reclaimed the hospital, so this hard-fought victory was ephemeral. The film elicited a firestorm of criticism, not so much about the one-dimensional characterization of the Chechens but for its relentless, egregious violence.[19]

Purgatory's notoriety was deserved. Criticisms of the same type have been leveled against Aleksei Balabanov's War, which strikes me as a work of a different order, despite its high level of violence. Balabanov (b. 1959) became an international name with his blockbuster The Brother (Brat', 1997), a cartoonishly violent but well-made action film very much in the American style. Reminiscent of The Afghan, The Brother and its inferior sequel, The Brother 2, follow the adventures of a young Russian veteran of the Chechen wars who returns home to St. Petersburg, to the only job he can find—as a hit man for his brother, a Russian mobster. Both starred Sergei Bodrov Jr., the charismatic young actor who had come to fame in The Prisoner of the Caucasus. The two Brother films, which were sensationally popular in Russia, are entertainment, not art, but the kind of mass-market filmmaking that deserves serious attention by social historians.

Like Nevzorov, Balabanov is a harsh critic of the post-Soviet Russian state, whose policies have, in his view, led to corruption, poverty, and crime. Balabanov is also considered to be a nationalist in the Russian context, that is, a "Great Russian chauvinist," to borrow from the parlance of Soviet times. In the context of present-day cultural politics, Balabanov is an outsider—an upstart from Siberia who is supposedly driven by the desire to extract profits from the proletariat by pandering to their basest instincts.

When *War* was released in 2002, many Russian critics were predictably alarmed, not only by its gritty violence ("a film to watch with your eyes closed"),[20] but also by what they saw as its racist depiction of Chechens. For them, the messages of *War*, a film about "blacks" (as the Chechens are pejoratively called) and "whites" (Russians), was also "black and white" in terms of its messages, which were blasted as "ideological," "immoral," "not politically correct," and "anti-artistic."[21] Ironically, the vitriolic attacks on *War*, which are eerily reminiscent of the ways films were lambasted in the darkest days of Stalinism, may in fact serve as indirect evidence that the film is more complex than some Russian intellectuals wanted to admit. Regardless, it struck a nerve.

Balabanov borrows the narrative structure of the classic American Western of the 1950s for *War*, with the Chechens as Indians and the Russian army as the cavalry.[22] The Caucasus's rugged and dangerous terrain, with its high peaks, rushing rivers, and glaciers, resembles the American West's mountain regions and is even more spectacular. The narrative tropes of the Western are turned upside down—and then sideways, so that by the end, we have a sneaking suspicion that for Balabanov, everyone is the enemy.

War is an extremely violent film about the Chechen slave trade. Unlike the soldiers in the *Prisoner of the Mountains*, we see rank-and-file soldiers with no ransom value sold as slaves to work for the Chechens. The film, which is constructed as a flashback, centers on Ivan, a young Siberian from a working-class background, who is being held by a Chechen clan chieftain, Aslan Gugaev. Ivan is useful to Gugaev because he can operate a computer and knows a little English besides. The Chechen leader has captured other human prizes who promise monetary reward: two British editors, including a woman, plus a Russian officer (played by Sergei Bodrov Jr. in his last role before his 2002 death in an avalanche in Dagestan) and a Jewish businessman.

Ivan is released with the Englishman, also named "John," to obtain ransom for the woman, Margaret. Back home in England, John cannot raise anywhere near the £2 million that Aslan demands, but he is promised £100,000 from a television company if he films the rescue effort. John returns to Russia, locates Ivan in Tobolsk, and easily persuades him to go on a commando-style rescue mission. Unable to find a job, discriminated against because he is a veteran of the Chechen conflict, Ivan does not have anything better to do. After many, many Chechens are killed, Margaret and the Russian captain are rescued, but John turns on Ivan. At the end of the film (as at the beginning), Ivan is in prison awaiting trial—as a war criminal.

War is a scathing indictment of post-Soviet Russian society, its desolation, poverty, alienation, crime, and drugs. Does Ivan hate Chechens? Yes. Why? They are trying to kill him. Does he believe Russians are superior to Chechens? Yes. What would the point of the war be otherwise? Of course, Ivan could reflect, analyze, dissect, but as he says to John after they have ambushed a Chechen family on the road, "Don't think, John. It's war." Ivan does, however, respect his Chechen foes—he understands why they fight: it is their land, after all. As with the protagonist of *Brother*, war has turned this intelligent but unsophisticated young man into a killing machine.

War offers a scathing indictment of the hypocrisy, pretense, and cowardice of the West, in this case represented by the British. John, unlike Ivan or any of the Chechens, is half a man—high-flown talk, without action to back it up. He hires Ivan to do his dirty work for him and then turns him in to the authorities when the going gets too bloody. Why did Ivan fail to pay any attention to the video camera that John is wielding like a weapon? Done in by his naïveté and contempt for the foreigner, Ivan has badly underestimated John.

Finally, through Aslan Gugaev, Balabanov offers a more complex portrayal of Chechen motivations than have other Russian films. Unlike *Purgatory*'s Israpilov, who is depicted as a rock star rebel, Gugaev is a grizzled thug, a clan leader like the Chechen rebel Shamil Basaev, feared not only by the Russian army but also by Chechens who belong to other clans. Nonetheless, Gugaev is also a Chechen patriot, as he demonstrates early in the picture. In a monologue to Ivan, Gugaev expands on the themes raised by Israpilov to Suvorov in *Purgatory*.

The Chechen explains to Ivan why he has executed the two Russian soldiers. One of them had killed his brother, but the other was just a kid who had made the mistake of wandering off in search of vodka. Gugaev sees the execution of the new recruit as equally just because the boy was too self-involved to deserve to live: "There's a war on and he leaves his post." Warming to his subject, he informs Ivan that Russians are "weak and stupid, led by half-wits." After all, "you've given away half the country for free" (referring to the dissolution of the USSR). "Why do you fight so badly?" Aslan asks, pausing for effect before answering his own question. "Because you're not fighting for your motherland [rodina]. You've been herded here like sheep."

Ivan does not bother to argue; he knows Gugaev is right. Gugaev continues, leaning forward, growling: "*I know my ancestors going back seven* generations. This is my land [zemlia]. I'll fight until there's not a Russian left from here to Volgograd." The intentional irony is that Russian nationalists would agree with Gugaev's assessment of the new Russia and the apparent lack of patriotism in the new Russians. What is the future for a nation and a people that have forgotten their past?

War is an ugly film, befitting an ugly, ill-defined war. It makes viewers and critics uncomfortable, as it should. War, Balabanov argues, has no heroes. It is no wonder that so many Russian critics recoiled in horror and dismissed it as a nationalist propaganda film from a commercial director. Yet the fact that the journal Notes on Cinema Studies (Kinovedcheskie zapiski) devoted six essays to attacking War indicates the critics' recognition of the film's importance even though they loathed it.[23]

The most balanced of the Chechen war films, and arguably the best, is Checkpoint, whose director Aleksandr Rogozhkin (b. 1950) has been pointedly critical of the Soviet war film heritage. "Truth be told," he said in an interview, "I have not seen even one normal Soviet war film."[24] In Checkpoint, ordinary people—both Russian and Chechen—find themselves in a situation that they do not understand and cannot control. The film centers on a group of young draftees manning a checkpoint in a remote outpost. They have gotten themselves in trouble with the locals for shooting a woman (in her legs) who is screaming at them after a house is blown up (probably by a suicide bomber). As a result, they have been sentenced to forty-five days' duty at a checkpoint in a spectacularly beautiful mountain valley.

Although the few Chechens who pass the checkpoint obviously resent their presence, there does not seem to be much danger. Lacking real business to tend to, the boy-soldiers drink, smoke pot, play cards, and occasionally kick a ball around.[25] The atmosphere is so casual that they know each other only by nicknames. With the exception of the narrator, Pepel ("Ashes"), the young men are good-hearted, but not particularly well educated or intelligent. Clearly, as we saw in Sprays of Champagne or, going farther back, The Cranes Are Flying, most of the "smart ones" figure out how to avoid service.

Two Chechen women regularly visit the checkpoint: Manimat, whom the soldiers dub "Masha," and her cousin, who is deaf and mute (and therefore presumed by the men to be simpleminded). Manimat pimps her cousin for bullets and occasionally for free, in order to ingratiate herself with the soldiers. The film ends when Manimat, who is a rebel sniper, accidentally shoots and kills Yurist ("Lawyer"), the one Russian soldier whom she genuinely likes. She intended to shoot Pepel, who sports a foxtail from his helmet, but that day Yurist wore his friend's helmet. As she realizes to her horror what she has done, her cousin steps on a mine and is blown up.

Checkpoint is a deceptively low-key film; its ending comes as a shock to the viewer, who has been lulled into the dull rhythms of war in this kind of conflict. This is not the Great Patriotic War. The soldiers have no idea why they are there. Although Chechnya is "Russian" territory, they feel like the invaders. Soviet citizens often drew analogies between the Afghan conflict and the U.S. war in Vietnam; such comparisons are also made vis-à-vis Chechnya.

Rogozhkin's view of the Russian military command is hardly flattering. In the film's most compelling scene, we see that the Russian command has no scruples about how to appease local authorities. The Russian general offers up one of the boys as a sacrifice to the Chechen police for the shooting of the Chechen woman at the beginning of the picture. We have no idea who shot the woman, but it does not really matter. The Chechens want a scapegoat; the general selects one, Krysa ("Rat"), over the protests of their platoon commander. Krysa's body is dumped at the checkpoint, wrapped in a sheepskin. Yelena Stishova praised Checkpoint for its lack of tendentiousness—and, interestingly, for being the anti–Saving Private Ryan.[26]

All these films—even Purgatory—make the same ultimate point in different ways: this conflict is not winnable. Although there are too few films over too short (and too recent) a period to draw meaningful generalizations, the emphasis on Russian soldiers as prisoners in these films (whether about the Afghan or Chechen conflicts) is noteworthy. Unlike the POWs in World War II, these prisoners seem to symbolize the loss of independence, autonomy, and power that many Russians feel in the post-Soviet period.

Given the current political situation in Russia, movies that critique the situation in Chechnya, such as Checkpoint or even War, may become increasingly rare. As of this writing, the most recent film to look into the conflict is Natalia Metlina's undeniably nationalist television documentary A Cocktail for Dudaev (Kokteil' dlia Dudaeva, 2004), which seeks to demolish three "myths" about the wars: that Chechens genuinely seek independence, that they are motivated by their Islamic faith, and that the Russian government is driven by its quest for oil. A Cocktail for Dudaev is relatively sophisticated propaganda by Soviet standards. Not only is the film visually and aurally interesting, but Metlina admits to certain sore points in Chechen-Russian-Soviet relations, like the Chechen deportation to Kazakhstan in

1944. However, she leaves out much critical detail that could influence viewers against the state's position.

Setting the Record Straight on World War II

In the new Russia, the Great Patriotic War is increasingly called the Second World War or the Russo-German War. Sixty years after its end, it remains a minefield for Russian historians. A glasnost-era plan to revise the official history of the war collapsed in a furious debate (reminiscent of the American debate over the Enola Gay exhibit at the Smithsonian) over whether a more critical history would "slander" the Party and veterans. As Russian historian Alter Litvin has written, "The first casualty of any war is truth, and to arrive at an understanding of what really went on in those tragic years will take a long time."[27]

In 1995, Litvin recalled the mood of ordinary citizens and veterans as "pessimistic," despite the official pomp and circumstance surrounding the fiftieth anniversary of Victory Day, and especially President Clinton's visit to Moscow for the celebration. Litvin went on to note that "the dominant emotion was not pride but sorrow."[28] New research has only added to the sorrow. Russian citizens are now aware, as the West has long known, that the German attack on 22 June 1941, could not have been a "surprise," and that Soviet culpability for the war began on 23 August 1939, with the signing of the Molotov-Ribbentrop Pact. New research also makes it certain that the number of Soviet deaths is much higher than the canonical "20 million," on the order of 27 million or even more. More than 500,000 men were sentenced to certain death in the penal battalions (shtrafbaty), often for very minor offenses. Between 4 and 5 million soldiers were either captured or missing in action.[29] The grim list goes on and on.

By the fifty-fifth anniversary of Victory Day in May 2000, Russian film critics were deploring the lack of films about the Great Patriotic War.[30] Since then, there has been an upsurge in cinematic treatments. Television has taken a particularly important role in popularizing the new history of the war. STV's documentary series Kremlin-9 (Kreml'-9) has devoted a number of episodes to the subject. Especially noteworthy is the one concerning the siege of Leningrad, titled The Unknown Blockade (Neizvestnaia blokada, 2003), which draws on reports from the NKVD archives. This forty-minute documentary not only shows newsreel footage of the dead and dying but also provides evidence from letters, which the NKVD seized and never allowed to be sent, showing that the mood of the public was as much defeatist and anti-Soviet as it was stalwart and heroic. *The Unknown Blockade* speaks openly about cannibalism and suicide, not to mention the NKVD's recommendation to the government that the military should destroy the entire city and its inhabitants rather than allow it to fall to the Germans. Another film in the series, *Snipers on the Towers* (Snaipery na bashniakh, 2001), is less sensational than *The Unknown Blockade* but frankly acknowledges "chaos" and "panic" in Moscow after the 15 October 1941, announcement that the government was being evacuated from the capital. Again, none of this is news to scholars specializing on the war, but these issues had not previously entered public discourse about World War II inside Russia.

Fictional television serials dominated the war films released in 2004–2005 for the sixtieth anniversary of the Victory. Three were exceptionally important: Nikolai Dostal's eleven-part RTV series, *Penal Battalion* (Shtrafbat, 2004); Vladimir Fatianov's *Major Pugachov's Last Battle* (Poslednii boi maiora Pugachëva, 2005, four parts) for NTV; and Vladilen Arsenev's *Echelon* (Eshelon, 2005, four parts) for Telekanal Rossia.[31] All were harsh exposés, but exposés packaged for the mass audience.

The most powerful and moving revelations came in *Penal Battalion*, adapted by Eduard Volodarsky from his novel by that name.[32] Aleksei Serebriakov stars as Vasily Stepanovich, a Red Army officer who falls into German hands, refuses to join the Vlasovites, escapes execution, and rejoins the Red Army only to be arrested. He becomes the *kombat* of a penal battalion consisting chiefly of common criminals, who are very rough types. Predictably but believably, Vasily turns these men into real soldiers—assuming that they live long enough to learn something from his leadership. *Penal Battalion* is an odd kind of comrades film, with betrayals on all sides. In the gripping, hellish finale, they are massacred (except for the itinerant priest whom they have picked up along the way). Some viewers may believe that Vasily has unaccountably survived, but I suggest that Dostal (b. 1946) is paying homage to Aleksandr Dovzhenko's *Arsenal* and Boris Barnet's *Borderlands*, in which the soldier-heroes indubitably die but appear to live on.

Each episode offers Vasily and his men a different, historically authentic trial, in addition to the trial of fighting the Germans. They have two enemies to face—the Germans and the NKVD—and they themselves are regarded as "enemies of the people" (vragi naroda) they are fighting to save. This issue becomes even more complicated when real "politicals" provide reinforcements to the battalion. The men have nothing. Vasily must beg for weapons, and his sergeant Antip Petrovich (who turned to crime when his peasant father was arrested as a kulak during collectivization) steals food to feed the battalion. One soldier murders a comrade over a dispute at cards; another shoots himself in the leg in a vain effort to avoid fighting; another rapes a young girl (who hangs herself in shame); another is a stool pigeon. They are often in an alcoholic stupor; they rob the dead. Dostal even dares to openly depict anti-Semitism: one soldier assigned to the *shtrafbat* is a Jew sentenced for slapping an officer who made an anti-Semitic slur.

Penal Battalion incorporates a fair amount of political commentary and discussion. The still idealistic Vasily begs the men to fight for "the land [*zemlia*], the motherland [*rodina*]," if they are not willing to fight for state and Party. The politicals debate Stalinism and the motivation for the "repressions," quoting "Comrade Stalin's" well-known aphorism "The death of one person is a tragedy. The death of a thousand is a statistic." Vasily remembers a long-ago argument he had with a skeptical friend about arrested acquaintances. "Are they all enemies of the people?" demanded the other man. "What if they said your oldest friend is an enemy of the people?" At that time Vasily had no answer. Now he understands the truth.

Vasily Stepanovich is a real hero, what Russians would call an "authentic person" (*nastoiashchii chelovek*). He does what he thinks is right, but he rarely plays by the rules. His shame at being excluded from the world of comrades—for example, he must address his superior as "citizen major" rather than "comrade major"—is painful to watch. He adapts, because he wants to live. He overlooks a lot—the stealing, the drunkenness, the priest. What does him in, however, is the remnant of his old-style humanist thinking. His unit captures some Vlasovites, including a friend from the German POW camp. Unlike Vasily, this man is a "real" traitor, yet Vasily takes pity on him, giving him a pistol and one bullet so that he can die with dignity. This act of mercy leads to Vasily's rearrest and torture. He survives, but as a broken man.

Dostal tries not to romanticize the only other character who is part of the film from beginning to end, Antip Petrovich. We learn through a flashback that Antip is not only a thief but also a murderer. By treating Antip with respect, Vasily has touched what remains of the human in him. Antip is very resourceful; in a different society, he might well have been a successful entrepreneur. And when he reveals his family history, we understand his anger when the battalion's politicals earnestly assure him that repression of ordinary peasants as supposed kulaks was nothing personal, merely "part of the Party's general line."

Penal Battalion is a great piece of popular filmmaking—entertaining, moving, informative. The ending, although trite, carries political weight: the priest sees a vision of the Holy Mother filling the heavens, telling him that they have "saved the Russian land." The film serves as a fitting tribute to the half-million men who fought the war as slaves but did not live to see their freedom. The final frames are a roll call of the 1,049 penal battalions. Interestingly, Penal Battalion was a featured film in the highbrow film journal the Art of the Cinema, with one of Russia's most important critics, Lev Anninsky, praising it as the "mirror of the Great Patriotic War."[33]

Major Pugachov's Last Battle reprises the prisoners motif. This time a Red Army POW is sent straight to the Gulag rather than to a penal battalion. Eduard Volodarsky, who wrote the screenplay for Penal Battalion, took the theme of Varlam Shalamov's story (part of the Kolyma Tales cycle) and filled in the details.[34] The film opens in a POW camp, with General Andrei Vlasov personally recruiting defectors. The next day, although one-third of the Soviet prisoners step forward, Major Pugachov and the rest decide that immediate death is better than dying a traitor. A few of them, including Pugachov, manage to escape the mass execution and find their way back to their own troops.

Quickly arrested, Pugachov discovers that he has now become the putative head of a fictitious counterrevolutionary organization; one of his men, under torture, confessed that Pugachov had been seen talking to Vlasov. Sent to the infamous camp at Kolyma, Pugachov finds a cohort of like-minded frontoviki, combat veterans unjustly imprisoned for a variety of imagined offenses. The soldiers plan to escape, but their plans are discovered by a member of the camp's large criminal element, with whom they are engaged in another kind of warfare. Pugachov does not hesitate to track down and stab this "enemy of the people." They make their break and, predictably, are all killed, save Pugachov, who commits suicide. But they have died free men, like human beings, not caged animals.

This gripping melodrama has two extraordinary scenes, in the first and last episodes. Pugachov and Vlasov do indeed converse at the POW camp. Vlasov has appealed to the prisoners as "Russians and Christians" to fight for their homeland against the Bolsheviks. But Vlasov is silent when Pugachov asks him why he failed to protest Stalin's excesses. Vlasov was, after all, in a position of power when Stalin and his cohort waged terror against

the Soviet people. Why, asks Pugachov, did Vlasov look the other way during the military purge "when [General Vasily] Bliukher and others were
shot?" Vlasov is not romanticized as a conflicted Russian patriot, but rather
depicted as the garden-variety Soviet opportunist that he was.

The second revelatory scene occurs at the end. The prisoners' escape has
been discovered, and the camp's commander engages in an extraordinary
conversation with the camp doctor. The general expresses his surprise that
this is the first escape attempt at Kolyma because in his view "the *frontoviki*
are a different breed from the naive revolutionary intelligentsia [referring to
the politicals swept up in the 1920s and the Great Terror]." Taken aback by
this comment, the nervous doctor responds cautiously, and the conversation continues this way:

Doctor: It's another Civil War.
General: Another? It hasn't ended since 1917.
Doctor: I don't understand what you mean.
General: It's a war of power [*vlast'*] against the people [*narod*].

Soviet power (*vlast' sovetskaia*) was supposed to be the people's power, of
course, not a weapon *against* the people. This conversation does not appear
in Shalamov's story, although Shalamov certainly would have shared Volodarsky's views. The general's interpretation of Soviet history is remarkably
similar to what is now the prevailing historiographical view—that the origins of the Terror lay in the Civil War, with Lenin and Trotsky as well as with
Stalin, and continued, with ebbs and flows, until Stalin's death.

The third example of the post-Soviet multipart television exposé, *Echelon*,
features a stubbornly nonconformist protagonist, Senior Lieutenant Petya
Glushkov, whose unit is sent to the Far East in summer 1945 after the war
in Europe has ended. This assignment is punishment for Glushkov's affair
with Erna, a German woman whom he saved from being raped by Soviet
soldiers. (Naturally, she immediately falls in love with him and wants to
bear his child.) The son of an enemy of the people, Glushkov is under constant surveillance, and unfortunately, Erna also has problematic parentage;
her father is a well-known Nazi.

Echelon is an odyssey film, most of it taking place on the train east, but the
adventures of Glushkov and his men are not as heartwarming as Alyosha's
in *Ballad of a Soldier*. Glushkov's soldiers are an unruly lot, constantly getting
into trouble on their various stops, their lack of discipline implicitly encouraged by their lieutenant's glowering malaise. They get into a brawl trying

to prevent drunken soldiers from raping an equally drunken nurse. They murder the informer (*stukach*) who has turned over the notebook of their young poet comrade, which includes a rendition of Osip Mandelstam's famous and foolhardy "ode" to Stalin: "His thick fingers fat as worms/And his words certain as stone weights/He laughs through his cockroach mustache."[35] They shelter two homeless girls in their rail car. They attempt to cover up the absence of their alcoholic comrade, who has missed the train at one stop and steals a peasant's horse to catch up with them.

Glushkov is an interesting but not entirely sympathetic character. A terrible officer, his failure to discipline his men leads to worse trouble for them. For example, Glushkov overheard the boy poet reciting banned works; if he had acted to warn him, he might have prevented the boy's eventual arrest as a "spy for Japan." Despite his condescending air of moral superiority, Glushkov always intervenes too late to be of any use. We are told that he is a great field officer (hence his release after his brief arrest), but it is difficult to imagine that this could be true.

Echelon is a curious contribution to the genre. The first Russian feature film (of which I am aware) to make any allusion to the mass rapes of German women by Soviet soldiers at the end of the war, it is also the first to allude to the fact that Soviet soldiers died in the brief, belated, and opportunistic confrontation with Japan. More than any other Russian war film, *Echelon* demonstrates the oppressive presence of political watchdogs among the rank and file. But it also illustrates anarchy behind the facade of order, an anarchy that it would seem necessary to bring under control, especially in wartime. If there were too many lieutenants like Glushkov, a subversive reading of the film might suggest that the Red Army *needed* oversight—as well as a major overhaul.

World War II as Entertainment

Most other Russian World War II films of the first years of the twenty-first century have had more modest aims than *The Penal Battalion*, *Major Pugachov's Last Battle*, and *Echelon*. They fall into two general categories: big, romantic, action-packed pictures and the small and thoughtful. Among the best examples of the war-as-adventure films are four from 2004: Vitaly Vorobev's *Unofficial Business* (Nesluzhebnoe zadanie), Viacheslav Nikiforov's *On the Nameless Heights* (Na bezymiannoi vysote), Aleksandr Aravin's *The Red Choir*

(Krasnaia kapella, also known in English as *The Red Chapel*); and Andrei Ma-
liukov's *The Saboteur* (Diversant).[36] Little distinguishes these pictures from
those of any other combatant nation, and that is precisely the point. For
some directors, the Great Patriotic War has become "World War II," the
source of story lines for commercial films, not the symbolic mainstay of
state power.

Three of the four films feature lots of action, with good-looking young
people as scouts and snipers. The poster for *The Saboteur* reads: "We will
beat the enemy to the last drop of blood," a reasonably accurate reflection
of the film's content. *Unofficial Business* is somewhat more interesting. Set in
Germany *after* the Germans have formally surrendered, it makes the point
that peace was hard to find, with dangerous mop-up operations continuing
for some time.

On the Nameless Heights, a four-part television film, is more ambitious
than *Unofficial Business* and *The Saboteur*. *Nameless Heights* attempts to be an
exposé as well as a thriller, but its serious elements are not well integrated
into what is essentially pulp fiction. The gorgeous (and highly skilled) female sniper has become a stock character in films of this kind. However,
Nameless Heights introduced Russians uninterested in thought-provoking
entertainment—or, indeed, even going out to a movie theater—to some
important topics. These include panic among undertrained (or untrained)
fresh recruits, overconfident officers, wartime liaisons, NKVD interference
in operations, and so on.

The final film of the four, *The Red Choir*, is a sixteen-episode television
soap opera set in occupied Paris. In terms of visual authenticity, it is almost laughable—sets, costumes, makeup, hairstyles are amateurish and
anachronistic. The dramatic conflict is straight from a John Le Carré novel:
two top agents, Karl Gieren and "Jean Gilbert" (the pseudonym of the Soviet "resident" in Paris), set their wits at each other. In an unprecedented
development for a Russian film, the most interesting and sympathetic
character is the enemy Gieren, who is dying from throat cancer but is determined to bring his adversary down. His determination and focus contrasts sharply with that of his Soviet counterpart, the lovestruck Gilbert.
Gilbert's infatuation with the beautiful French artist Hélène nearly results
in the dismantling of the USSR's entire continental intelligence network.
Gieren's suicide at series' end is rendered more poignantly than the news
that "Jean Gilbert" spent a decade in the Lubianka prison after his return
home and never saw Hélène again. For viewers old enough to remember

the tormented Soviet agent "Stirlitz" in Lioznova's TV miniseries *Seventeen Moments of Spring* (1973), "Gilbert" is sophomoric by comparison. (Interestingly, *Seventeen Moments of Spring*, a far superior treatment of this theme, was rereleased in 2004 on DVD, and a statue of Stirlitz is being erected in Lubyanka Square in Moscow.)[37]

The most popular film of the action-and-romance type, however, is Nikolai Lebedev's *The Star* (Zvezda, 2002). *The Star* is based on the story by Emmanuil Kazakevich, previously filmed in 1949 by Aleksandr Ivanov. Ivanov's version was banned, supposedly because the soldiers, who are in a reconnaissance unit, are shown disobeying orders. It was, however, released after Stalin's death and enjoyed great success, ranking sixth at the box office in 1953, with 28.9 million viewers.[38]

Although Ivanov's scouts are middle-aged, Lebedev's are youths, an attempt to appeal to a different audience. The film carefully individualizes each of them, as well as the young woman who is their radio operator. As in *And the Dawns Are Quiet Here*, all are lost, and the loss of each life matters. The picture's tragic romanticism is enhanced by a swooning, sentimental score and lush cinematography that focuses as much on the beauties of nature as on the beauty of these young people who are sacrificed in their prime. It is a tragedy, but unlike *The Penal Battalion*, a tragedy that allows Russians to feel good about their past.

In the same issue of *Notes on Cinema Studies* in which Balabanov's *War* was viciously attacked, *The Star* was pointedly praised. Aleksandr Troshin found the film "poetic"; for Nina Dymshits, it was "simple, living, warm."[39] Irina Shilova appreciated the way the young heroes "fulfilled their duty" and "preserved their honor," yet "remained children."[40] Just as *War* was attacked with the vitriol of Stalinist film criticism, so *The Star* was praised with its saccharine sweetness.[41] The acerbic Russian critic Aleksandr Shpagin, however, saw *The Star* as one of a number of recent Russian films that have "ceased to recognize reality." He labeled Lebedev's film an example of "wartime socialist realism comparable to what was turned out by the Dovzhenko Film Studios in the [1940s]."[42]

World War II as Art

Conventional story films designed for mass audiences like *The Star* fit well into the national revival that the Putin government is trying to encourage in the face of declining patriotism and support for the military.[43] Although some Russian scholars and filmmakers privately express concerns about subtle and not-so-subtle pressures toward the patriotic turn, films that treat more complex wartime themes are still being made. The best known of these pictures, *The Cuckoo* (Kukushka, 2002), comes from the director of *Checkpoint*, Aleksandr Rogozhkin. *The Cuckoo* was widely shown at international film festivals, and Rogozhkin received the Best Director award at the Moscow Film Festival in 2002.

The Cuckoo is a lighthearted and optimistic look at a serious subject: the futility of war. Set in Finland in fall 1944, the story is about a unique ménage à trois: Veiko, a Finnish sniper; Ivan, a Red Army officer; and Anni, a self-reliant young Sami (Lap) war widow. "Cuckoo" is Russian military slang for a Finnish sniper. Veiko has been chained to a rock by the Germans for cowardice. After thirty-five minutes of screen time, Veiko frees himself. In the meantime, we meet another condemned man: Ivan, who was on his way to be court-martialed when German bombing kills the driver and the officious young officer escorting him.

These two stories converge at Anni's isolated hut by a lake. As Anni is burying the Soviet soldiers, she realizes that Ivan is still alive and drags him home. Veiko also finds his way to her place. Since none of the three speaks the other's language, hilarious misunderstandings occur. Veiko is a chatterbox who talks nonstop even though neither Anni nor Ivan understands him. Ivan is insulted when Veiko, trying to find out his name, suggests that it might be "Ivan," the generic Red Army soldier. Irritated, he tells Veiko to go to hell—"Poshël ty"—so Anni and Veiko believe his name is "Posholty" and call him that for the rest of the film. (In a lighthearted way, this motif of failed communications recalls Alov and Naumov's *Peace to Him Who Enters*.)

Sexual competition for Anni drives the two men even further apart than nationality, language, or (presumed) ideology; Anni takes the young, handsome Veiko as her lover. But after Ivan shoots Veiko in an argument, she realizes why Ivan is so angry. She nurses Veiko back to health, sleeps with Ivan, and after the two men have left her to return to their respective homes, she gives birth to fraternal twin boys whom she names Veiko and "Posholty" after their fathers. Although this film is a lovely fairy tale, its underlying message is fraught with conservative romanticism.[44] The simple earth mother, untouched by the evils of civilization, solves the problem of male aggression through sex and the birth of new life. (Rogozhkin also shies away from Ivan's undoubtedly unhappy fate if he actually managed to reach his home.)

Some of *The Cuckoo*'s themes are reprised in Pyotr Todorovsky's *In the Constellation of Taurus* (V sozvedii byka, 2003; also known in English as *In the Constellation of the Ox*).[45] Todorovsky directed *A Wartime Romance*, discussed in the previous chapter; this time, his wartime romance is also a triangle, but of teenagers rather than adults. The ox herder Vanya competes with Igor, a city boy evacuated from Rostov to live with his mentally disturbed aunt, for the attentions of Kalya, the village beauty. The first half of the film presents a timeless conflict, the unkindness of adolescents: Igor really enjoys playing the little prince to Vanya's uncouth farm boy. We discover Igor's true vulnerability when Kalya wants to have sex with him; despite his pretended sophistication, the rosy-cheeked city boy is shocked. All the while Vanya skulks outside, peering through windows, enraged to the point that we fear that he will harm Igor.

The fear is realized when the two boys are sent out across the steppe to get some hay. Igor is sleeping so soundly that Vanya rolls him off the sleigh, to leave him there to freeze to death. Angry and jealous though Vanya is at his rival, he is a decent kid who cannot follow through with his intentions; he returns to pick up Igor before any harm is done. The boys pass perilously close to some Germans and then stumble across a frightened, lost German soldier, who accidentally shoots Igor. The rest of the film concerns their joint struggle for survival. Igor is dying, but all three suffer from the extreme cold and lack of food, not to mention the strafing by German planes.

As in *The Cuckoo*, the focus from this point on is communication and how both language and class divide as well as unite. Otto, the German soldier (who turns out to be a medic), understands the importance of establishing a human connection with his captors. He introduces himself, wants to know their names. Coming from an educated family, Igor knows a bit of German; he and Otto exchange the names of their favorite composers, a bond that excludes Vanya. Otto is a good listener; both Igor and Vanya engage him in long monologues, confessing their former dislike of each other. Ashamed of his behavior, Igor admits to Otto that he does not really love Kalya and used her to hurt Vanya. Otto, who cannot follow a word but senses their emotions, nods sympathetically. The two Russians boys are only able to reveal their feelings to someone who does not understand Russian.

The situation looks grim for the three youths, and the ending is ambiguous. It seems that a group of village women is approaching, but they have seen mirages before on this ghastly trek. Igor is still alive, but Vanya has collapsed in the snow. They are showered with red leaflets announcing that the Soviet armies at Stalingrad have joined ranks, forecasting the eventual victory.

A Time to Gather Stones (Vremia sobirat' kamni, 2005, dir. Aleksei Karalin) provides a final example of recent films that both humanize and interrogate the concept of the enemy.[46] The story is a simple one. In late spring 1945, after the war has ended, Rudolf Ohnesorg ("without a care"), a German officer, is taken back to the USSR as a mine sweeper. Accompanied by a brusque, crude Soviet captain and an attractive female lieutenant-interpreter, the deeply depressed Ohnesorg (played by the German actor David Bunners) is subjected to compassion, hatred, and curiosity from Soviet citizens as he goes about his deadly business. Blown up by a mine, he is buried with respect (and a cross) by his Soviet comrades. This quiet melodrama, predictable by "Western" standards, is noteworthy for its depiction of the anger and desire for vengeance that permeated the populace of the formerly occupied territories of the USSR at the end of the war, as well as for its reference to Ecclesiastes 3:5, which is not so much a call for forgiveness as a call for "moving on." This is not a very Soviet sentiment.

Two darker and more complex films, both concerning the German occupation, have excited interest and controversy. Our Own (Svoi, 2004), directed by Dmitry Meskhiev (b. 1963), was named Best Film at the Moscow Film Festival, even though it was not universally well received by Russian critics.[47] This deceptively simple psychological drama compellingly recombines the oft-visited themes of prisoners and collaborators. Three Soviet soldiers (including an NKVD officer and a Jewish commissar) escape from German captivity in August 1941 and hide with the family of the youngest of them, Mitka. Mitka's father, who has served time in the Gulag as a kulak and is currently working for the Germans, is distinctly unhappy to see them. This may well be the most dangerous "refuge" they could have chosen.

The Germans and other collaborators scour the village for them, then take Mitka's sisters hostage. Who is "svoi"? The nation? The village? The family? What happens when all are divided? Although the father joins the soldiers to free the girls (and kill the collaborators), Meskhiev leaves these questions unanswered. We are not to believe that the father has had a political change of heart; he simply wants to save his daughters.

Even more troubling and provocative is Andrei Kudinenko's *Occupation. Mysterium* (Okkupatsiia. Misterii, 2003).[48] A Belarusian, rather than Russian, film, it is included here because of its history. Banned by Belarus's authoritarian government, *Occupation* was shown at the Moscow Film Festival in 2004 and is being commercially distributed on DVD in the Russian Federation. This puts Russia in the novel position of challenging, rather than supporting, censorship of the arts.[49]

The film's subtitle—"an existential drama with elements of a thriller"—describes it well. Like Macedonian director Milcho Manchevski's much-praised *Before the Rain* (Pred dozhdot, 1994), this grim tale, which deconstructs myths about partisans and collaborators, is told out of chronological order, with interlocking narratives. Although *Come and See* had hinted at some of the tactics the partisans used to recruit members (remember that young Flor did not leave with his mother's permission), in the subsequent two decades, the partisans had remained a sacrosanct subject.

Kudinenko's partisans are a band of nihilistic marauders who roam the countryside dispensing "frontier justice" when they believe that someone is a collaborator. They are reminiscent of the bandit gangs that preyed upon refugees during the Russian Civil War, and the film's oppressive atmosphere reminds us of Smirnov's *The Angel*. Kudinenko's partisans are also morally indistinguishable from the film's collaborators. *Occupation* ends as it begins, with imminent death. Given that the "end" of the film is actually its chronological beginning, the message is obvious.

Arguably the most unusual of the recent war films, *The Last Train* (Poslednii poezd, 2004), is directed by Aleksei Alekseevich Gherman. A. A. Gherman's artistic lineage is distinguished: his father is Aleksei Gherman of *Trial on the Road* and *Twenty Days without War* fame, his grandfather, the war writer Yury Gherman. Aleksei Gherman Sr. had, of course, been a pathbreaking director in the days of film censorship, so the bar for his son was set very high.[50] Could Gherman Jr. irritate and confuse the average moviegoer as much as his father? Yes, he could—by making a film with a German army doctor as the protagonist.

In early winter 1944, the German army is fleeing the Soviet advance. Dr. Fischbach and postmaster Kreutzer are stranded. Now they are the refugees, wandering in inhospitable territory in deep winter, surrounded by enemies, including rampaging partisans. Their efforts to survive are complicated by Fischbach's morbid obesity; he can hardly walk in the best of circumstances. Even when the two Germans find shelter in a log house, they must share the space with helpless partisans dying from diphtheria. After a few desultory "adventures," Kreutzer, Fischbach, and everyone else they have encountered are dead or dying. The Last Train is not so much an antiwar movie as an "anti–war movie" movie. Humanizing the enemy is one thing, but Gherman Jr. does not condescend to do that. Fischbach and Kreutzer are enigmas, not characters. Gherman seems to be sounding the death knell for the war film, a point noted by at least one Russian critic.[51] Although The Last Train is filmed in black-and-white, its messages are anything but.

Whither the Russian War Film?

The post-Soviet Russian war film is too new to have a history. Historians are skilled at predicting the past, but we are notoriously poor prognosticators of the future. Until the spectacular success of Company 9, it seemed likely that the Afghan-Soviet War would fade into the recesses of history, in a way reminiscent of the Korean War for the United States, about which very few films were made. There are signs, however, that new films about the Chechen conflict are being quietly discouraged, so it is possible that Afghanistan may stand in for Chechnya in future productions.

The Great Patriotic War, it seems, will have a new life in film, but a life that draws from the best of the Russo-Soviet tradition. Some recent films, such as the television miniseries The Penal Battalion and Major Pugachov's Last Battle, bring the crimes of the Stalin era to viewers who are unlikely to read books on the same topics. On the other hand, The Star and films of its ilk are Russian versions of Saving Private Ryan, part of the wave of nostalgia for the simpler days of the Good War. Just as many Americans resent the revisionist history of the United States, many Russians yearn for a usable past, one that inspires pride rather than shame. The revelations about the Great Patriotic War that have been popularized in film and television are heartbreaking, but they enhance rather than diminish the heroism and sacrifices of the Soviet people during those terrible years. By personalizing, dramatizing, and visualizing the successes and failures of the war years, the movies have enabled the postwar generation to understand that the statistic of the 27 million dead is, in the end, the tragedy of one.

Conclusion:
"A Kind of Solution"

And now, what's going to happen to us, without barbarians?
They were, those people, a kind of solution.
C. P. Cavafy, "Waiting for the Barbarians"[1]

The sixtieth anniversary of Victory Day in May 2005 was marked not only by a resurgence of interest in the Great Patriotic War as a subject for the new Russian cinema but also by a revival of the wartime canon. A month after the Victory Day celebrations, the Twenty-seventh Moscow International Film Festival hosted a retrospective of the wartime war films, featuring a varied selection, including movies that figured prominently in chapter 3: *She Defends the Motherland, The Rainbow, The Invasion, Malakhov Hill, Moscow Skies*, and *Six o' Clock in the Evening after the War*.[2] Their appeal is easy to understand, especially in uncertain times. As we have seen, the often imperfect citizens who populated these films are not the cardboard heroes and heroines of cold war clichés. Their cinematic suffering and sacrifice represent real suffering and sacrifice. Moreover, their sacrifices had a purpose: to save their homeland and their people by destroying a clear and present foe.

At the same time, critic Aleksandr Shpagin sought to counteract the wave of nostalgia with a provocative two-part essay for the *Art of the Cinema* titled "The Religion of War: Subjective Notes on God-Seeking in War Cinema" (Religiia voiny: sub"ektivnye zametki o bogoiskatel'stve v voennom kinematografe). In it, Shpagin seeks to explode the "great myth" that "the war is one of the best pages of our history."[3] By "the war," he meant, of course, the "Great Patriotic." Through an examination of the quasi-religious imagery and plots of Russian war films, Shpagin argues that art film directors contributed as much, if not more, to the "religion of war" (Tumarkin's "cult") as did the directors of middle-brow films. This is even true, he asserts, when the film's message was overtly antiwar. In the second part of his disquisition, he focuses on Elem Klimov's 1985 masterpiece *Come and See*. Whereas

I labeled *Come and See* "the apogee of the Soviet war film," Shpagin sees it as "the apogee of war as religion."[4] Are these different ways of saying the same thing? Were Soviet war films no more than constituent parts of the iconostasis of this religion/cult, which was celebrated in "the cathedral of death [beneath] the empty heavens"?[5] For Shpagin, films like *The Cuckoo*, *Our Own*, and *The Last Train* signify not nihilism but hope because the "religious ecstasy of war is nowhere to be found" in them.[6]

In these closing pages, which will address the significance of war cinema in Russian culture and society, I would like to consider the war films and their contribution to the war cult somewhat differently. As Cavafy so eloquently argues in his famous poem, "barbarians" can be very useful. Throughout its short history, the USSR was arguably more concerned with barbarians than most states (save, perhaps, the United States), whether they were real or fabricated, internal or external. After the fall of the Soviet Union, the uneasy quiet in the new Russia made it possible to believe, even if only for a moment, that "some who have just returned from the border say: there are no barbarians any longer."[7] Then along came the Chechen conflict. And if there were no Chechens? "Those people" are, after all, "a kind of solution."[8]

Enemies and Heroes

Because war must have an enemy, war films are ideal vehicles to explore the cultural construction of the enemy. Russian and Soviet war films have certainly reinforced prevailing images of the enemy, but, as importantly, they also subverted them. This was clear from World War I on. In late czarist cinema, what I call the "culture of absence"—the declining number of war films from 1915 to 1917—speaks volumes, especially given the increasing popularity of the movies in Russia's cities. The czarist government desired more patriotic films, but they were unable to compel the studios to comply.

The arrival of the Bolsheviks and their labeling of World War I as an "imperialist" conflict further complicated the historiophoty of the Great War. In this interpretation, German rank-and-file soldiers were not necessarily the "enemy," even though their officers, rulers, and other warmongers clearly were. Boris Barnet's *Borderlands* illustrates the conundrum of the Soviet World War I film very well. How can the German soldiers shooting at the Russians *not* be the enemy? Yet far from the battlefield, the German POW Müller is depicted as a nice kid, warmhearted and hardworking.

The Civil War had no shortage of enemies, but they too were difficult to define, given the Bolshevik emphasis on class instead of nationality. White officers, drawn mainly from the Russian upper classes, are clearly "enemies." But what about the rank-and-file White soldier, like the illiterate peasant batman in *Chapaev*? Is this benighted soul, Russian to his core, an "enemy" of the Reds? Then there are the foreign interventionists in the early Civil War films. Their officers are enemies—as in Pudovkin's *The Heir to Genghis Khan*—but Pudovkin handily skirts the issue of rank and file. As was the case in World War I, working-class enemy soldiers—like the British soldier pressed into counterrevolutionary intervention—present a conundrum. They are fighting the Reds, to be sure, but they are also part of the international proletarian brotherhood.

Later Civil War films avoided this conundrum by focusing on the Civil War as a national tragedy—Russians killing Russians, more out of fear, greed, or ignorance than class hatred. *The Angel* is the best example of the paradoxes and cruelty of the Civil War, and it was banned for this very reason. Other films, like *In the Dangerous Backwoods*, also depict the terrible violence that indelibly marked Soviet Russia. Were starving peasants really the enemy? By the end of the Soviet period, Soviet directors seemed not to think so. Their Civil War, like the "real" Civil War, defies simplistic determinism.

War film directors privileged the Great Patriotic War for many reasons, but one important factor is that in this war the enemy was incontrovertible and obvious. The Germans and their foreign allies invaded; they can be distinguished visually (their uniforms), and aurally (their language), as well as by their savage cruelty and racist ideology. It helped that the Party no longer professed to believe that the German rank and file were "brothers" compelled to betray their class, and so in early World War II films the German enemy could be portrayed as monsters. But as time went on, even this trope became unstable: the Germans were idiots, then "disappeared," before finally reappearing as human beings.

In addition, the wartime war films emphasized the internal enemy: collaborators, defeatists—and, worse, the Whites returning after years abroad like crows to feast on the carrion the Germans left in their wake. After Stalin's death, films about the Great Patriotic War often centered on the collaborators, traitors, deserters, and especially returning POWs, not necessarily to condemn, but to question the definition of the internal enemy. In recent years, the POW has been heroicized in Russian war films as the exemplar of sacrifice, suffering—and betrayal by the state. The NKVD has become as much an enemy of the Soviet people during the war as the Germans.

The crudest cinematic caricatures of the wartime enemy can be found in the post-Soviet Russian films about the Afghan and Chechen conflicts. This is particularly ironic given that recent television serials about World War II (like *The Red Choir* and *Echelon*) or movies like *A Time to Gather Stones* work hard to create sympathetic Germans. *Purgatory* and *Company 9* are the most extreme examples from a very small body of work about Afghanistan and Chechnya, but the racism and xenophobia implicit in them are disturbing harbingers of what may lie ahead.

The construction of the hero (or heroine) is, of course, as essential to the war film as the depiction of the enemy. As Soviet cinema's ambiguous heroes demonstrate, hero-making proved problematic. The louder state cultural organs shouted for "positive heroes," the more complex cinematic war heroes became. The shell-shocked, almost simpleminded Filimonov in Ermler's *The Fragment of an Empire* could not really be a hero. What about Mariutka, who shoots her White lover in Protazanov's *The Forty-first*? By the 1930s, dead war heroes worked best: Timosh in Dovzhenko's *Arsenal* is a good example from the late silent films. From the early talkies, *Chapaev*, Commissar Martynov in *We Are from Kronstadt*, and *Shchors* all fulfill what could have been the maxim of the Stalin era: the only useful hero is a dead hero. Yet Chapaev, the most famous hero in all of Soviet cinema, sets the standard for most future Soviet war film heroes, whether or not they survive: an unruly, spontaneous individual who answers only to himself.

This marked anarchistic streak, at odds with the state's increasing authoritarianism under Stalin, served the heroes and heroines of the wartime war films very well. From Comrade P. in *She Defends the Motherland* to Streltsov in *Moscow Skies*, Soviet war heroes are not waiting for someone to tell them what to do, not even when partisans give way to uniformed troops. Of course, the map-obsessed generals of the late forties films stay close by the telephone waiting for Comrade Stalin to enlighten them, but they are the exception, not the rule. From the Thaw to the end of the USSR, the Soviet cinematic war hero, even at his or her most heroic, was closer to what Yury Khaniutin called "not-a-hero" than to an automaton like Shchors. Tarkovsky's Ivan provides a chilling and unforgettable example: a child who does as he pleases, driven by hatred and revenge, outside adult control.

This is not to argue that early Soviet war films were openly subversive. On the surface, most of them appeared to conform to the Party's general line as well as to Stalin's personal tastes. We know that Stalin loved *Chapaev*, *We Are from Kronstadt*, and *Shchors*, as well as Arnshtam's *Girlfriends*. Soviet audiences, however, liked what they liked. There is no credible evidence that *Shchors* attracted a willing audience, whereas long after Stalin's death, film buffs continued to watch *Chapaev* and *We Are from Kronstadt*.

The wartime war films, with their early emphasis on women and partisans, conformed to the state's needs at that time. They also, however, reflected *popular* sentiments and, to some extent, "reality." Even though Stalin had finished with women, partisans, and all truly ordinary people as heroes by the late forties, *filmmakers* were not "finished," nor were audiences. The popularity of foreign films and Soviet musical comedies in the immediate postwar era provides ample evidence that Soviet moviegoers, like moviegoers everywhere, sought genuine entertainment and believable characters.

As the Thaw's war films demonstrate, Soviet directors longed to provide audiences with more profound explorations of the Great Patriotic War than had been possible in the late forties and early fifties. Real people and real situations quickly reemerged in war films from the midfifties on. The Thaw war films focused on wartime as much as war, and their protagonists represented a cross section of the Soviet population: faithless lovers (Veronika in *The Cranes Are Flying*), Gulag survivors (Serpilin in *The Living and the Dead*), POWs (Astakhov in *Clear Skies*), and so on.

The human focus continued during the Stagnation. Even though cultural bureaucrats under Brezhnev sought to co-opt cinema to support the reification of the war cult, the war films of the late sixties and particularly the seventies indicate a mixed degree of success. Conservative directors like Yury Ozerov could churn out overblown war epics, like *Liberation*, on demand, but audiences did not want to see them, even when they were strongly encouraged to do so by their unions. Stalinism had not provided many moviegoing options, but Brezhnev's "developed socialism" did. Blockbusters were definitely not propaganda films.

The end of full-fledged state terror after Stalin's death meant that the price to pay for truly transgressive films was much lower: a stymied career, rather than prison or execution. With the exception of the unfortunate Askoldov (and the even more unfortunate Sergei Paradjanov, who was incarcerated in a mental institution), the most independent-minded directors continued working, even if at a much slower pace. The banning of

Aleksei Gherman Sr.'s *Trial on the Road* did not mean the end of his career, and *Twenty Days without War* followed a few years later.

In sum, despite the vagaries of regime change, there has been a great deal of continuity in the Soviet cinematic tradition. Whether through large-scale, mass-market movies like *And the Dawns Are Quiet Here* or small art films like *The Ascent*, Soviet directors continued to plumb the human dimensions of war and wartime after the Thaw, creating a memorable body of work. But how much "history" can be learned from these films?

Film as History

As we have seen, the Soviet war film had a slow start. This is not as counterintuitive as it appears. In the 1920s, both the Great War and the Civil War were too close in time to allow historically minded filmmakers any perspective. In addition, the Pokrovsky school of historiography that dominated the decade was mechanistically Marxist; hence both the Great War and the Civil War were forced into a rigidly materialist interpretive model. Since individual actions were supposed to be predetermined by class origin, on the surface, there seemed to be little latitude for exploring human agency in wartime. Even when the directors of the 1920s chose to privilege the individual over the collective, their heroes lack autonomy: Bair in *The Heir to Genghis Khan*, Mariutka in *The Forty-first*, Filimonov in *The Fragment of the Empire*.

The advent of socialist realism in the 1930s supported the return of individuals and stories to the screen. *Chapaev* provides the best example: a rousing adventure with a lovable hero. Not only was *Chapaev* a more entertaining film than *Shchors*, Chapaev was also a more typical example of the kind of raw human material the Bolsheviks sought to mold into Red commanders: unlettered men (and women) of the people. There is not, however, a large enough body of work on the Civil War to constitute a true historiophoty of the Civil War on film.

This changed with the Great Patriotic War. Newer wars notwithstanding, the Great Patriotic has yet to be supplanted as the quintessential war for Russian war films. With the exception of the late Stalin period, Soviet World War II films, from the war to the present, have been remarkably authentic microhistories, and their evolution remarkably seamless.

The wartime war films were, of course, foundational in establishing themes and style. The unparalleled disaster of the invasion and encirclement required the state to loosen constraints on filmmakers. Directors wanted to make the same kinds of films that people wanted to see: films that were optimistic yet believable. Through 1943, therefore, the women-and-partisan films reflect a kind of reality: ordinary citizens operating on their own initiative to save their motherland, drawing on whatever resources they can, including religious belief. The eventual shift away from autonomous heroes and heroines, toward uniformed soldiers, tracked the actual changes in the Red Army's fortunes. Even when the wartime war films began to center on soldiers, sailors, and pilots (after Stalingrad), their rank-and-file soldiers and their field officers exhibit a high degree of autonomy and a camaraderie that defies rank. "Spit-and-polish" and other forms of military discipline did not enter the cinematic picture until 1945.

The war films of the late forties were the ones that were most tightly controlled by the central authorities and are, therefore, the most divorced from the reality of wartime. Yet it would be a mistake to dismiss their historical validity entirely. The generals were, of course, central to the war effort, as was Stalin (for good and for ill). Although Stalin's heavy-handed interventions are portrayed in these films as signs of his genius, he was indeed omnipresent. One could also turn this "evidence" on its head, to support the argument that the Supreme Command needed to fight Stalin as well as Hitler in order to win the war. However, the overall *absence* of a war cinema in the late 1940s is as important as the *presence* of Stalin in the few war films that were made.

As a result, after Stalin's death, there was pent-up desire to explore war, especially the Great Patriotic War, on the screen in new ways. Many of the greatest successes of Thaw cinema, whether artistic or commercial, were war films. From the Thaw on, the cinematic space of war narrowed quite dramatically, even as the Great Patriotic became increasingly ritualized in public commemorations; microhistories like *The Living and the Dead* replaced epics like *The Fall of Berlin*. As the war's history was cast in stone, literally as well as figuratively, war films became more iconoclastic and individualized, even after Khrushchev's ouster and the return of more stringent film censorship.

One way to demonstrate this point is to look at how the Battle of Stalingrad is dissected in films like *Burning Snow* and *They Fought for the Motherland*. In both, the story of Stalingrad is told from the ground level, without any sense of the larger scheme, in other words, in defiant opposition to *The Great Turning Point* and *The Battle of Stalingrad*. Local histories of the war like

Burning Snow provide a partial picture but one that is more significant than that in *The Great Turning Point*. Most soldiers—and their lieutenants—fight and die without fully understanding or experiencing the large-scale operational strategies.

Another hallmark of the post-Stalin combat film was its focus on soldiers who were young, unprepared, and frightened. In these films, the kids are often placed in leadership positions, left to their own devices. They mostly die. To the postwar generation, this sacrifice is more heartbreaking and pointless than heroic, especially after the debunking of Stalin as a military genius.

Although combat films continued to be the most common type of Soviet war film, home front movies also humanized the war effort from the midfifties on. Films set in the occupation were relatively rare, but stories situated in the evacuation and the siege of Leningrad allowed directors to explore the impact of war on noncombatants, especially children. The soldier-on-leave variant provided another window on the world behind the lines.

The increasing focus in the post-Stalin war films on collaborators and POWs and their postwar fates is also noteworthy. Millions of political prisoners were released from the Gulag in the 1950s; many were formally rehabilitated, which provided concrete evidence of what some had long suspected—that most "enemies of the people" were in fact innocent. For believers, however, this news was devastating. Whom to believe? What to believe? If so many were innocent, what had the vast network of spies, informers, police, and intelligence officers been doing all these years? Long before academic historians in the USSR could turn to these painful issues, Soviet filmmakers were exploring them and bringing the crimes of the Stalin era to the attention of millions of people.

Film as Political Discourse

In the Soviet era, as we have seen through the lens of war films, movies might be banned, but filmmakers were never automatons. Even in the worst of times, there was much genuine humanity in Soviet cinema. Because war and wartime have built-in pathos and patriotism, it was arguably easier for directors to combine humanism and political correctness in war films than it was in other genres. Because Soviet cinema was a nationalized industry in an authoritarian state, movies were always "political," especially when they seemed not to be.[9] Subtle deviations from the norm are therefore exceptionally important, as when Zakhar Agranenko inserted one minute of documentary footage of starving Leningraders during the blockade into his otherwise unremarkable film *The Leningrad Symphony.*

By comparison, post-Soviet Russia is a "free" society, in which films need not deliver their subversive political messages subtly (often to the detriment of their artistic impact). The themes of the Russo-Soviet war film have continued in the new Russian cinema. The prisoners theme dominates films about World War II, not only in the relentlessly grim serials like *Penal Battalion* and *Major Pugachov's Last Battle* but also in the upbeat fairy tale *The Cuckoo,* where the protagonists are both accused men: Veiko chained to a rock as a coward, Ivan arrested for crimes unknown.

The prisoners theme continues in post-Soviet films about the Afghan and Chechen wars. The emphasis has shifted, however, reflecting the alienation of Russian society from the military. In the glasnost era, the brutal conditions in the Soviet army, especially the hazing and deaths of recruits, reached public attention. Although scenes of training camp hazing dominate the first half of *Company 9*, a main focus of the Afghan and Chechen films has been the betrayal of Russian soldiers by their commanders and by the state. The POWs in *The Peshawar Waltz*, *The Prisoner of the Caucasus*, and *War* are all abandoned by their country; *The Muslim* features a former POW who does not want to be repatriated. In *Checkpoint*, the Russian commanders randomly select a soldier to be sacrificed to the Chechen civilian authorities. The degree of disaffection from the military (and, by association, the state) that these recent films represent is pronounced.

Even though *Company 9* ostensibly concerns the Soviet war in Afghanistan, the setting is disingenuous. Few viewers—and certainly none with draft-age sons—could believe that the Russian army has resolved its problems. It is not obvious that sentimental wartime romances like *The Star* can counteract the effects of *Company 9* and create the patriotic culture that the Putin government so ardently desires.

When I began the research for this book, I secretly hoped for a story with a linear plot, clearly defined characters, and a tidy, if not happy, ending. As we have seen, binary categories like art/entertainment, subversive/conformist, true/false are only partly useful tools for analysis of Russian cinema. Thankfully for those who love Russian film, it has proved hard to subjugate, even when the subject seems tailor-made to conform to the state's policies.

FILMOGRAPHY

By Title

English title	Russian title	Director	Year	War
And the Dawns Are Quiet Here	A zori zdes' tikhie	Rostotskii, Stanislav	1972	WWII
Angel	Angel/Nachalo nevedomogo veka, 2	Smirnov, Andrei	1967	Civil War
Arsenal	Arsenal	Dovzhenko, Aleksandr	1929	WWI
Ascent	Voskhozhdenie	Shepitko, Larissa	1976	WWII
At a Dangerous Line	U opasnoi cherty	Georgiev, V.	1983	WWII
At Home among Strangers, a Stranger at Home	Svoi sredi chuzhikh, chuzhoi sredi svoikh	Mikhalkov, Nikita	1974	Civil War
Autumn Season	Barkhatnoi sezon	Pavlovich, V.	1978	Spain
Ballad of a Soldier	Ballada o soldate	Chukhrai, Grigorii	1959	WWII
Baltic Skies, 2 parts	Baltiiskoe nebo	Vengerov, Vladimir	1960	WWII
Battle for Berlin	Bitva za Berlin/ Osvobozhdenie, 4	Ozerov, Iurii	1971	WWII
Battle of Local Significance	Boi mestnogo znachenie/ A zori zdes' tikhie, 2	Rostotskii, Stanislav	1972	WWII
Battle of Stalingrad	Stalingradskaia bitva	Petrov, Vladimir	1949	WWII
Belorussian Station	Belorusskii vokzal	Smirnov, Andrei	1972	WWII
Berlin	Berlin	Raizman, Iulii	1945	WWII
Borderlands	Okraina	Barnet, Boris	1933	WWI
Brave People	Smelye liudi	Iudin, Konstantin	1950	WWII
Breakthrough	Proryv/Osvobozhdenie, 2	Ozerov, Iurii	1968	WWII
Brother	Brat'	Balabanov, Aleksei	1997	Chechnya
Burn, Burn, My Star	Gori, gori, moia zvezda	Mitta, Aleksandr	1969	Civil War
Burning Snow	Goriachii sneg	Egiazarov, Gavriil	1972	WWII
Cadets	Kursanty	Kavun, Andrei	2005	WWII
Celestial Sloth	Nebesnyi tikhokhod	Timoshenko, Semën	1945	WWII
Chapaev	Chapaev	Vasilev, Georgii and Sergei	1934	Civil War
Checkpoint	Blokpost	Rogozhkin, Aleksandr	1998	Chechnya
Chief of Chukchi	Nachal'nik Chukotki	Melnikov, Vitalii	1966	Civil War
Chronicle of a Dive Bomber	Khronika pikiruiushchego bombardirovshchika	Birman, Naum	1967	WWII
Cities and Years	Goroda i gody	Cherviakov, Evgenii	1930	Civil War
Clear Skies	Chistoe nebo	Chukhrai, Grigorii	1961	WWII
Cocktail for Dudaev	Kokteil' dlia Dudaeva	Metlina, N.; Pankratov, V.	2004	Chechnya
Come and See	Idi i smotri	Klimov, Elem	1985	WWII
Commander of the Lucky "Pike"	Komandir schastlivoi "Shchuki"	Volchek, Vladimir	1972	WWII
Commissar	Kommissar	Askoldov, Aleksandr	1966	Civil War
Communist	Kommunist	Raizman, Iulii	1958	Civil War

English title	Russian title	Director	Year	War
Company 9	Deviataia rota	Bondarchuk, Fëdor	2005	Afghan
Cranes Are Flying	Letiat zhuravli	Kalatozov, Mikhail	1957	WWII
Crown of the Russian Empire	Korona rossiiskoi imperii	Keosaian, Edmond	1970–71	Civil War
Cuckoo	Kukushka	Rogozhkin, Aleksandr	2002	WWII
Death Bay	Bukhta smerti	Room, Abram	1926	Civil War
Defeat of the German-Fascist Troops near Moscow	Razgrom nemetsko-fashistskikh voisk pod Moskvy	Varlamov, L.; Kopalin, I.	1942	WWII
Directing the Main Blow	Napravlenie glavnogo duga/ Osvobozhdenie, 3	Ozerov, Iurii	1970	WWII
Echelon	Eshelon	Arsenev, Vladilen	2005	WWII
Elusive Avengers	Neulovimye mstiteli	Keosaian, Edmond	1967	Civil War
End of St. Petersburg	Konets Sankt-Peterburga	Pudovkin, Vsevolod	1927	WWI
Everyone Knows Kadkin	Kadkina vsiakii znaet	Vekhotko, Anatolii	1976	WWII
Exploits of an Intelligence Officer	Podvig razvedchika	Barnet, Boris	1947	WWII
Fall of Berlin	Padenie Berlina	Chiaureli, Mikhail	1949	WWII
Fate of a Man	Sud'ba cheloveka	Bondarchuk, Sergei	1959	WWII
Father of a Soldier	Otets soldata	Chkheidze, Rezo	1965	WWII
First after God	Pervyi posle Boga	Chiginskii, Vasilii	2005	WWII
Flaming Arc	Ognënnaia duga/Osvobozhdenie, 1	Ozerov, Iurii	1968	WWII
Flight	Beg	Alov, A.; Naumov, V.	1970	Civil War
Forty-first	Sorok pervyi	Protazanov, Iakov	1927	Civil War
Forty-first	Sorok pervyi	Chukhrai, Grigorii	1956	Civil War
Fourth Year of the War Came	Shël chetvërtyi god voiny	Nikolaenko, Georgii	1983	WWII
Fragment of the Empire	Oblomok imperii	Ermler, Fridrikh	1929	WWI
Girlfriends	Podrugi	Arnshtam, Leo	1935	Civil War
Glory to Us, Death to the Enemy	Slava nam—smert'vragam	Bauer, Evgenii	1914	WWI
Gold	Zoloto	Viatich-Berezhnykh, D.	1969	WWII
Great Turning Point	Velikii perelom	Ermler, Fridrikh	1945	WWII
Hard Little Nut	Krepkii oreshëk	Vul'fovich, Teodor	1967	WWII
Heir to Genghis Khan	Potomok Chingis-khana	Pudovkin, Vsevolod	1928	Civil War
His Excellency's Adjutant	Adiutant ego prevoskhoditel'stva	Tashkov, Evgenii	1969	Civil War
Homecoming	Vozvrashchenie	Chubakova, Tatiana	1987	Afghan
House I Live In	Dom v ktorom ia zhivu	Kulidzhanov, Lev	1957	WWII
House of Fools	Dom durakov	Konchalovskii, Andrei	2003	Chechnya
In June of '41	V iiune 41go	Ptashuk, Mikhail	2004	WWII
In the Constellation of Taurus	V sozvedii byka	Todorovskii, Pëtr	2003	WWII
In the Dangerous Backwoods	V streliaiushchei glushi	Khotinenko, Vladimir	1986	Civil War
In the Second Echelon	V vtorom eshelon/A zori zdes' tikhie, 1	Rostotskii, Stanislav	1972	WWII
Intervention	Interventsiia	Poloka, Gennadii	1967	Civil War
Invasion	Nashestvie	Room, Abram	1944	WWII

English title	Russian title	Director	Year	War
It Was the Month of May	Byl' mesiats mai	Khutsiev, Marlen	1970	WWII
Ivan Nikulin, Russian Sailor	Ivan Nikulin, russkii matros	Savchenko, Igor	1944	WWII
Ivan's Childhood	Ivanovo detstvo	Tarkovskii, Andrei	1962	WWII
Kindergarten	Detskii sad	Evtushenko, Evgenii	1984	WWII
King, the Law, and Freedom	Korol', zakon, i svoboda	Chardynin, Pëtr	1914	WWI
Konstantin Zaslonov	Konstantin Zaslonov	Faintsimmer, A.; Korsh-Sablin, V.	1949	WWII
Last Line	Poslednii rubezh/Shchit i mech, 4	Basov, Vladimir	1967–68	WWII
Last Storm/Liberation, 5	Poslednii shturm/Osvobozhdenie, 5	Ozerov, Iurii	1971	WWII
Last Train	Poslednii poezd	German, Aleksei Jr.	2004	WWII
Legal Marriage	Zakonnyi brak	Mkrtchian, Albert	1985	WWII
Leningrad Symphony	Leningradskaia simfoniia	Agranenko, Zakhar	1957	WWII
Liberation	Osvobozhdenie	Ozerov, Iurii	1968–71	WWII
Lily of Belgium	Liliia Belgii	Starewicz, Władysław	1915	WWI
Little Red Devils	Krasnye d'iavoliata	Perestiani, Ivan	1923	Civil War
Living and the Dead	Zhivye i mërtvye	Stolper, Aleksandr	1963	WWII
Major Pugachov's Last Battle	Poslednii boi maiora Pugachëva	Fatianov, Vladimir	2005	WWII
Malakhov Hill	Malakhov Kurgan	Zarkhi, A.; Kheifits, I.	1944	WWII
Man of War	Chelovek voiny	Muradov, Aleksei	2005	WWII
Mashenka	Mashen'ka	Raizman, Iulii	1942	Winter War
Military Machine Crew	Ekipazh mashiny boevoi	Vasilevskii, Vitalii	1983	WWII
Moonzund	Moonzund	Muratov, Aleksandr	1987	WWI
Moscow Skies	Nebo Moskvy	Raizman, Iulii	1944	WWII
Murder on Dante Street	Ubiistvo na ulitse Dante	Romm, Mikhail	1956	WWII
Muslim	Musulmanin	Khotinenko, Vladimir	1995	Afghan
My Dear Man	Dorogoi moi chelovek	Kheifits, Iosif	1958	WWII
New Adventures of the Elusive	Novye prikliucheniia neulovimykh	Keosaian, Edmond	1968	Civil War
No Crossing under Fire	V ogne broda net	Panfilov, Gleb	1969	Civil War
Not Subject to Appeal	Obzhalovaniiu ne podlezhit/ Shchit i mech, 3	Basov, Vladimir	1967–68	WWII
Occupation. Mysterium	Okkupatsiia. Misterii	Kudinenko, Andrei	2003	WWII
Officers	Offitsery	Rogovoi, V.	1971	WWII
On the Road to Berlin	Na puti v Berlin	Ershov, Mikhail	1969	WWII
On the Unknown Heights	Na besymiannoi vysote	Nikiforov, Viacheslav	2003	WWII
Once at Night	Odnazhdii nochiu/Nashi devushki, 2	Kozintsev, Grigorii	1942	WWII
Once There Was a Girl	Zhila-byla devochka	Eisymont, Viktor	1944	WWII
Only the Old Go to Battle	V boi idut odni stariki	Bykov, Leonid	1973	WWII
Our Girls	Nashi devushki	Room, A.; Kozintsev, G.	1942	WWII
Our Own	Svoi	Meskhiev, Dmitrii	2004	WWII
Pavel Korchagin	Pavel Korchagin	Alov, A.; Naumov, V.	1956	Civil War
Peace to Him Who Enters	Mir vkhodiashchemu	Alov, A.; Naumov, V.	1961	WWII
Penal Battalion	Shtrafbat	Dostal, Nikolai	2004	WWII

English title	Russian title	Director	Year	War
Person No. 217	Chelovek no. 217	Romm, Mikhail	1944	WWII
Peshawar Waltz	Peshavarskii val's	Bekmambetov, Timur	1993	Afghan
Prisoner of the Caucasus	Kavkazkii plennik	Bobrov, Sergei	1996	Chechnya
Property of the Republic	Dostoianie respubliki	Bychkov, Vladimir	1971	Civil War
Purgatory	Chistilishche	Nevzorov, Aleksandr	1997	Chechnya
Quagmire	Triasina	Chukhrai, Grigorii	1977	WWII
Quiet Don	Tikhii Don	Gerasimov, Sergei	1957–58	Civil War
Rainbow	Raduga	Donskoi, Mark	1943	WWII
Red Choir	Krasnaia kapella	Aravin, Aleksandr	2004	WWII
Regional Party Secretary	Sekretar raikoma	Pyrev, Ivan	1942	WWII
Remember Your Name	Pomni imia svoë	Kolosov, Sergei	1974	WWII
Retribution	Vozmedie	Stolper, Aleksandr	1967	WWII
Riders	Vsadniki	Savchenko, Igor	1939	Civil War
Saboteur	Diversant	Maliukov, Andrei	2004	WWII
Seventeen Moments of Spring	Semnadtsat' mgnovenii vesny	Lioznova, Tatiana	1973	WWII
Shchors	Shchors	Dovzhenko, Aleksandr	1939	Civil War
She Defends the Motherland	Ona zashchishchaet rodinu	Ermler, Fridrikh	1943	WWII
Shield and Sword	Shchit i mech	Basov, Vladimir	1967–68	WWII
Six o' Clock in the Evening after the War	V shest' chasov vechera posle voiny	Pyrev, Ivan	1944	WWII
Slave of Love	Raba liubvyi	Mikhalkov, Nikita	1975	Civil War
Snipers on the Towers	Snaipery na bashniakh	Ivannikov, Maksim	2004	WWII
Sprays of Champagne	Bryzgi shampanskogo	Govorukhin, Stanislav	1988	WWII
Star	Zvezda	Lebedev, Nikolai	2002	WWII
Story of a Real Man	Povest' o nastoiashchem cheloveke	Stolper, Aleksandr	1948	WWII
Tehran-43	Tegeran-43	Alov, A.; Naumov, V.	1980	WWII
There the Soldiers Went	Aty-baty shli soldaty	Bykov, Leonid	1976	WWII
They Fought for the Motherland	Oni srazhalis' za rodinu	Bondarchuk, Sergei	1975	WWII
Third Blow	Tretii udar'	Savchenko, Igor	1948	WWII
Time to Gather Stones	Vremia sobirat' kamni	Karelin, Aleksei	2005	WWII
To Survive Orders	Prikazanov—vyzhit/Shchit i mech, 2	Basov, Vladimir	1967–68	WWII
Torpedo Bombers	Torpedonostsy	Aranovich, Semën	1983	WWII
Trial on the Road	Proverka na doragakh	German, Aleksei	1971	WWII
Tripol Tragedy	Tripol'skaia tragediia	Anoshchenko, Aleksandr	1926	Civil War
Twenty Days without War	Dvadtsat' dnei bez voiny	German, Aleksei	1976	WWII
Twenty-Six Commissars	Dvadtsat shest kommissarov	Shengelaia, Nikolai	1932	Civil War
Two Comrades Served	Sluzhili dva tovarishcha	Karelov, Evgenii	1968	Civil War
Two Days	Dva dnia	Stabovoi, Georgii	1927	Civil War
Two Fyodors	Dva Fedora	Khutsiev, Marlen	1958	WWII
Two Warriors	Dva boitsa	Lukov, Leonid	1943	WWII
Unforgettable Year 1919	Nezabyvaemyigod 1919	Chiaureli, Mikhail	1950	Civil War
Unknown Blockade	Neizvestnaia blokada	Ivannikov, Maksim	2004	WWII
Unknown Pages from the Life of a Scout	Neizvestnye stranitsy iz zhizni razvedchika	Chebotarëv, V.	1990	WWII

English title	Russian title	Director	Year	War
Unofficial Business	Nesluzhebnye zadanye	Vorobev, Vitalii	2004	WWII
Volunteers	Dobrovol'tsy	Egorov, Iurii	1958	WWII
Wait for Me	Zhdi menia	Stolper, Aleksandr	1943	WWII
War	Voina	Balabanov, Aleksei	2002	Chechnya
Wartime Romance	Voenno-polevoi roman	Todorovskii, Pëtr	1983	WWII
We Are from Kronstadt	My iz Kronshtadta	Dzigan, Efim	1936	Civil War
We Draw Fire on Ourselves	Vyzyvaem ogon' na sebia	Kolosov, Sergei	1963–64	WWII
Wedding in Malinovka	Svad'ba v Malinovke	Tytyshkin, Andrei	1967	Civil War
White Sun of the Desert	Beloe solntse pustyni	Motyl, Vladimir	1969	Civil War
Wild Honey	Dikii mëd	Chebotarëv, V.	1966	WWII
Wind	Veter	Sheffer, L.	1926	Civil War
Wings	Krylia	Shepitko, Larissa	1966	WWII
Without the Right to Be Oneself	Bez prava byt soboi/Shchit i mech, 1	Basov, Vladimir	1967–68	WWII
Wounded Birds	Podranki	Gubenko, Nikolai	1977	WWII
Young Guard	Molodaia gvardiia	Gerasimov, Sergei	1947	WWII
Zhenya, Zhenechka and "Katiusha"	Zhenia, Zhenechka i "Katiusha"	Motyl, Vladimir	1967	WWII
Zoya	Zoia	Arnshtam, Leo	1944	WWII

By Director

Director	Year	English title	Russian title	War
Agranenko, Zakhar	1957	Leningrad Symphony	Leningradskaia simfoniia	WWII
Alov, A.; Naumov, V.	1956	Pavel Korchagin	Pavel Korchagin	Civil War
Alov, A.; Naumov, V.	1961	Peace to Him Who Enters	Mir vkhodiashchemu	WWII
Alov, A.; Naumov, V.	1970	Flight	Beg	Civil War
Alov, A.; Naumov, V.	1980	Tehran-43	Tegeran-43	WWII
Anoshchenko, Aleksandr	1926	Tripol Tragedy	Tripol'skaia tragediia	Civil War
Aranovich, Semën	1983	Torpedo Bombers	Torpedonostsy	WWII
Aravin, Aleksandr	2004	Red Choir	Krasnaia kapella	WWII
Arnshtam, Leo	1935	Girlfriends	Podrugi	Civil War
Arnshtam, Leo	1944	Zoya	Zoia	WWII
Arsenev, Vladilen	2005	Echelon	Eshelon	WWII
Askoldov, Aleksandr	1966	Commissar	Kommissar	Civil War
Balabanov, Aleksei	1997	Brother	Brat'	Chechnya
Balabanov, Aleksei	2002	War	Voina	Chechnya
Barnet, Boris	1933	Borderlands	Okraina	WWI
Barnet, Boris	1947	Exploits of an Intelligence Officer	Podvig razvedchika	WWII
Basov, Vladimir	1967–68	Last Line	Poslednii rubezh/Shchit i mech, 4	WWII
Basov, Vladimir	1967–68	Not Subject to Appeal	Obzhalovaniiu ne podlezhit/Shchit i mech, 3	WWII
Basov, Vladimir	1967–68	Shield and Sword	Shchit i mech	WWII

Director	Year	English title	Russian title	War
Basov, Vladimir	1967–68	To Survive Orders	Prikazanov—vyzhit/Shchit i mech, 2	WWII
Basov, Vladimir	1967–68	Without the Right to Be Oneself	Bez prava byt soboi/Shchit i mech, 1	WWII
Bauer, Evgenii	1914	Glory to Us, Death to the Enemy	Slava nam—smert'vragam	WWI
Bekmambetov, Timur	1993	Peshawar Waltz	Peshavarskii val's	Afghan
Birman, Naum	1967	Chronicle of a Dive Bomber	Khronika pikiruiushchego bombardirovshchika	WWII
Bobrov, Sergei	1996	Prisoner of the Caucasus	Kavkazkii plennik	Chechnya
Bondarchuk, Fëdor	2005	Company 9	Deviataia rota	Afghan
Bondarchuk, Sergei	1959	Fate of a Man	Sud'ba cheloveka	WWII
Bondarchuk, Sergei	1975	They Fought for the Motherland	Oni srazhalis' za rodinu	WWII
Bychkov, Vladimir	1971	Property of the Republic	Dostoianie respubliki	Civil War
Bykov, Leonid	1973	Only the Old Go to Battle	V boi idut odni stariki	WWII
Bykov, Leonid	1976	There the Soldiers Went	Aty-baty shli soldaty	WWII
Chardynin, Petr	1914	King, the Law, and Freedom	Korol', zakon, i svoboda	WWI
Chebotarëv, Vladimir	1966	Wild Honey	Dikii mëd	WWII
Chebotarëv, Vladimir	1990	Unknown Pages from the Life of a Scout	Neizvestnye stranitsy iz zhizni razvedchika	WWII
Cherviakov, Evgenii	1930	Cities and Years	Goroda i gody	Civil War
Chiaureli, Mikhail	1949	Fall of Berlin	Padenie Berlina	WWII
Chiaureli, Mikhail	1950	Unforgettable Year 1919	Nezabyvaemyigod 1919	Civil War
Chiginskii, Vasilii	2005	First after God	Pervyi posle Boga	WWII
Chkheidze, Rezo	1965	Father of a Soldier	Otets soldata	WWII
Chubakova, Tatiana	1987	Homecoming	Vozvrashchenie	Afghan
Chukhrai, Grigorii	1956	Forty-first	Sorok pervyi	Civil War
Chukhrai, Grigorii	1959	Ballad of a Soldier	Ballada o soldate	WWII
Chukhrai, Grigorii	1961	Clear Skies	Chistoe nebo	WWII
Chukhrai, Grigorii	1977	Quagmire	Triasina	WWII
Donskoi, Mark	1943	Rainbow	Raduga	WWII
Dostal, Nikolai	2004	Penal Battalion	Shtrafbat	WWII
Dovzhenko, Aleksandr	1929	Arsenal	Arsenal	WWI
Dovzhenko, Aleksandr	1939	Shchors	Shchors	Civil War
Dzigan, Efim	1936	We Are from Kronstadt	My iz Kronshtadta	Civil War
Egiazarov, Gavriil	1972	Burning Snow	Goriachii sneg	WWII
Egorov, Iurii	1958	Volunteers	Dobrovol'tsy	WWII
Eisymont, Viktor	1944	Once There Was a Girl	Zhila-byla devochka	WWII
Ermler, Fridrikh	1929	Fragment of the Empire	Oblomok imperii	WWI
Ermler, Fridrikh	1943	She Defends the Motherland	Ona zashchishchaet rodinu	WWII
Ermler, Fridrikh	1945	Great Turning Point	Velikii perelom	WWII
Ershov, Mikhail	1969	On the Road to Berlin	Na puti v Berlin	WWII
Evtushenko, Evgenii	1984	Kindergarten	Detskii sad	WWII
Faintsimmer, A.; Korsh-Sablin, V.	1949	Konstantin Zaslonov	Konstantin Zaslonov	WWII
Fatianov, Vladimir	2005	Major Pugachov's Last Battle	Poslednii boi maiora Pugachëva	WWII

Director	Year	English title	Russian title	War
Georgiev, V.	1983	At a Dangerous Line	U opasnoi cherty	WWII
Gerasimov, Sergei	1947	Young Guard	Molodaia gvardiia	WWII
Gerasimov, Sergei	1957–58	Quiet Don	Tikhii Don	Civil War
German, Aleksei	1971	Trial on the Road	Proverka na doragakh	WWII
German, Aleksei	1976	Twenty Days without War	Dvadtsat' dnei bez voiny	WWII
German, Aleksei Jr.	2004	Last Train	Poslednii poezd	WWII
Govorukhin, Stanislav	1988	Sprays of Champagne	Bryzgi shampanskogo	WWII
Gubenko, Nikolai	1977	Wounded Birds	Podranki	WWII
Iudin, Konstantin	1950	Brave People	Smelye liudi	WWII
Ivannikov, Maksim	2004	Snipers on the Towers	Snaipery na bashniakh	WWII
Ivannikov, Maksim	2004	Unknown Blockade	Neizvestnaia blokada	WWII
Kalatozov, Mikhail	1957	Cranes Are Flying	Letiat zhuravli	WWII
Karelin, Aleksei	2005	Time to Gather Stones	Vremia sobirat' kamni	WWII
Karelov, Evgenii	1968	Two Comrades Served	Sluzhili dva tovarishcha	Civil War
Kavun, Andrei	2005	Cadets	Kursanty	WWII
Keosaian, Edmond	1967	Elusive Avengers	Neulovimye mstiteli	Civil War
Keosaian, Edmond	1968	New Adventures of the Elusive	Novye prikliucheniia neulovimykh	Civil War
Keosaian, Edmond	1970–71	Crown of the Russian Empire	Korona rossiiskoi imperii	Civil War
Kheifits, Iosif	1958	My Dear Man	Dorogoi moi chelovek	WWII
Khotinenko, Vladimir	1986	In the Dangerous Backwoods	V streliaiushchei glushi	Civil War
Khotinenko, Vladimir	1995	Muslim	Musulmanin	Afghan
Khutsiev, Marlen	1958	Two Fyodors	Dva Fedora	WWII
Khutsiev, Marlen	1970	It Was the Month of May	Byl' mesiats mai	WWII
Klimov, Elem	1985	Come and See	Idi i smotri	WWII
Kolosov, Sergei	1963–64	We Draw Fire on Ourselves	Vyzyvaem ogon' na sebia	WWII
Kolosov, Sergei	1974	Remember Your Name	Pomni imia svoë	WWII
Konchalovskii, Andrei	2003	House of Fools	Dom durakov	Chechnya
Kozintsev, Grigorii	1942	Once at Night	Odnazhdii nochiu/ Nashi devushki, 2	WWII
Kudinenko, Andrei	2003	Occupation. Mysterium	Okkupatsiia. Misterii	WWII
Kulidzhanov, Lev	1957	House I Live In	Dom v ktorom ia zhivu	WWII
Lebedev, Nikolai	2002	Star	Zvezda	WWII
Lioznova, Tatiana	1973	Seventeen Moments of Spring	Semnadtsat' mgnovenii vesny	WWII
Lukov, Leonid	1943	Two Warriors	Dva boitsa	WWII
Maliukov, Andrei	2004	Saboteur	Diversant	WWII
Melnikov, Vitalii	1966	Chief of Chukchi	Nachal'nik Chukotki	Civil War
Meskhiev, Dmitrii	2004	Our Own	Svoi	WWII
Metlina, N.; Pankratov, V.	2004	Cocktail for Dudaev	Kokteil' dlia Dudaeva	Chechnya
Mikhalkov, Nikita	1974	At Home among Strangers, a Stranger at Home	Svoi sredi chuzhikh, chuzhoi sredi svoikh	Civil War
Mikhalkov, Nikita	1975	Slave of Love	Raba liubvyi	Civil War
Mitta, Aleksandr	1969	Burn, Burn, My Star	Gori, gori, moia zvezda	Civil War
Mkrtchian, Albert	1985	Legal Marriage	Zakonnyi brak	WWII

Director	Year	English title	Russian title	War
Motyl, Vladimir	1967	Zhenya, Zhenechka and "Katiusha"	Zhenia, Zhenechka i "Katiusha"	WWII
Motyl, Vladimir	1969	White Sun of the Desert	Beloe solntse pustyni	Civil War
Muradov, Aleksei	2005	Man of War	Chelovek voiny	WWII
Muratov, Aleksandr	1987	Moonzund	Moonzund	WWI
Nevzorov, Aleksandr	1997	Purgatory	Chistilishche	Chechnya
Nikiforov, Viacheslav	2003	On the Unknown Heights	Na besmiannoi vysote	WWII
Nikolaenko, Georgii	1983	Fourth Year of the War Came	Shël chetvërtyi god voiny	WWII
Ozerov, Iurii	1968	Breakthrough/Liberation, 2	Proryv/Osvobozhdenie, 2	WWII
Ozerov, Iurii	1968	Flaming Arc/Liberation, 1	Ognënnaia duga/ Osvobozhdenie, 1	WWII
Ozerov, Iurii	1970	Directing the Main Blow/ Liberation, 3	Napravlenie glavnogo duga/ Osvobozhdenie, 3	WWII
Ozerov, Iurii	1971	Battle for Berlin/ Liberation, 4	Bitva za Berlin/ Osvobozhdenie, 4	WWII
Ozerov, Iurii	1971	Last Storm/Liberation, 5	Poslednii shturm/ Osvobozhdenie, 5	WWII
Ozerov, Iurii	1968–71	Liberation	Osvobozhdenie	WWII
Panfilov, Gleb	1969	No Crossing under Fire	V ogne broda net	Civil War
Pavlovich, V.	1978	Autumn Season	Barkhatnoi sezon	Spain
Perestiani, Ivan	1923	Little Red Devils	Krasnye d'iavoliata	Civil War
Petrov, Vladimir	1949	Battle of Stalingrad	Stalingradskaia bitva	WWII
Poloka, Gennadii	1967	Intervention	Interventsiia	Civil War
Protazanov, Iakov	1927	Forty-first	Sorok pervyi	Civil War
Ptashuk, Mikhail	2004	In June of '41	V iiune 41go	WWII
Pudovkin, Vsevolod	1927	End of St. Petersburg	Konets Sankt-Peterburga	WWI
Pudovkin, Vsevolod	1928	Heir to Genghis Khan	Potomok Chingis-khana	Civil War
Pyrev, Ivan	1942	Regional Party Secretary	Sekretar raikoma	WWII
Pyrev, Ivan	1944	Six o' Clock in the Evening after the War	V shest' chasov vechera posle voiny	WWII
Raizman, Iulii	1942	Mashenka	Mashen'ka	Winter War
Raizman, Iulii	1944	Moscow Skies	Nebo Moskvy	WWII
Raizman, Iulii	1945	Berlin	Berlin	WWII
Raizman, Iulii	1958	Communist	Kommunist	Civil War
Rogovoi, V.	1971	Officers	Offitsery	WWII
Rogozhkin, Aleksandr	1998	Checkpoint	Blokpost	Chechnya
Rogozhkin, Aleksandr	2002	Cuckoo	Kukushka	WWII
Romm, Mikhail	1944	Person No. 217	Chelovek no. 217	WWII
Romm, Mikhail	1956	Murder on Dante Street	Ubiistvo na ulitse Dante	WWII
Room, A.; Kozintsev, G.	1942	Our Girls	Nashi devushki	WWII
Room, Abram	1926	Death Bay	Bukhta smerti	Civil War
Room, Abram	1944	Invasion	Nashestvie	WWII
Rostotskii, Stanislav	1972	And the Dawns Are Quiet Here	A zori zdes' tikhie	WWII
Rostotskii, Stanislav	1972	Battle of Local Significance And the Dawns, 2	Boi mestnogo znachenie/ A zori zdes tikhie, 2	WWII

Director	Year	English title	Russian title	War
Rostotskii, Stanislav	1972	In the Second Echelon And the Dawns, 1	V vtorom eshelon/A zori zdes' tikhie, 1	WWII
Savchenko, Igor	1939	Riders	Vsadniki	Civil War
Savchenko, Igor	1944	Ivan Nikulin, Russian Sailor	Ivan Nikulin, russkii matros	WWII
Savchenko, Igor	1948	Third Blow	Tretii udar'	WWII
Sheffer, L.	1926	Wind	Veter	Civil War
Shengelaia, Nikolai	1932	Twenty-Six Commissars	Dvadtsat shest kommissarov	Civil War
Shepitko, Larissa	1966	Wings	Krylia	WWII
Shepitko, Larissa	1976	Ascent	Voskhozhdenie	WWII
Smirnov, Andrei	1967	Angel	Angel/Nachalo nevedomogo veka, 2	Civil War
Smirnov, Andrei	1972	Belorussian Station	Belorusskii vokzal	WWII
Stabovoi, Georgii	1927	Two Days	Dva dnia	Civil War
Starewicz, Władysław	1915	Lily of Belgium	Liliia Belgii	WWI
Stolper, Aleksandr	1943	Wait for Me	Zhdi menia	WWII
Stolper, Aleksandr	1948	Story of a Real Man	Povest'o nastoiashchem cheloveke	WWII
Stolper, Aleksandr	1963	Living and the Dead	Zhivye i mërtvye	WWII
Stolper, Aleksandr	1967	Retribution	Vozmedie	WWII
Tarkovskii, Andrei	1962	Ivan's Childhood	Ivanovo detstvo	WWII
Tashkov, Evgenii	1969	His Excellency's Adjutant	Adiutant ego prevoskhoditel'stva	Civil War
Timoshenko, Semën	1945	Celestial Sloth	Nebesnyi tikhokhod	WWII
Todorovskii, Pëtr	1983	Wartime Romance	Voenno-polevoi roman	WWII
Todorovskii, Pëtr	2003	In the Constellation of Taurus	V sozvedii byka	WWII
Tytyshkin, Andrei	1967	Wedding in Malinovka	Svad'ba v Malinovke	Civil War
Varlamov, L.; Kopalin, I.	1942	Defeat of the German-Fascist Troops near Moscow	Razgrom nemetsko-fashitskikh voisk pod Moskvy	WWII
Vasilev, Georgii and Sergei	1934	Chapaev	Chapaev	Civil War
Vasilevskii, Vitalii	1983	Military Machine Crew	Ekipazh mashiny boevoi	WWII
Vekhotko, Anatolii	1976	Everyone Knows Kadkin	Kadkina vsiakii znaet	WWII
Vengerov, Vladamir	1960	Baltic Skies	Baltiiskoe nebo	WWII
Viatich-Berezhnykh, Damir	1969	Gold	Zoloto	WWII
Volchek, Vladimir	1972	Commander of the Lucky Pike	Komandir schastlivoi "Shchuki"	WWII
Vorobev, Vitalii	2004	Unofficial Business	Nesluzhebnye zadanye	WWII
Vul'fovich, Teodor	1967	Hard Little Nut	Krepkii oreshëk	WWII
Zarkhi, A.; Kheifitz, I.	1944	Malakhov Hill	Malakhov Kurgan	WWII

Note: For Yegiazarov, see Egiazarov; Yegorov, see Egorov; Yevtushenko, see Evtushenko; Yudin, see Iudin.

By War

War	English title	Russian title	Director	Year
Afghan	Homecoming	Vozvrashchenie	Chubakova, Tatiana	1987
Afghan	Peshawar Waltz	Peshavarskii val's	Bekmambetov, Timur	1993

War	English title	Russian title	Director	Year
Afghan	Muslim	Musilmanin	Khotinenko, Vladimir	1995
Afghan	Company 9	Deviataia rota	Bondarchuk, Fëdor	2005
Chechnya	Prisoner of the Caucasus	Kavkazkii plennik	Bobrov, Sergei	1996
Chechnya	Brother	Brat'	Balabanov, Aleksei	1997
Chechnya	Purgatory	Chistilishche	Nevzorov, Aleksandr	1997
Chechnya	Checkpoint	Blokpost	Rogozhkin, Aleksandr	1998
Chechnya	War	Voina	Balabanov, Aleksei	2002
Chechnya	House of Fools	Dom durakov	Konchalovskii, Andrei	2003
Chechnya	Cocktail for Dudaev	Kokteil' dlia Dudaeva	Metlina, N.; Pankratov, V.	2004
Civil War	Little Red Devils	Krasnye d'iavoliata	Perestiani, Ivan	1923
Civil War	Death Bay	Bukhta smerti	Room, Abram	1926
Civil War	Tripol Tragedy	Tripol'skaia tragediia	Anoshchenko, Aleksandr	1926
Civil War	Wind	Veter	Sheffer, L.	1926
Civil War	Forty-first	Sorok pervyi	Protazanov, Iakov	1927
Civil War	Two Days	Dva dnia	Stabovoi, Georgii	1927
Civil War	Heir to Genghis Khan	Potomok Chingis-khana	Pudovkin, Vsevolod	1928
Civil War	Cities and Years	Goroda i gody	Cherviakov, Evgenii	1930
Civil War	Twenty-Six Commissars	Dvadtsat shest kommissarov	Shengelaia, Nikolai	1932
Civil War	Chapaev	Chapaev	Vasilev, Georgii and Sergei	1934
Civil War	Girlfriends	Podrugi	Arnshtam, Leo	1935
Civil War	We Are from Kronstadt	My iz Kronshtadta	Dzigan, Efim	1936
Civil War	Riders	Vsadniki	Savchenko, Igor	1939
Civil War	Shchors	Shchors	Dovzhenko, Aleksandr	1939
Civil War	Unforgettable Year 1919	Nezabyvaemyigod 1919	Chiaureli, Mikhail	1950
Civil War	Forty-first	Sorok pervyi	Chukhrai, Grigorii	1956
Civil War	Pavel Korchagin	Pavel Korchagin	Alov, A.; Naumov, V.	1956
Civil War	Quiet Don	Tikhii Don	Gerasimov, Sergei	1957–58
Civil War	Communist	Kommunist	Raizman, Iulii	1958
Civil War	Chief of Chukchi	Nachal'nik Chukotki	Melnikov, Vitalii	1966
Civil War	Commissar	Kommissar	Askoldov, Aleksandr	1966
Civil War	Angel	Angel/Nachalo nevedomogo veka, 2	Smirnov, Andrei	1967
Civil War	Elusive Avengers	Neulovimye mstiteli	Keosaian, Edmond	1967
Civil War	Intervention	Interventsiia	Poloka, Gennadii	1967
Civil War	Wedding in Malinovka	Svad'ba v Malinovke	Tytyshkin, Andrei	1967
Civil War	New Adventures of the Elusive	Novye prikliucheniia neulovimykh	Keosaian, Edmond	1968
Civil War	Two Comrades Served	Sluzhili dva tovarishcha	Karelov, Evgenii	1968
Civil War	Burn, Burn, My Star	Gori, gori, moia zvezda	Mitta, Aleksandr	1969
Civil War	His Excellency's Adjutant	Adiutant ego prevoskhoditel'stva	Tashkov, Evgenii	1969
Civil War	No Crossing under Fire	V ogne broda net	Panfilov, Gleb	1969
Civil War	White Sun of the Desert	Beloe solntse pustyni	Motyl, Vladimir	1969
Civil War	Flight	Beg	Alov, A.; Naumov, V.	1970
Civil War	Crown of the Russian Empire	Korona rossiiskoi imperii	Keosaian, Edmond	1970–71
Civil War	Property of the Republic	Dostoianie respubliki	Bychkov, Vladmir	1971
Civil War	At Home among Strangers, a Stranger at Home	Svoi sredi chuzhikh, chuzhoi sredi svoikh	Mikhalkov, Nikita	1974

War	English title	Russian title	Director	Year
Civil War	Slave of Love	Raba liubvyi	Mikhalkov, Nikita	1975
Civil War	In the Dangerous Backwoods	V streliaiushchei glushi	Khotinenko, Vladimir	1986
Spain	Autumn Season	Barkhatnoi sezon	Pavlovich, V.	1978
Winter War	Mashenka	Mashen'ka	Raizman, Iulii	1942
WWI	Glory to Us, Death to the Enemy	Slava nam—smert' vragam	Bauer, Evgenii	1914
WWI	King, the Law, and Freedom	Korol', zakon, i svoboda	Chardynin, Petr	1914
WWI	Lily of Belgium	Liliia Belgii	Starewicz, Władysław	1915
WWI	End of St. Petersburg	Konets Sankt-Peterburga	Pudovkin, Vsevolod	1927
WWI	Arsenal	Arsenal	Dovzhenko, Aleksandr	1929
WWI	Fragment of the Empire	Oblomok imperii	Ermler, Fridrikh	1929
WWI	Borderlands	Okraina	Barnet, Boris	1933
WWI	Moonzund	Moonzund	Muratov, Aleksandr	1987
WWII	Defeat of the German-Fascist Troops near Moscow	Razgrom nemetsko-fashistskikh voisk pod Moskvy	Varlamov, L.; Kopalin, I.	1942
WWII	Once at Night	Odnazhdii nochiu/Nashi devushki, 2	Kozintsev, Grigorii	1942
WWII	Our Girls	Nashi devushki	Room, A.; Kozintsev, G.	1942
WWII	Regional Party Secretary	Sekretar raikoma	Pyrev, Ivan	1942
WWII	Rainbow	Raduga	Donskoi, Mark	1943
WWII	She Defends the Motherland	Ona zashchishchaet rodinu	Ermler, Fridrikh	1943
WWII	Two Warriors	Dva boitsa	Lukov, Leonid	1943
WWII	Wait for Me	Zhdi menia	Stolper, Aleksandr	1943
WWII	Invasion	Nashestvie	Room, Abram	1944
WWII	Ivan Nikulin, Russian Sailor	Ivan Nikulin, russkii matros	Savchenko, Igor	1944
WWII	Malakhov Hill	Malakhov Kurgan	Zarkhi, N.; Kheifits, I.	1944
WWII	Moscow Skies	Nebo Moskvy	Raizman, Iulii	1944
WWII	Once There Was a Girl	Zhila-byla devochka	Eisymont, Viktor	1944
WWII	Person No. 217	Chelovek no. 217	Romm, Mikhail	1944
WWII	Six o' Clock in the Evening after the War	V shest'chasov vechera posle voiny	Pyrev, Ivan	1944
WWII	Zoya	Zoia	Arnshtam, Leo	1944
WWII	Berlin	Berlin	Raizman, Iulii	1945
WWII	Celestial Sloth	Nebesnyi tikhokhod	Timoshenko, Semën	1945
WWII	Great Turning Point	Velikii perelom	Ermler, Fridrikh	1945
WWII	Exploits of an Intelligence Officer	Podvig razvedchika	Barnet, Boris	1947
WWII	Young Guard	Molodaia gvardiia	Gerasimov, Sergei	1947
WWII	Story of a Real Man	Povest' o nastoiashchem cheloveke	Stolper, Aleksandr	1948
WWII	Third Blow	Tretii udar'	Savchenko, Igor	1948
WWII	Battle of Stalingrad	Stalingradskaia bitva	Petrov, Vladimir	1949
WWII	Fall of Berlin	Padenie Berlina	Chiaureli, Mikhail	1949
WWII	Koustantin Zaslonov	Koustantin Zaslonov	Faintsimmer, A.	1949
WWII	Brave People	Smelye liudi	Iudin, Konstantin	1950
WWII	Murder on Dante Street	Ubiistvo na ulitse Dante	Romm, Mikhail	1956
WWII	Cranes Are Flying	Letiat zhuravli	Kalatozov, Mikhail	1957
WWII	House I Live In	Dom v ktorom ia zhivu	Kulidzhanov, Lev	1957
WWII	Leningrad Symphony	Leningradskaia simfoniia	Agranenko, Z.	1957

War	English title	Russian title	Director	Year
WWII	My Dear Man	Dorogoi moi chelovek	Kheifits, Iosif	1958
WWII	Two Fyodors	Dva Fedora	Khutsiev, Marlen	1958
WWII	Volunteers	Dobrovol'tsy	Egorov, Iurii	1958
WWII	Ballad of a Soldier	Ballada o soldate	Chukhrai, Grigorii	1959
WWII	Fate of a Man	Sud'ba cheloveka	Bondarchuk, Sergei	1959
WWII	Baltic Skies	Baltiiskoe nebo	Vengerov, Vladimir	1960
WWII	Peace to Him Who Enters	Mir vkhodiashchemu	Alov, A.; Naumov, V.	1961
WWII	Clear Skies	Chistoe nebo	Chukhrai, Grigorii	1961
WWII	Ivan's Childhood	Ivanovo detstvo	Tarkovskii, Andrei	1962
WWII	Living and the Dead	Zhivye i mertvye	Stolper, Aleksandr	1963
WWII	We Draw Fire on Ourselves	Vyzyvaem ogon' na sebia	Kolosov, Sergei	1963–64
WWII	Father of a Soldier	Otets soldata	Chkheidze, Rezo	1965
WWII	Wild Honey	Dikii mëd	Chebotarëv, Vladimir	1966
WWII	Wings	Krylia	Shepitko, Larissa	1966
WWII	Chronicle of a Dive Bomber	Khronika pikiruiushchego bombardirovshchika	Birman, Naum	1967
WWII	Retribution	Vozmedie	Stolper, Aleksandr	1967
WWII	Hard Little Nut	Krepkii oreshëk	Vul'fovich, Teodor	1967
WWII	Zhenya, Zhenechka and "Katiusha"	Zhenia, Zhenechka i "Katiusha"	Motyl, Vladimir	1967
WWII	Last Line	Poslednii rubezh/Shchit i mech, 4	Basov, Vladimir	1967–68
WWII	Not Subject to Appeal	Obzhalovaniiu ne podlezhit/Shchit i mech, 3	Basov, Vladimir	1967–68
WWII	Shield and Sword	Shchit i mech	Basov, Vladimir	1967–68
WWII	To Survive Orders	Prikazanov—vyzhit/Shchit i mech, 2	Basov, Vladimir	1967–68
WWII	Without the Right to Be Oneself	Bez prava byt soboi/Shchit i mech, 1	Basov, Vladimir	1967–68
WWII	Breakthrough/Liberation, 1	Proryv/Osvobozhdenie, 2	Ozerov, Iurii	1968
WWII	Flaming Arc/Liberation, 2	Ognënnaia duga/Osvobozhdenie, 1	Ozerov, Iurii	1968
WWII	Liberation	Osvobozhdenie	Ozerov, Iurii	1968–71
WWII	Gold	Zoloto	Viatich-Berezhnykh, Damir	1969
WWII	On the Road to Berlin	Na puti V Berlin	Ershov, Mikhail	1969
WWII	It Was the Month of May	Byl' mesiats mai	Khutsiev, Marlen	1970
WWII	Directing the Main Blow/Liberation, 3	Napravlenie glavnogo duga/Osvobozhdenie, 3	Ozerov, Iurii	1970
WWII	Battle for Berlin/Liberation, 4	Bitva za Berlin/Osvobozhdenie, 4	Ozerov, Iurii	1971
WWII	Last Storm/Liberation, 5	Poslednii shturm/Osvobozhdenie, 5	Ozerov, Iurii	1971
WWII	Officers	Offitsery	Rogovoi, V.	1971
WWII	Trial on the Road	Proverka na doragakh	German, Aleksei	1971
WWII	And the Dawns Are Quiet Here	A zori zdes' tikhie	Rostotskii, Stanislav	1972
WWII	Battle of Local Significance	Boi mestnogo znachenie/A zori zdes tikhie, 2	Rostotskii, Stanislav	1972
WWII	Belorussian Station	Belorusskii vokzal	Smirnov, Andrei	1972
WWII	Burning Snow	Goriachii sneg	Egiazarov, Gavriil	1972
WWII	Commander of the Lucky Pike	Komandir schastlivoi "Shchuki"	Volchek, Vladimir	1972

War	English title	Russian title	Director	Year
WWII	In the Second Echelon	V vtorom eshelon/A zori zdes' tikhie, I	Rostotskii, Stanislav	1972
WWII	Only the Old Go to Battle	V boi idut odni stariki	Bykov, Leonid	1973
WWII	Seventeen Moments of Spring	Semnadtsat' mgnovenii vesny	Lioznova, Tatiana	1973
WWII	Remember Your Name	Pomni imia svoë	Kolosov, Sergei	1974
WWII	They Fought for the Motherland	Oni srazhalis za rodinu	Bondarchuk, Sergei	1975
WWII	Ascent	Voskhozhdenie	Shepitko, Larissa	1976
WWII	Everyone Knows Kadkin	Kadkina vsiakii znaet	Vekhotko, Anatolii	1976
WWII	There the Soldiers Went	Aty-baty shli soldaty	Bykov, Leonid	1976
WWII	Twenty Days without War	Dvadtsat dnei bez voiny	German, Aleksei	1976
WWII	Quagmire	Triasina	Chukhrai, Grigorii	1977
WWII	Wounded Birds	Podranki	Gubenko, Nikolai	1977
WWII	Tehran-43	Tegeran-43	Alov, A.; Naumov, V.	1980
WWII	At a Dangerous Line	U opasnoi cherty	Georgiev, V.	1983
WWII	Fourth Year of the War Came	Shël chetvërtyi god voiny	Nikolaenko, Georgii	1983
WWII	Military Machine Crew	Ekipazh mashiny boevoi	Vasilevskii, Vitalii	1983
WWII	Torpedo Bombers	Torpedonostsy	Aranovich, Semën	1983
WWII	Wartime Romance	Voenno-polevoi roman	Todorovskii, Pëtr	1983
WWII	Kindergarten	Detskii sad	Evtushenko, Evgenii	1984
WWII	Come and See	Idi i smotri	Klimov, Elem	1985
WWII	Legal Marriage	Zakonnyi brak	Mkrtchian, Albert	1985
WWII	Sprays of Champagne	Bryzgi shampanskogo	Govorukhin, Stanislav	1988
WWII	Unknown Pages from the Life of a Scout	Neizvestnye stranitsy iz zhizni razvedchika	Chebotarëv, Vladimir	1990
WWII	Cuckoo	Kukushka	Rogozhkin, Aleksandr	2002
WWII	Star	Zvezda	Lebedev, Nikolai	2002
WWII	In the Constellation of Taurus	V sozvedii byka	Todorovskii, Pëtr	2003
WWII	Occupation. Mysterium	Okkupatsiia. Misterii	Kudinenko, Andrei	2003
WWII	On the Unknown Heights	Na besymiannoi vysote	Nikiforov, Viacheslav	2003
WWII	In June of '41	V iiune 41go	Ptashuk, Mikhail	2004
WWII	Last Train	Poslednii poezd	German, Aleksei Jr.	2004
WWII	Our Own	Svoi	Meskhiev, Dmitrii	2004
WWII	Penal Battalion	Shtrafbat	Dostal, Nikolai	2004
WWII	Red Choir	Krasnaia kapella	Aravin, Aleksandr	2004
WWII	Saboteur	Diversant	Maliukov, Andrei	2004
WWII	Snipers on the Towers	Snaipery na bashniakh	Ivannikov, Maksim	2004
WWII	Unknown Blockade	Neizvestnaia blokada	Ivannikov, Maksim	2004
WWII	Unofficial Business	Nesluzhebnye zadanye	Vorobev, Vitalii	2004
WWII	Cadets	Kursanty	Kavun, Andrei	2005
WWII	Echelon	Eshelon	Arsenev, Vladilen	2005
WWII	First after God	Pervyi posle Boga	Chiginskii, Vasilii	2005
WWII	Major Pugachov's Last Battle	Poslednii boi maiora Pugachëva	Fatianov, Vladmir	2005
WWII	Man of War	Chelovek voiny	Muradov, Aleksei	2005
WWII	Time to Gather Stones	Vremia sobirat' kamni	Karelin, Aleksei	2005

NOTES

Preface and Acknowledgments

1. There is newsreel footage of the Russo-Japanese War, but no fiction films. The one fiction film about the short Winter War with Finland, *Mashenka*, was released in 1942 and is discussed in chapter 3.

2. Aleksei German, "Pravda—ne skhodstva, a otkrytie," *Iskusstvo Kino* [hereafter *IK*], no. 12 (December 2001): 79, reprinted from *IK*, no. 2 (February 1979).

3. Ibid., 81.

4. Pierre Sorlin, *The Film in History: Restaging the Past* (Totowa, N.J.: Barnes and Noble, 1980); Marc Ferro, *Film and History*, trans. Naomi Greene (Detroit, Mich.: Wayne State University Press, 1988).

5. Robert Brent Toplin, *Reel History: In Defense of Hollywood*, Culture America (Lawrence: University Press of Kansas, 2002), and *History by Hollywood: The Use and Abuse of the American Past* (Urbana: University of Illinois Press, 1996); John E. O'Connor, *The Image as Artifact: The Historical Analysis of Film and Television* (Malabar, Fla.: Krieger, 1990); John E. O'Connor and Martin E. Jackson, eds., *American History, American Film: Interpreting the Hollywood Image* (New York: Continuum, 1988); Peter Rollins, ed., *Hollywood as Historian: American Film in a Cultural Context* (Lexington: University Press of Kentucky, 1983); and Rollins, ed., *Columbia Companion to American History on Film: How the Movies Have Portrayed the American Past* (New York: Columbia University Press, 2003).

6. Robert A. Rosenstone, *Visions of the Past: The Challenge of Film to Our Idea of History* (Cambridge, Mass.: Harvard University Press, 1995); Rosenstone, ed., *Revisioning History: Film and the Construction of a New Past* (Princeton, N.J.: Princeton University Press, 1995); Leger Grindon, *Shadows on the Past: Studies in the Historical Fiction Film* (Philadelphia: Temple University Press, 1994); Vivian Sobchack, ed., *The Persistence of History: Film and the Modern Event* (New York: Routledge, 1996); Marcia Landy, *Cinematic Uses of the Past* (Minneapolis: University of Minnesota Press, 1996); and Landy, ed., *The Historical Film: History and Memory in Media* (New Brunswick, N.J.: Rutgers University Press, 2000).

7. E.g., an essay on *Repentance* that appeared in Rosenstone, *Revisioning History*, and an essay on *Andrei Rublёv* that appeared in Sobchack, *Persistence of History*.

8. Hayden White, "Historiography and Historiophoty," *American Historical Review* 93 (December 1988): 1193–1199.

9. Frank Manchel, *Film Study: An Analytical Bibliography* (Rutherford, N.J.: Fairleigh Dickinson University Press, 1990). The war film is the subject of chapter 2. My understanding of genre has also been shaped by Dudley Andrew, *Concepts in Film Theory* (Oxford: Oxford University Press, 1984), chap. 7; and Thomas Schatz, *Hollywood Genres: Formulas, Filmmaking, and the Studio System* (Philadelphia: Temple University Press, 1981), chap. 2.

10. Jeanine Basinger, *The World War II Combat Film: Anatomy of a Genre*, rev. ed. with updated filmography by Jeremy Arnold (Middletown, Conn.: Wesleyan University Press, 2003). Also see Roger Manvell, *Films and the Second World War*

(South Brunswick, N.J.: A. S. Barnes, 1974); Clayton R. Koppes and Gregory D. Black, *Hollywood Goes to War: How Politics, Profits, and Propaganda Shaped World War II Movies* (New York: Free Press/Macmillan, 1987); Thomas Doherty, *Projections of War: Hollywood, American Culture, and World War II* (New York: Columbia University Press, 1993).

11. David Bordwell, *Narration in the Fiction Film* (Madison: University of Wisconsin Press, 1985), chap. 9.

12. Katerina Clark, *The Soviet Novel: History as Ritual* (Chicago: University of Chicago Press, 1981).

13. Roger Pethybridge, *The Social Prelude to Stalinism* (New York: St. Martin's Press, 1974), chap. 3.

14. Mark von Hagen, *Soldiers in the Proletarian Dictatorship: The Red Army and the Soviet Socialist State, 1917–1930* (Ithaca, N.Y.: Cornell University Press, 1990); Roger R. Reese, *Stalin's Reluctant Soldiers: A Social History of the Red Army, 1925–1941* (Lawrence: University Press of Kansas, 1996); David R. Stone, *Hammer and Rifle: The Militarization of the Soviet Union, 1926–1933* (Lawrence: University Press of Kansas, 2000); Richard W. Harrison, *The Russian Way of War: Operational Art, 1904–1940* (Lawrence: University Press of Kansas, 2001).

15. Iurii Khaniutin, *Preduprezhdenie proshlogo* (Moscow: Iskusstvo, 1968); Vatslav Smal, *Chelovek, voina, podvig* (Minsk: Nauka i tekhnika, 1979); Aleksandr Kamshalov, *Geroika podviga na ekrane: Voenno-patrioticheskaia tema v sovetskom kinematografe* (Moscow: Iskusstvo, 1986).

16. Nina Tumarkin, *The Living and the Dead: The Rise and Fall of the Cult of World War II in Russia* (New York: Basic Books, 1994).

17. Sheila Fitzpatrick, *The Commissariat of Enlightenment: Soviet Organization of Edu-*cation *and the Arts under Lunacharskii, October 1917–1921* (Cambridge: Cambridge University Press, 1970); Fitzpatrick, ed., *Cultural Revolution in Russia* (Bloomington: Indiana University Press, 1978) Fitzpatrick, *Everyday Stalinism: Ordinary Life in Extraordinary Times: Soviet Russia in the 1930s* (Oxford: Oxford University Press, 1999); Jeffrey Brooks, *Thank You, Comrade Stalin! Soviet Public Culture from Revolution to Cold War* (Princeton, N.J.: Princeton University Press, 2000); Karen Petrone, *Life Has Become More Joyous, Comrades! Celebrations in the Time of Stalin* (Bloomington: Indiana University Press, 2000); David L. Hoffmann, *Stalinist Values: The Cultural Norms of Soviet Modernity, 1917–1941* (Ithaca, N.Y.: Cornell University Press, 2003).

18. Richard Stites, *Russian Popular Culture: Entertainment and Society since 1900* (Cambridge: Cambridge University Press, 1992); and Stites, ed., *Culture and Entertainment in Wartime Russia* (Bloomington: Indiana University Press, 1995).

19. In Russian, see Valerii Golovskoi, *Mezhdu ottepel'iu i glasnost'iu: Kinematograf 70-kh* (Moscow: Materik, 2004).

20. Denise J. Youngblood, *The Magic Mirror: Moviemaking in Russia, 1908–1918* (Madison: University of Wisconsin Press, 1999); Youngblood, *Soviet Cinema in the Silent Era, 1918–1935* (Austin: University of Texas Press, 1991); Youngblood, *Movies for the Masses: Popular Cinema and Soviet Society in the 1920s* (Cambridge: Cambridge University Press, 1992).

21. Peter Kenez, *Cinema and Soviet Society from the Revolution to the Death of Stalin* (London: I. B. Tauris, 2001); Josephine Woll, *Real Images: Soviet Cinema and the Thaw* (London: I. B. Tauris, 2000); Anna Lawton, *Kinoglasnost: Soviet Cinema in Our Time* (Cambridge: Cambridge University Press, 1992); and Lawton, *Imaging Russia*

2000: Film and Facts (Washington, D.C.: New Academia Publishing, 2004). Lawton's *Kinoglasnost* has been republished in a slightly revised edition under the title *Before the Fall: Soviet Cinema in the Gorbachev Years* (Washington, D.C.: New Academia Publishing, 2002).

22. See, e.g., Richard Taylor and Ian Christie, eds., *Inside the Film Factory: New Approaches to Russian and Soviet Cinema* (London: Routledge, 1991); Richard Taylor and Derek Spring, eds., *Stalinism and Soviet Cinema* (London: Routledge, 1993). Other works by Taylor are cited in chapter source notes.

23. L. M Budiak, ed., *Rossiiskii illiuzion* (Moscow: Materik, 2003) [hereafter RI]; L. Kh. Mamatova, ed., *Kino: Politika i liudi 30-e gody* (Moscow: Materik, 1995); V. I. Fomin, comp., *Kino na voine: Dokumenty i svidetel'stva* (Moscow: Materik, 2005).

24. Sergei Zemlianukhin and Miroslava Segida, *Domashniaia sinemateka: Otechestvennoe kino, 1918–1996* (Moscow: Dubl'-D, 1996) [hereafter DS].

Introduction

1. C. P. Cavafy, *Collected Poems*, rev. ed., trans. Edmund Keeley and Philip Sherrard, ed. George Savidis (Princeton, N.J.: Princeton University Press, 1992), 18. This poem was written in 1904.

2. In 2002, Polit.ru and the OGI publishing company sponsored a symposium on this subject; the conference papers appear in Lev Gudkov, comp., *Obraz vraga* (Moscow: OGI, 2005).

3. Omitted are the Russo-Japanese War (1904–1905) and the Winter War with Finland (1939), although *Mashenka*, which was released during World War II, will be discussed in chapter 3. Because of my focus on the impact of war on Russian and Soviet society, I have also excluded films about the Spanish civil war, such as V. Pavlovich's thriller *Autumn Season* (Barkhatnyi sezon, 1978), as well as films about World War II in Europe that lack Russian characters, like *Murder on Dante Street* (Ubiistvo na ulitse Dante), Mikhail Romm's 1956 melodrama about a French actress who learns that her beloved only child is a fascist collaborator.

4. Only a few documentaries will be discussed in these pages; a potentially controversial exclusion is Mikhail Romm's *Ordinary Fascism* (Obyknovennyi fashizm, 1965), an important compilation documentary, but one that chronicles the rise of Nazism in Germany, not the impact of Nazism in the USSR. Nonfiction films were not part of the cinematic dialogue about war films as art or entertainment between the 1920s and glasnost. The best analysis in English of the Soviet documentary is Graham Roberts, *Forward Soviet! History and Non-fiction Film in the USSR* (London: I. B. Tauris, 1999). Roberts discusses the "not so strange death of the Soviet documentary" in chapter 7.

5. As an example, George O. Liber's recent biography of Aleksandr (Oleksandr) Dovzhenko is based on Ukrainian archival material, *Alexander Dovzhenko: A Life in Soviet Film* (London: BFI Publishing, 2002). Joshua First is presently researching a doctoral dissertation at the University of Michigan on the revival of Ukrainian cinema in the Brezhnev era.

6. Andrew Horton, "The Star That Didn't Shine," *Kinoeye* 2, no. 13 (2002), http://www.kinoeye.org/02/13/horton13 part4.php. This quotation, which comes from the opening paragraph of Horton's review of the 2002 film *The Star* (to be discussed in chapter 9), reflects a widely held view that I hope to dispel.

7. Hayden White, "Historiography and Historiophoty," *American Historical Review* 93 (December 1988), 1193.

8. Ibid.

9. Petre Petrov, "The Freeze of Historicity in Thaw Cinema," *KinoKultura*, no. 8 (April 2005): 1/9, http://www.kinokultura.com/articles/apr05-petrov.html.

10. See Denise Youngblood, *Movies for the Masses: Popular Cinema and Soviet Society in the 1920s* (Cambridge: Cambridge University Press, 1992), chap. 2.

11. My highly condensed discussion of "classical narration" is based on David Bordwell, *Narration in the Fiction Film* (Madison: University of Wisconsin Press, 1985), chap. 9. On the master plot of socialist realism, see Katerina Clark, *The Soviet Novel: History as Ritual* (Chicago: University of Chicago Press, 1981), chap. 1.

12. Likewise, my discussion of "art-cinema narration" is distilled from Bordwell, *Narration in the Fiction Film*, chap. 10.

13. Ibid., 207.

14. Petrov, "Freeze of Historicity in Thaw Cinema," 1.

Chapter One

1. This chapter is based in part on research first presented in my books *The Magic Mirror, Movies for the Masses*, and *Soviet Cinema in the Silent Era*. For other works on Russian and Soviet silent cinema, see, e.g., Semën Ginzburg, *Kinematografii dorevoliutsionnoi Rossii* (Moscow: Iskusstvo, 1963); Yuri Tsivian, *Early Cinema in Russia and Its Cultural Reception*, trans. Alan Bodger, ed. Richard Taylor (London: Routledge, 1994); Nikolai Lebedev, *Ocherk istorii kino SSSR*, vol. 1, *Nemoe kino* (Moscow: Goskinoizdat, 1947); Rostislav Iurenev, *Kratkaia istoriia sovetskogo kino* (Moscow: Biuro propagandy sovetskogo kinoiskusstva, 1979); Jay Leyda, *Kino: A History of the Russian and Soviet Film* (New York: Collier, 1973); Richard Taylor, *The Politics of the Soviet Cinema, 1917–1929* (New York: Cambridge University Press, 1979); Richard Taylor and Ian Christie, eds., *The Film Factory: Russian and Soviet Cinema in Documents, 1896–1939*, trans. Richard Taylor (Cambridge, Mass.: Harvard University Press, 1988); Peter Kenez, *Cinema and Soviet Society from the Revolution to the Death of Stalin* (London: I. B. Tauris, 2001).

2. Ginzburg, *Kinematografii dorevoliutsionnoi Rossii*, 157; Lebedev, *Ocherk istorii kino SSSR*, 35.

3. Lebedev, *Ocherk istorii kino SSSR*, 33.

4. "Teatr i kinematografii," *Vestnik kinematografii*, no. 87 (1 April 1914): 19; M. Brailovskii, "Dvenadtsat' millionov," *Sine-fono*, no. 3 (9 November 1913): 21–22.

5. This section of this chapter is adapted from my article "A War Forgotten: The Great War in Russian and Soviet Cinema," in Michael Paris, ed., *The First World War and Popular Cinema: 1914 to the Present* (New Brunswick, N.J.: Rutgers University Press, 2000), 172–175.

6. Lebedev, *Ocherk istorii kino SSSR*, 35; Ginzburg, *Kinematografii dorevoliutsionnoi Rossii*, 157.

7. Lebedev, *Ocherk istorii kino SSSR*, 5.

8. Ginzburg, *Kinematografii dorevoliutsionnoi Rossii*, 46.

9. Ibid., 191–192. For a detailed discussion of this issue, see Hubertus F. Jahn, *Patriotic Culture in Russia during World War I* (Ithaca, N.Y.: Cornell University Press, 1995), chap. 3; for an overview, see Peter Kenez, "Russian Patriotic Films," in Karel Dibbets and Bert Hogenkamp, eds., *Film and the First World War* (Amsterdam: Amsterdam University Press, 1995), 36–42.

10. Viktor Listov, "Early Soviet Cinema: The Spontaneous and the Planned, 1917–1924," trans. and ed. Richard Taylor and Derek Spring, *Historical Journal of Film, Radio and Television* 11, no. 2 (1991): 22. Listov goes on to say: "The proposals were such that 30 years later Stalin and Zhdanov could have put their names to many of the Tsar's instructions."

11. Quoted in Yuri Tsivian, Paolo Cherchi Usai, Lorenzo Codelli, Carlo Montanaro, and David Robinson, eds., *Silent Witnesses: Russian Films, 1909–1919* (Pordenone and London: Edizione Biblioteca dell'Imagine/BFI Publishing, 1989), 224.

12. Ibid.

13. Kenez, "Russian Patriotic Films," 40.

14. The first revolution in 1917 occurred in February, according to the Julian calendar then in use in Russia; in March, according to the Gregorian calendar. Likewise, the Great October Revolution took place on 7–8 November 1917 by the Gregorian calendar.

15. For a colorful account of the Civil War (as well as the Great War and the Revolutions), see Orlando Figes, *A People's Tragedy: The Russian Revolution, 1891–1924* (New York: Penguin, 1998); a more sober-minded scholarly overview of the Civil War may be found in Evan Mawdsley, *The Russian Civil War* (Boston: Unwin Hyman, 1987).

16. For a description of the most important examples, see Nikolai Iezuitov, "Agitki epokhi grazhdanskoi voiny," IK, no. 5 (May 1940): 47–51.

17. Youngblood, *Soviet Cinema*, 18–19.

18. A. Strel'chenko, "Krasnye d'iavoliata na dorogakh voiny" [letter to the editor], *Sovetskii ekran* [hereafter SE], no. 20 (1985): 17.

19. For a recent analysis, see Richard Taylor, *October: Oktiabr'* (London: BFI Publishing), 2002.

20. This discussion is adapted from Youngblood, "A War Forgotten," 175–176. For a recent analysis, see Vance Kepley Jr., *The End of St. Petersburg* (London: I. B. Tauris, 2003).

21. This is the first depiction of post-traumatic stress disorder in Soviet cinema. For a more complete discussion of this film and the circumstances surrounding its production, see Youngblood, *Movies for the Masses*, 149–152.

22. For a recent appraisal, see Ekaterina Khokhlova, "Oblomok imperii," in RI, 99–104.

23. "Why is it counted the highest artistic achievement to give a picture a thick layer of symbolism? . . . This obviously leads to a break with realistic forms in the mind of the mass viewer"; Iakov Rudoi, "Nasha kinematografiia i massovoi zritel'," SE, no. 37 (1929): 17.

24. Ippolit Sokolov, "Korni formalizma," *Kino*, no. 17 (1930): 3; for his earlier views, see Sokolov, "Oblomok imperii," *Kino*, no. 38 (1929): 2.

25. See, e.g., Fitzpatrick, *Russian Revolution*.

26. Youngblood, *Soviet Cinema*, 88–90. An earlier example that drew some notice was *Father Knysh's Band*; see the review V. G., "Banda bat'ka Knysha," *Pravda*, 4 June 1924.

27. P. A., "Oshibka Vasiliia Guliavina (Veter)," *Kino*, no. 43 (1926); Ippolit Sokolov, "Veter," *Kino*, no. 45 (1926): 3; S. Ermolinskii, "Veter (Oshibka Vasiliia Guliavina)," *Pravda*, 4 November 1926.

28. A. German, "Tripol'skaia tragediia," *Kino*, no. 15 (1926): 3.

29. Youngblood, *Soviet Cinema*, 88–89, 153; for a review of *Two Days* that praises

its realism, see Khrisanf Khersonskii, "VUFKU na perelome: *Spartak, Dva dnia, Zvenigora,*" *Pravda,* 10 February 1928.

30. For more details, see Youngblood, *Soviet Cinema,* 214; and Konstantin Fedin, *Cities and Years,* trans. Michael Scammell (New York: Dell, 1962).

31. Boris Alpers, "*Goroda i gody,*" *Kino i zhizn'* no. 34/35 (1930): 7–8.

32. Boris Lavrenev, *The Forty-first* (Moscow: Foreign Languages Publishing House, 1958). Its initial publication date was 1924.

33. A. I. Troianovskii and R. I. Egiarovskii, *Izuchenie kino-zritelia: Po materialam issledovatel'skoi teatral'noi masterskoi* (Moscow: Narkompros, 1928), 31; Arsen, "Sorok pervyi," *Kino-front,* no. 6 (1927): 15–19; Youngblood, *Movies for the Masses,* 113–114. An appreciative review can be found in Boris Gusman, "*Sorok pervyi,*" *Pravda,* 18 March 1927.

34. The British also appear as villains in Nikolai Shengelaya's film *The Twenty-six Commissars* (Dvadtsat'shest' komissarov, 1933), which was based on the historical events surrounding the 1918 execution of the Baku Soviet by counter-revolutionaries. This film was criticized for its "formalism" and symbolism; see Youngblood, *Soviet Cinema,* 213. Yakov Protazanov's *Tommy* (Tommi, 1932) portrays the softer side of the British— a young English soldier defects to the Reds; see Ian Christie and Julian Graffy, eds., *Protazanov and the Continuity of Russian Cinema* (London: BFI/NFT, 1993), 74.

35. "K itogam sezona," *Kino i zhizn',* no. 15 (1930): 3–5; Youngblood, *Soviet Cinema,* 212–213. For a critical review, see S. Ermolinskii, "*Potomok Chingiz-Khana,*" *Pravda,* 5 December 1928.

36. This discussion has been adapted in part from "A War Forgotten," 176–177. The best analysis of this film may be found in Vance Kepley Jr., *In the Service of the State: The Cinema of Alexander Dovzhenko* (Madison: University of Wisconsin Press, 1986), chap. 5; for the circumstances surrounding its production, see George O. Liber, *Alexander Dovzhenko: A Life in Soviet Film* (London: BFI Publishing, 2002), 94–102.

37. See Viktor Geiman, "Pochemu zriteliu nravitsia odno, a kritiku—drugoe," *Kino,* no. 19 (1929): 2–3; and M. Rafes's remarks in Rossiiskii Gosudarstvennyi Arkhiv Literatury i Iskusstva (RGALI), f. 2494, op. 1, ed. khr. 2134, "Stenogramma zasedaniia rezhisserskoi sekstii ARRK o stsenarnom krisize (1929)," 5–9. For a more tempered review, see Khrisanf Khersonskii, "Novoe slovo ukrainskoi kinematografii: Fil'ma [sic] *Arsenal,*" *Pravda,* 14 February 1929 (note to Russian speakers: the word *fil'm* was not consistently gendered masculine until the 1930s). My translation of the titles is based on a Soviet print rather than on the print available in the United States.

38. Denise J. Youngblood, *Soviet Cinema,* Appendix 2.

39. Roger Pethybridge, *The Social Prelude to Stalinism* (New York: St. Martin's Press, 1974), 83.

40. Not surprisingly, émigré Russians had a different response. See Aaron J. Cohen, "Oh, That! Myth, Memory, and World War I in the Russian Emigration and the Soviet Union," *Slavic Review* 62, no. 1 (Spring 2003): 69–86.

Chapter Two

1. Youngblood, *Soviet Cinema in the Silent Era, 1918–1935* (Austin: University of Texas Press, 1991), appendix 1.

2. Ibid., chap. 9; Peter Kenez, *Cinema and Soviet Society from the Revolution to the Death of Stalin* (London: I. B. Tauris, 2001), chap. 5. For an excellent discussion of how socialist realism's "positive hero" was translated cinematically, see Richard Taylor, "Red Stars, Positive Heroes, and Personality Cults," in *Stalinism and Soviet Cinema*, ed. Richard Taylor and Derek Spring (London: Routledge, 1993), chap. 5.

3. Peter Kenez provides the most complete English-language survey of Soviet cinema in the 1930s in *Cinema and Soviet Society*, chaps. 6–8. For a view from a prominent Russian critic and film scholar, see Maia Turovskaia, "The 1930s and 1940s: Cinema in Context," in Taylor and Spring, *Stalinism and Soviet Cinema*, chap. 3. Jay Leyda was a student at VGIK in the midthirties; Jay Leyda, *Kino: A History of the Russian and Soviet Film* (New York: Collier, 1973), chap. 4, provides many interesting details on various personalities. For an exhaustive account of Stalin's obsession with movies, see Grigorii Mariamov, *Kremlevskii tsenzor: Stalin smotrit kino* (Moscow: Kinotsentr', 1992).

4. One important example was Sergei Eisenstein's *Bezhin Meadow* (Bezhin lug, 1937), which was banned even though its subject was the martyrdom of the peasant boy Pavlik Morozov, who was murdered, ostensibly for threatening to betray his family's anti-Soviet activities. See Ekaterina Khokhlova, "Forbidden Films of the 1930s," in Taylor and Spring, *Stalinism and Soviet Cinema*, chap. 6; Natacha Laurent, *L'Œil du Kremlin: Cinéma et censure en URSS sous Staline (1928–1953)* (Paris: Editions Privat, 2000), chap. 2.

5. Shumiatsky (executed in 1939) even wanted to create a Soviet Hollywood in the Crimea. See Richard Taylor, "Boris Shumyatsky and Soviet Cinema in the 1930s," in Taylor and Ian Christie, eds., *Inside the Film Factory: New Approaches to Russian and Soviet Cinema*, Soviet Cinema (London: Routledge, 1991), chap. 11.

6. The revival of selected Russian heroes at this time was part of Stalin's plan to establish himself as a Russian as well as Soviet leader, as an heir to the czars as well as to Lenin. To name a well-known example, Sergei Eisenstein likewise found a "safe" historical subject in *Alexander Nevsky* (Aleksandr Nevskii, 1938), a film about the thirteenth-century Russian prince who repelled the Teutonic knights. This movie's fate paralleled political developments. Intended as a warning against German fascism and militarism, it was withdrawn after the Molotov-Ribbentrop Pact of 1939, to be rereleased only after the German invasion in June 1941.

7. The two leading directors of the musical comedy were Grigory Aleksandrov and Ivan Pyrev. The versatile and politically astute Ivan Pyrev becomes an important figure for this book during the war; for a discussion of his films in the 1930s, see Maia Turovskaia, "I. A. Pyr'ev i ego muzykal'nye komedii: K probleme zhanra," *Kinovedcheskie zapiski* [hereafter KZ], no. 1 (1988): 111–146; Richard Taylor, "Singing on the Steppes for Stalin: Ivan Pyr'ev and the Kolkhoz Musical in Soviet Cinema," *Slavic Review* 58, no. 1 (Spring 1999): 143–159; and John Haynes, *New Soviet Man: Gender and Masculinity in Stalinist Soviet Cinema* (Manchester: Manchester University Press, 2003), chap. 4.

8. Kenez, "Soviet Cinema in the Age of Stalin," in Taylor and Spring, *Stalinism and Soviet Cinema*, 56.

9. Sergei Yutkevich's *The Man with the Gun* (Chelovek s ruzhëm, 1938) is one of

the better examples of films of this type. According to this reinterpretation of recent history, the Party, rather than the people, became instrumental in the Revolution. Not only was Lenin now ubiquitous in movies about the Revolution, but Stalin began appearing in places where he never was in reality.

10. Kenez, *Cinema and Soviet Society*, 117.

11. See, e.g., A. Erlikh, "*Okraina*," *Pravda*, 8 April 1933.

12. Mikhail Bleiman et al., "Bez chetkogo ideinogo zamysla (ob *Okraine*)," *Kino*, no. 23 (1933). Other reactions from the Soviet film press are translated into French in François Albera and Roland Cosandey, eds., *Boris Barnet: Ecrits, documents, études, filmographie* (Locarno: Editions du Féstivale Internationale du Film, 1985), 132–133.

13. Mark Kushnirov, *Zhizn' i fil'my Borisa Barneta* (Moscow: Iskusstvo, 1977), 112–113, says that Kuzmina, who at the time was married to Barnet, insisted that Barnet rewrite the role as an ingenue part. Kuzmina, on the other hand, asserts in an interview with Bernard Eisenschitz that it was Barnet's idea and that she was uncomfortable with the change; Eisenschitz, "A Fickle Man, or Portrait of Boris Barnet as Soviet Director," in Taylor and Christie, *Inside the Film Factory*, 152–153.

14. Translated in Richard Taylor and Ian Christie, eds., *The Film Factory: Russian and Soviet Cinema in Documents, 1896–1939* (Cambridge, Mass.: Harvard University Press, 1988), 234–235. Also see Christie, "Making Sense of Early Soviet Sound," in Taylor and Christie, *Inside the Film Factory*, chap. 10. *Borderlands* is mentioned briefly on page 191.

15. For a recent appreciation of this film by a Russian film scholar, see Evgenii Margolit, "*Okraina*," *RI*, 111–116.

16. Lewis Milestone was born Lev Milshtein in Kishenev, Russian Bessarabia (now Moldova), in 1895. He emigrated to the United States in 1913 and served in the U.S. Army during World War I; Ephraim Katz, *The Film Encyclopedia*, 2nd ed. (New York: Harper and Row, 1994), 941.

17. Maia Turovskaia discusses the popularity of *Chapaev* and its competitors in "The Tastes of Soviet Moviegoers during the 1930s," in Thomas Lahusen, ed., *Late Soviet Culture: From Perestroika to Novostroika*, Post-Contemporary Interventions (Durham, N.C.: Duke University Press, 1993), 95–107.

18. The Vasilevs were neither brothers nor even related.

19. Jeremy Hicks, "The International Reception of Early Soviet Sound Cinema: *Chapaev* in Britain and America," *Historical Journal of Film, Radio and Television* 25 (June 2005): 273–289.

20. A. S. Troshin, ed., "'Kartina sil'naia, khoroshaia no ne *Chapaev*': Zapiski besed B. Z. Shumiatskogo s I. V. Stalynym posle kinoprosmotrov 1935–1937," *KZ*, no. 62 (2002): 168. Also see Fëdor Razzakov, *Nashe liubimoe kino: Tainoe stanovitsia iavnym* (Moscow: Algoritm, 2004), 27. This number is derived from Boris Shumiatsky's notes detailing the conversations Stalin had with Shumiatsky and various Politburo members after film screenings; Shumiatsky, then the head of Soiuzkino, was responsible for arranging Stalin's screenings. This is the continuation of Troshin's work with the notebooks; see note 25 for the citation to a prior installment.

21. Dmitrii Furmanov, *Chapaev*, in Nicholas Luker, ed., *An Anthology of the Classics of Socialist Realism: From Furmanov to Sholokhov* (Ann Arbor, Mich.: Ardis, 1988), 45–125.

22. As distinct from *The Forty-first*, which is not a combat film.

23. "Vstrecha literatorov s uchastnikami fil'ma *Chapaev*," *Pravda*, 26 November 1934.

24. "*Chapaeva* posmotrit vsia strana," *Pravda*, 22 November 1934.

25. Aleksandr Troshin, ed., "'A driani podrobno *Garmon*' bol'she ne stavite?' Zapiski besed B. Z. Shumiatskogo s I. V. Stalinym posle kinoprosmotrov 1934," *KZ*, no. 61 (2002): 309–334.

26. *Sovetskoe kino* (Moscow: Iskusstvo, 1937).

27. In *SE*, no. 9 (1980), see G. Beregovoi, "Nasha pobeda," 7, and Iu. Nikulin, "*Chapaev* s nami," 17. Beregovoi was a much-decorated pilot, twice a Hero of the Soviet Union. See also Anonymous, *A Woman in Berlin: Eight Weeks in the Conquered City, a Diary*, trans. Philip Boehm (New York: Henry Holt, 2005), 254–255, who says *Chapaev* opened in Berlin immediately after the fall of the city.

28. See, e.g., in *IK*, which was founded in 1931 and by the midthirties was the only Soviet film journal until 1957: I. Dolinskii, "*Chapaev*: Literaturnoe proizvedenie i fil'm," no. 7/8 (July/August 1940): 51–57; Sergei Gerasimov, "Sila Stalinskikh idei," no. 6 (June 1949): 13–18; Nikolai Lebedev, "Na podstupakh k *Chapaevu*," no. 2 (February 1951): 9–14; S. Freilikh, "Po puti sotsialisticheskogo realizma: *Izbrannye stsenarii sovetskogo kino v shesti tomakh*," no. 4 (April 1952): 109–122. For post-Stalin views, see R. Iurenev, "*Chapaev*," *IK*, no. 11 (November 1964): 10–19; "Kartina zhivët!" *SE*, no. 21 (1974): 14–15. For a twenty-first-century Russian view on the film, see Aleksandr Karaganov, "*Chapaev*," in *RI*, 117–122.

29. "Konkurs-77," *SE*, no. 10 (1978): 13. In the 1978 survey it dropped to thirty-third place, still impressive for a thirty-four-year-old film; "Konkurs SE-78," *SE*, no. 9 (1979): 12–13.

30. Troshin, "'Kartina sil'naia,'" 153, 168.

31. Vsevolod Vishnevskii, "*My iz Kronshtadta*," *Pravda*, 22 August 1935.

32. Efim Dzigan, "Chetvert veka: *My iz Kronshtadta*," *SE*, no. 8 (1961): 4–5.

33. Ibid., 8.

34. I. Ermolinskii, "*My iz Kronshtadta* (Avtor stsenarii Vsevolod Vishnevskii, rezhissër Ef. Dzigan, proizvodstvo studii Mosfil'm, 1936): Zamechatel'nyi fil'm," *Pravda*, 3 March 1936; "Uspekh zamechatel'nogo fil'ma: Pervyi den' demonstratsii *My iz Kronshtadta*," *Pravda*, 22 March 1936.

35. Troshin, "'Kartina sil'naia,'" 166–167.

36. "*My iz Kronshtadta* na parizhskikh ekranakh," *Pravda*, 4 June 1936.

37. From Eisenstein's diary as quoted by Oksana Bulgakowa, *Sergei Eisenstein: A Biography*, trans. Anne Dwyer (Berlin: PotemkinPress, 2001), 182.

38. E.g., Vsevolod Vishnevskii, "Pistatel' i rezhissër: Iz pisem k E. Dziganu (publikatsiia)," *IK*, no. 6 (June 1954): 56–76; German Kremlev, "1936-xxx-1966:" *My iz Kronshtadta*," *SE*, no. 6 (1966): 20. Much more recently, the picture has also been reaffirmed as a classic of Russian cinema by Lev Parfenov, "*My iz Kronshtadta*," in *RI*, 159–164.

39. A. Strel'chenko, "*Krasnye d'iavoliata na dorogakh voiny*" [letter to the editor], *SE*, no. 20 (1985): 17.

40. Evgenii Margolit and Viacheslav Shmyrov, *Iz'iatoe kino: Katalog sovetskikh igrovykh kartin, nevypushchennykh vo vsesoiuznyi prokat po zavershenii v proizvodstve ili iz'iatykh iz deistvuiushchego fil'mofonda v god vypuska na ekran (1924–1953)* (Moscow: Dubl'-D, 1995), 74–75.

41. Vance Kepley Jr., *In the Service of the State: The Cinema of Alexander Dovzhenko* (Madison: University of Wisconsin Press, 1986), chap. 9, provides the best cinematic analysis of the film. George O. Liber, *Alexander Dovzhenko: A Life in Soviet Film* (London: BFI Publishing, 2002), chap. 7, details the full history of the ill-starred production. The Soviet movie-going public was unaware of this history until the midseventies. See A. Mishurin, "Na s"emakh *Shchorsa*," *IK*, no. 9 (September 1974): 49–58.

42. Kepley, *In the Service of the State*, 121.

43. Liber, *Alexander Dovzhenko*, 158.

44. Ibid., 156.

45. Ibid., 157–164.

46. Ibid., 164–165.

47. Sergei Gerasimov, "Beseda re-zhissëra so stsenaristom," *IK*, no. 11 (November 1953): 67. Gerasimov does, however, consider *Shchors* to be Dovzhenko's best sound film.

48. David L. Hoffmann, *Stalinist Values: The Cultural Norms of Soviet Modernity, 1917–1941* (Ithaca, N.Y.: Cornell University Press, 2003), 85.

49. Leo Arnshtam, "*Shchors*: Novyi fil'm A. Dovzhenko, proizvodstvo Kievskoi kinostudii," *Pravda*, 25 January 1939. Also see note 52, below.

50. Liber, *Alexander Dovzhenko*, 164–165.

51. I. Manevich, "Tvorcheskii put' I. A. Savchenko," *IK*, no. 1 (January 1951): 17.

52. His name was "Leo," not the Russian "Lev." See "Arnshtam, Leo Oskarovich," *Kino*, 30. Sergei Yutkevich supervised the film's production and is sometimes erroneously credited as director. See also note 47.

53. Hoffmann discusses the emphasis on feminine dress and behavior and the importance of motherhood (in chapter 3 of *Stalinist Values*) and mentions in pass-ing (111–112) a few of the ways this was reinforced by visual culture.

54. Troshin, "'Kartina sil'naia,'" 153. Stalin praised Arnshtam's direction and cut Shumiatsky off when he suggested that Arnshtam's mentor Sergei Yutkevich had helped Arnshtam quite a bit and should be given most of the credit for the success of *Girlfriends*. The date was 25 December 1935; Stalin watched *Chapaev* (again) right after the screening of *Girlfriends*.

Chapter Three

1. John Barber and Mark Harrison, *The Soviet Home Front, 1941–1945: A Social and Economic History of the USSR in World War II* (London: Longman, 1991), 39–44. Another good source for the social history of the war is Robert W. Thurston and Bernd Bonwetsch, eds., *The People's War: Responses to World War II in the Soviet Union* (Urbana: University of Illinois Press, 2000).

2. The mythologization of the war is the subject of Nina Tumarkin's *The Living and the Dead: The Rise and Fall of the Cult of World War II in Russia* (New York: Basic Books, 1994), a seminal work that is comprehensive in every manifestation of the cult, except for cinema, which Tumarkin discusses only in passing.

3. V. Golovnia, "Mosfil'm v gody Velikoi otechestvennoi voiny," *IK*, no. 7 (July 1979): 12. For accounts of the evacuation, see V. I. Fomin, comp., *Kino na voine: Dokumenty i svidetel'stva* (Moscow: Materik, 2005), 85–133.

4. Golovnia, "Mosfil'm v gody Velikoi otechestvennoi voiny," 11; Peter Kenez, "Black and White: The War on Film," in Richard Stites, ed., *Culture and Entertainment in Wartime Russia* (Bloomington: Indiana University Press, 1995), 164.

5. Natacha Laurent, *L'Œil du Kremlin: Cinéma et censure en URSS sous Staline (1928–1953)* (Paris: Editions Privat, 2000), chaps. 4–5.

6. Valerii Fomin has collected nearly 400 documents in *Kino na voine*, most of which deal with picayune criticisms of films that could by no means be construed as harmful to the war effort. See, e.g., Grigorii Aleksandrov's report on *She Defends the Motherland*, 352. Director Mikhail Romm even wrote to Stalin in January 1943 protesting the situation (538–540).

7. I. G. Bol'shakov, *Sovetskoe kinoiskusstvo v gody Velikoi otechestvennoi voiny (1941–1945)* (Moscow: Goskinoizdat, 1948), 142–144. In addition, Bolshakov lists eighty-seven documentaries and fifty-one "most important" educational and scientific films (144–148).

8. Peter Kenez, *Cinema and Soviet Society from the Revolution to the Death of Stalin* (London: I. B. Tauris, 2001), 175. The other major genres were filmed operas and concerts and historical dramas, notably Sergei Eisenstein's *Ivan the Terrible* (Ivan Groznyi, part 1, 1944), which Stalin himself had commissioned.

9. Ibid., 167, based on Dorothy Jones's analysis in *Hollywood Quarterly*, no. 1 (1945/46). Jones identified 374 titles out of 1,212. British production was naturally much smaller, averaging only 42 titles annually over the course of the war. Fewer than half of these were war films, and the percentage of war films declined during the last two years of the war; see Robert Murphy, "The British Film Industry: Audiences and Producers," in Philip M. Taylor, ed., *Britain and the Cinema in the Second World War* (New York: St. Martin's Press, 1988), 31; Murphy, *British Cinema and the Second World War*

(London: Continuum, 2000), 14. German feature film production during the war consisted primarily of musicals, historical epics, and family melodramas; see Eric Rentschler, *The Ministry of Illusion: Nazi Cinema and Its Afterlife* (Cambridge, Mass.: Harvard University Press, 1996); and Rolf Giesen, *Nazi Propaganda Films: A History and Filmography* (Jefferson, N.C.: McFarland, 2003).

10. Bol'shakov, *Sovetskoe kinoiskusstvo v gody Velikoi otechestvennoi voiny*, 40.

11. Jay Leyda, *Kino: A History of the Russian and Soviet Film* (New York: Collier, 1973), 389.

12. The British also made films about the Resistance in France and elsewhere in occupied Europe; Murphy, *British Cinema*, chap. 4.

13. Kenez, "Black and White," 161.

14. Barber and Harrison, *Soviet Home Front*, 127–133.

15. See, e.g., Alexander Dallin, *German Rule in Russia, 1941–1945: A Study in Occupation Policies*, 2nd ed. rev. (Boulder, Colo.: Westview Press, 1981); and Omer Bartov, *The Eastern Front, 1941–45: German Troops and the Barbarisation of Warfare* (New York: St. Martin's Press, 1986).

16. For a detailed study of the partisan movement, see Matthew Cooper, *The Nazi War against Soviet Partisans, 1941–1944* (New York: Stein and Day, 1979); an overview may be found in Richard Overy's highly readable *Russia's War: A History of the Soviet War Effort, 1941–1945* (New York: Penguin, 1998), 143–153. On the role of women in the partisan movement, see John Erickson, "Soviet Women at War," in John Garrard and Carol Garrard, eds., *World War 2 and the Soviet People* (New York: St. Martin's Press, 1993), 50–76; Kazimiera J. Cottam, *Women in War and Resistance: Selected Biographies of Soviet*

Women Soldiers (Nepean, Ont.: New Military Publishing, 1998), 278–395; Susanne Conze and Beate Fieseler, "Soviet Women as Comrades-in-Arms: A Blind Spot in the History of the War," in Thurston and Bonwetsch, People's War, 210–234.

17. For contradictory views on this point, in Lynne Attwood, ed., Red Women on the Silver Screen: Soviet Women and Cinema from the Beginning to the End of the Communist Era (London: Pandora, 1993), see Attwood, "The Stalin Era," 67, who acknowledges the predominance of heroines, and Oksana Bulgakowa, "The Hydra of the Soviet Cinema: The Metamorphoses of the Soviet Film Heroine," 163, who unaccountably denies it.

18. Kenez, Cinema and Soviet Society, 174.

19. Evgenii Margolit and Viacheslav Shmyrov, Iz'iatoe kino: Katalog sovetskikh igrovykh kartin, nevypushchennykh vo vsesoiuznyi prokat po zavershenii v proizvodstve ili iz'iatykh iz deistvuiushchego fil'mofonda v god vypuska na ekran (1924–1953) (Moscow: Dubl'-D, 1995), 88.

20. Ibid.; also DS, 273.

21. The essays in Stites, Culture and Entertainment, give a good overview of Soviet wartime culture as a whole; for a condensed version, see Richard Stites, Russian Popular Culture: Entertainment and Society since 1900 (Cambridge: Cambridge University Press, 1992), 98–116. On the role of the war cult in wartime, see Tumarkin, The Living and the Dead, chap. 4. Press culture is well covered in Jeffrey Brooks, Thank You, Comrade Stalin! Soviet Public Culture from Revolution to Cold War (Princeton, N.J.: Princeton University Press, 2000), chap. 7. For a discussion that focuses more explicitly on patriotic culture (but one that curiously omits the war films), see David Brandenberger, Na-

tional Bolshevism: Stalinist Mass Culture and the Formation of Modern Russian National Identity, 1931–1956 (Cambridge, Mass.: Harvard University Press, 2002), chap. 9.

22. The role of Russian women in combat during the Great War is the subject of Laurie S. Stoff's book They Fought for the Motherland: Russia's Women Soldiers in World War I and the Revolution (Lawrence: University Press of Kansas, 2006).

23. The only full-length scholarly monograph to date on any aspect of women in combat during the Russo-German War is Reina Pennington, Wings, Women, and War: Soviet Airwomen in World War II Combat (Lawrence: University Press of Kansas, 2001). Kazimiera J. Cottam has done more than any other scholar to keep the memory of these women alive; in addition to her Women in War and Resistance, see, e.g., Cottam, ed. and trans., Defending Leningrad: Women behind Enemy Lines, rev. ed. (Nepean, Ont.: New Military Publishing, 1998); and Z. M. Smirnova-Medvedeva, On the Road to Stalingrad: Memoirs of a Woman Machine Gunner, ed. and trans. Kazimiera J. Cottam, rev. ed. (Nepean, Ont.: New Military Publishing, 1997).

24. Director Mikhail Kalatozov was sent to Hollywood in July 1943 to promote Soviet war films. In letters to Ivan Bolshakov, he reported that the favorable American reception of She Defends the Motherland enabled him to sell Two Warriors and Wait for Me in 1944; Kalatozov, "Druzhba zakliatykh vragov: Pis'ma iz Gollivud," ed. Valerii Fomin, IK, no. 8 (August 2005): 134. Two American fiction films from 1943 appeared on Soviet screens during the war, Michael Curtiz's Mission to Moscow and Lewis Milestone's North Star, as did two documentaries, Frank Capra's Battle for Russia and Song

about Russia; Vladimir Kozlov, comp., and Aleksandr Dorozhevich, ed., "Spisok amerikanskikh fil'mov v sovetskom i rossiiskom prokate, 1929–1998," *Kinograf*, no. 16 (2005): 176.

25. Konstantin Rudnitsky also drew this comparison, saying that the war is remembered primarily in two images: Dmitry Moor's recruiting poster and Vera Maretskaya as Comrade P.; K. Rudnitskii, "O Vere Maretskoi," *IK*, no. 1 (January 1979): 119.

26. It is worth noting at this point that "Fridrikh Ermler" was Vladimir Breslav's nom de guerre. Breslav, of Latvian Jewish (not German) heritage, had served the Red Army as a spy during the Civil War and used this name as he infiltrated German lines. He later served in the Cheka.

27. At least one contemporary reviewer found her performance "profoundly true and authentic"; Sergei Borodin, "Ona zashchishchaet rodinu," *Pravda*, 24 May 1943.

28. For the views of other scholars on *She Defends the Motherland* and some of the other movies discussed in this chapter, see Kenez, "Black and White," 157–175, or *Cinema and Soviet Society*, chap. 9; Leyda, *Kino*, 364–388; David Gillespie, *Russian Cinema* (Harlow: Longman, 2003), chap. 7; Paul Babitsky and John Rimberg, *The Soviet Film Industry* (New York: Praeger, 1955), 177–187. For the Soviet viewpoint, see Bol'shakov, *Sovetskoe kinoiskusstvo v gody Velikoi otechestvennoi voiny*, chaps. 3–5; Iurii Khaniutin, *Preduprezhdenie iz proshlogo* (Moscow: Iskusstvo, 1968), 22–146; Neia Zorkaia, *The Illustrated History of the Soviet Cinema* (New York: Hippocrene, 1989), chap. 4; Rostislav Iurenev, "Kinoiskusstvo voennykh let," in *Sovetskaia kul'tura v gody velikoi otechestvennoi voiny* (Moscow:

Nauka, 1976), 235–251; or Iurenev, *Kratkaia istoriia sovetskogo kino* (Moscow: Biuro propagandy sovetskogo kinoiskusstva, 1979), 128–136.

29. Maretskaia, quoted by Rudnitskii, "O Vere Maretskoi," 119.

30. Mark Donskoi, "Raduga," *SE*, no. 3 (1969): 18; Donskoi, "My srazhalis' svoim iskusstvom," in *Sovetskaia kul'tura*, 252–254.

31. This is an extremely interesting comment, coming as it does from a clearly Ukrainian character.

32. Donskoi, "Raduga," 19; and Semën Freilikh, "Etot neistovyi Mark Donskoi," *IK*, no. 6 (June 1971): 40; recounted (without source citation) in Iurenev, *Kratkaia istoriia*, 132, and Zorkaia, *Illustrated History*, 189. See also John Haynes's discussion of the picture in *New Soviet Man: Gender and Masculinity in Stalinist Soviet Cinema* (Manchester: Manchester University Press, 2003), 165–169.

33. As Rosalinde Sartorti observes in her survey of the wartime cult heroes, Zoya is the most famous of the World War II icons. Yet in 1991, as the last gasp of glasnost before the fall of the USSR, even the sacred Zoya myth came under attack, with some claiming that she had been stoned to death by villagers angry at the partisans, which, if true, would mean that the famous photograph by Sergei Strunnikov showed another dead girl. See Sartorti, "The Making of Heroes, Heroines, and Saints," in Stites, *Culture and Entertainment*, 182–186, 188–190; also see Tumarkin, *The Living and the Dead*, 76–78.

34. Vadim Kozhevnikov, "Zoia," *Pravda*, 22 September 1944.

35. DS, 169.

36. Reviewers praised it for its future-mindedness; see P. Lidov, "Mashen'ka," *Pravda*, 19 April 1942.

37. Liliia Mamatova, "Mashen'ka i zombi: Mifologiia soveskoi zhenshchiny," IK, no. 6 (June 1991): 118.

38. DS, 242. This film was also selected for inclusion in RI; see Valeriia Gorelova, "Mashen'ka," 213–218.

39. This fragment is quoted from Stites, Russian Popular Culture, 101.

40. Many survivor memoirs have been translated into English, e.g., Aleksandr Fadeev, Leningrad in the Days of the Blockade, trans. R. D. Charques (Westport, Conn.: Greenwood Press, 1971); Vera Inber, Leningrad Diary, trans. Serge M. Wolff and Rachel Grieve (New York: St. Martin's Press, 1971); Elena Kochina, Blockade Diary, trans. and intro. Samuel C. Ramer (Ann Arbor, Mich.: Ardis, 1990); Lidia Ginzburg, Blockade Diary, trans. Alan Myers (London: Harvill Press, 1995). The definitive account of the military operations is David M. Glantz, The Battle for Leningrad, 1941–1944 (Lawrence: University Press of Kansas, 2002).

41. Valeriia Gorelova, "Zhila-byla devochka," in RI, 237–244.

42. Bol'shakov, Sovetskoe kinoiskusstvo v gody Velikoi otechestvennoi voiny, 40.

43. As Kenez notes, The Regional Party Secretary is unusual among the wartime war films in having a Party bureaucrat as its hero (Cinema and Soviet Society, 179).

44. Ladynina was one of the most beloved stars of the Soviet screen from the midthirties to the fifties. Her work with Pyrev has recently been commemorated by Liana Polukhina, Marina Ladynina i Ivan Pyr'ev (Moscow: Eksmo/Algoritm, 2004).

45. Anna Karavaeva, "Sekretar' raikoma," Pravda, 13 December 1942.

46. Rostislav Iurenev, "Ivan Aleksandrovich Pyr'rev: Biograficheskii ocherk," in Ivan Pyr'ev v zhizni i na ekrane: Stranitsy vospominanii (Moscow: Kinotsentr, 1994), 38.

47. Leonid Leonov, "Invasion," in Four Soviet War Plays (London: Hutchinson, 1944), 58–117.

48. Iurii Khaniutin, "Kogda pushki streliaiut," IK, no. 5 (May 1965): 20.

49. Anna Karavaeva, "Nashestvie," Pravda, 1 March 1945.

50. "Ob ideinosti v kinoiskusstve," Pravda, 29 September 1943; Vsevolod Pudovkin, "O fil'me Dva boitsa," Pravda, 6 October 1943. (Leading directors were often called upon to praise the films of less well known artists.)

51. The film's staying power is attested to in Anatolii Volkov, "Dva boitsa," in RI, 219–224.

52. Sergei Narovchatov, "Dvadtsat' let spustia," IK, no. 2 (February 1965): 51.

53. See in SE, no. 9 (1980), G. Beregovoi, "Nasha pobeda," 7, and Iu. Nikulin, "Chapaev s nami," 17, who, despite the title of his reminiscence, says that Two Warriors was "the best film that I saw at the front."

54. Babitsky and Rimberg, Soviet Film Industry, 182.

55. Haynes, New Soviet Man, 54.

56. Vadim Kozhevnikov, "Nebo Moskvy," Pravda, 2 June 1944.

57. DS, 276.

58. See, e.g., N. Sirivlia, "Nebo nad Moskvy," IK, no. 8 (August 1997): 38–40.

59. Bol'shakov, Sovetskoe kinoiskusstvo v gody Velikoi otechestvennoi voiny, 64. Babitsky and Rimberg assert that Malakhov Hill was banned (184–185). This is not, however, corroborated in Margolit and Shmyrov Iz'iatoe Kino, where the film is not listed, nor by DS, 236. The film may, however, have had a restricted distribution. For an explanation of Bolshakov's role in central film administration, see Babitsky and Rimberg, Soviet Film Industry, 44, 47, 49.

60. This detail was recalled by the star

herself in Marina Ladynina, "Vo vremia voiny iskusstvo voiuet!" SE, no. 9 (1980): 7.

61. Anonymous, A Woman in Berlin: Eight Weeks in the Conquered City, a Diary, trans. Philip Boehm (New York: Henry Holt, 2005), 254–255. "Anonymous," a German journalist who spoke Russian, also enjoyed the film.

62. D. Zaslavskii, "V shest' chasov vechera posle voiny," Pravda, 19 November 1944. Grigory Aleksandrov includes a still from the film, although he does not actually discuss it, in his article on the development of the comedy genre; G. Aleksandrov, "Printsipy sovetskoi kinokomedii," IK, no. 5 (May 1949): 12–16.

63. Aleksandr Deriabin, "Rannie otechestvennye tsvetnye fil'my, 1931–1945: Fil'mografa," KZ, no. 56 (2002): 322–348; and DS, 173. The second part of Sergei Eisenstein's Ivan the Terrible (1945) was filmed partly in color, but it was banned until 1958; ibid., 172.

64. Kenez, Cinema and Soviet Society, 182.

Chapter Four

1. Reina Pennington, Wings, Women, and War: Soviet Airwomen in World War II Combat (Lawrence: University Press of Kansas, 2001), chap. 7.

2. DS, 276.

3. For another view on The Great Turning Point and other films discussed in this chapter, see Iurii Khaniutin, Preduprezhdenie proshlogo (Moscow: Iskusstvo, 1968), 146–213.

4. My discussion of the background of the film's production is drawn from Jay Leyda, Kino: A History of the Russian and Soviet Film (New York: Collier, 1973), 391–393.

5. M. Galaktionov, "Velikii perelom," Pravda, 31 January 1946.

6. Quoted by Leyda, Kino, 392; this article appeared in Soviet Literature (Sovetskaia literatura) in 1946.

7. See Nina Tumarkin, The Living and the Dead: The Rise and Fall of the Cult of World War II in Russia (New York: Basic Books, 1994), 95–100, for a brief overview. The disillusionments of the decade after the war are the subject of Elena Zubkova's excellent monograph Russia after the War: Hopes, Illusions, and Disappointments, 1945–1957, trans. and ed. Hugh Ragsdale (Armonk, N.Y.: M. E. Sharpe, 1998). The most vivid analysis of Soviet society in the late 1940s through the early 1950s as reflected in Soviet literature remains Vera S. Dunham's classic In Stalin's Time: Middleclass Values in Soviet Fiction (Cambridge: Cambridge University Press, 1976).

8. Tumarkin, The Living and the Dead, 104. Victory Day became a holiday again in 1965.

9. An insightful discussion of the revival of the Stalin cult and its relationship to the war may be found in Jeffrey Brooks, Thank You, Comrade Stalin! Soviet Public Culture from Revolution to Cold War (Princeton, N.J.: Princeton University Press, 2000), chap. 8. See also Tumarkin, The Living and the Dead, chap. 5.

10. Peter Kenez, Cinema and Soviet Society from the Revolution to the Death of Stalin (London: I. B. Tauris, 2001), 205.

11. Ibid., 165.

12. Babitsky and Rimberg, Soviet Film Industry, 243.

13. Natacha Laurent, L'Œil du Kremlin: Cinéma et censure en URSS sous Staline (1928–1953) (Paris: Editions Privat, 2000), chaps. 6–10.

14. For a vivid discussion of Eisenstein's travails, see Oksana Bulgakowa, Sergei Eisenstein: A Biography, trans. Anne

Dwyer (Berlin: PotemkinPress, 2001), 217–224.

15. Maia Turovskaia, "Soviet Films of the Cold War," in Richard Taylor and Derek Spring, eds., *Stalinism and Soviet Cinema* (London: Routledge, 1993), 131–141. See also Babitsky and Rimberg, *Soviet Film Industry*, 188–212.

16. DS, 63, 219.

17. Khaniutin, *Preduprezhdenie proshlogo*, 212.

18. Kenez, *Cinema and Soviet Society*, 215; Babitsky and Rimberg, *Soviet Film Industry*, 191–192.

19. Quoted by Babitsky and Rimberg, *Soviet Film Industry*, 191.

20. Ibid., 192–193. *The Girl of My Dreams* appears as part of the historical background in Tatiana Lioznova's popular 1973 television miniseries about the war, *Seventeen Moments of Spring* (Semnadtsat' mgnovenii vesny).

21. Ibid., 200.

22. DS, 333. Another film of this period with a hero who is neither disabled nor killed is *Konstantin Zaslonov* (Konstantin Zaslonov, dir. Aleksandr Faintsimmer [Feinzimmer] and Vladimir Korsh-Sablin, 1949). In this "true story" of a Belorussian partisan who pretends to collaborate with the Germans in order to sabotage their supply trains, Zaslonov is a true-to-type socialist realist hero. Although less stuffy than Shchors, Zaslonov is just as "perfect." *Konstantin Zaslonov* was also awarded a Stalin Prize, in 1950.

23. Boris Polevoi, *A Story about a Real Man*, trans. J. Fineberg (Westport, Conn.: Greenwood Press, 1970); Aleksandr Fadeev, *The Young Guard*, trans. Violet Dutt (Moscow: Foreign Languages Publishing House, 1958).

24. In *Kino*, 394–395, Leyda notes

that criticism of the apparently "panicky" Soviet withdrawal from Krasnodon that Fadeev described had to be revised after part 1 of Gerasimov's film had been completed; see also Babitsky and Rimberg, *Soviet Film Industry*, 195–196. What happened to the Young Guard of Krasnodon is still a source of controversy; see I. A. Ioffe and N. K. Petrova, eds., *Molodaia gvardiia (g. Krasnodon): Khudozhestvennaia obraz i istoricheskaia real'nost': Sbornik dokumentov i materialov* (Moscow: Veche, 2003). Fadeev, who was allegedly drunk the entire time he investigated the story, committed suicide in 1946.

25. Stolper followed Polevoi's spelling of the hero's surname in the film. As a result, many sources use "Meresev" whether describing the "real man" or the character.

26. Stolper's other two wartime war films were *A Lad from Our Town* (Paren' iz nashego goroda, 1942) and *Days and Nights* (Dni i nochi, 1945), both of which were based on works by Konstantin Simonov. Also see note 40 below.

27. For one Soviet officer's account of his time in a military hospital, where the doctors were "mostly ladies," see Evgeni Bessonov, *Tank Rider: Into the Reich with the Red Army*, trans. Bair Irincheev (London: Greenhill and Mechanicsburg, Pa.: Stackpole, 2003), 226–227. Bessonov also recalls watching movies in the hospital, but, alas, does not mention any titles.

28. DS, 331.

29. P. Pavlenko, "Poema o sovetskom cheloveke," *Pravda*, 23 November 1948.

30. Pavel Kadochnikov, "Na frontovykh dorogakh," IK, no. 3 (March 1975): 69–73. Kadochnikov was not a veteran himself, but he drew from his wartime experiences that often brought him into contact with frontline soldiers.

31. "Posle voiny," SE, no. 22 (1967), 18–19.

32. DS, 253–254.

33. Their eyes were gouged out, etc.

34. Nonna Mordiukova recalled this in "Posle voiny," 18.

35. E.g., in Pravda, 1948: "Molodaia gvardiia," 26 August; "Molodaia gvardiia," 10 October; "Ogromnyi uspekh fil'ma Molodaia gvardiia," 12 October. This film continued to be touted long after its release; in IK, see Iulii Raizman, "O tvorcheskom roste molodykh kinoakterov," no. 4 (April 1952): 93; Il'ia Kopalin, "Na festivale sovetskikh fil'mov v Vengrii," no. 6 (June 1954): 109–110. A present-day reevaluation can be found in Valeriia Gorelova, "Molodaia gvardiia," in RI, 255–261.

36. Semën Freilikh, "Molodost' fil'ma," IK, no. 1 (January 1965): 1–6.

37. John Erickson, The Road to Stalingrad: Stalin's War with Germany, vol. 1 (New York: Harper and Row, 1975), 372. In this section of his magnum opus, Erickson provides a great deal of useful information about the hypercentralization of the command and "the gap between decisions taken at the centre and the requirements of the fronts" (372).

38. A German soldier's view of the battle for the Crimea may be found in Gottlob Herbert Bidermann, In Deadly Combat: A German Soldier's Memoir of the Eastern Front, trans. and ed. Derek S. Zumbro (Lawrence: University Press of Kansas, 2000).

39. Vadim Kozhevnikov, "Tretii udar," Pravda, 3 May 1948.

40. The first feature film about the Battle of Stalingrad was Aleksandr Stolper's Days and Nights (Dni i nochi, 1945), which was an adaptation of the novel by Konstantin Simonov, Days and Nights,

trans. Joseph Barnes (New York: Simon and Schuster, 1945).

41. For a German soldier's view of the Battle of Stalingrad, see Günther K. Koschorrek, Blood Red Snow: The Memoirs of a German Soldier on the Eastern Front (Mechanicsburg, Pa.: Stackpole, 2000).

42. "Stalingradtsy o kinofil'me Stalingradskaia bitva," Pravda, 11 May 1949.

43. V. Koroteev, "Stalingradskaia bitva," Pravda, 20 December 1949.

44. For the definitive analysis of this movie as an aspect of the Stalin cult, see Richard Taylor, Film Propaganda: Soviet Russia and Nazi Germany, 2nd ed. rev. (London: I. B. Tauris, 1998), chap. 9. For an account of the fall of Berlin by a Soviet soldier, see Bessonov, Tank Rider, 197–224.

45. Liliia Mamatova, "Mashen'ka i zombi: Mifologiia sovetskoi zhenshchiny," IK, no. 6 (June 1991): 115–116.

46. Quoted by Leyda, Kino, 401.

47. DS, 316.

48. Kenez, Cinema and Soviet Society, 207.

49. "Zamechatel'noe proizvedenie sovetskogo kinoiskusstva: Zriteli o fil'me Padenie Berlina," Pravda, 25 January 1950.

50. V. Shcherbina, "Fil'm o velikom pobede," Pravda, 25 January 1950.

51. L. Pogozheva, "Padenie Berlina," IK, no. 1 (January 1950): 11–12. In the same journal, also see M. Andzhaparidze and V. Tsirgiladze, "Kak sozdavalsia fil'm Padenie Berlina," no. 4 (April 1950): 22–26; A. Groshev, "Obraz nashego sovremennika v kinoiskusstve," no. 4 (April 1951): 14.

52. Taylor, Film Propaganda, 100.

53. Neia Zorkaia, The Illustrated History of the Soviet Cinema (New York: Hippocrene, 1989), 196. Her frank characterization was, of course, "safe" in the glasnost era, when this book appeared.

54. Quoted by Leyda, Kino, 401.

55. DS, 278.

56. Boris Polevoi, author of The Story of a Real Man, reviewed the picture for Pravda, "Nezabyvaemyi 1919 god," 4 May 1952. In IK (1951), see Vsevolod Vishnevskii, Mikhail Chiaureli, and A. Filimonov, "Nezabyvaemyi 1919-i," no. 5, 31–42, and no. 6, 18–29 (this is the literary scenario); I. Rachuk and I. Ol'shanskii, "Stsenarii o nezabyvaemom," no. 6, 13–17. In IK (1952), see Iu. Kalashnikov, "Traditsii geroicheskogo epokha," no. 7, 3–25; Igor' Belza, "Zametki o muzyke fil'ma Nezabyvaemyi 1919 god," no. 9, 87–91; L. Kosmatov, "Izobrazitel'noe reshenie fil'ma Nezabyvaemyi 1919 god," no. 9, 101–110.

57. The other contender would be Ivan Pyrev's Cossack musical, The Kuban Cossacks (Kubanskie kazaki, 1949, released 1950).

58. DS, 413.

59. Pavel Kuznetsov, "Fil'm o smelykh liudiakh," Pravda, 8 September 1950. Also see L. Pogozheva, "O prostykh i smelykh liudiakh," IK, no. 4 (April 1950): 27.

Chapter Five

1. Background for this chapter has been drawn primarily from Josephine Woll's excellent study of Thaw cinema, Real Images: Soviet Cinema and the Thaw (London: I. B. Tauris, 2000), and secondarily from Iurii Khaniutin, Preduprezhdenie proshlogo (Moscow: Iskusstvo, 1968), 215–283, and Evgenii Margolit, "Kinematograf 'ottepeli': K portretu fenomena," KZ, no. 67 (2001): 195–230. Margolit's essay can also be found (but untranslated) in Nancy Condee, producer, Thaw Cinema, CD-ROM (Pittsburgh: Artima Studio/University of Pittsburgh, n.d.).

2. Nina Tumarkin, The Living and the Dead: The Rise and Fall of the Cult of World War II in Russia (New York: Basic Books, 1994), 110.

3. Woll, Real Images, 3–11. According to Neia Zorkaia, The Illustrated History of the Soviet Cinema (New York: Hippocrene, 1989), 196, the push for an increase in film production had been under way since 1952.

4. Il'ia Erenburg, The Thaw, trans. Manya Harari (Chicago: Regnery, 1955).

5. See, e.g., the following reviews of The Fate of a Man, which are filled with canned phrases: B. Polevoi, "Sud'ba cheloveka," Pravda, 17 April 1959, and Georgii Beridze, "Pesn' o muzhestve," Pravda, 9 March 1960.

6. Woll, Real Images, 30–31.

7. Ibid., 60.

8. This was the second time the story had been filmed. Mark Donskoy made a conventional, forgettable screen version in 1942 (which was not included in DS). In 1973, a six-part television series directed by Nikolai Mashchenko from a script by Alov and Naumov appeared. This was so successful that it was released for the big screen as a two-part film in 1975; DS, 189.

9. Woll, Real Images, 36.

10. "Savchenko, Igor' Andreevich," in Kino-slovar' v dvukh tomakh, 2 vols. (Moscow: Izd-vo Sovetskaia entsiklopediia, 1970), 2:498–499.

11. Ia. Varshavskii, "Za chto boretsia fil'm," IK, no. 4 (April 1958): 27–38.

12. Woll, Real Images, 36–37.

13. L. Pogozheva, "Novoe prochtenie romana," IK, no. 2 (February 1957): 83–97.

14. Ibid., 86–87.

15. DS, 205, 316.

16. Ibid., 205.

17. Zorkaia, *Illustrated History*, 218; Woll, *Real Images*, 38.

18. Woll, *Real Images*, 39.

19. For an appreciation of this film in aesthetic terms as a romantic epic, see ibid., 40–41; and Iurii Tiurin, "*Sorok per-vyi*," in *RI*, 279–284.

20. Iurii Tiurin, "*Tikhii Don*," in *RI*, 297–302.

21. Ibid., 297.

22. DS, 420.

23. Ibid., 449.

24. S. Freilikh, "Sud'ba Grigoriia Me-lekhova," *IK*, no. 1 (January 1958): 20–35, and no. 9 (September 1958): 91–100.

25. Woll, *Real Images*, 63.

26. See, e.g., ibid., 73–78; Woll, *The Cranes Are Flying* (London: I. B. Tauris, 2003); *Letiat' zhuravli* (Moscow: Iskusstvo, 1972); Anatolii Volkov, "*Letiat zhuravli*," in *RI*, 285–290; Iurii Bogomolov, *Mikhail Kalatozov: Stranitsy tvorcheskoi biografii* (Moscow: Iskusstvo, 1989), 157–182; A. Batalov, *Sud'ba i remeslo* (Moscow: Iskusstvo, 1984), 119–136; G. Kremlev, *Mikhail Kalatozov* (Moscow: Iskusstvo, 1964), 161–203.

27. For a discussion of this issue, see, e.g., in John Garrard and Carol Garrard, eds., *World War 2 and the Soviet People* (New York: St. Martin's Press, 1993): Frank Ellis, "Army and Party in Conflict: Soldiers and Commissars in the Prose of Vasilii Grossman," 180–201, and Arnold McMillin, "Recovery of the Past and Struggle for the Future: Vasil' Bykaw's [sic] Recent War Fiction," 202–212.

28. Woll, *Real Images*, 71–73.

29. Lev Anninskii, *Shestidesiatniki i my* (Moscow: Soiuz Kinematografistov SSSR, 1991), 8–43. The quotation is the opening line, 8.

30. Woll, *Real Images*, 78–79.

31. Maia Turovskaia, "'Da' i 'net,'" *IK*, no. 12 (December 1957): 14–18; Rostislav

Iurenev, "Vernost'," *IK*, no. 12 (December 1957): 5–14.

32. DS, 227.

33. Woll, *Real Images*, 89. Sholokhov's story was finally published in 1956.

34. For other analyses of this film, see Woll, *Real Images*, 88–91; Zorkaia, *Illustrated History*, 220–223; and Marina Kuznetsova, "Sud'ba cheloveka," in *RI*, 315–320.

35. For other views, see Woll, *Real Images*, 96–99; Zorkaia, *Illustrated History*, 217–220; Liudviga Zakrzhevskaia, "Ballada o soldate," in *RI*, 309–314.

36. On *The Fate of a Man*, see "Vtoraia zhizn' literaturnogo obraza," *IK*, no. 6 (June 1959): 88–94, a roundtable discussion featuring many well-known critics. For the discussion of *The Ballad of a Soldier*, see "Podprobnyi razgovor," *IK*, no. 1 (January 1960): 65–80.

37. DS, 432.

38. Ibid., 28.

39. "Tarkovskii, Andrei Arsen'evich," *Kino-slovar' v dvukh tomakh*, 2:632.

40. Vida T. Johnson and Graham Petrie, *The Films of Andrei Tarkovsky: A Visual Fugue* (Bloomington: Indiana University Press, 1994), 67. This work is the definitive analysis of Tarkovsky's oeuvre.

41. Marlen Khutsiev's *The Two Fyodors* (*Dva Fëdora*, 1958) is a lovely little film set in the first postwar months showing the difficulty of adjusting to peacetime for newly demobilized Big Fyodor (the writer Vasily Shukshin in his first role) and the orphaned Little Fyodor. Their relationship becomes complicated when Big Fyodor falls in love. DS does not record an attendance figure (107).

42. Ibid., 173.

43. "Urbanskii, Evgenii Iakovlevich," *Kino-slovar' v dvukh tomakh*, 2:710–711; Zorkaia, *Illustrated History*, 202.

44. DS, 496.

45. See, e.g., N. Ignateva, "Liudi i vremia," *IK*, no. 7 (July 1961): 33–39; and Tatiana Bachelis, "Realnost' schast'ia," *IK*, no. 8 (August 1961): 71–78.

46. Woll, *Real Images*, 123.

47. DS, 245.

48. This phrase comes from a later critic, Vatslav Smal, *Chelovek, voina, podvig* (Minsk: Nauka i tekhnika, 1979), 62. Smal also labeled *Ivan's Childhood* as "abstract humanism."

49. V. Kardin, "Liudi i simvoly," *IK*, no. 10 (October 1961): 60, 62. Ironically, Ia. Varshavsky, writing in the fan magazine *Soviet Screen*, admired *Peace*'s allegory; see Varshavskii, "Mir vkhodiashchemu," SE, no. 19 (1961): 6–7, 13.

50. L. A. Alova, comp., *Aleksandr Alov i Vladimir Naumov: Stat'i, svidetel'stva, vyskazyvaniia* (Moscow: Iskusstvo, 1989), 70–89.

51. Woll, *Real Images*, 79.

52. DS, 128.

53. Zorkaia, *Illustrated History*, 210.

54. In *Kino-slovar' v dvukh tomakh*, see "Kulidzhanov, Lev Aleksandrovich," 1:866, and "Segel, Iakov Aleksandrovich," 2:522.

55. Iurii German, *The Staunch and the True*, trans. Olga Shartse (Moscow: Progress Publishers, n.d.). (The publisher obviously decided on a more stalwart title for the English-speaking audience than "My Dear Man.") For a first-person account of conditions in a World War II field hospital, see Nikolai Amosov, *PPG 2266: A Surgeon's War*, trans. George St. George (Chicago: Regnery, 1975).

56. DS, 131. *My Dear Man* was seen by 32 million viewers and was named the third-best film of the year in the *Soviet Screen* readers' poll.

57. Ibid., 125. *Volunteers* drew 26.6 million viewers, finishing in seventeenth place at the box office in 1959.

58. Nikolai Chukovskii, *Baltic Skies*, trans. R. Daglish (Moscow: Foreign Languages Publishing House, 1956).

59. "Vengerov, Vladimir Iakolevich," *Kino-slovar' v dvukh tomakh*, 1:278.

60. See, e.g., Leonid Kozlov, "K chemu stremilsia khudozhnik?" *IK*, no. 12 (December 1957): 38–44.

61. DS, 28.

62. Konstantin Simonov, *The Living and the Dead*, trans. Alex Miller (Moscow: Progress Publishers, 1975).

63. "The highest flight of truth for me was Stolper's film *The Living and the Dead*." Aleksei German, "Pravda—ne skhodstvo, a otkrytie," *IK*, no. 12 (December 2001): 82. This is a reprint of an article that first appeared in *IK* in 1979. A more recent appreciation of the film and its influence, especially on its director Gherman, can be found in Vera Shitova, "Zhivye i mërtvye," SE, no. 24 (1987): 14–15.

64. DS, 146.

65. Vladimir Baskakov, "Geroicheskoe v kino," *IK*, no. 8 (August 1964): 39.

66. Ian Bereznitskii, "Radi zhizni na zemle," *IK*, no. 3 (March 1964): 5–6.

67. Examples of Simonov's wartime reportage can be found in Ilya Ehrenburg [Il'ia Epenburg] and Konstantin Simonov, *In One Newspaper: A Chronicle of Unforgettable Years*, trans. Anatol Kagan (New York: Sphinx, 1985).

68. Baskakov, "Geroicheskoe v kino," 39.

69. "Kolosov, Sergei Nikolaevich," in *Kino: Entsiklopedicheskii slovar'* (Moscow: Sovetskaia entsiklopediia, 1986), 207.

Chapter Six

1. Josephine Woll, *Real Images: Soviet Cinema and the Thaw* (London: I. B. Tauris, 2000), 203–204.

2. By the late seventies, Brezhnev was also building a cult of Brezhnev.

3. Anna Lawton, *Kinoglasnost: Soviet Cinema in Our Time* (Cambridge: Cambridge University Press, 1992), 9–10.

4. Ibid., 11.

5. Nina Tumarkin, *The Living and the Dead: The Rise and Fall of the Cult of World War II in Russia* (New York: Basic Books, 1994), 133.

6. Konstantin Rokossovskii, "Armiia i kino," SE, no. 3 (1959): 1.

7. A. Groshev "40 let sovetskogo kino," SE, no. 16 (1959): 2–3; Efim Dzigan, "Chetvert veka: My iz Kronshtadta," SE, no. 8 (1961): 4–5.

8. Rostislav Iurenev, "*Chapaev*," IK, no. 11 (November 1964): 10–19.

9. Vladimir Baskakov, "Geroicheskoe v kino," IK, no. 8 (August 1964): 7–12. It is interesting that Baskakov would dismiss *The Young Guard* (or even *Story of a Real Man*) as a film of the same order as *The Fall of Berlin*. Later articles in the *Art of the Cinema* and *Soviet Screen* defended Gerasimov's picture; see S. Freilikh, "Molodost' fil'ma," IK, no. 1 (January 1965): 1–6; and "Posle voiny," SE, no. 22 (1967): 18–19. *Soviet Screen* also had kind words about *The Story of a Real Man*.

10. Iurii Khaniutin, "Kogda pushki streliaiut," IK, no. 5 (May 1965): 2 (for the quotation), 8–9, 10–13.

11. Ibid., 13–19.

12. Semën Freilikh, "Etot neistovyi Mark Donskoi," IK, no. 6 (June 1971): 40.

13. Khaniutin, 20–23 (the quotation appears on page 20).

14. See, e.g., "Velikaia otechestvennaia," SE, no. 20 (1967): 18–20; Mark Donskoi, "*Raduga*," SE, no. 3 (1969): 18–19.

15. Tumarkin, *The Living and the Dead*, chap. 6.

16. Ibid., 135.

17. There were many Soviet cold war spy thrillers; I am referring here only to spy thrillers set during World War II.

18. DS, 509. No box office is recorded for *Retribution*, 71–72. Critics considered *Retribution* a disappointing sequel to *The Living and the Dead*; see, e.g., Vatslav Smal, *Chelovek, voina, podvig* (Minsk: Nauka i tekhnika, 1979), 89.

19. "Konkurs 68 itogi," SE, no. 10 (1969): 2–3. There were 40,000 ballots returned in the 1968 competition. It is important to keep in mind, however, that this is far from a scientific sample: 71 percent of the respondents were twenty-five or younger; 95 percent lived in cities; 80 percent were female; 64 percent saw thirty to seventy films per year, with another 20 percent seeing more than seventy per year. This is the profile of hard-core film fans.

20. "Vul'fovich, Teodor Iur'evich," in *Kino: Entsiklopedicheskii slovar'* (Moscow: Sovetskaia entsiklopediia, 1986), 84.

21. DS, 144, 214–215.

22. It drew 49.6 million viewers; ibid., 27.

23. "Chkheidze, Revaz Davidovich," *Kino-slovar' v dvukh tomakh*, 2 vols. (Moscow: Izd-vo Sovetskaia entsiklopediia, 1970), 2:913.

24. DS, 310.

25. Ibid., 481.

26. Ibid., 122.

27. "Viatich-Berezhnykh, Damir Alekseevich," *Kino*, 86.

28. DS, 167, does not record an attendance figure for this film.

29. No attendance recorded; ibid., 267.

30. "Ershov, Mikhail Ivanovich," *Kino*, 138; DS, 41.

31. "Keosaian, Edmond Gareginovich," *Kino*, 177.

32. DS, 209–210, 283, 286.

33. One of these films, *The White Sun of the Desert*, has been included in *Russian Illusion*'s pantheon of Russian film classics; see Marina Kuznetsova, "*Beloe solntse pustyni*," *RI*, 459–464.

34. DS, 392. *The Property of the Republic* drew 47.14 million (DS, 132); *The White Sun of the Desert*, 34.5 million (DS, 34).

35. DS, 411.

36. See, e.g., Mark Zak, "Epokha i litsa," *IK*, no. 8 (August 1968): 19–23.

37. A. Karaganov, "Geroika podviga, kharakter voiny," *IK*, no. 7 (July 1969): 43.

38. For a sample of the reviews, see L. A. Alova, comp., *Aleksandr Alov i Vladimir Naumov: Stat'i, svidetel'stva, vyskazyvaniia* (Moscow: Iskusstvo, 1989), 146–169; see also Aleksandr Karaganov, "Beg," *RI*, 471–476.

39. *The Flight* was seen by 19.7 million (DS, 30).

40. Liudviga Zakrzhevskaia, "V ogne broda net," in *RI*, 429–434.

41. "Poloka, Gennadii Ivanovich," *Kino*, 327.

42. A later, more conventional effort to bring the world of the revolutionary theater to the screen, Aleksandr Mitt's tragicomedy *Burn, Burn My Star* [Gori, gori, moia zvezda, 1969] focused on a quixotic but deeply humane actor/director with Bolshevik sympathies and enjoyed considerable popularity.

43. Woll, *Real Images*, 202.

44. In Russian, Ognev's query is a play on words. The film was *neprazdnichnyi* (literally "not festive"), to which Ognev replied "*Razve revoliutsiia byla prazdnik?*"; Vladimir Ognev, "Dvadtsat' let nazad," *IK*, no. 1 (January 1988): 39.

45. Ibid.

46. Elena Stishova, "Strasti po Komissaru," *IK*, no. 1 (January 1989): 119.

47. "V gorode Berdicheve," in Vasilii Grossman, *Povesty, rasskazy, ocherki* (Moscow: Voennoe izd-vo Ministerstvo oborony soiuza SSR, 1958), 88–103. Askoldov changed the main characters' names from Khaim-Abram to Yefim and Beila to Maria.

48. Stishova, "Strasti po Komissaru," 110. For a discussion of the "arrest" of Grossman's war novel, see Tumarkin, *The Living and the Dead*, 113–117. For the novel in English, see Vasily [Vasilü] Grossman, *Life and Fate*, trans. Robert Chandler (New York: Harper and Row, 1985).

49. Discussed in Tumarkin, *The Living and the Dead*, 19–24.

50. Stishova, "Strasti po Komissaru," 110.

51. The most important of these documents appear in V. I. Fomin, comp., *Polka: Dokumenty, svidetel'nost', kommentarii* (Moscow: Nauchno-issledovatel'skii institut kinoiskusstva, 1992), 46–76; also see the discussion in Evgenii Margolit, "Kommissar," *RI*, 423–428.

52. Stishova, "Strasti po Komissaru," 117–118.

53. Chernenko, *Krasnaia zvezda*, 229–230.

54. Ibid., 114.

55. Ibid., 112.

56. Lawton, *Kinoglasnost*, 163–164; Lawton's analysis of the film appears on pages 160–163.

57. DS, 305; Richard Stites, *Russian Popular Culture: Entertainment and Society since 1900* (Cambridge: Cambridge University Press, 1992), 169.

58. "Konkurs-70 itogi," SE, no. 10 (1971): 1–2.

59. DS, 305.

60. "Konkurs-71 itogi," SE, no. 10 (1972): 18.

61. "Ozerov, Iurii Nikolaevich," *Kino*, 264.

62. Tumarkin, *The Living and the Dead*, 134.

63. Note that Jews are not mentioned as a category and that part of the Holocaust death toll is folded in here.

64. This was especially true with the later parts, as attendance was flagging. See Dal Orlov, "Zavershenie epopei," IK, no. 2 (February 1972): 6–14, on parts 4–5.

65. Marina Chechneva, "Pravda o voine," SE, no. 9 (1970): 2–4. Chechneva was a Hero of the Soviet Union.

66. Iurii Ozerov, "Vosslavit podvig naroda," IK, no. 2 (February 1971): 1, 3.

67. Semën Freilikh, "Litso geroia," IK, no. 4 (April 1971): 100–101.

68. Ibid., 105–106. A few years later, Yury Khaniutin flatly stated that war films in the style of *Liberation* had no future; Khaniutin, "Vozvrashchennoe vremia," IK, no. 7 (July 1977): 96.

Chapter Seven

1. DS, 11; "Konkurs SE-72 itogi," SE, no. 10 (1973): 12–13.

2. Lev Anninskii, "Ikh kroviu: Fil'm i kontekst (*A zori zdes' tikhie . . .*)," IK, no. 1 (January 1973): 23.

3. Vadim Sokolov, "Vagrianye zori," SE, no. 24 (1972): 4. For a recent Russian evaluation, see Mark Zak, "A zori zdes' tikhie," RI, 507–512.

4. Mark Zak, "Tol'ko ob odnom srazhenii," IK, no. 3 (March 1973): 32.

5. "Konkurs 'SE-73'-itogi," SE, no. 9 (1974): 18–19. It drew an audience of 22.9 million; DS, 98.

6. DS, 48.

7. During World War II, a few wartime documentaries received "special awards" from the Academy.

8. Aleksandr Karaganov, "Oni srazhalis' za rodinu," RI, 537–542.

9. "Konkurs-75," SE, no. 10 (1976): 18–19; DS, 301.

10. Nina Tumarkin, *The Living and the Dead: The Rise and Fall of the Cult of World War II in Russia* (New York: Basic Books, 1994), 137.

11. DS, 340.

12. Ibid., 25.

13. Tumarkin, *The Living and the Dead*, 141–145.

14. DS, 460.

15. Ibid.

16. F. Markova, "Razrushenie lichno," SE, no. 23 (1978): 6–7; "Konkurs SE-78," SE, no. 9 (1979): 12–13.

17. The Russian word *svoi* is as evocative as it is difficult to translate into English; it literally means "one's own," not "at home."

18. DS, 395. For an extensive analysis, see Birgit Beumers, *Nikita Mikhalkov: Between Nostalgia and Nationalism* (London: I. B. Tauris, 2005), 21–29.

19. A detailed analysis may be found in Beumers, *Nikita Mikhalkov*, 29–37.

20. For the censorship documents, see V. I. Fomin, comp., *Polka: Dokumenty, svidetel'nost', kommentarii* (Moscow: Nauchno-issledovatel'skii institut kinoiskusstva, 1992), 110–132; for a recent Russian analysis, see Evgenii Margolit, "Proverka na dorogakh," RI, 513–518.

21. Iurii German, "Ekho voiny," IK, no. 4 (April 1975): 15–16.

22. Iurii Khaniutin, "Vozvrashchennoe vremia," IK, no. 7 (July 1977): 91–92. For a recent Russian perspective, see Aleksandr Karaganov, "Dvadtsat' dnei bez voiny," RI, 555–560.

23. Shepitko was killed, along with the most important members of her

crew, in an accident that several of my acquaintances in the Soviet film industry believed was not "accidental." No one has produced any evidence of this, but it demonstrates the paranoia of the times. For a tribute, see "Pamiati tovarishcha: Larissa Shepitko, Vladimir Chukhnov, Iurii Fomenko," IK, no. 12 (December 1979): 143–145.

24. Liudviga Zakrzhevskaia, "Krylia," RI, 387–392.

25. "Kryl'ia: Podrobnyi razgovor," IK, no. 10 (October 1966): 12–29.

26. Her husband, Elem Klimov, completed her final film, which was in progress at the time of her death.

27. Josephine Woll, Real Images: Soviet Cinema and the Thaw (London: I. B. Tauris, 2000), 205; Vasyl Bykaŭ, "Sotnikov," in his Povesti, trans. author (Moscow: Khudozhestvennaia literatura, 1984), 5–110. Bykaŭ's name is rendered "Vasil Bykov" in Russian.

28. Tumarkin discusses some of the overtly religious symbolism in patriotic paintings of this time; The Living and the Dead, 140–141.

29. Solonitsyn (1934–1982) is best known in the West for his work with Tarkovsky: Andrei Rublëv, Solaris, and The Mirror.

30. See, e.g., L. Karakhan, "Krutoi put Voskhozhdenii," IK, no. 10 (October 1976): 85–105; Zoia Kutorga and Ovidii Gorchakov, "Vozvrashchennoe proshloe," IK, no. 5 (May 1977): 55–59.

31. Elena Stishova, "Khronika i legenda (Voskhozhdenie)," IK, no. 9 (September 1977): 32.

32. Ibid., 36; Khaniutin, "Vozvrashchennoe vremia," 96. For a recent Russian view, see Liudviga Zakrzhevskaia, "Voskhozhdenie," RI, 549–555.

33. Khaniutin, "Vozvrashchennoe vremia," 96.

34. Vadim Sokolov, "Venchanie tekh talantov, razviazka tekh legend," SE, no. 9 (1977): 3.

35. "Voskhozhdenie k pravde," SE, no. 1 (1978): 2.

36. In SE, 1978, see "Konkurs-77," no. 10, 10, and Inna Levshina, "Konkurs-77: Kommentarii kritika," no. 11, 8–9.

37. DS, 76. No figures are given for Twenty Days without War (107).

Chapter Eight

1. Nina Tumarkin, The Living and the Dead: The Rise and Fall of the Cult of World War II in Russia (New York: Basic Books, 1994), 169.

2. Unless one also counts Varlamov and Kopalin's The Defeat of the German-Fascist Troops near Moscow, which won a special Oscar (not Best Foreign Picture), or Japanese director Akira Kurosawa's Dersu Uzala, a Japanese-Soviet coproduction. For a recent evaluation, see Nadezhda Aleksandrova, "Moskva slezam ne verit," RI, 579–584.

3. Evgenii Matveev, "Rodiny radi," IK, no. 5 (May 1980): 5–6. He also included two wartime war films that I have not seen: A Lad from Our Town and The Front.

4. DS, 446; "Konkurs SE-81," SE, no. 10 (1982): 12.

5. No attendance recorded, DS, 463.

6. Zima, Irkutsk province.

7. No attendance date recorded, DS, 119.

8. No attendance date recorded; ibid., 503.

9. "Torpedonostsy," SE, no. 16 (1983): 4–5; DS, 452.

10. DS, 69.

11. Attendance was 15.5 million; ibid., 187.

12. For a brief discussion of this film, see Anna Lawton, Kinoglasnost: Soviet Cin-

ema in Our Time (Cambridge: Cambridge University Press, 1992), 45–46. Attendance was 20.3 million; DS, 335.

13. Todorovsky's original title for the film (for which he had written the screenplay two decades earlier) was "Field Wife"; see Neia Zorkaia, *The Illustrated History of the Soviet Cinema* (New York: Hippocrene, 1989), 302.

14. See the photospread in SE, no. 21 (1983): 10–11; for a recent review, see Natal'ia Miloserdova, "Voenno-polevoi roman," RI, 621–626.

15. "Konkurs-84," SE, no. 10 (1985): 2.

16. No attendance figures recorded; DS, 39.

17. Vladimir Baskakov, "Trudnyi put k pobede," IK, no. 11 (November 1985): 13–20. Baskakov had formerly been deputy head of Goskino and at this time was the director of VNIIK, the All-Union Scientific Institute for Film Research. See Lawton, *Kinoglasnost*, 66. DS, 39–40, does not record attendance data.

18. The legal, but fictitious, marriage is a time-honored tradition. In the nineteenth century, liberal-minded men would marry women to free them from their families; in the Soviet period, fictitious marriages tended to be for the purpose of obtaining residency permits in choice locales, like Moscow or Leningrad.

19. DS, 155. However, no attendance figures are recorded.

20. Elem Klimov and Ales Adamovich, "Trud po sgushcheniiu dobra," IK, no. 6 (June 1984): 50–51.

21. Adamovich particularly wanted to bring this aspect of the war to the attention of the West; ibid., 56. My analysis of *Come and See* is revised from my article "A War Remembered: Soviet Films of the Great Patriotic War," *American Historical Review* 105 (June 2001): 852–854.

22. See John Barber and Mark Harrison, *The Soviet Home Front, 1941–1945: A Social and Economic History of the USSR in World War II* (London: Longman, 1991), 73–76, for a discussion of some recruiting tactics for the "volunteer" forces.

23. E. Gromov, "Nabat Khatyni," SE, no. 18 (1985): 8–9.

24. DS, 176.

25. Lawton, *Kinoglasnost*, 53–54.

26. Ibid., 66–67.

27. Lev Anninskii, "Tikhie vzryvy: polemicheskie zametki," IK, no. 5 (May 1985): 58.

28. Ibid., 68.

29. Ibid., 58.

30. One might also argue, of course, that Khrushchev did as well.

31. The background material in this section is drawn from Lawton, *Kinoglasnost*, chap. 2, particularly 53–65.

32. Viacheslav Shmyrov, "*Molodaia gvardiia SSSR* (1948)," IK, no. 11 (November 1988): 106–107.

33. Miron Chernenko, "*Sorok pervyi*," IK, no. 7 (July 1987): 94.

34. Valentin Mikhailovich, "*Potomok Chingis-khana*," IK, no. 5 (May 1988): 99.

35. Sergei Lavrent'ev, "*Sud'ba cheloveka*," IK, no. 1 (January 1989): 122–124; Liudmila Donets, "*Ballada o soldate*," IK, no. 1 (January 1989): 125–127.

36. This article, which appeared in IK, no. 6 (June 1988), has been translated in Michael Brashinsky and Andrew Horton, *Russian Critics on the Cinema of Glasnost* (Cambridge: Cambridge University Press, 1994), 11–17. My quotation comes from the translation, 14–15.

37. On the revolution in the historical profession, see R. W. Davies, *Soviet History in the Gorbachev Revolution* (Bloomington: Indiana University Press, 1989). Lawton, *Kinoglasnost*, chap. 7, provides

an overview of the documentaries made during this period.

38. See Tumarkin, *The Living and the Dead*, 175–181.

39. Ibid., 167; DS, 236–237.

40. DS, 75, 180; Lawton's figures are much higher, *Kinoglasnost*, 192–193.

41. Lawton, *Kinoglasnost*, 210–213.

42. No attendance recorded in DS, 279.

43. No attendance recorded in DS, 254. Muratov is the former husband of the well-known art film director Kira Muratova.

44. No attendance recorded in DS, 45.

45. No attendance recorded in DS, 53.

46. Tumarkin, *The Living and the Dead*, 168.

47. Ibid., 99–200.

48. Ibid., 206.

49. Ibid., 203.

50. Georgian director Lana Gogoberidze made this comment to me in spring 1988 during a visit to Stanford University. George Faraday treats the trials of this period in *Revolt of the Filmmakers: The Struggle for Artistic Autonomy and the Fall of the Soviet Film Industry* (University Park: Pennsylvania State University Press, 2000).

51. Oleg Rudnev, "What Kind of Cinema Will Dr. Tagi-Zade Prescribe for Us?" *Current Digest of the Soviet Press* 43, no. 18 (1991): 10–11, originally published in *Izvestiia*, 6 May 1991. For more detail on the competition with foreign films, see Youngblood, "'Americanitis': The Amerikanshchina in Soviet Cinema," *Journal of Popular Film and Television* 19, no. 4 (Winter 1992): 153.

Chapter Nine

1. In Lev Gudkov, comp., *Obraz vraga* (Moscow: OGI, 2005), see Aleksei Levin-son, "'Kavkaz' podo mnoiu: Kratkie zametki po formirovaniiu i prakti-cheskomu ispol'zovaniiu 'obraza vraga' v otnoshenii lits kavkazskoi natsional'nosti," 276–301, and Galina Zvereva, "Chechenskaia voina v diskur-sakh massovoi kul'tury v Rossii: formy representatsii vraga," 302–335.

2. Based on my own observations in Moscow, April 1995.

3. Anna Lawton, *Imaging Russia 2000: Film and Facts* (Washington, D.C.: New Academia Publishing, 2004), 22–23.

4. For the definitive textual analysis, see Birgit Beumers, *Burnt by the Sun* (London: I. B. Tauris, 2000); for an overview, see Denise J. Youngblood, "The Cosmopolitan and the Patriot: The Brothers Mikhalkov-Konchalovsky and Russian Cinema," *Historical Journal of Film, Radio and Television* 25, no. 1 (2003): 27–41.

5. The new Russian cinema and society are the subjects of Anna Lawton's most recent book, *Imaging Russia 2000*.

6. This was followed by *The Afghan-2* in 1994. See DS, 25.

7. Lawton, *Imaging Russia*, 227.

8. DS, 261.

9. For an extremely laudatory review, see Valerii Kichin, "9 rota Fëdora Bondarchuka v zerkale dushi i pressy," http://www.film.ru/article.asp?ID=4263. Although the film has yet to be released in the United States, it was such a "sensation" in Russia that major American newspapers picked up the story; see Peter Finn, "From Bitter Memories, a Russian Blockbuster," *Washington Post*, 20 October 2005, A16; Sophia Kishkovsky, "From a Bitter War Defeat Comes Russia's Latest Blockbuster Action Movie," *New York Times*, 29 October 2005, A23.

10. See, e.g., [interview with the scenarist] Iurii Korotkev, "Instinkt voiny

zhivët v kazhdom cheloveke," *IK*, no. 7 (July 2005): 84–95.

11. According to this source, a person whom I consider to be a reliable informant but who shall remain unnamed, Bondarchuk thought it prudent to change the venue to Afghanistan.

12. *DS*, 187, no attendance recorded.

13. Andrei Plakhov, "Plennik gory i zalozhnik uspekh," *IK*, no. 6 (June 1996): 8, 10. V. Pritulenko also raised these issues in an interview with Bodrov, "Ia khotel sdelat' gumannuiu kartinu," *IK*, no. 6 (June 1996): 13–15, in which Bodrov is accused of caring more about success than art.

14. T. Sergeeva, E. Stishova, and O. Shervud, comps., "Na toi voine nezna-menitoi," *IK*, no. 7 (July 2000): 6.

15. See Youngblood, "The Cosmo-politan and the Patriot," for a discussion of Konchalovskii's American career.

16. See, e.g., Valerii Kichin, "Liubite vragov vashikh," http://www.film.ru/authors/article.asp?ID=3525.

17. Lawton, *Imaging Russia*, 230–231.

18. Lawton also notes that Suvorov's missing eye recalls another military hero of yore, Mikhail Kutuzov; ibid., 234.

19. For Lawton's analysis of this film, see ibid., 231–234.

20. Nina Tsyrkun, "Sestra talanta i eë brat," *KZ*, no. 57 (2002): 13.

21. Aleksandr Deriabin, "Besson-nitsa," *KZ*, no. 57 (2002): 20. A similar point of view from an American scholar and critic can be found in Andrew Horton, "War, What Is It Good For?" *Kinoeye*, vol. 2, no. 18 (2002), http://www.kinoeye.org/02/18/horton18 mp3.php.

22. Valerii Kichin, "Biznes-plan voen-nykh deistvii," http://www.film.ru/article.asp?ID=3209; and Sergei Lavrent'ev, "Aleksei Balabanov: *War* (Voina, 2002),"

KinoKultura (February 2003), http://kinokultura.com/reviews/Rwar.html.

23. *KZ*, no. 57 (2002): 6–32.

24. Sergeeva, Stishova, and Shervud, "Na toi voine neznamenitoi," 20.

25. The summer camp atmosphere is markedly different from Khusein Erkenov's controversial 1990 film *One Hundred Days before the Command* (Sto dnei do prikaza), an attack on the brutal conditions inside Soviet military training camps that also broke the Russian taboo against depicting homosexuality on-screen. *DS*, 427, provides no attendance data for this difficult and disturbing film, which was "suppressed" even though censorship had supposedly ended.

26. Elena Stishova, "Zapiski s kavkaz-skoi voiny," *IK*, no. 1 (January 1999): 21–25.

27. Alter L. Litvin, *Writing History in Twentieth-Century Russia: A View from Within*, trans. and ed. John L. H. Keep (New York: Palgrave, 2001), 106. Chapter 7 covers World War II.

28. Ibid.

29. Ibid., 106–107.

30. See, e.g., I. I. Sukhachev, "Velikaia Otechestvennaia vsegda byla riadom," *IK*, no. 5 (May 2000): 5–11.

31. Andrei Kavun's ten-part serial *The Cadets* (Kursanty, 2004), which is based on director Pyotr Todorovsky's memoirs of his experiences in a World War II officer training camp, is arguably another example of its type. It shows NKVD omnipresence in the camp, which features in a subplot, but the main plotline is the romance between the good-looking protagonist and a local girl, which leads to their wedding.

32. Eduard Volodarskii, *Shtrafbat* (Moscow: Vagrius, 2004). I suspect that the novel and the series were developed simultaneously.

33. Lev Anninskii, "Shtrafbat kak zerkalo Velikoi Otechestvennoi," IK, no. 11 (November 2004): 9–13. Anninsky noted in particular Dostal's frankness in dealing with anti-Semitism (11), and the role of Russian Orthodox faith, 12–13. The journal devoted thirty pages to the series (4–34).

34. Varlam Shalamov, "Major Pugachov's Last Battle," in Kolyma Tales, trans. John Glad (London: Penguin, 1994), 241–256.

35. Mandelstam, "We Live and Do Not Feel the Country under Our Feet," quoted from Victor Sonkin's excellent new translation of the poem in his article "Never Anyone's Contemporary," Russian Life (January/February 2006): 43.

36. Another example is Aleksei Muradov's twelve-part serial Man of War (Chelovek voiny, 2005). Its plot is a hodgepodge combination of spy thriller and partisan exposé, but it is more visually interesting than most films of this type. In the title sequence, "Chelovek voiny" fades into "vek voiny," which changes the meaning from "man of war" to "century of war."

37. "Stirlitz Has Come to Stay," Russian Life, May/June 2006, 8.

38. Evgenii Margolit and Viacheslav Shmyrov, Iz'iatoe kino: Katalog sovetskikh igrovykh kartin, nevypushchennykh vo vsesoiuznyi prokat po zavershenii v proizvodstve ili iz'iatykh iz deistvuiushchego fil'mofonda v god vypuska na ekran (1924–1953) (Moscow: Dubl'-D, 1995), 102–103; DS, 159.

39. In KZ, no. 57 (2002), see Aleksandr Troshin, "Koordinaty Zvezda," 34; Nina Dymshits, "Chelovecheskoe kino," 36.

40. Irina Shilova, "Vozvrashchenie k prostote," KZ, no. 57 (2002): 47.

41. For a markedly different viewpoint from an American film scholar and critic, see Andrew Horton, "The Star That Didn't Shine," Kinoeye 2, no. 13 (2002): 1–2, http://www.kinoeye.org/02/13/horton13 part4.php. Horton concludes that "Zvezda is a remarkably empty film" (2).

42. Aleksandr Shpagin, "Newly Sprouting Seedlings in the Rustling Fields of Domestic Cinema," trans. Vladimir Padunov, KinoKultura, no. 10 (October 2005): 2. http://www.kinokultura .com/articles/oct05-kinotavr.html

43. See, e.g., in Russia Profile, 2, no. 8 (October 2005): Viktor Litovkin, "An Army without Patriots: Why the Young Don't Want to Serve in Russia's Armed Forces" (11), and "The Problem of Patriotism: Russia Profile Round Table" (27–30); and also "Rastim patriotov Rossii," Polit.Ru, 15 August 2005, http://www .polit.ru/dossie/2005/07/20/patria.html, which reprints documents connected to the government's program for patriotic education, to which 497.8 million rubles have been budgeted for the years 2006–2010.

44. As Vida Johnson has noted, memo to author, February 2006, a feminist reading is also possible; Anni does not really need these men, except as sperm donors. For a scholarly review of this film in English, see Daniel H. Wild, "Aleksandr Rogozhkin: Cuckoo (Kukushka), 2002," KinoKultura (April 2004), http://www.kinokultura.com/reviews/ R44cuckoo.html.

45. Taurus illuminates the Northern Hemisphere most brightly in winter.

46. My thanks to Birgit Beumers for introducing me to this film.

47. See, e.g., Marina Drozdova, "Kody dostupa," IK, no. 9 (September 2004): 33–35. Drozdova disliked its moral ambiguity and chilly, detached tone. For a positive review, see Valerii

Kichin, "MMKF-2004: V avguste 41-go: Konkursnyi fil'm *Svoi* pokazal nam druguiu voinu," http://www.film.ru/article.asp?ID=3954; for a balanced one, see Elena Prokhorova, "Dmitrii Meskhiev: *Our Own, aka Us and Ours [Svoi]*, 2004," *KinoKultura* (January 2005), http://www.kinokultura.com/reviews/R1-05svoi.html. Prokhorova is especially insightful in exploring the multiple meanings of *svoi* in the context of the film. For a more general discussion of the importance of the concept *svoi* in Russian culture, see anthropologist Alexei Yurchak's *Everything Was Forever, until It Was No More: The Last Soviet Generation* (Princeton, N.J.: Princeton University Press, 2006), 108–114.

48. The Latin word *mysterium* has several meanings, including "secret rites" or "brotherhood," as well as referring to the Passion.

49. Another Belarusian film that has been saved from oblivion through Russian intervention is Mikhail Ptashuk's last film, the English-language *In June '41* (V iiune 41-go). This Belarusian/American coproduction was finished in 2002 shortly before Ptashuk was killed in a car accident, but it failed to find a distributor until 2004. The Russian release provides a Russian-language voice-over (meaning that the English is audible in the background, and two actors read all the parts). *In June '41* tells the story of a young American girl, Rose Ashkenazy, of Belorussian-Jewish heritage, who is visiting relatives in a shtetl in Belorussia (now Belarus) when the Germans invade the Soviet Union. She alone escapes the extermination of the shtetl's population and joins up with a Russian soldier and a Belorussian child. This is a terrible film,

poorly acted and packed with sentimental clichés, but nevertheless worth mentioning for its treatment of the "Jewish question," which is still a taboo subject in many of the former Soviet territories.

50. Birgit Beumers deals with the father-son issue in her insightful review of this film, "Aleksei Gherman, Jr.: *The Last Train (Poslednii poezd)*, 2003," *KinoKultura* (January 2004), http://www.kinokultura.com/reviews/R14train.html.

51. Aleksandr Shpagin, "Religiia voiny: sub"ektivnye zametki o bogoiskatel'stve v voennom kinematografe," pt. 2, IK, no. 6 (June 2005): 89.

Conclusion

1. C. P. Cavafy, *Collected Poems*, rev. ed., trans. Edmund Keeley and Philip Sherrard, ed. George Savidis (Princeton, N.J.: Princeton University Press, 1992), 19.

2. The other three films shown at the festival were *Antosha Rybkin* (Antosha Rybkin, 1942), *Once at Night* (Odnazhdy nochiu, 1945), and *Submarine T-9* (Pod vozhnaia lodka T-9, 1943); http://www.miff.ru/27/eng/moscow/films/364.

3. Aleksandr Shpagin, "Religiia voiny," IK, no. 5 (May 2005): 57.

4. Aleksandr Shpagin, "Religiia voiny," IK, no. 6 (June 2005): 88.

5. Ibid.

6. Ibid., 89.

7. Cavafy, *Collected Poems*, 19.

8. And not only for Russians, of course.

9. Here I am using *political* in its narrow sense, referring to state power. One might easily argue that the commercial imperatives of the Hollywood studio system were also "political."

BIBLIOGRAPHY

Primary Sources

Agranovskii, A. "Pobeda zvukovogo kino: Zlatye gory." Pravda, 26 November 1931.

Albera, François, and Roland Cosandey, eds. Boris Barnet: Ecrits, documents, études, filmographie. Locarno: Editions du Féstivale Internationale du Film, 1985.

Aleksandrov, G. "Printsipy sovetskoi kinokomedii." IK, no. 5 (May 1949): 12–16.

Aleksandrov, O., and B. Galanter. "Pobeda za nami." Pravda, 6 August 1941.

———. "Rasskazy o muzhestve i geroizme: Novyi kinosbornik." Pravda, 26 August 1941.

Alov, Aleksandr, and Vladimir Naumov. Stat'i, svidetel'stva, vyskazyvaniia. Moscow: Iskusstvo, 1989.

Alova, L. A., comp. Aleksandr Alov i Vladimir Naumov: Stat'i, svidetel'stva, vyskazyvaniia. Moscow: Iskusstvo, 1989.

Alpers, B. V. Dnevnik kinokritika, 1928–1937. Moscow: Fond Novoe tysiachletie, 1995.

———. "Goroda i gody." Kino i zhizn', no. 34/35 (1930): 7–8.

Amosov, Nikolai. PPG 226: A Surgeon's War. Trans. George St. George. Chicago: Regnery, 1975.

Andzhaparidze, M., and V. Tsirgiladze. "Kak sozdavalsia fil'm Padenie Berlina." IK, no. 4 (April 1950): 22–26.

Anninskii, Lev. "Ikh kroviu: Fil'm i kontekst (A zori zdes' tikhie . . .)." IK, no. 1 (January 1973): 21–33.

———. Shestidesiatniki i my. Moscow: Soiuz kinematografistov SSSR, 1991.

———. "Shtrafbat kak zerkalo Velikoi Otechestvennoi." IK, no. 11 (November 2004): 9–13.

———. "Tikhie vzryvy: polemicheskie zametki." IK, no. 5 (May 1985): 56–69.

Anonymous. A Woman in Berlin: Eight Weeks in the Conquered City, a Diary. Trans. Philip Boehm. New York: Henry Holt, 2005.

Arnshtam, L. "Shchors: Novyi fil'm A. Dovzhenko, proizvodstvo Kievskoi kinostudii." Pravda, 25 January 1939.

Arossev, A. Soviet Cinema. Moscow: VOKS, 1935.

Arsen. "Sorok-pervyi." Kino-front, no. 6 (1927): 15–19.

Bachelis, Tatiana. "Realnost' schast'ia." IK, no. 8 (August 1961): 71–81.

Baskakov, Vladimir. "Geroicheskoe v kino." IK, no. 8 (August 1964): 34–40.

———. "Trudnyi put k pobede." IK, no. 11 (November 1985): 13–20.

Batalov, Aleksei. Sud'ba i remeslo. Moscow: Iskusstvo, 1984.

Belza, Igor'. "Zametki o muzyke fil'ma Nezabyvaemyi 1919 god." IK, no. 9 (September 1952): 87–91.

Beregovoi, G. "Nasha pobeda." SE, no. 9 (1980): 7.

Bereznitskii, Ian. "Radi zhizni na zemle." IK, no. 3 (March 1964): 4–11.

Beridze, Georgii. "Pesn' o muzhestve." Pravda, 9 March 1960.

Bessonov, Evgeni. *Tank Rider: Into the Reich with the Red Army.* Trans. Bair Irincheev. Mechanicsburg, Pa.: Stackpole, 2003.

Bidermann, Gottlob Herbert. *In Deadly Combat: A German Soldier's Memoir of the Eastern Front.* Trans. and ed. Derek S. Zumbro. Lawrence: University Press of Kansas, 2000.

Bleiman, Mikhail, et al. "Bez chetkogo ideinogo zamysla (ob *Okraine*)." *Kino*, no. 23 (1933).

Bodrov, Sergei, and V. Pritulenko. "Ia khotel sdelat' gumannuiu kartinu." *IK*, no. 6 (June 1996): 13–15.

Bol'shakov, I. G. *Sovetskoe kinoiskusstvo v gody Velikoi otechestvennoi voiny (1941–1945).* Moscow: Goskinoizdat, 1948.

Borodin, Sergei. "*Ona zashchishchaet rodinu.*" *Pravda*, 24 May 1943.

Brailovskii, M. "Dvenadtsat' millionov." *Sine-fono*, no. 3 (9 November 1913): 21–22.

Bulgakov, Mikhail. *The Early Plays of Mikhail Bulgakov.* Ed. Ellendea Proffer. Trans. Carl R. Proffer and Ellendea Proffer. Bloomington: Indiana University Press, 1972.

Bykaŭ, Vasyl [Bykov, Vasil]. *Povesti.* Trans. V. Bykaŭ. Moscow: Khudozhestvennaia literatura, 1984.

"*Chapaev* posmotrit vsia strana." *Pravda*, 22 November 1934.

Chechneva, Marina. "Pravda o voine." *SE*, no. 9 (1970): 2–4.

Chirskov, B. "Nas uchit Partiia." *IK*, no. 6 (June 1949): 22–26.

Chukovskii, Nikolai. *Baltic Skies.* Trans. R. Daglish. Moscow: Foreign Languages Publishing House, 1956.

Cottam, Kazimiera J., ed. and trans. *Defending Leningrad: Women behind Enemy Lines.* Rev. ed. Nepean, Ont.: New Military Publishing, 1998.

Deriabin, Aleksandr. "Bessonnitsa." *KZ*, no. 57 (2002): 16–22.

———. "Rannie otechestvennye tsvetnye fil'my 1931–1945: Fil'mografa." *KZ*, no. 56 (2002): 322–348.

Dikii, A. "Pochëtnyi dolg sovetskikh khudozhnikov." *IK*, no. 6 (June 1949): 9–12.

———. "Tvorcheskaia radost'." *IK*, no. 3 (March 1949): 23–27.

Dolinskii, I. "*Chapaev*: Literaturnoe proizvedenie i fil'm." *IK*, no. 7/8 (July/August 1940): 51–57.

Donskoi, Mark. "My srazhalis' svoim iskusstvom." In *Sovetskaia kul'tura v gody velikoi otechestvennoi voiny*, 252–254. Moscow: Nauka, 1976.

———. "*Raduga.*" *SE*, no. 3 (1969): 18–19.

Drozdova, Marina. "Kody dostupa." *IK*, no. 9 (September 2004): 34–37.

Dymshits, Nina. "Chelovecheskie kino." *KZ*, no. 57 (2002): 34–37.

Dzigan, Efim. "Chetvert veka: *My iz Kronstadta.*" *SE*, no. 8 (1961): 4–5, 8.

Ehrenburg, Ilya, and Konstantin Simonov. *In One Newspaper: A Chronicle of Unforgettable Years.* Trans. Anatol Kagan. New York: Sphinx, 1985.

Erlikh, A. "*Okraina.*" *Pravda*, 8 April 1933.

———. "*Pobeda za nami: Novyi kinosbornik.*" *Pravda*, 11 August 1941.

Ermolinskii, I. "*My iz Kronshtadta* (Avtor stsenarii Vsevolod Vishnevskii, rezhissër Ef. Dzigan, proizvodstvo studii Mosfil'm, 1936): Zamechatel'nyi fil'm." *Pravda*, 3 March 1936.

Ermolinskii, S. "*Potomok Chingiz-khana,*" *Pravda*, 5 December 1928.

———. "*Veter.*" *Pravda*, 4 November 1926.

Erukhimovich, I. "My iz Kronshtadta: Zametchatel'nyi fil'm." *Pravda*, 3 March 1936.

Fadeev, Aleksandr. *Leningrad in the Days of the Blockade*. Trans. R. D. Charques. Westport, Conn.: Greenwood Press, 1971.

———. *The Young Guard*. Trans. Violet Dutt. Moscow: Foreign Languages Publishing House, 1958.

Fedin, Konstantin. *Cities and Years*. Trans. Michael Scammell. New York: Dell, 1962.

"Fil'm Nebo Moskvy," *Pravda*, 2 June 1944.

Fomin, V. I., comp. *Kino na voine: Dokumenty i svidetel'stva*. Moscow: Materik, 2005.

———. *Polka: Dokumenty, svidetel'nost', kommentarii*. Otechestvennoe kino v dokumentakh. Moscow: Nauchno-issledovatel'skii institut kinoiskusstva, 1992.

Freilikh, Semën. "Etot neistovyi Mark Donskoi." *IK*, no. 6 (June 1971): 39–43.

———. "Litso geroia." *IK*, no. 4 (April 1971): 94–109.

———. "Molodost' fil'ma." *IK*, no. 1 (January 1965): 1–6.

———. "Po puti sotsialisticheskogo realizma: Izbrannye stsenarii sovetskogo kino v shesti tomakh." *IK*, no. 4 (April 1952): 109–122.

———. "Sud'ba Grigoriia Melekhova." *IK*, no. 1 (January 1958): 20–35, and no. 9 (September 1958): 91–100.

Galaktionov, M. "Velikii perelom." *Pravda*, 31 January 1946.

Gardin, Vladimir. "V zhizhni i v iskusstve." *IK*, no. 12 (December 1954): 99–125.

Geiman, Viktor. "Pochemu zriteliu nravitsia odno, a kritiku—drugoe." *Kino*, no. 19 (1929): 2–3.

Gerasimov, Sergei. "Beseda rezhissëra so stsenaristom." *IK*, no. 11 (November 1953): 67.

———. "Sila Stalinskikh idei." *IK*, no. 6 (June 1949): 13–18.

———. "Sovetskaia kinodramaturgiia." *IK*, no. 1 (January 1955): 3–31.

———. "Za voploshchenie prednachertanii partii!" *IK*, no. 10 (October 1952): 20–24.

German, A. "Tripol'skaia tragediia." *Kino*, no. 15 (1926): 3.

German, Aleksei. "Pravda—ne skhodstva, a otkrytie." *IK*, no. 12 (December 2001): 76–93.

German, Iurii. "Ekho voiny." *IK*, no. 4 (April 1975): 15–16.

———. *Eternal Battle*. Trans. Olga Shartse. Moscow: Progress, 1967.

———. *The Staunch and the True*. Trans. Olga Shartse. Moscow: Progress, 1967.

Ginzburg, Lidia. *Blockade Diary*. Trans. Alan Myers. London: Harvill Press, 1995.

Golovnia, V. "Mosfil'm v gody Velikoi otechestvennoi voiny." *IK*, no. 7 (July 1979): 11–32.

Gosfil'mofond Rossii. *Sovetskie khudozhestvennye fil'my: Annotirovannyi katalog, 1968–1969*. Moscow: Niva Rossii, 1995.

———. *Sovetskie khudozhestvennye fil'my: Annotirovannyi catalog, 1970–1971*. Moscow: Niva Rossii, 1996.

Gosfil'mofond SSSR. *Letiat' zhuravli*. Moscow: Iskusstvo, 1972.

———. *Sovetskie khudozhestvennye fil'my: Annotirovannyi katalog*. Vols. 1–5, 1918–1965. Moscow: Iskusstvo, 1960–1979.

Gromov, E. "Nabat Khatyni." *SE*, no. 18 (1985): 8–9.

Groshev, A. "Obraz nashego sovremennika v kinoiskusstve." *IK*, no. 4 (April 1951): 14–16.

———. "40 let sovetskogo kino." *SE*, no. 16 (1959): 1–3, 12.

Grossman, Vasily. *Life and Fate*. Trans. Robert Chandler. New York: Harper and Row, 1985.

———. *Povesti, rasskazy, ocherki*. Moscow: Voennoe izd-vo Ministerstvo oborony soiuza SSR, 1958.

Gusman, Boris. "Sorok pervyi." *Pravda*, 18 March 1927.

Ignat'eva, N. "Liudi i vremia." *IK*, no. 7 (July 1961): 33–39.

Inber, Vera. *Leningrad Diary*. Trans. Serge M. Wolff and Rachel Grieve. New York: St. Martin's Press, 1971.

Ioffe, I. A., and N. K. Petrova, eds. *Molodaia gvardiia (g. Krasnodon): Khudozhestvennaia obraz i istoricheskaia real'nost': Sbornik dokumentov i materialov*. Moscow: Veche, 2003.

Iurenev, Rostislav. "Chapaev." *IK*, no. 11 (November 1964): 10–19.

———. "Rasskaz o nezabyvaemom." *Pravda*, 25 January 1964.

———. "Vernost'." *IK*, no. 12 (December 1957): 5–14.

"K itogam sezona." *Kino i zhizn'*, no. 15 (1930): 3–5.

Kadochnikov, Pavel. "Na frontovykh dorogakh." *IK*, no. 3 (March 1975): 69–73.

Kalashnikov, Iu. "Traditsii geroicheskogo epokha." *IK*, no. 7 (1952): 3–25.

Kalatozov, Mikhail. "Druzhba zakliatykh vragov: Pis'ma iz Gollivud." Ed. Valerii Fomin. *IK*, no. 8 (August 2005): 123–134.

Karaganov, A. "Geroika podviga, kharakter voiny." *IK*, no. 7 (July 1969): 43.

Karakhan, L. "Krutoi put *Voskhozhdenii*," *IK*, no. 10 (October 1976): 85–105.

Karavaeva, Anna. "Nashestvie." *Pravda*, 1 March 1945.

———. "Sekretar' raikoma." *Pravda*, 13 December 1942.

Kardin, V. "Liudi i simvoly." *IK*, no. 10 (October 1961): 58–62.

Khaniutin, Iurii. "Kogda pushki streliaiut." *IK*, no. 5 (May 1965): 1–24.

———. "Vozvrashchennoe vremia." *IK*, no. 7 (July 1977): 86–97.

Khersonskii, Khrisanf. "Novoe slovo ukrainskoi kinematografii: Fil'ma [sic] *Arsenal*." *Pravda*, 14 February 1929.

———. "VUFKU na perelome: *Spartak, Dva dnia, Zvenigora*." *Pravda*, 10 February 1928.

Kichin, Valerii. "Biznes-plan voennykh deistvii." http://www.film.ru/authors/article.asp?ID=3209.

———. "*9 rota* Fëdora Bondarchuka v zerkale dushi i pressy." http://www.film.ru/article.asp?ID=4263.

———. "Liubite vragov vashikh." http://www.film.ru/authors/ article.asp?ID=3525.

———. "MMKF-2004: V avguste 41-go: Konkursnyi fil'm *Svoi* pokazal nam druguiu voinu." http://www.film.ru.authors/article.asp?ID=3954.

Kino: Entsiklopedicheskii slovar'. Moscow: Sovetskaia entsiklopediia, 1986.

Kino-slovar' v dvukh tomakh. 2 vols. Moscow: Sovetskaia entsiklopediia, 1966, 1970.

Klimov, Elem, and Ales Adamovich. "Trud po sgushcheniiu dobra." *IK*, no. 6 (June 1984): 50–65.

Kochina, Elena. *Blockade Diary*. Trans. and intro. Samuel C. Ramer. Ann Arbor, Mich.: Ardis, 1990.

Kopalin, Il'ia. "Na festivale sovetskikh fil'mov v Vengrii." *IK*, no. 6 (June 1954): 109–110.

Koroteev, V. "Stalingradskaia bitva." *Pravda*, 20 December 1949.

Korotkev, Iurii. "Instinkt voiny zhivët v kazhdom cheloveke." *IK*, no. 7 (July 2005): 84–95.

Koschorrek, Günther K. *Blood Red Snow: The Memoirs of a German Soldier on the Eastern Front*. Mechanicsburg, Pa.: Stackpole, 2002.

Kosmatov, L. "Izobrazitel'noe reshenie fil'ma *Nezabyvaemyi 1919 god*." *IK*, no. 9 (September 1952): 101–117.

Kozhevnikov, Vadim. "*Nebo Moskvy*." *Pravda*, 10 June 1944.

———. "*Tretii udar*." *Pravda*, 3 May 1948.

———. "*Zoia*." *Pravda*, 22 September 1944.

Kozlov, Leonid. "K chemu stremilsia khudozhnik?" *IK*, no. 12 (December 1957): 38–44.

Kozlov, Vladimir, comp., and Aleksandr Dorozhevich, ed. "Spisok amerikanskikh fil'mov v sovetskom i rossiiskom prokate, 1929–1998." *Kinograf*, no. 16 (2005): 175–208.

"*Kryl'ia*: Podrobnyi razgovor." *IK*, no. 10 (October 1966): 12–29.

Kutorga, Zoia, and Ovidii Gorchakov. "Vozvrashchennoe proshloe." *IK*, no. 5 (May 1977): 55–59.

Kuznetsov, P. "Fil'm o smelykh liudiakh." *Pravda*, 8 September 1950.

Ladynina, Marina. "Vo vremia voiny iskusstvo voiuet!" *SE*, no. 9 (1980): 6–7.

Lavrenev, Boris. *The Forty-first*. Moscow: Foreign Languages Publishing House, 1958.

Lebedev, Nikolai. "Na podstupakh k *Chapaevu*." *IK*, no. 2 (February 1951): 9–14.

Leningradskii Gosudarstvennyi Institut Teatra, Muzyki i Kinematografii. *Molodye rezhissëry sovetskogo kino: Sbornik statei*. Leningrad: Iskusstvo, 1962.

Leonov, Leonid. "Invasion." In *Four Soviet War Plays*, 58–117. London: Hutchinson, 1944.

Levshina, Inna. "Konkurs-77: Kommentarii kritika." *SE*, no. 11 (1978): 8–9.

Lidov, P. "*Mashen'ka*." *Pravda*, 19 April 1942.

Litovkin, Viktor. "An Army without Patriots: Why the Young Don't Want to Serve in Russia's Armed Forces." *Russia Profile* 2, no. 8 (October 2005): 11.

Luker, Nicholas, ed. *An Anthology of the Classics of Socialist Realism: From Furmanov to Sholokhov*. Ann Arbor, Mich.: Ardis, 1988.

Macheret, A. "Natal'ia Uzhvii." *IK*, no. 7 (July 1954): 31–42.

Mandelstam [Mandel'shtam], Osip. "We Live and Do Not Feel. . . . " Trans. in Victor Sonkin, "Never Anyone's Contemporary." *Russian Life*, January/February 2006, 43.

Manevich, I. "Tvorcheskii put' I. A. Savchenko." *IK*, no. 1 (January 1951): 16–18.

Margolit, Evgenii, and Viacheslav Shmyrov. *Iz'iatoe kino: Katalog sovetskikh igrovykh kartin, nevypushchennykh vo vsesoiuznyi prokat po zavershenii v proizvodstve ili iz'iatykh iz deistvuiushchego fil'mofonda v god vypuska na ekran (1924–1953)*. Moscow: Dubl'-D, 1995.

Markova, F. "Razrushenie lichno." *SE*, no. 23 (1978): 6–7.

Matveev, Evgenii. "Rodiny radi." *IK*, no. 5 (May 1980): 4–17.

"*Molodaia gvardiia*." *Pravda*, 26 August 1948.

"*Molodaia gvardiia*." *Pravda*, 10 October 1948.

"*My iz Kronshtadta* na parizhskikh ekranakh." *Pravda*, 22 March 1936.

Narovchatov, Sergei. "Dvadtsat' let spustia." *IK*, no. 2 (February 1965): 50–52.

Nikulin, Iu. "*Chapaev* s nami." *SE*, no. 9 (1980): 17.

"Ob ideinosti v kinoiskusstve." *Pravda*, 29 September 1943.

Ognev, Vladimir. "Dvadtsat let nazad." *IK*, no. 1 (January 1988): 32–39.

"Ogromnyi uspekh fil'ma *Molodaia gvardiia*." *Pravda*, 12 October 1948.

Orlov, Dal. "Zavershenie epopei." *IK*, no. 2 (February 1972): 6–14.

Ozerov, Iurii. "Vosslavit podvig naroda." *IK*, no. 2 (February 1972): 1–4.

P. A. "Oshibka Vasiliia Guliavina (*Veter*)." *Kino*, no. 43 (1926).

"Pamiati tovarishcha: Larissa Shepitko, Vladimir Chukhnov, Iurii Fomenko." *IK*, no. 12 (December 1979): 143–145.

Pavlenko, P. "Poema o sovetskom cheloveke." *Pravda*, 23 November 1948.

Pervomaiskyi, Leonid. *Dikii mëd: Sovremennaia ballada*. Trans. L. Pervomaiskyi and A. Gromova. Moscow: Khudozhestvennaia literatura, 1968.

Petrov, V. "Fil'm o geroicheskom srazhenii." *IK*, no. 3 (March 1949): 22.

Pikul', Valentin. *Moonzund: Roman-khronika*. Moscow: Sovetskaia Rossiia, 1985.

Plakhov, Andrei. "Plennik gory i zalozhnik uspekh." *IK*, no. 6 (June 1996): 5–10.

"Podprobnyi razgovor." *IK*, no. 1 (January 1960): 65–80.

Pogozheva, L. "Fil'm o smelykh liudiakh." *IK*, no. 4 (April 1950): 27–29.

———. "Novoe prochtenie romana." *IK*, no. 2 (February 1957): 83–97.

———. "O prostykh i smelykh liudiakh." *IK*, no. 4 (April 1950): 27.

———. "*Padenie Berlina*." *IK*, no. 1 (January 1950): 10–14.

Polevoi, Boris. "*Nezabyvaemyi 1919 god*." *Pravda*, 4 May 1952.

———. *A Story about a Real Man*. Trans. J. Fineberg. Westport, Conn.: Greenwood Press, 1970.

———. "*Sud'ba cheloveka*." *Pravda*, 17 April 1959.

"Posle voiny." *SE*, no. 22 (1967): 18–19.

"The Problem of Patriotism: *Russia Profile* Round Table." *Russia Profile* 2, no. 8 (October 2005): 27–30.

Pudovkin, Vsevolod. "O fil'me *Dva boitsa*." *Pravda*, 6 October 1943.

Rachuk, I., and I. Ol'shanskii. "Stsenarii o nezabyvaemom." *IK*, no. 6 (June 1951): 13–17.

Raizman, Iulii. "O tvorcheskom roste molodykh kinoakterov." *IK*, no. 4 (April 1952): 92–104.

"Rastim patriotov Rossii." *Polit.Ru* (15 August 2005). http://www.polit.ru/dossie/ 2005/07/20/patria/html.

Rokossovskii, Konstantin. "Armiia i kino." *SE*, no. 3 (1959): 1.

Rossiiskii Gosudarstvennyi Arkhiv Literatury i Iskusstva, f. 2494, op. 1, ed. khr. 2134. "Stenogramma zasedaniia rezhisserskoi sektsii ARRK o stsenarnom krisize (1929)," 5–9.

Rudnev, Oleg. "What Kind of Cinema Will Dr. Tagi-Zade Prescribe for Us?" *Current Digest of the Soviet Press* 43, no. 18 (1991): 10–11.

Rudoi, Iakov. "Nasha kinematografiia i massovoi zritel'." *SE*, no. 37 (1929): 17.

S. Es. "*Tiazhëlye gody*." *Pravda*, 10 December 1925.

Sajer, Guy. *The Forgotten Soldier*. Washington, D.C.: Brassey's, 2000.

Sergeeva, T., E. Stishova, and O. Shervud, comps. "Na toi voine neznamenitoi." *IK*, no. 7 (July 2000): 5–25.

Shalamov, Varlam. "Major Pugachov's Last Battle." In *Kolyma Tales*, trans. John Glad, 241–256. London: Penguin, 1994.

Shcherbina, V. "Fil'm o velikom pobede." *Pravda*, 25 January 1950.

Shevelev, S. "*Pobeda za nami!* Boevoi kinosbornik No. 5." *Pravda*, 3 October 1941.

Shilova, Irina. . . . *i moe kino: piatidesiatye, shestidesiatye, semidesiatye*. Moscow: NIIK/ Kinovedcheskie zapiski, 1993.

———. "Vozvrashchenie k prostote." *KZ*, no. 57 (2002): 37–42.

Sholokhov, Mikhail. *One Man's Destiny and Other Stories, Articles, and Sketches, 1923–1963*. Trans. H. C. Stevens. New York: Knopf, 1966.

Shpagin, Aleksandr. "Newly Sprouting Seedlings in the Rustling Fields of Domestic Cinema." Trans. Vladimir Padunov. *KinoKultura*, no. 10 (October 2005). http://www .kinokultura.com/articles/oct05-kinotavr.html.

———. "Religiia voiny: sub"ektivnye zametki o bogoiskatel'stve v voennom kinemato- grafe." *IK*, no. 5 (May 2005): 56–68, and no. 6 (June 2005): 72–89.

Simmons, Cynthia, and Nina Perlina, eds. *Writing the Siege of Leningrad: Women's Diaries, Memoirs, and Documentary Prose*. Pittsburgh: University of Pittsburgh Press, 2002.

Simonov, Konstantin. *Days and Nights*. Trans. Joseph Barnes. New York: Simon and Schuster, 1945.

———. *The Living and the Dead*. Trans. Alex Miller. Moscow: Progress, 1975.

Smirnov, S. S. "Zhivye i bessmertnye." *Pravda*, 16 January 1964.

Smirnova-Medvedeva, Z. M. *On the Road to Stalingrad: Memoirs of a Woman Machine Gunner*. Rev. ed. Ed. and trans. Kazimiera J. Cottam. Nepean, Ont.: New Military Publishing, 1997.

Sokolov, Ippolit. "Korni formalizma." *Kino*, no. 17 (1930): 3.

———. "*Oblomok imperii*." *Kino*, no. 38 (1929): 2.

———. "*Veter*." *Kino*, no. 45 (1926): 3.

Sokolov, Vadim. "Vagrianye zori." *SE*, no. 24 (1972): 4–5.

———. "Venchanie tekh talantov, razviazka tekh legend." *SE*, no. 9 (1977): 2–3.

Sovetskoe kino. Moscow: Iskusstvo, 1937.

"Stalingradtsy o kinofil'me *Stalingradskaia bitva*." *Pravda*, 11 May 1949.

Stishova, Elena. "Khronika i legenda (*Voskhozhdenie*)." *IK*, no. 9 (September 1977): 30–41.

———. "Strasti po *Komissaru*." *IK*, no. 1 (January 1989): 110–121.

———. "Zapiski s kavkazskoi voiny." *IK*, no. 1 (January 1999): 21–25.

Strel'chenko, A. "*Krasnye d'iavoliata na dorogakh voiny*." *SE*, no. 20 (1985): 17.

Sukhachev, I. I. "Velikaia Otechestvennaia vsegda byla riadom." *IK*, no. 5 (May 2000): 5–11.

Taylor, Richard, and Ian Christie, eds. *The Film Factory: Russian and Soviet Cinema in Docu- ments, 1896–1939*. Trans. Richard Taylor. Cambridge, Mass.: Harvard University Press, 1988.

"Teatr i kinematografii." *Vestnik kinematografii*, no. 87 (1 April 1914): 19.

"*Torpedonostsy*." *SE*, no. 16 (1983): 4–5.

Troianovskii, A. I., and R. I. Egiarovskii. *Izuchenie kino-zritelia: Po materialam issledovatel'skoi teatral'noi masterskoi*. Moscow: Narkompros, 1928.

Troshin, Aleksandr, ed. "'A driani podrobno *Garmon'* bol'she ne stavite?' Zapiski besed B. Z. Shumiatskogo s I. V. Stalinym posle kinoprosmotrov 1934," *KZ*, no. 61 (2002): 281–346.

———. ed. "'Kartina sil'naia, khoroshaia no ne *Chapaev*': Zapiski besed B. Z. Shumiatskogo s I. V. Stalinym posle kinoprosmotrov, 1935–1937," *KZ*, no. 62 (2003): 115–187.

———. "Koordinaty *Zvezda*." *KZ*, no. 57 (2002): 33–34.

Tsivian, Yuri, Paolo Cherchi Usai, Lorenzo Codelli, Carlo Montanaro, and David Robinson. *Silent Witnesses: Russian Films, 1909–1919*. Pordenone: Edizione Biblioteca dell'Imagine/BFI Publishing, 1989.

Tsyrkun, Nina. "Sestra talanta i eë brat." *KZ*, no. 57 (2002): 13.

Turovskaia, Maia. "'Da' i 'net.'" *IK*, no. 12 (December 1957): 14–18.

"Uspekh zamechatel'nogo fil'ma: Pervyi den' demonstratsii *My iz Kronshtadta*." *Pravda*, 22 March 1936.

V. G. "*Banda Bat'ka Knysha*." *Pravda*, 4 June 1924.

———. "*V tylu u belykh*." *Pravda*, 18 February 1925.

Varshavskii, Ia. "*Mir vkhodiashchemu*." *SE*, no. 19 (1961): 6–7, 13.

———. "Za chto boretsia fil'm." *IK*, no. 4 (April 1958): 27–38.

Vasil'ev, G., and Vasil'ev, S. *Chapaev*. In *Izbrannye stsenarii sovetskogo kino*. Vol. 1. Moscow: Goskinoizdat, 1949.

"Velikaia otechestvennaia." *SE*, no. 20 (1967): 18–20.

Viktorov, Ia. "Litso fashistskogo 'novogo poriadka.'" *Pravda*, 10 December 1941.

Vishnevskii, Vsevolod. "*My iz Kronshtadta*." *Pravda*, 22 August 1935.

———. *My iz Kronshtadta. Izbrannye stsenarii sovetskogo kino.* Vol. 1. Moscow: Goskinoizdat, 1942.

———. "Pisatel' i rezhissër: Iz pisem k E. Dziganu (publikatsiia)." *IK*, no. 6 (June 1954): 56–76.

Vishnevskii, Vsevolod, Mikhail Chiaureli, and A. Filimonov. "*Nezabyvaemyi 1919-i*." *IK*, no. 5 (May 1951): 31–42, and no. 6 (June 1951): 12–19.

Vishnevskii, Vsevolod, and Efim Dzigan. "Kak my stavili fil'm." *Pravda*, 3 March 1936.

Volodarskii, Eduard. *Shtrafbat*. Moscow: Vagrius, 2004.

"Voskhozhdenie k pravde." *SE*, no. 1 (1978): 2–3.

"Vstrecha literatorov s uchastnikami fil'ma *Chapaev*." *Pravda*, 26 November 1934.

"Vtoraia zhizn' literaturnogo obraza." *IK*, no. 6 (June 1959): 88–94.

Zak, Mark. "Epokha i litsa." *IK*, no. 8 (August 1968): 19–23.

———. "Tol'ko ob odnom srazhenii." *IK*, no. 3 (March 1973): 24–32.

"Zamechatel'noe proizvedenie sovetskogo kinoiskusstva: Zriteli o fil'me *Padenie Berlina*." *Pravda*, 25 January 1950.

Zaslavskii, D. "V shest' chasov vechera posle voiny." *Pravda*, 19 November 1944.

Zemlianukhin, Sergei, and Miroslava Segida, comps. *Domashniaia sinemateka: Otechestvennoe kino, 1918–1996*. Moscow: Dubl'-D, 1996.

Secondary Sources

Andrew, Dudley. *Concepts in Film Theory*. Oxford: Oxford University Press, 1984.

Attwood, Lynne, ed. *Red Women on the Silver Screen: Soviet Women and Cinema from the Beginning to the End of the Communist Era*. London: Pandora, 1993.

Babitsky, Paul, and John Rimberg. *The Soviet Film Industry*. New York: Praeger, 1955.

Barber, John, and Mark Harrison. *The Soviet Home Front, 1941–1945: A Social and Economic History of the USSR in World War II*. London: Longman, 1991.

Bartov, Omer. *The Eastern Front, 1941–45: German Troops and the Barbarisation of Warfare*. New York: St. Martin's Press, 1986.

Basinger, Jeanine. *The World War II Combat Film: Anatomy of a Genre*. 2nd rev. ed. Middletown, Conn.: Wesleyan University Press, 2003.

Beumers, Birgit. "Aleksei Gherman, Jr.: *The Last Train* (*Poslednii poezd*), 2003." *KinoKultura*, January 2004. http://www.kinokultura.com/reviews/R14train.html.

————. *Burnt by the Sun*. London: I. B. Tauris, 2000.

————. "Myth-Making and Myth-Taking: Lost Ideals and the War in Contemporary Russian Cinema." *Canadian Slavonic Papers* 42, nos. 1–2 (March–June 2000): 171–189.

————. *Nikita Mikhalkov: Between Nostalgia and Nationalism*. London: I. B. Tauris, 2005.

————. ed. *Russia on Reels: The Russian Idea in Post-Soviet Cinema*. London: I. B. Tauris, 1999.

Bogomolov, Iu. *Mikhail Kalatozov: Stranitsy tvorcheskoi biografii*. Moscow: Iskusstvo, 1989.

Bordwell, David. *Narration in the Fiction Film*. Madison: University of Wisconsin Press, 1985.

Brandenberger, David. *National Bolshevism: Stalinist Mass Culture and the Formation of Modern Russian National Identity, 1931–1956*. Cambridge, Mass.: Harvard University Press, 2002.

Brashinsky, Michael, and Andrew Horton. *Russian Critics on the Cinema of Glasnost*. Cambridge: Cambridge University Press, 1994.

Broekmeyer, Marius. *Stalin, the Russians, and Their War, 1941–1945*. Trans. Rosalind Buck. Madison: University of Wisconsin Press, 2004.

Brooks, Jeffrey. *Thank You, Comrade Stalin! Soviet Public Culture from Revolution to Cold War*. Princeton, N.J.: Princeton University Press, 2000.

Budiak, L. M., ed. *Rossiiskii illiuzion*. Moscow: Materik, 2003.

Bulgakowa, Oksana. *Sergei Eisenstein: A Biography*. Trans. Anne Dwyer. Berlin: PotemkinPress, 2001.

Carnes, Mark C., ed. *Past Imperfect: History according to the Movies*. New York: Henry Holt, 1996.

Chambers, John Whiteclay, II, and David Culbert, eds. *World War II, Film, and History*. New York: Oxford University Press, 1996.

Chernenko, Miron. *Krasnaia zvezda, zhëltaia zvezda: Kinematograficheskaia istoriia evreistva v Rossii (1919–1999)*. Vinnitsa: Globus-Press, 2003.

————. "Sorok pervyi." *IK*, no. 7 (July 1987): 93–95.

Clark, Katerina. *The Soviet Novel: History as Ritual*. Chicago: University of Chicago Press, 1981.

Cohen, Aaron J. "Oh, That! Myth, Memory, and World War I in the Russian Emigration and the Soviet Union." *Slavic Review* 62, no. 1 (Spring 2003): 69–86.

Condee, Nancy, producer. *Thaw Cinema*. CD-ROM. Pittsburgh: Artima Studio/University of Pittsburgh, n.d.

Cooper, Matthew. *The Nazi War against Soviet Partisans, 1941–1944*. New York: Stein and Day, 1979.

Cottam, Kazimiera J. *Women in War and Resistance: Selected Biographies of Soviet Women Soldiers*. Nepean, Ont.: New Military Publishing, 1998.

Dallin, Alexander. *German Rule in Russia, 1941–1945: A Study in Occupation Policies*. 2nd ed., rev. Boulder, Colo.: Westview Press, 1981.

Davies, R. W. *Soviet History in the Gorbachev Revolution*. Bloomington: Indiana University Press, 1989.

Dibbets, Karel, and Bert Hogenkamp, eds. *Film and the First World War*. Amsterdam: Amsterdam University Press, 1995.

Doherty, Thomas. *Projections of War: Hollywood, American Culture, and World War II*. Film and Culture. New York: Columbia University Press, 1993.

Donets, Liudmila. "*Ballada o soldate*." IK, no. 1 (January 1989): 125–127.

Dunham, Vera S. *In Stalin's Time: Middleclass Values in Soviet Fiction*. Cambridge: Cambridge University Press, 1976.

Erenburg, Il'ia. *The Thaw*. Trans. Manya Harari. Chicago: Regnery, 1955.

Erickson, John. *The Road to Stalingrad: Stalin's War with Germany*. Vol. 1. New York: Harper and Row, 1975.

Faraday, George. *Revolt of the Filmmakers: The Struggle for Artistic Autonomy and the Fall of the Soviet Film Industry*. University Park: Pennsylvania State University Press, 2000.

Ferro, Marc. *Film and History*. Trans. Naomi Greene. Detroit, Mich.: Wayne State University Press, 1988.

Figes, Orlando. *A People's Tragedy: The Russian Revolution, 1891–1924*. New York: Penguin, 1998.

Finn, Peter. "From Bitter Memories, a Russian Blockbuster." *Washington Post*, 20 October 2005, A-16.

Fitzpatrick, Sheila. *The Commissariat of Enlightenment: Soviet Organization of Education and the Arts under Lunacharskii, October 1917–1921*. Cambridge: Cambridge University Press, 1970.

———. ed. *Cultural Revolution in Russia*. Bloomington: Indiana University Press, 1978.

———. *Everyday Stalinism: Ordinary Life in Extraordinary Times: Soviet Russia in the 1930s*. Oxford: Oxford University Press, 1999.

———. *The Russian Revolution, 1917–1932*. Oxford: Oxford University Press, 1982.

———. *Tear Off the Masks! Identity and Imposture in Twentieth-Century Russia*. Princeton, N.J.: Princeton University Press, 2005.

Garrard, John, and Carol Garrard, eds. *World War 2 and the Soviet People*. New York: St. Martin's Press, 1993.

Giesen, Rolf. *Nazi Propaganda Films: A History and Filmography*. Jefferson, N.C.: McFarland, 2003.

Gillespie, David. *Russian Cinema*. Harlow: Longman, 2003.

Ginzburg, Semën. *Kinematografii dorevoliutsionnoi Rossii*. Moscow: Iskusstvo, 1963.

Glantz, David M. *The Battle for Leningrad, 1941–1944*. Lawrence: University Press of Kansas, 2002.

————. *Stumbling Colossus: The Red Army on the Eve of World War.* Lawrence: University Press of Kansas, 1998.

Glantz, David M., and Jonathan M. House. *When Titans Clashed: How the Red Army Stopped Hitler.* Lawrence: University Press of Kansas, 1995.

Golovskoi, Valerii. *Mezhdu ottepel'iu i glasnost'iu: Kinematograf 70-kh.* Moscow: Materik, 2004.

Goulding, Daniel J., ed. *Post New Wave Cinema in the Soviet Union and Eastern Europe.* Bloomington: Indiana University Press, 1989.

Grindon, Leger. *Shadows on the Past: Studies in the Historical Fiction Film.* Philadelphia: Temple University Press, 1994.

Gudkov, Lev, comp. *Obraz vraga.* Moscow: OGI, 2005.

Harrison, Richard W. *The Russian Way of War: Operational Art, 1904–1940.* Lawrence: University Press of Kansas, 2001.

Haynes, John. *New Soviet Man: Gender and Masculinity in Stalinist Soviet Cinema.* Manchester: Manchester University Press, 2003.

Hicks, Jeremy. "The International Reception of Early Soviet Sound Cinema: *Chapaev* in Britain and America." *Historical Journal of Film, Radio and Television* 25, no. 2 (June 2005): 273–289.

Higham, Robin, and Frederick W. Kagan. *The Military History of the Soviet Union.* New York: Palgrave, 2002.

Hoffmann, David L. *Stalinist Values: The Cultural Norms of Soviet Modernity, 1917–1941.* Ithaca, N.Y.: Cornell University Press, 2003.

Horton, Andrew. "The Star That Didn't Shine." *Kinoeye* 2, no. 13 (2002). http://www .kinoeye.org/02/13/horton13 part4.php.

————. "War, What Is It Good For?" *Kinoeye* 2, no. 18 (2002). http://www.kinoeye .org/02/18/horton18 no.3php.

Horton, Andrew, and Michael Brashinsky. *The Zero Hour: Glasnost and Soviet Cinema in Transition.* Princeton, N.J.: Princeton University Press, 1992.

Iezuitov, Nikolai. "Agitki epokhi grazhdanskoi voiny." *IK,* no. 5 (May 1940): 47–51.

Institut istorii iskusstv ministerstva kul'tury SSSR. *Istoriia sovetskogo kino, 1917–1967.* Vol. 2, 1931–1941. Moscow: Iskusstvo, 1973.

Iurenev, Rostislav. "Ivan Aleksandrovich Pyr'ev: Biograficheskii ocherk." In *Ivan Pyr'ev v zhizni i na ekrane: Stranitsy vospominanii,* 5–73. Moscow: Kinotsentr, 1994.

————. "Kinoiskusstvo voennykh let." In *Sovetskaia kul'tura v gody velikoi otechestvennoi voiny,* 235–251. Moscow: Nauka, 1976.

————. *Kratkaia istoriia sovetskogo kino.* Moscow: Biuro propagandy sovetskogo kinoiskusstva, 1979.

Jahn, Hubertus F. *Patriotic Culture in Russia during World War I.* Ithaca, N.Y.: Cornell University Press, 1995.

Johnson, Vida T., and Graham Petrie. *The Films of Andrei Tarkovsky: A Visual Fugue.* Bloomington: Indiana University Press, 1994.

Kamshalov, Aleksandr. *Geroika podviga na ekrane: Voenno-patrioticheskaia tema v sovetskom kinematografe.* Moscow: Iskusstvo, 1986.

Kane, Kathryn. *Visions of War: The Hollywood Combat Films of World War II.* Ann Arbor, Mich.: UMI Research Press, 1982.

"Kartina zhivët!" SE, no. 21 (1974): 14–15.

Kenez, Peter. *Cinema and Soviet Society from the Revolution to the Death of Stalin.* London: I. B. Tauris, 2001.

———. "Russian Patriotic Films." In *Film and the First World War,* ed. Karel Dibbets and Bert Hogenkamp, 36–42. Amsterdam: Amsterdam University Press, 1995.

Kepley, Vance, Jr. *The End of St. Petersburg.* London: I. B. Tauris, 2003.

———. *In the Service of the State: The Cinema of Alexander Dovzhenko.* Madison: University of Wisconsin Press, 1986.

Khaniutin, Iurii. *Preduprezhdenie proshlogo.* Moscow: Iskusstvo, 1968.

———. *Sergei Bondarchuk.* Moscow: Iskusstvo, 1962.

Kishkovsky, Sophia. "From a Bitter War Defeat Comes Russia's Latest Blockbuster Action Movie." *New York Times,* 29 October 2005, A23.

Koppes, Clayton R., and Gregory D. Black. *Hollywood Goes to War: How Politics, Profits, and Propaganda Shaped World War II Movies.* New York: Free Press/Macmillan, 1987.

Kremlev, German. *Mikhail Kalatozov.* Moscow: Iskusstvo, 1964.

———. "1936-xxx-1966: My iz Kronshtadta." SE, no. 6 (1966): 20.

Kushnirov, Mark. *Zhizn' i fil'my Borisa Barneta.* Moscow: Iskusstvo, 1977.

Landy, Marcia. *Cinematic Uses of the Past.* Minneapolis: University of Minnesota Press, 1996.

———. ed. *The Historical Film: History and Memory in Media.* New Brunswick, N.J.: Rutgers University Press, 2000.

Laurent, Natacha. *L'Œil du Kremlin: Cinéma et censure en URSS sous Staline (1928–1953).* Paris: Editions Privat, 2000.

Lavrent'ev, Sergei. "Aleksei Balabanov: War (Voina, 2002)." *KinoKultura,* February 2003. http://www.kinokultura.com/reviews/Rwar.html.

———. "Sud'ba cheloveka." *IK,* no. 1 (January 1989): 122–124.

Lawton, Anna. *Before the Fall: Soviet Cinema in the Gorbachev Years.* Washington, D.C.: New Academia Publishing, 2002.

———. *Imaging Russia 2000: Film and Facts.* Washington, D.C.: New Academia Publishing, 2004.

———. *Kinoglasnost: Soviet Cinema in Our Time.* Cambridge: Cambridge University Press, 1992.

Lebedev, Nikolai. *Ocherk istorii kino SSSR.* Vol. 1, *Nemoe kino.* Moscow: Goskinoizdat, 1947.

Leyda, Jay. *Kino: A History of the Russian and Soviet Film.* New York: Collier, 1973.

Liber, George O. *Alexander Dovzhenko: A Life in Soviet Film.* London: BFI Publishing, 2002.

Lincoln, W. Bruce. *Passage through Armageddon: The Russians in War and Revolution, 1914–1918.* New York: Oxford University Press, 1994.

Listov, Viktor. "Early Soviet Cinema: The Spontaneous and the Planned, 1917–1924." Trans. and ed. Richard Taylor and Derek Spring. *Historical Journal of Film, Radio and Television* 11, no. 2 (1991): 21–27.

Litvin, Alter L. *Writing History in Twentieth-Century Russia: A View from Within*. Trans. and ed. John L. H. Keep. New York: Palgrave, 2001.

Mamatova, L. Kh., ed. *Kino: Politika i liudi (30-e gody)*. Moscow: Materik, 1995.

———. "Mashen'ka i zombi: Mifologiia sovetskoi zhenshchiny." *IK*, no. 6 (June 1991) 110–118.

Manchel, Frank. *Film Study: An Analytical Bibliography*. Rutherford, N.J.: Fairleigh Dickinson University Press, 1990.

Manvell, Roger. *Films and the Second World War*. South Brunswick, N.J.: A. S. Barnes, 1974.

Margolit, Evgenii. "Kinematograf 'ottepeli': K portretu fenomena." *Kinovedcheskie zapiski*, no. 67 (2001): 195–230.

Mariamov, Grigorii. *Kremlevskii tsenzor: Stalin smotrit kino*. Moscow: Kinotsentr', 1992.

Mawdsley, Evan. *The Russian Civil War*. Boston: Unwin Hyman, 1987.

Menashe, Louis. "Patriotic Gauze, Patriotic Gore: Russians at War." *Cineaste*, Summer 2004, 26–29.

Mikhailovich, Valentin. "*Potomok Chingis-khana*." *IK*, no. 5 (May 1988): 99–101.

Mishurin, A. "Na s"emakh *Shchorsa*." *IK*, no. 9 (September 1974): 49–58.

Murphy, Robert. *British Cinema and the Second World War*. London: Continuum, 2000.

———. "The British Film Industry: Audiences and Producers." In *Britain and the Cinema in the Second World War*, ed. Philip Taylor, 31–41. New York: St. Martin's Press, 1988.

O'Connor, John E. *The Image as Artifact: The Historical Analysis of Film and Television*. Malabar, Fla.: Krieger, 1990.

O'Connor, John E., and Martin E. Jackson, eds. *American History, American Film: Interpreting the Hollywood Image*. New York: Continuum, 1988.

Overy, Richard. *Russia's War: A History of the Soviet War Effort, 1941–1945*. New York: Penguin, 1998.

Paris, Michael, ed. *The First World War and Popular Cinema: 1914 to the Present*. New Brunswick, N.J.: Rutgers University Press, 2000.

Pennington, Reina. *Wings, Women, and War: Soviet Airwomen in World War II Combat*. Lawrence: University Press of Kansas, 2001.

Pethybridge, Roger. *The Social Prelude to Stalinism*. New York: St. Martin's Press, 1974.

Petrone, Karen. *Life Has Become More Joyous, Comrades! Celebrations in the Time of Stalin*. Bloomington: Indiana University Press, 2000.

Petrov, Petre. "The Freeze of Historicity in Thaw Cinema." *KinoKultura*, no. 8 (April 2005) http://www.kinokultura.com/articles/apr05-petrov.html.

Polukhina, Liana. *Marina Ladynina i Ivan Pyr'ev*. Moscow: Eksmo/Algoritm, 2004.

Prokhorova, Elena. "Dmitrii Meskhiev: Our Own, aka Us and Ours [Svoi], 2004." *KinoKultura*, January 2005. http://www.kinokultura.com/reviews/R1-05svoi.html.

Razzakov, Fëdor. *Nashe liubimoe kino: Tainoe stanovitsia iavnym*. Moscow: Algoritm, 2004.

Reese, Roger R. *Stalin's Reluctant Soldiers: A Social History of the Red Army, 1925–1941*. Lawrence: University Press of Kansas, 1996.

Rentschler, Eric. *The Ministry of Illusion: Nazi Cinema and Its Afterlife*. Cambridge, Mass.: Harvard University Press, 1996.

Roberts, Geoffrey. *Victory at Stalingrad*. London: Longman, 2002.

Roberts, Graham. *Forward Soviet! History and Non-fiction Film in the USSR*. London: I. B. Tauris, 1999.

Rollins, Peter, ed. *Columbia Companion to American History on Film: How the Movies Have Portrayed the American Past*. New York: Columbia University Press, 2003.

———. ed. *Hollywood as Historian: American Film in a Cultural Context*. Lexington: University Press of Kentucky, 1983.

Rosenstone, Robert A., ed. *Revisioning History: Film and the Construction of a New Past*. Princeton, N.J.: Princeton University Press, 1995.

———. *Visions of the Past: The Challenge of Film to Our Idea of History*. Cambridge, Mass.: Harvard University Press, 1995.

Rudnitskii, Konstantin. "O Vere Maretskoi." IK, no. 1 (January 1979): 112–125.

Schatz, Thomas. *Hollywood Genres: Formulas, Filmmaking, and the Studio System*. Philadelphia: Temple University Press, 1981.

Shitova, Vera. "Zhivye i mërtvye." SE, no. 24 (1987): 14–15.

Shmyrov, Viacheslav. "Moldaia gvardiia SSSR (1948)." IK, no. 11 (November 1988): 106–107.

Sirivlia, N. "Nebo nad Moskvy." IK, no. 8 (August 1997): 38–40.

Smal, Vatslav. *Chelovek, voina, podvig*. Minsk: Nauka i tekhnika, 1979.

Sobchack, Vivian, ed. *The Persistence of History: Film and the Modern Event*. New York: Routledge, 1996.

Sokolov, I. V., ed. *Istoriia sovetskogo kino iskusstva zvukovogo perioda: Po vyskazyvaniiam masterov kino i otzyvam kritikov*. Vol. 1, 1930–1941. Moscow: Goskinoizdat, 1946.

Sorlin, Pierre. *The Film in History: Restaging the Past*. Totowa, N.J.: Barnes and Noble, 1980.

Sovetskaia kul'tura v gody velikoi otechestvennoi voiny. Moscow: Nauka, 1976.

Stites, Richard., ed. *Culture and Entertainment in Wartime Russia*. Bloomington: Indiana University Press, 1995.

———. *Russian Popular Culture: Entertainment and Society since 1900*. Cambridge: Cambridge University Press, 1992.

Stoff, Laurie S. *They Fought for the Motherland: Russia's Women Soldiers in World War I and the Revolution*. Lawrence: University Press of Kansas, 2006.

Stone, David R. *Hammer and Rifle: The Militarization of the Soviet Union, 1926–1933*. Lawrence: University Press of Kansas, 2000.

Szovjet játékfilmek katalógusa. Budapest: Magyar Filmtudományi Intézet és Filmarchívum, 1977.

Taylor, Richard. *Film Propaganda: Soviet Russia and Nazi Germany*. 2nd ed. rev. London: I. B. Tauris, 1998.

———. *October: Oktiabr'*. London: BFI Publishing, 2002.

———. *The Politics of the Soviet Cinema, 1917–1929*. New York: Cambridge University Press, 1979.

———. "Singing on the Steppes for Stalin: Ivan Pyr'ev and the Kolkhoz Musical in Soviet Cinema." *Slavic Review* 58, no. 1 (Spring 1999): 143–159.

Taylor, Richard, and Ian Christie, eds. *Inside the Film Factory: New Approaches to Russian and Soviet Cinema*. London: Routledge, 1991.

Taylor, Richard, and Derek Spring, eds. *Stalinism and Soviet Cinema*. London: Routledge, 1993.

Thurston, Robert W., and Bernd Bonwetsch, eds. *The People's War: Responses to World War II in the Soviet Union.* Urbana: University of Illinois Press, 2000.

Toplin, Robert Brent. *History by Hollywood: The Use and Abuse of the American Past.* Urbana: University of Illinois Press, 1996.

———. *Reel History: In Defense of Hollywood.* Lawrence: University Press of Kansas, 2002.

Troianovskii, V., ed. *Kinematograf ottepeli.* Vol. 1. Moscow: Materik, 1996.

Tsivian, Yuri. *Early Cinema in Russia and Its Cultural Reception.* Trans. Alan Bodger. Ed. Richard Taylor. London: Routledge, 1994.

Tumanova, N. "Geroini sovetskogo ekran." *IK*, no. 12 (December 1975): 20–33.

Tumarkin, Nina. *The Living and the Dead: The Rise and Fall of the Cult of World War II in Russia.* New York: Basic Books, 1994.

Turovskaia, Maia. "I. A. Pyr'ev i ego muzykal'nye komedii: K probleme zhanra." *KZ*, no. 1 (1988): 111–146.

———. "The Tastes of Soviet Moviegoers during the 1930s." In *Late Soviet Culture: From Perestroika to Novostroika*, ed. Thomas Lahusen, 95–107. Durham, N.C.: Duke University Press, 1993.

Von Hagen, Mark. *Soldiers in the Proletarian Dictatorship: The Red Army and the Soviet Socialist State, 1917–1930.* Ithaca, N.Y.: Cornell University Press, 1990.

White, Hayden. "Historiography and Historiophoty." *American Historical Review* 93, no. 3 (December 1988): 1193–1199.

Wild, Daniel H. "Aleksandr Rogozhkin: Cuckoo (Kukushka), 2002." *KinoKultura*, April 2004. http://www.kinokultura.com/reviews/R44cuckoo.html.

Woll, Josephine. *The Cranes Are Flying.* London: I. B. Tauris, 2003.

———. *Real Images: Soviet Cinema and the Thaw.* London: I. B. Tauris, 2000.

Youngblood, Denise J. "'Americanitis': The Amerikanshchina in Soviet Cinema." *Journal of Popular Film and Television* 19, no. 4 (Winter 1992): 149–156.

———. "The Cosmopolitan and the Patriot: The Brothers Mikhalkov-Konchalovsky and Russian Cinema." *Historical Journal of Film, Radio and Television* 25, no. 1 (2003): 27–41.

———. *The Magic Mirror: Moviemaking in Russia, 1908–1918.* Madison: University of Wisconsin Press, 1999.

———. *Movies for the Masses: Popular Cinema and Soviet Society in the 1920s.* Cambridge: Cambridge University Press, 1992.

———. *Soviet Cinema in the Silent Era, 1918–1935.* Austin: University of Texas Press, 1991.

———. "A War Forgotten: The Great War in Russian and Soviet Cinema." In *The First World War and Popular Cinema: 1914 to the Present*, ed. Michael Paris, 172–196. New Brunswick, N.J.: Rutgers University Press, 2000.

———. "A War Remembered: Soviet Films of the Great Patriotic War." *American Historical Review* 105, no. 5 (June 2001): 839–856.

Yurchak, Alexei. *Everything Was Forever, until It Was No More: The Last Soviet Generation.* Princeton, N.J.: Princeton University Press, 2006.

Zorkaia, Neia. *The Illustrated History of the Soviet Cinema.* New York: Hippocrene, 1989.

Zubkova, Elena. *Russia after the War: Hopes, Illusions, and Disappointments, 1945–1957.* Trans. and ed. Hugh Ragsdale. Armonk, N.Y.: M. E. Sharpe, 1998.

INDEX